What's Wrong with Sociology?

What's Wrong with Sociology?

Stephen Cole
editor

Transaction Publishers
New Brunswick (U.S.A.) and London (U.K.)

Copyright © 2001 by Transaction Publishers, New Brunswick, New Jersey.

All rights reserved under International and Pan-American Copyright Conventions. No part of this book may be reproduced or transmitted in any form or by any means, electronic or mechanical, including photocopy, recording, or any information storage and retrieval system, without prior permission in writing from the publisher. All inquiries should be addressed to Transaction Publishers, Rutgers—The State University, 35 Berrue Circle, Piscataway, New Jersey 08854-8042.

This book is printed on acid-free paper that meets the American National Standard for Permanence of Paper for Printed Library Materials.

Library of Congress Catalog Number: 00-053257
ISBN: 0-7658-0039-X
Printed in the United States of America

Library of Congress Cataloging-in-Publication Data

What's wrong with sociology? / edited with an introduction by Stephen Cole.
    p. cm.
    Includes bibliographical references.
    ISBN 0-7658-0039-X (alk. paper)
    1. Sociology. I. Cole, Stephen, 1941-.

HM585 .W53 2001
301—dc21   00-053257

Contents

Introduction
The Social Construction of Sociology

Stephen Cole

In some ways this is a very personal book; it represents my own views as to who would have interesting things to say on the problems currently facing the discipline of sociology and as to which already published articles dealing with this topic were worth reprinting. Eight of the chapters in this book were originally published in 1994 as a special issue of *Sociological Forum*, the journal of the Eastern Sociological Society, of which I was editor at the time. These are the chapters by S. Cole, Collins, Davis, Lipset, Molotch, Rule, the Simpsons, and Stinchcombe. One chapter, that by Zald, was an invited contribution to a follow-up discussion of the special issue appearing in the same journal. Two of the chapters, those by M. Cole and Ellis and Bochner are original essays which I commissioned for this book. The other chapters, those by Becker and Rau, Berger, Felson, Henry, and Huber were previously published articles. The essay by Henry was part of a special issue of *Sociological Forum* devoted to the views of African American sociologists on the current state of sociology which I commissioned when I was editor. The Huber essay was the Centennial Essay published in the *American Journal of Sociology* (AJS) in 1995. There were other people whom I asked to contribute to both the special issue and this volume who declined.

The many hundreds of other sociologists whom I might have asked to contribute would have, perhaps, written quite different essays— stressing different themes. Many would have felt that there was nothing really wrong with sociology except that we were being treated poorly by university administrators and state governments. There are some sociologists who feel that the field has never been in better shape; that is not true of the people who wrote the essays in this volume nor does it represent my point of view.

Although this introduction and the essays in this collection are critical of the current state of sociology, this should not be taken as evidence for our disenchantment with the discipline. The authors whose essays are contained in this volume truly love the discipline of sociology and it is because of their strong commitment to the discipline that some of us are deeply concerned about what we see as current shortcomings in the discipline. Criticizing some aspects of the way in which sociology is currently practiced does not mean that we do not appreciate the good work which is currently being done by many sociologists or that we do not see the discipline as having great insights to add to our understanding of human behavior. These criticisms are offered in a constructive way with the hope that they will be of some value in overcoming some of what we see as problems existing in the discipline today.

My main work has been in the specialty of the sociology of science. My last monograph, *Making Science: Between Nature and Society* (1992) contained a detailed critique of a position which has now become dominant in the sociology of science — social constructivism. Based upon a relativist epistemology, constructivists argue that there is no "truth" and rather than nature influencing what scientists come to believe as true, social processes among scientists influence how we come to define nature. In the course of thinking through whether the natural sciences are socially constructed, it occurred to me to ask whether sociology was completely socially constructed. What exactly would this mean? It would mean that what sociologists believe to be true about human behavior has very little to do with evidence from the empirical world; rather it is mostly a result of ideology, power, authority, and other social processes. I gradually came to believe that although this view was not an accurate depiction of the natural sciences it was a relatively accurate portrayal of sociology and I believe that the essays in this book offer much support for such a conclusion. The many friends and colleagues to whom I have shown prior drafts of this introduction have frequently asked whether there was something inherent in the discipline of sociology which made it necessary that it be socially constructed or could it operate more according to the principles of the natural sciences. My answer is that, of course, there is nothing inherent in sociology which makes it a socially constructed body of knowledge but that it is unlikely that the discipline would do what would be necessary for the current situation to change. What such changes would be will be outlined in the concluding section of this introduction.

Before beginning my discussion of the themes which run through the sixteen essays in this book, it is important to let the reader know exactly what are and what are not the aims of this book. First, it is important to recognize that the essays presented here are those of opinion. Thus, not every statement made in these essays or in this introduction is backed up with empirical evidence or a series of citations. In the introduction particularly I make some statements and reach some conclusions that are not based upon a systematic study of the field; but rather the views of the authors of the essays in this book and my own thirty plus years of experience. Opinion, of course, is more interesting if it is based upon evidence than if it comes out of the blue. And wherever possible the authors of the essays and I in the introduction attempt to cite examples or references which back up our opinions; but these are not journal articles of the type normally published in the *American Sociological Review*.

Second, in reading the introduction, the reader should understand that I am trying to summarize the views of sixteen very diverse writers some of which I agree with and others which I do not. This brings us to the third and final point: the authors of these essays, selected to represent diverse views of sociology, disagree with each other. Every reader will find some essays more in line with their own views; but the particular essays chosen will differ from reader to reader. There was a good deal of diversity of reaction to the essays presented in this book among the referees who reviewed the book prior to publication. Some said that certain essays should be excluded; but those were the favorite essays of other reviewers. It has always been my view that this book should reflect the diversity of opinion in the field. The original essays published in *Sociological Forum* did not represent this diversity as well as the expanded version published here. As essays of opinion, this book is aimed at stimulating thought about what problems face the discipline of sociology and what the future of the discipline will be. They may even stimulate some readers to go out and do empirical research to show that the opinions expressed in one or more of the essays are incorrect or need modification.

The themes which are most important in the essays in this book are ideology, progress and consensus, the level of generality, the causal model and the appropriate unit of analysis, the post-modernist turn, the use of literary technique, the quality of sociology students, the lack of civility among disagreeing sociologists, the contradiction between American culture and sociology, sociological ethnocentrism and methodological faddism. There is one over-arching theme that connects many, although not all of the sub-themes that I will discuss in the introduction and that is the extent to which sociology is socially constructed.

Of course, it should be obvious that probably none of the authors of the 15 chapters in this book (other than my own) would agree with all my views expressed in this introduction and some of them would agree with none of them. I have tried to have people who represent different positions contribute to this book. Thus, Padget Henry (Chapter 15) and Carolyn Ellis and Art Bochner (Chapter 16) are post-modernists who believe that the problem with sociology is that it has failed to embrace the lessons of recent postmodernist intellectual developments. Harvey Molotch (Chapter 8) is a sociologist who identifies with the left and has co-authored a prize winning neo-Marxist interpretation of urban sociology (Logan and Molotch, 1987). He also is a leading qualitative researcher. Randall Collins is one of the country's leading conflict theorists. Joan Huber and Carolyn Ellis are feminists.

The Problem of Ideology

Let me now turn to the highly provocative papers that are published in this book. Rather than summarize each paper individually, I will point out common themes, and thus, since many of the papers contain multiple themes, I will refer to them several times as they become relevant. The most frequent theme to be found in these essays is that sociology has become too ideological. As a result, it has lost credibility among university administrators, politicians, and the general public. Our work is seen as not being objective; but as a justification of predominantly liberal or left-wing political sympathies.

Marty Lipset (Chapter 12), in an autobiographical account, describes his days at Columbia where he was influenced by Robert Lynd, a socialist who strongly believed that sociologists should keep their politics separate from their work, as well as by Merton and Lazarsfeld. He also describes the events of the late sixties, the student rebellions, and what he sees as the negative influence they had and continue to have on sociology.

In an analysis of the history of the American Sociological Association (ASA) Ida Simpson and Richard Simpson show how that organization has become increasingly influenced by politics. Whereas in the old days, when the professional oganization was known by the name of the American Sociological Society (ASS), the profession did not take communal stands on political issues of the day, today the ASA is constantly doing so. They also point out that, in election to office and appointment to committees, gender and racial politics frequently play a greater role than contribution to the discipline. The Simpsons present data which show that a smaller proportion of ASA resources is currently being devoted to cognitive problems of the discipline than was the case in the past. As an intellectual force the ASA is being surpassed by its many sections, which seem to be growing exponentially and are contributing to the sense of disciplinary fragmentation that many authors, including Art Stinchcombe (Chapter 3), refer to.

Joan Huber (Chapter 14) looks at sociology from the point of view of university administrators. Citing the article in this book by the Simpsons, Huber concurs that the ASA is overly concerned with political issues and under concerned with the cognitive problems of the discipline. Huber asks what the taxpayers get in return for their support of sociology in public universities. And she concludes that most university administrators don't think they get very much. One of the problems she points out is the attractiveness of the discipline to radicals, both students and professors. This gives the discipline at least the image of being ideological. Huber doesn't want to change the social reformist tendencies of sociologists; she feels that people committed to social change will always be attracted to sociology; but she does point this out as a serious problem in the public relations of the discipline.

The main point of Richard Felson's essay (Chapter 11) is that as a result of ideology, sociologists have been discouraged from studying certain problems and if they dare to study them in a particular way they end up being punished. Felson distinguishes "blame analysis" from "causal analysis". The former is concerned with how to partition the blame for a disadvantaged group's (what he calls a "protected" group) being disadvantaged. Thus, some feminists want to put the blame on men or the "capitalist class" for all the disadvantages and discrimination that women have experienced. Felson sees blame analysis as being part of ideological agendas, having no legitimate place in the social sciences. Causal analysis, on the other hand, tries to use empirical evidence to disentangle the multiple causes which result in the outcome that a particular group is disadvantaged. Sociologists can only study these "protected" groups or what others have called "victims" if their answers to the causal question are politically acceptable. If not, they are accused of being sexists, homophobes, or racists, who blame the victim for their disadvantage.

In my contribution (Chapter 1) I argue that sociologists generally do not choose their research topics in order to answer theoretically relevant questions but rather on personal and ideological grounds. Quoting Kuhn I argue that when topics are picked on such grounds they frequently lead the researcher to work on what Lieberson (1985) calls "undoable" projects. I also argue that, since sociological audiences evaluate work using ideological criteria, that there is a disincentive to try to develop better empirical solutions to many problems because they will be rejected on ideological grounds. Stinchcombe (Chapter 3) agrees with this conclusion:

> Much of the variation in interestingness of facts in sociology has to do with their moral value. Because much of sociology is interested in contemporary facts about things the government and the economy do not have under control, about 'social problems' (if they were under control political scientists or economists would study them), a disproportionate share of the facts we study are matters of ideological import, especially facts about what conservative institutions are to be blamed for."(pp. 284-5)

He goes on to give an example: gender and race differences in earnings are similar to age differences in earnings; yet there is no study of the latter fact because "most people in the society have no particular moral or ideological objection to seniority discrimination..." (p. 285).

James Rule makes a similar point when he concludes that "on politically charged theoretical issues... the doctrines of social scientists often sound suspiciously like abstracted versions of the conflicting prejudices of non-specialists." (p.242) Rule sees the increasing popularity of what he calls theory as an expression of social experience rather than as an objective description of the social world as being a result of ideology and a relativistic epistemology which is seeping into sociology. He also sees ideology as the explanation for changes in the popularity of various theories of civil violence. He discusses the shift from non-rational to rational explanations of civil disorder and concludes that the change was not a result of new discoveries or empirical evidence but rather a change in the ideological climate:

> In the 1940s and 1950s, students of militant action were preoccupied with movements like Stalinism, Nazism, and McCarthyism— phenomena with which they had little sympathy. By the 1960s, students of militant action were attending more to movements for civil rights, racial equality, and international peace— developments that they were likely to support. The new generation of theorists simply found it unsatisfactory to embrace views that seemed to place these things in a negative light..."(p. 247)

In my (Cole, 1975) analysis of the reception and use of Merton's famous paper "Social Structure and Anomie" (1957) I conclude that change in the political climate had more to do than empirical evidence with the fields ultimately losing interest in anomie theory and turning its attention instead to the more politically compatible labeling theory of the symbolic interactionists. When ideology overshadows empirical evidence in determining which theories we adopt, is it any wonder that an observer might be concerned about the extent to which the beliefs of sociologists are constrained by evidence from the empirical world?

There are other contributors to this volume, who, although they do not make the ideological nature of sociology their main point, do mention it. For example, Davis (Chapter 4) when he says that sociology has a "weak immune system" refers to Marxism as an infection: "It was not until the post-Vietnam period that Marx loomed larger than, say, Ibn-Khaldun. The Marxian infection came with the use of academia as a sheltered workshop for intellectual refugees from the Vietnam turmoil." (p.189) Randall Collins (Chapter 2) in talking about the attempts of sociologists to offer policy advice concludes: "Applied social science consists to a large extent of exhortation — e.g., the study of stratification is ammunition for social reform movements, and the study of revolution has been an encouragement to make one. Applied sociology frequently takes the form of intervening on a particular side in social conflicts, giving an ideological appeal for one interest and thereby alienating the other." (p. 170)

One of the main points raised by Peter Berger (Chapter 9) is that sociologists have failed to predict or even understand the major world events of the last thirty years, such as the social movements of the late 1960s, the collapse of Communism, the rise of Japan and the southeast Asian tigers (now he might add the severe financial difficulties faced by these tigers in 1998), and the Iranian revolution. Berger sees these failures as being a result of the ideological bias of contemporary sociology along with its parochialism, triviality, and rationality. He sees these four conditions as being responsible for sociologists' making no attempt to be "value free" in their research, and their ideologically driven research has prevented them from understanding what is going on in the society in which they live. He accuses sociology of failing to answer the big questions.

Maria Cole (Chapter 10), influenced by Berger, applies his critique to an analysis of the sociology of gender research. She argues that general macrostructural theory of gender stratification is ethnocentric and ideologically biased. It mistakenly applies generalizations based upon conditions which have existed at certain times in the United States to all societies at all times. I will discuss her case study of women in the military below when I analyze another theme, that of the generalizability of sociological theory.

The Problem of Progress and Consensus

Complaints about the ideological nature of much sociological writing is the most frequently occurring theme in these essays. Perhaps the second most emphasized is the perceived failure of sociology as a discipline to have consensus and to make "progress", its failure to develop a core of agreed upon knowledge, and in general its cognitive incoherence. In my essay, I distinguish between the frontier of science which is characterized by high levels of disagreement in all sciences, and the core, the few facts, theories, exemplars which the field accepts as important and representing the "truth." Examples of core knowledge would be Watson and Crick's model of DNA or Darwin's theory of evolution. I believe that sociology has little or no core and I try to explain why it does not develop one as the natural sciences do. The two major problems are: 1) we select topics on non-theoretical grounds; and 2) we are shooting at a moving target. Whereas a discipline such as physics studies phenomena which are constant (the structure of the atom) and sciences like astronomy, geology and evolutionary biology study things which change very slowly, we study phenomena which change very rapidly.

I give as an example an attempt to develop a theory of gender inequality. A theory which was correct in 1965 would be totally incorrect in 2000 because the phenomenon has changed before we could develop an adequate theory of it. Harvey Molotch (Chapter 8) agrees with me that the phenomena we are studying change very quickly; but he believes that sociology actually causes some of this change.

Both Huber and Davis agree that sociology lacks a developed intellectual core and Huber believes that if we cannot develop and maintain an intellectual core, our future is in danger. Becker and Rau and Stinchcombe express similar beliefs. Huber asks what it is that administrators want from an academic department. She lists three things: centrality, quality of faculty, and quality of students. On all three sociology is currently experiencing difficulty. Centrality has to do with whether or not a discipline is necessary to run a liberal arts program. Math and English, for example, are highly central disciplines which other departments require their students to take courses in. Sociology owns no special subject matter and it is not difficult for an administrator to imagine running his or her university without a sociology department. As far as the quality of faculty goes, there is so much disagreement in sociology, that it is almost impossible to get consensus that any particular people would be good to have on one's faculty. And as far as students go, Lipset reports the results of a survey where deans rate sociology as last in both the quality of faculty and students. The quality of students is an issue I will discuss in more detail below.

Randall Collins distinguishes between scientific fields which are characterized by high consensus and rapid discovery like physics and those, which he believes to be more common, which do not display consensus and rapid discovery, like science prior to the seventeenth century and contemporary sociology. Collins does not think that the reason that we fail to develop consensus has anything to do with lack of empiricism, measurement problems, failure to develop mathematical formulations, or our inability to use the experimental method for most of our problems. He concludes that "by itself empirical research does not lead to consensus or rapid discovery." (p.166) Rather, he sees the condition of sociology as a result of the lack of technological devices which have the ability constantly to discover new phenomena which need to be explained. He sees conversation analysis and artificial intelligence as the two areas which have the greatest possibility for developing into consensual-rapid discovery type fields.

Perhaps most interestingly, Collins argues that some areas of sociology like comparative research have made impressive gains, but that the social structure of sociology is not conducive to turning these gains into a high consensus-rapid discovery field. This is because the relatively small number of research sociologists are spread too thin among thousands of topics (unlike physics, for example, where thousands of physicists work on a single problem) and our discipline is plagued by:

> the ideology that no scientific knowledge exists in these fields. The reality that is being reflected upon here is the social structure of the field, rather than a description of its cognitive contents. It is feasible, on the epistemological level, to apply canons of generalizability, explanatory power, and coherence, and to extract from the myriad sociological publications some materials that have a higher scientific quality than others. On the substantive level, there is no need to be a relativist. Some of the contents of sociology are scientific. But they do not become the focus of a social consensus, because they are not linked into rapid-discovery chains. Lacking that social support, they are merely one strand among many others. (pp. 169-70).

I agree with Collins on this and see it as part of the explanation why, despite the fact that much excellent empirical work has been done in sociology, this work seems to have little impact on the beliefs of sociologists.

Perhaps Collins provides an explanation for Molotch's wistful complaint that good studies are done in sociology, problems are solved, facts are established and then nobody pays any attention to them. Molotch (Chapter 8) uses as an example his own work on racial integration in Chicago (1972). In that book, Molotch shows that at least in the areas of Chicago that he studied in the 1960s segregation was not a result of white flight. But despite the excellence of his study and the convincing nature of the evidence he assembles, many sociologists are not aware of the Molotch book and still believe that racial segregation is primarily a result of white flight. This is an example where what sociologists believe might have been constrained by empirical evidence; but where this evidence was for the most part ignored. Again, I am not arguing that there is something inherent in the discipline which makes it necessary that it be socially constructed but that the way in which the discipline is played out produces this result.

Another example where evidence which I would see as relatively conclusive seems to be ignored in sociology can be found in the field of status attainment and social mobility. Literally some of the best empirical research ever done in sociology was done on this topic. I refer, of course, to the ground breaking work of Blau and Duncan (1967), the re-analysis by Christopher Jencks, et.al. (1972), and the follow up by Featherman and Hauser (1978). All these studies based upon huge data sets, carefully analyzed by some of the most competent sociologists, all showed that in the contemporary United States, at least for white males, class of origin explains only sixteen percent of the variance on income as an adult (and the bulk of this is indirect through the influence of class of origin on education). Yet my personal experience and reading of the stratification literature suggests to me that a significant number of sociologists don't accept these findings as true. In fact, some more recent research by Erikson and Goldthorpe (1992) has raised some important methodological critiques of the American work on social stratification. I do not believe that these criticisms are significant enough to negate the conclusions, but they do illustrate how difficult it is to establish "facts" in sociological research. Evidence seems to have no influence on what many sociologists believe to be true, if that evidence contradicts dearly held ideologically connected positions. Prior readers of this introduction have suggested that the more eminent members of the community would accept the conclusions of the status attainment research; but my experience has shown that it is one's political predisposition rather than one's eminence which influences how one treats the large body of status attainment research. This field also presents us with another example of how rapid social change makes it difficult to develop core knowledge. Apparently in the last twenty years since most of the status attainment research has been done, economists have found a stronger relationship between class of origin and the individual's own position in the stratification system. (See the discussion of this literature in the first part of Herrnstein and Murray, 1995).

Davis (Chapter 4) also agrees that sociology is intellectually incoherent and that we are faddish, abandoning topics when we get bored. Davis says that the only ideas that have ever been "proven" wrong in sociology are status inconsistency and relative deprivation. (I wish Davis had provided a reference for this last item, since his own 1966 paper offers support for the theory of relative deprivation.) This is a serious problem in sociology. There really is little premium placed on solving problems rather than addressing them. Thus, much sociological work, even highly thought of work, succeeds in raising interesting questions and in the best cases provides some partial understanding of the problem, but usually does not succeed in answering them. In the natural sciences scientists get no credit simply for raising problems; but for developing solutions which other scientists believe to be true and accept as fact. Davis points out that in sociology there is no conflict over priority as is found in other disciplines. This is because it is hard to identify a "discovery" and very few people work on the same problem. Thus there is little cumulation and Davis agrees with Lieberson (1985) that many sociologists work on "undoable" problems.

Molotch points out that sociology, rather than being based upon confirmed empirical evidence (of any variety) is often based upon assertions which are later cited as facts. My personal favorite example of this is Rosabeth Kanter's book, *Men and Women of the Corporation* (1977), which is frequently cited as having "proved" or "shown" that opportunity causes aspirations rather than the other way around, despite the fact that there is no evidence in her book or anywhere else to support this conclusion. It is easy to find multiple other examples where assertions or hypotheses get transformed into facts, findings, conclusions, etc. without the benefit of empirical verification— another example of how what we believe to be true is socially constructed rather than the result of research. I do not want to compare sociology with an overly idealized image of the natural sciences. Indeed, the natural sciences differ significantly in the extent to which the acceptance of theories is dependent upon empirical evidence. An example of a theory which is currently entering the core in evolutionary biology with very little empirical support is the Eldredge and Gould theory of punctuated equilibrium (Wotherspoon, 1997).

The main theme of Rule's contribution (Chapter 7) is that sociology is characterized by little if any progress and that there is little cumulation of theoretical ideas. He uses as his primary example his work on civil violence, a book in which he examines the history of sociological work done on civil violence and concludes that there has been little progress and what there has been has been influenced more by fashion than by empirical evidence. Rule contrasts two ways of approaching sociology. One emphasizes the subjective experience of individuals and he calls this the "expressive" approach; this would characterize most of the post-modernist influences on sociology and fields like feminist research. He compares this with what he calls the "coping" approach which is essentially a positivistic attempt to solve social problems using empirical data and evaluating theories on the basis of the extent to which they are supported by the evidence and to which they are useful.

For Rule, utility is a fundamental component of progress. He gives some examples of theories which he believes to be "useful." I personally would not want to see utility used as a criterion for evaluating sociological research. If we aim our research at "solving" social problems we get caught in two dilemmas. First, we must be drawn into ideological and political controversies because the solutions to all social problems involve making value judgements about what is good or bad. Should we legalize all currently illegal recreational drugs? Sociologists might be able to say what the consequences would be of legalization or maintaining the current approach to recreational drug use; but they could not tell society what to do — because this decision involves not scientific evidence but value judgments and here our values are no better or more important than anyone else's.

Second, if we focus our research on utility we will be drawn into working on "undoable" research. I believe an example of this is the problem of capital punishment. Most of the sociologists who have studied this problem are liberals and have concluded on the basis of evidence that capital punishment doesn't work (e.g. Archer and Gartner, 1984). Economists who have studied this problem and are substantially more conservative than sociologists have concluded on the basis of empirical evidence that capital punishment does work (Ehrlich, 1975). (For the record, I personally oppose capital punishment.) This, to me, is an example of an undoable problem. In order for this study to be done you have to do it historically and cross-culturally (as the Archer and Gartner study does); however, the data are so poor and non-comparable and the specific historical, structural, and cultural conditions existing in the various societies at various times which influence whether or not capital punishment is effective are too complex to be dealt with given existing data, methods, and theories. In other words, it would be impossible to get the liberal sociologists and the more conservative economists together and have them design a doable empirical study which would answer the question so that both groups would accept the results as true. It is possible to use theory to guess whether capital punishment might work or not; but it is not possible to address the question empirically in a conclusive way.

Mayer Zald (Chapter 6) also focuses on the problems of progress and cumulation which he sees as different. He seems to be using progress in the traditional sense of "advance" and cumulation to mean that we know more about a particular area although our theoretical understanding of that area may not advance. Cumulation is more the addition of new facts (something which Davis says should be our primary concern). Zald has been significantly influenced by post-positivist philosophy of science, particularly Kuhn (1970) and Rorty (1980). He disagrees with some of the other contributors to this volume and argues that although sociology might not make progress in the traditional positivist sense (which he sees as being naive), that it does make community based progress. That means, that within a community, working on a particular problem, let us say, social movements (the field in which Zald has done a lot of his research)— the community will agree that they have more and better knowledge now than they did in the past. This is a judgment, Zald stresses, which is community based. In other words, someone from outside the community might look at all the work and conclude that there is not much, if any, progress.

The positions of Zald and Rule are at loggerheads. Rule would insist that there must be some universal objective standard to judge whether progress has been made; Zald is willing to accept the judgment of the sociologists working in the field. Zald freely admits that the state of a field is socially and historically constructed. Zald agrees that sociology as a whole is what he calls an "adhocracy", i.e. there is little consensus and progress looking at the field as a whole, which is too fractionated for there to be agreement. But he gives examples of progress in several sub-fields. He argues that real progress was made in ethnomethodology; but then the field seemed to lose steam and disintegrate. He sees substantial progress in historical sociology; but is not very specific about what it consists of. He convincingly argues that demography is a field which seems to have made progress. Demography, which has almost become a separate discipline, does indeed seem to be an exception to most sociological fields. And finally, he argues that there has been progress in his field of collective behavior and gives some examples that he believes illustrate this progress.

The issue raised by Zald and touched upon by Stinchcombe when he talks about sociology being a fragmented field is a serious and interesting one: is sociology really one field, or is it like the former field of biology, a bunch of separate fields with their own theories, methods, and facts of interest lumped together under one disciplinary umbrella for institutional reasons? If sociology were as useful for society as biological research is for medicine and health, there is little doubt in my mind that sociology would be in the process of breaking up into perhaps as many as ten to fifteen separate fields. If this were to happen (an impossibility because of the lack of financial resources and the unwillingness of society to provide them and also the lack of a sufficient number of students to people the divided fields), then it might be possible to develop consensus and have progress within these separate fields. Perhaps the lesson to be learned from Zald's analysis is that we should not ask whether there is progress in sociology; but whether there is progress in particular specialties.

The fragmentation of sociology is discussed by Becker and Rau and is a major theme of Stinchcombe. But after being highly critical of the current state of sociology and concluding that the field is hopelessly fragmented Stinchcombe ends his essay by saying that this is a good thing — let a thousand flowers bloom.

The Level of Generality Problem

Another theme which emerges in several of the essays including Berger (Chapter 9), S. Cole (Chapter 1), M. Cole (Chapter 10), and Davis (Chapter 4) concerns the level of generality of sociological work. Berger criticizes American sociology for being parochial, trivial, overly dependent upon a rational model of behavior, and as I pointed out above, ideological. He believes that we should study the "big" problems and that such study absolutely demands looking at other societies or cultures and using comparative historical cross-cultural analysis. Although the amount of this type of research is increasing in sociology, American sociologists frequently write general theory which is based upon knowledge of only one society, their own; and an arrogant implicit assumption that other societies are like their own or are not worth equal attention. It is interesting to note that the United States is only one of over 150 nations (we generally equate nations with societies) in the contemporary world; yet I would guess that more than 75 percent of sociological writing has concentrated only on the United States and not asked whether observed correlations or causal mechanisms might be different in some other society. From a theoretical point of view there is no reason why the United States should be more important than any other society and many reasons why it might be different from other societies.

Berger's article had a strong influence on Maria Cole's essay on gender theory. She conducts an analysis of general macrostructural theories of gender produced by American sociologists who argue that their theories are "panhistorical" and "cross cultural". Cole, who received her training and worked in Poland, and later in England, the United States and Australia believes that these attempts at general macrostructural theories are in fact ethnocentric and parochial, generalizing from American experience to the rest of the world. Rather than arguing abstractly she attempts to prove her point by looking at one generalization which American gender theorists have made: that women do not participate in war. Using historical and qualitative evidence from Poland she shows that this has not been the case in Poland or other European societies. She provides data which suggest that women have played a substantial role in wars, insurrections, and rebellions in Poland over the last two centuries.

Interestingly, some of the sources used by Cole in her essay are the books by journalist Eva Hoffman, *Lost in Translation* (1989), and *Exit into History: A Journey through the New Eastern Europe* (1993). Hoffman was born in Warsaw and then moved to Canada as a teenager. Her observations on the comparative role played by women in Poland and the United States provide evidence which contradict some of the generalizations made by American sociologists who write on gender. The basic point is that if you really want to do general theory or comparative analysis, make sure that you have knowledge of societies other than your own. This is a point strongly emphasized by Berger.

A broader question raised by the essays of both Coles is: Is explanatory general theory really possible? Maria Cole suggests that the general theories of gender inequality which exist fail to explain the significance of gender in societies other than the United States. I go further in my essay. I argue that it may be impossible to develop general theory which has explanatory power. The only general theory that we have tells us things which are obvious and for which we have no need for sociology in order to know. (I do not mean that it is impossible to develop general orientations, as opposed to specific theories, which might prove useful in guiding some empirical research.)

I use as my prime example what I consider to be one of the most successful and praiseworthy attempts at general theory I am familiar with the research program of Michael Hannan and his collaborators who try to develop a population ecology theory of organizations. I show how their theory leads to results which are obvious and that even the details of their theory are obvious to anyone familiar with the type of organization being described. I argue that coming up with obvious findings may be legitimate if one is doing descriptive research; but obvious theoretical work is not a new contribution to knowledge (Laudan, 1977). The work of Hannan and his colleagues is not a failure because they didn't do a good job; they have done an excellent job. It is a failure because it is impossible to produce non-obvious general theory. This is because the only variables which will apply to all cases must be essentially obvious tautologies. Another example is Skocpol's theory that we have a social revolution when the state breaks down (1979).

The latter is measured by the occurrence of the revolution. The most interesting things that we want to know as sociologists are historically and culturally specific and require detailed analysis of specific cultures and historical periods. Thus, the most we can hope for is middle-range theory; but even at this level we may have to give up explanatory power. Sociologists might have to settle for theories of phenomena which are historically and culturally unique. Thus, I argue that we are more like historians than we are like physicists and there is no way for us to be different.

Problems with the Causal Model and the Appropriate Unit of Analysis

My position would probably resonate with Davis who thinks that in general sociologists pay too much attention to "theory" and not enough attention to finding the facts. He says that much of sociology tells us the theory behind the "research", the methods utilized; but very little in the way of findings. What did you find out? That is what he wants to know— not what theories you tacked on up front and in the conclusion or what methods you used— but your findings. Yet Davis doesn't really want sociology to be purely descriptive. His complaint about theory is based upon an old fashioned view of what a theory is. I can agree with him that we don't want or need that kind of theory. If we think of theory as an explanation of an empirical problem (Laudan, 1977), then I think that Davis really wants sociology to be theoretical.

Causal analysis is the primary theory style of contemporary sociology. And this is actually what Davis wants us to do. He wants us to take some interesting two variable correlations and explain them by introducing additional variables into the analysis. He tells us some of the relationships he would like to see explained. First, he wants to know a zero-order correlation: what is the relationship between married women's labor force participation (independent variable) and strength of marital bonds (dependent variable). Second, there is a correlation between cohort and verbal skills (recent cohorts have lower verbal skills) controlling for education. Here we already have three variables; Davis wants us to explain this correlation. Third, there is a correlation between self-reported health and socioeconomic status. Why? Fourth, there is a correlation in the contemporary U.S. between race and marital status. Why? Married people are happier than unmarried people and white people are happier than African Americans. Why? And why is the former correlation getting smaller over time?

I will raise some other correlations that interest me for which explanations have not been found: the correlation between gender and scientific productivity among American scientists, the correlation between gender and performance on the quantitative part of the Scholastic Aptitude Test, the correlation between race and IQ (this is one of Felson's forbidden topics because it deals with a "protected" group and the blame analysts will stop us from studying it), or the correlation between Jewish/Christian and income or any other measure of attainment (maybe we would be allowed to do this research because Jews, the minority, are not a protected group, and anyway their incomes are higher.)

I like Davis' suggestion. This is the type of causal analysis that I wanted to do when I entered sociology. These were the kinds of questions for which Lazarsfeld's logic of causal analysis and elaboration scheme are perfect for analyzing. I wish I had the time to analyze every one of them. But here I would like to raise a question for Davis and any other sociologist, methodologist, or otherwise, to answer. If you look in the methods textbooks for examples of meaningful two variable relationships (e.g. like gender and number of publications for scientists) which are washed out by third variables, why do you invariably find hypothetical rather than real examples? I use such hypothetical examples in my own methods book; so does everybody else. When I analyze an example from *Union Democracy* which claimed to be a washout of a two-variable relationship, I showed how it was not a legitimate analysis (Cole, 1976, pp. 64-6). In order to make it look like the third variable reduced the size of the two variable relationship in the partials, the authors of *Union Democracy* changed the measure of the dependent variable. When the analysis is done properly we see that they fail to wash out the two-variable relationship. In fact the explanation that the authors state for the correlation they try to explain is not supported by any data. And these are some of our best sociological analysts of empirical data.

You can find real examples in texts of two-variable relationships that don't wash out and plenty of real examples of specification or interaction; but it is difficult to find examples of two-variable relationships which wash out when a real independent third or fourth variable is controlled (or in regressions when larger numbers of variables are controlled). Even in Davis's famous "Frog Pond" paper (1966), his test factor, "flair", only reduces the gammas in the many partials in an elaborate five variable table. And because it even reduces the gammas it is interesting.

It is possible that the inability of sociologists to wash out a two variable relationship by introducing additional variables into the analysis may not be because we have failed to identify the proper third variables; but perhaps it is because correlations like these can't be washed out no matter what additional independent variables are used.

If we can't find examples where correlations between basic demographic variables like gender and race are washed out when controlling for legitimately independent variables, doesn't this raise serious questions about how we are applying the causal model? To do causal research on these types of questions requires the assumption that you can specify the social or cultural aspects of variables like gender, race, and religion and control for them and wash out the correlation. But what if the reason for these correlations has to do with cultural or structural factors on which there is no individual variance? I believe this to be the case for gender, the only one of these basic variables which I have studied in depth. I believe that virtually every woman growing up in a particular society is influenced by the gender norms of that society and that, therefore, there is little variance on the key independent variable which characterizes a society rather than individuals (Cole and Fiorentine, 1991). If this is true, then we can't use survey research to answer many of the most important questions. Because the unit of analysis has to be a specific society in a specific historical period. Survey research would become only one small part in an immensely difficult comparative historical analysis in which it is difficult to get data on more than a few cases and where the other uncontrolled variables that might influence the dependent variable are numerous and impossible to control.

Contradiction Between American Culture and Sociology

This is a point raised by Molotch which deserves emphasis. Molotch says that the reason that sociology is having problems in the United States is that the society in its essential culture is basically hostile to sociological ways of thinking. What he means is that our culture, with its emphasis on individualism and seeing the causes of social problems as being a result of individual as opposed to social failure, is incompatible with a sociological view of how and why things happen. We need a better society, concludes Molotch.

Now many readers of this book would probably agree with Molotch on this point. I have one problem with it, however. Other societies, particularly some of the Western European societies and Japan place a much greater emphasis on social causation in their culture and this can be seen in their highly developed state welfare programs. Many of these societies are wealthy, meaning that they have the resources to develop high quality and different sociology. But one must ask whether European or Japanese sociology is any better than American sociology. Some post-modernists might say yes (at least for European sociology). But for much of sociology in the rest of the world, American sociology has been used as the model. So, although I think that Molotch raises an interesting question, one which deserves to be analyzed, I am not sure what the answer will be.

The Post Modernist Turn

Padget Henry (Chapter 15) believes that sociology is in serious trouble; but the reasons he gives are diametrically opposed to what most of the other contributors to this volume believe. He rejects the notion that the problem of sociology is that it is too ideological or that it is not technically adequate (as Henry interprets the Collins argument) because the period of its greatest growth was also the time when ideology became more important and, in his opinion, methodology made great strides forward. Henry makes a convincing argument, as do others like Davis and Molotch, that sociology has no subject matter which is its exclusive property. Economics owns the economy and political science the state; but sociology studies everything and owns nothing. He argues that sociologists have recently paid attention to work being done in economics; but he sees us as taking more from that field than what that field has taken from us. Therefore, we have a "negative balance of trade" with economics. Because there is no subject matter which is exclusively ours, we are open to being raided by new and emerging disciplines.

These new disciplines are based upon post-modern theorizing characterized by an emphasis on hermeneutics and language. Henry argues that sociology has failed to pay attention to these new developments, hoping they would just go away. The result has been that we have lost market share to new programs such as Africana Studies, Women's Studies, other programs emphasizing ethnicity, and the humanities, which, as a result of post-modernist developments, are now addressing some of the problems that used to be primarily the property of sociologists. He sees us particularly vulnerable to other disciplines taking away students who are interested in race/ethnicity, gender, third world development, and the arts. The new disciplines have been receptive to post-modernist ideas and are more attractive to students than sociology. Although post-modernist theories do not particularly appeal to me, I believe that Henry may be correct in his argument. Whether this means that sociology should adopt post-modernist theories and approaches and train more meta-theorists, as Henry suggests, or that we should mount a counter-offensive which I think people like Davis and Rule and perhaps other contributors to this book would favor is something which deserves to be debated.

Use of Literary Techniques

Post-modernists have been criticized for writing in a turgid impenetrable style. The writings of Donna Harraway are a good example. But some post-modernists such as Ellis and Bochner criticize traditional sociological writing for being boring and ignoring the problems faced by real people. Ellis and Bochner define themselves as being on the periphery of sociology as opposed to what they call the center (I think there is less of a coherent center than they perceive). Bochner is a Professor of Communication and Ellis has a joint appointment in the Departments of Sociology and Communication; although at one time he tried to have her appointment switched solely to the latter department. They have given up hope for what they see as the core or traditional sociology. To them it is unnecessarily abstract and boring, and it ignores the problems of real people. I am very sympathetic to their assessment of "traditional" sociology. But what they propose to do to make sociology more relevant, useful, and interesting is something which most contributors to this volume, as Ellis and Bochner guess in their innovative essay, will probably reject; that is, to do sociology by merging auto-biography and fiction writing with sociological concerns.

Carolyn Ellis's book, *Final Negotiations* (1995) is an autobiographical account of the relationship between Carolyn and Gene Weinstein. Carolyn describes their changing relationship as Gene became more and more ill with terminal emphysema. Now, Ellis and Bochner want to know if "we", the center, consider something like *Final Negotiations* to be sociology. I will give an honest answer. I don't really know; but what I do know is that this book is extraordinarily well written— to the standards of the best contemporary popular memoirs. I also know that *Final Negotiations* was more enjoyable to read and more enlightening about the human condition than the great majority of sociology books I have read in the last twenty years. Now obviously writing autobiography or fiction isn't going to give us a high consensus-rapid discovery field described by Collins or the type of progress which Rule would like to see or any laws such as physicists have. But, like good fiction, it does provide great insight into human behavior and thus deserves a place in sociology. If literature departments can steal our subjects, then certainly we can appropriate some of their techniques. I would love to see more books like *Final Negotiations* written. I believe that the use of literature written by professional writers as well as literature written by professional sociologists can do a lot to inform us about the human condition. Henry (Chapter 15) I believe would be very sympathetic to the approach of Ellis and Bochner because he several times cites the words of

C. Wright Mills: "As Mills often reminded us, the cultural significance of sociology is realized when through its lenses people see their personal troubles and public issues in a new and more familiar light." (p. 650). And I am sure these words of Mills would resonate with Ellis and Bochner.

The Quality of Sociology Students

This brings us to another theme in several of the essays, including that of Becker and Rau and Huber. The quality of students going into sociology both at the undergraduate and graduate level has been getting lower and lower. If we look at Graduate Record Examination (GRE) scores, sociology graduate students now have the lowest mean scores except for social work and criminology. One reason why we don't have any young Mertons, Parsons, Lazarsfelds, or Goffmans is that most very smart people don't want to become sociologists. And given the low prestige and serious problems of the discipline, who can blame them?

Our undergraduate programs are so bad, as Becker and Rau point out, that we can't expect to attract the best and brightest undergraduates. In fact, our courses have been dumbed down in order to bring in sufficient numbers to prevent the further decline in size of our departments. Even with the dumbed down courses we hesitate to give realistic grades and many sociologists make bargains with their students: I'll give you all A's and B's and you won't have to do any work so long as you won't bother me or complain about me to the chair. This is the same kind of contract between pupils and teachers which can be found in our high schools. For evidence see one of the finest examples of qualitative research, *The Shopping Mall High School* (Powell, et. al. 1985). This book and the other book I use to teach about education, such as *The Learning Gap* (Stevenson and Stigler, 1992) were not written by sociologists but by educational researchers and psychologists respectively. In fact, an indicator of the poor state of sociology is the difficulty in finding good books written by sociologists to assign to undergraduates. I find increasingly that I am using the work of other social scientists, historians, and journalists — which all seem to deal better with empirical problems than the writings of my disciplinary colleagues.

Several contributors to this volume, Becker and Rau and Stinchcombe, mention the poor introductory courses that are taught by most sociology departments. Examine any of the popular introductory texts; they all tend to be similar since they copy from one another, and marketing people at the big publishing houses usually control the production of the book. They usually have 21 or 22 chapters in which they try to "cover" the field. Pick one of these books up and ask whether you would be interested in sociology, if this were your first exposure to it. If I had taken an introductory sociology course with a standard 22 chapter text, it would have been my last sociology course. These books are incredibly boring. They are filled with hundreds and hundreds of citations. The average physics introductory text has fewer than 100 citations; the average sociology text has more than 800 (Cole, 1992). They are also filled with dozens and dozens of terms— jargon— which the students are forced to memorize so that they may answer the pre-packaged multiple choice questions which come with the teacher's manual. The examples used are brief and insufficient to develop a point adequately. The students who are forced to pay the exorbitant prices charged for these four color technically slick "books" forget everything they have read within a day or two of the final exam and sell their book back into the used book market; thus new editions every third year.

The approach to theory is pitiful in these introductory texts. Practically all of them pose three or four different theoretical orientations: structural-functional analysis, conflict theory, symbolic interactionism. These are abstract entities which have little meaning to the students. And most text books completely give up on the attempt to teach the students anything about sociological methods. Admittedly it is hard to teach methodology to introductory students, but sociology is a hard discipline and what's wrong with having some difficult material in the introductory course?

Joan Huber criticizes the quality of our graduate programs. She served on an ASA committee to find out what graduate programs were requiring and to make recommendations to improve them. In her article she publishes parts of her report, including the suggestion that graduate students not sit on committees that determine graduate curriculum. It is not hard to guess that the ASA ignored this report and refused to distribute it. There are very serious problems in many graduate programs based upon the unwillingness of many "liberal" sociologists to engage in evaluation. I'll leave the gory detail to the Huber essay.

Is it possible that because of the weakness of both our undergraduate and graduate programs and our aversion to evaluation that some (not all) relatively well known sociologists are not of the same intellectual caliber as stars of the past? Again, we come back to the social construction of the discipline. It is possible that some sociologists achieve positions of power and visibility not necessarily because of the brilliance of their minds illustrated in their writing; but because of their ideological position, their pleasant personalities, and networks of self-promoting friends. These factors play a role in all disciplines; but in a field like physics they won't make you a star if you don't produce the goods. And if you really produce the goods in physics, the other stuff won't matter. You can be an s.o.b and still win the Nobel Prize (see Taubes, 1986).

The Absence of Civility

Which brings us to still another theme mentioned by several writers (Lipset and Molotch): many sociologists just seem to enjoy stabbing each other in the back and engaging in vicious political fighting. (As members of English and anthropology departments can tell you, this is not something unique to sociology.) Science in general is competitive (there are many natural scientists who hate their competitors); but it is also collegial— the people in the community recognize that they have interests in common and are willing to admit they were wrong or accept an intellectual disagreement without letting it turn into a personal vendetta (See Peter Galison's *How Experiments End*, 1987). The type of behavior that we find in many sociology departments is simply suicidal and it appears as if some of us would rather see our departments retrenched than live in peace and civility with our colleagues.

Why is this? It could be because uncivil people self-select into sociology; but I prefer a more sociological explanation. The activities engaged in by natural scientists and social scientists at the research frontier are very similar; but the outcome is vastly different. Core knowledge is continually being produced in the natural sciences and not in sociology. This means that leaders in sociology have less communally recognized achievements to back up their status. In this situation the relative significance of political and social processes (social construction) is likely to be greater in a field like sociology. Whereas in a field like physics intellectual authority is based primarily upon contributions to the core, in a field like sociology it is primarily based on power within the discipline. This argument should not be overstated. The people who have the power tend to be those whose work has been most highly recognized. However, since the work is never accepted into the core there is always disagreement about its validity and significance. Consider, just for example, the extent of disagreement over the significance of the work of Merton and Parsons, the two most eminent sociologists in America in the post World War II period. There would not be such disagreement about the work of the most eminent physicists. This weakens the cognitive base on which authority is built in sociology. In other words, people in sociology tend to act nasty because there is not an underlying agreement upon good work which brings people into line. Thus, sociologists behave as Latour (1987) says that all scientists behave. They fight and war among each other; with the spoils going to the most powerful (the extent to which someone's ideas are right or wrong has no bearing on the battle).

Sociological Ethnocentrism

This is another point raised by Molotch and one with which I agree. Sociologists seem to believe that everything can be explained by sociological concepts. We have a particular aversion to biological explanations and some like Alice Rossi (1985) and Walter R. Gove (1994) believe that this is particularly damaging to sociology. What I tell students is that before they start to think of sociological explanations for a particular phenomenon they are interested in, they should first ask whether it could be explained by some more common sense approach.

Another type of sociological ethnocentrism is a failure by most sociologists to admit that a good part of individual human behavior is due to random factors which simply can't be explained sociologically. For example, when Jencks et. al. (1972) concluded that we can explain only 25 percent of the variance on income and that the rest is a result of specialized skills that sociologists don't measure or a result of "luck", some ridiculed him; but he was right. Sociologists haven't adequately introduced the notion of chance into their analyses and some of them like the social constructivists in science studies believe that sociology can explain everything, including the specific content of the "laws" of nature.

Methodological Faddism

Although some contributors to this volume see methodology as an area in which advance has been made (Rule and Henry), others such as Davis and myself see sociology as dominated by methodological faddism. Davis in his essay is very critical of the currently most popular method of analysis in the leading sociology journals, logistic regression. Davis sees logistic regression as a retrogression rather than an advance. Whereas fields like economics and psychology have long been obsessed with statistical significance— to the extent that in economics elaborate models are proposed which explain two percent of the variance on the dependent variable— sociology has managed to avoid this obsession and, although conducting tests of significance, has concentrated on the size and substantive meaning of effects. Logistic regression, as Davis points out, tells us nothing more than whether a particular variable in the regression equation has a direct effect on the dependent variable andwhether this effect is statistically significant. This is primarily a result of the sample size. With a big enough sample size, the tiniest relationship will be statistically significant.

I have been told that many sociologists analyze their data using ordinary least squares regression, and then when they have figured out what the data mean, they run the regression as a logistic one in order to satisfy the journal editors and their referees. The SPSS program for logistic regression will not even give you a measure of R squared. Thus, using this technique, you have no idea how much variance you have explained on your dependent variable. Some statisticians have figured out a way to compute an R-square equivalent from a logistic regression but it is a method which must be done by hand using a complex formula.

The question I have is this: who ever determined that multi-variate sociological analysis had to be done using logistic regression? The authorities who bless or banish particular methods are like the gnomes of the Swiss banks— they are invisible. There are many other ways of handling dichotomous dependent variables, including some of the ingenious ones utilized by Davis and even techniques like Probit Regression which at least gives you an R-square and an estimate of the size of the effect of each variable. I have a suggestion to make to the editors of the major journals. In order to encourage methodological diversity in the field, refuse to accept a criticism that one method should have been replaced by another, unless the critic is willing to take the data set and demonstrate that different substantive results would be obtained by using the "preferred" method. If the critic is not willing to do this, then his or her preference for one method over another should have no bearing upon editorial decisions about submitted articles. If we did this, we might see some interpretable analyses back in our major journals. Maybe people would even use tables instead of regressions. Why not use the simplest method possible rather than the most complex?

Again the answer lies in power within the discipline. There are some people who have positions of significant power in sociology based upon their greater statistical or mathematical skills. These people want to maintain their power and they do this by persuading sociologists to use techniques that are complex and, in the case of logistic regression, difficult to interpret. Many people tend to be slightly afraid of these powerful "quantoids" in sociology. But I suggest that if there had not been a displacement of goals, where the method becomes more important than the substantive finding, then quantoids who have few interesting ideas would not have the power that they do in contemporary sociology. How they have achieved and maintained this power is an interesting subject for empirical analysis.

Clearly, this introduction has not covered all the themes in the sixteen essays in this book; and it may not have done justice to some of them. But I hope that it provides a stimulating introduction to what I myself find to be a very interesting and readable set of essays on some of the current problems in our discipline. As you read these essays, ask yourself the question, is sociology socially constructed or is what we believe constrained in some way by the results of research? To say that sociology is socially constructed does not mean, as R. Collins points out, that there are not good examples of empirical work which should constrain what we believe to be true. But whether such work actually does shape our beliefs is questioned by several of the authors who have contributed essays to this book. If sociology is socially constructed, can (should) anything be done about it? How does the construction process operate?

It has been my impression that along with the end of the cold war there was a peaking in the extent to which sociology was politicized. There also seems to be a revival of interest in empirically based sociology. In my own department even politically "radical" students are complaining that they are not being taught enough about advanced quantitative methods in order for them to use the currently fashionable techniques in their research. What could we do if we wanted to see the extent to which sociology was socially constructed reduced? First, we should emphasize to both our graduate and undergraduate students the importance of subjecting our interpretations of human behavior to empirical verification. We should do this even if it means suspending our willingness to accept the currently popular views on the inability to establish "truth" even in the natural sciences. Physicists couldn't do their work if they believed that it was impossible to determine whether an idea was right or wrong. That is why Stephen Brush, the historian of science, says that the history of science should be rated X (Brush, 1975).

Second, we must place more emphasis than has in the past been put on the design phase of empirical research. My teacher, Paul Lazarsfeld, used to brag about how he could find interesting results in any set of data. This was true for a mind of Lazarsfeld's caliber but it is not the best way to advance knowledge. We must concentrate our efforts on what Merton calls "strategic research sites"— those which enable us to tell which of two conflicting theories or interpretations is empirically supported and which is not.

Third, we should change our laissez-faire policy on the selection by graduate students of dissertation topics. This is one area where imitating our colleagues in the natural sciences might be useful. Rather than allow our students (even encourage them) to select dissertation topics which they are "interested" in, we should guide them to selecting topics which are theoretically relevant, meaning that they will help answer an important question of debate in the field of research, and then guide them to doing "doable" as opposed to "undoable" research. One well designed doable theoretically relevant study is worth more than 100 poorly designed undoable studies on questions of doubtful significance. Rather than most of our students being independent entrepreneurs (a role which they are poorly equipped to play), they should become apprentices: learning the craft of sociology under the direction of an experienced and seasoned practitioner.

And fourth we should become more collegial and open minded in how we go about our professional work. A good dose of civility should go a long way towards increasing the morale and esprit de corps among our colleagues and this should make it easier to attract good undergraduates to select as their life's work what is still, after all, one of the most interesting fields of scholarly endeavor. Especially the more successful among our numbers should devote more of their time and energy towards recruiting new people into the field. This will be easier to do if the field is run on a more collegial basis. There is nothing inherently contradictory between maintaining high standards and maintaining high levels of civility. Finally, we should continue with a trend which has already begun: the emphasis on historical and cross-cultural approaches in which the unit of analysis will be something larger than the individual.

There is one small group of sociologists who are likely to have particularly negative attitudes to the views expressed in this book. These are the relatively few people, mostly younger, who have been highly rewarded by the discipline. After all, a discipline which has highly rewarded *their* work couldn't be in as bad shape as some of the authors of the essays in this volume believe. They might view these essays as simply the complaints of sociologists who feel that the discipline has not given them adequate recognition — a form of "sour grapes." Considering the very substantial success that has been achieved by many of the authors of these essays, this argument is hard to make. But finally I urge the readers to decide if these essays represent simply the opinions of some disgruntled members of the profession or serious problems that the profession currently faces.

Acknowledgements

My greatest debt in producing this book is to the authors of the included essays. They took the time to write what I believe to be interesting and thought provoking essays and were very patient when it took much longer than originally expected to get this book into print. I particularly want to thank Irving Louis Horowitz, the head of Transactions Press for agreeing to publish this book relatively quickly (and without asking me to delete some of the essays). The book could have in fact been published a year ago, had it not been for my obligation to complete another project before I had time to work on this one.

Annulla Linders, Assistant Professor of Sociology at the University of Cincinnati, was managing editor of Sociological Forum while I was editor and without her help I could not have run that journal or published this collection of essays. Finally, and perhaps most crucial in the book's publication, I want to thank Robert W. Cole and Sylvia Cole for setting this book in type and thoroughly proofreading the manuscript. This took many, many hours for which they were inadequately compensated. Without their skills and devotion, I would have given up on the book.

I thank Eliot Werner and Kluwer Academic/ Plenum Publishers for permission to reprint without fee the articles originally published in Sociological Forum. These are the articles by S. Cole, R. Collins, J. A. Davis, P. Henry, S.M. Lipset, H. Molotch, J. B. Rule, I. H. Simpson, R. L. Simpson, A. L. Stinchcombe, and M. Zald. I thank Irving Louis Horowitz and Transactions Press for permission to reprint without fee the articles originally published in Society. These are the articles by H. S. Becker and W. Rau, P. Berger, and R. B. Felson. I thank the University of Chicago Press for permission to reprint with a reduced fee the article by J. Huber. I thank M. Cole, A. Bochner, and C. Ellis for agreeing to write original essays for this book.

References

Archer, Dane and Rosemary Gartner. 1984. *Violence and Crime in Cross-National Perspective*. New Haven: Yale University Press.

Blau, Peter and Otis Dudley Duncan. 1967. *The American Occupational Structure*. New York: Wiley.

Brush, Stephen. 1975. "Should the History of Science be Rated X?" *Science*. 183: 1164-72.

Cole, Stephen. 1975. "The Growth of Scientific Knowledge: Theories of Deviance as a Case Study." pp.175-220 in Lewis Coser, ed. *The Idea of Social Structure: Papers in Honor of Robert K. Merton*. New York: Harcourt, Brace, Jovanovich.

——————. 1976. *The Sociological Method, 2nd Edition*. Chicago: Rand McNally.

——————. 1992. *Making Science: Between Nature and Society*. Cambridge, MA: Harvard University Press.

Cole, Stephen and Robert Fiorentine. 1991. "Discrimination Against Women in Science: The Confusion of Outcome with Process." pp. 205-226 in Harriet Zuckerman, Jonathan R. Cole, and John Bruer, eds. *The Outer Circle: Women in the Scientific Community*. New York: Norton.

Davis, James A. 1966. "The Campus as a Frog Pond: An Application of the Theory of Relative Deprivation to Career Decisions of College Men," *American Journal of Sociology* 72: 17-31.

Ehrlich, I. 1975. "The Deterrent Effect of Capital Punishment: A Question of Life and Death." *American Economic Review*. 65: 397-417.

Ellis, Carolyn. 1995. *Final Negotiations: A Story of Love, Loss, and Chronic Illness*. Philadelphia: Temple University Press.

Erikson, Robert and John H. Goldthorpe. 1992. *The Constant Flux: A Study of Class Mobility in Industrial Societies*. Oxford: Oxford University Press.

Galison, Peter. 1987. *How Experiments End*. Chicago. University of Chicago Press.

Featherman, David L and Robert M. Hauser. 1978. *Opportunity and Change*. New York: Academic Press.

Gove, Walter R. 1994. "Why We Do What We Do: A Biopsychosocial Theory of Human Motivation." *Social Forces* 73: 363-94.

Herrnstein, Richard and Charles Murray. 1995. *The Bell Curve*. New York: The Free Press.

Hoffman, Eva. 1989. *Lost in Translation: A Life in a New Language*. New York: E. P. Dutton.

——————. 1993. *Exit into History: A Journey through the New Eastern Europe*. New York: Viking Penguin.

Jencks, Christopher, Marshall Smith, Henry Acland, Mary Jo Bane, David Cohen, Herbert Gintis, Barbara Heyns, and Stephan Michelson. 1972. *Inequality: A Reassessment of the Effect of Family and Schooling in America*. New York: Basic Books.

Kanter, Rosabeth Moss. 1977. *Men and Women of the Corporation*. New York: Basic Books.

Kuhn, Thomas. [1962] 1970. *The Structure of Scientific Revolutions*. Chicago: The University of Chicago Press.

Latour, Bruno. 1987. *Science In Action*. Cambridge, MA: Harvard University Press.

Laudan, Larry. 1977. *Progress and Its Problems: Towards a Theory of Scientific Growth*. Berkeley, CA: University of California Press.

Lieberson, Stanley. 1985. *Making It Count: The Improvement of Social Research and Theory*. Berkeley: University of California Press.

Lipset, Seymour Martin, Martin A. Trow, and James S. Coleman. 1956. *Union Democracy*. Glencoe, IL: The Free Press.

Logan, John R. and Harvey L. Molotch. 1987. *Urban Fortunes: The Political Economy of Place*. Berkeley: University of California Press.

Merton, Robert K. [1938] 1957. "Social Structure and Anomie." pp. 131-160 in Robert K. Merton, *Social Theory and Social Structure*. Glencoe, IL: The Free Press.

Molotch, Harvey Luskin. 1972. *Managed Integration: Dilemmas of Doing Good in the City*. Berkeley: University of California Press.

Powell, Arthur, et.al. 1985. *The Shopping Mall High School*. Boston: Houghton Mifflin.

Rorty, Richard. 1980. *Philosophy and the Mirror of Nature*. Princeton: Princeton University Press.

Rossi, Alice (ed.). 1985. *Gender and the Life Course*. New York: Aldine

Skocpol, Theda. 1979. *States and Social Revolutions*. Cambridge. Cambridge University Press.

Stevenson, Harold W. and James W. Stigler. 1992. *The Learning Gap: Why Our Schools are Failing and What We Can Learn from Japanese and Chinese Education*. New York: Summit Books.

Taubes, Gary. 1986. *Nobel Dreams: Power, Deceit and the Ultimate Experiment*. Redmond, Wa.: Tempus Books.

Turner, Stephen Park and Jonathan H. Turner. 1990. "The Impossible Science: An Institutional Analysis of American Sociology." *Sage Library of Social Research*, 181. Newbury Park, CA: Sage.

Wotherspoon, Jane. 1997. "The Critical Reception of the Eldredge and Gould theory of punctuated equilibrium: The Interaction of Scientific and Social Factors in the Evaluation of New Knowledge," Honors Thesis, University of Queensland, Department of Anthropology and Sociology, Australia.

1

Why Sociology Doesn't Make Progress Like the Natural Sciences

Stephen Cole

In analyzing science it is crucial to make a distinction between two types of knowledge: the core and the research frontier (S. Cole, 1992). The core consists of a small group of theories, methods, and exemplars that are almost universally accepted by the relevant scientific community as being both true and important. Examples of parts of the core in physics would be quantum mechanics, the Weinberg, Salam and Glashow theory of weak interactions, or the Bardeen, Cooper, and Schrieffer theory of superconductivity. An example in molecular biochemistry would be the Watson and Crick model of DNA. And an example in evolutionary biology would be Darwin's theory of evolution.

The frontier consists of all newly produced knowledge. Most of this knowledge is ignored, a small part is paid attention to and most of that is discarded as being wrong. The core is connected to the frontier through the evaluation process. Only a tiny percentage of new knowledge moves from the frontier to the core, yet it is the core which is the basis of progress in all sciences. The core, similar to Kuhn's ([1962] 1970) concept of paradigm, is what is taught to new recruits and is the common ground upon which new science is developed.

Prior research which I have conducted suggests that at the research frontier there are not significant differences in the way in which natural sciences and social sciences proceed. The problem with fields like sociology is that they have virtually no core knowledge. Sociology has a booming frontier but none of the activity at that frontier seems to enter the core. There seems to be no sociological work which the great majority of the community will regard as both true and important.

Most sociologists will probably require no evidence to accept the validity of this conclusion. But for the few who may be skeptical I suggest examining introductory textbooks in fields like physics, chemistry, and sociology (S. Cole, 1983). In physics texts, for example, there are a relatively small number of references- about 100. In sociology texts there are usually more than 800 references. In physics texts most of the work cited was produced before the contemporary period; in sociology the overwhelming majority of work cited is relatively recent. The physics texts have very high overlap; the sociology texts have less overlap. The material covered in physics texts used 20 years ago is almost the same as the material covered in physics texts used today. In sociology there have been substantial changes in the material covered in texts used 20 years ago and those used today. In other words, the physics texts are reporting what is in the core and the sociology texts are reporting what is at the ever changing frontier.

In this paper I will argue that there are two variables influencing the development of core knowledge which differentiate the natural and social sciences. These are the extent to which the phenomena we study are mutable, and the extent to which problem choice and decisions made in solving problems are based upon cognitive as opposed to non-cognitive criteria. I will be comparing physics with sociology. Among the natural sciences, physics is the field in which the phenomena studied are least likely to be mutable and in which decisions are least likely to be made on non-cognitive criteria. I am aware that there is considerable variation among the natural sciences on these variables. Biology, for example, is in many ways intermediary between physics and sociology on these variables. Ecologists, for example, study phenomena which change over time. And fields like evolution and genetics, which have relevance for social and political issues, are more likely than physics to have decisions of scientists influenced by non-cognitive criteria. Also in fields like medicine, agricultural science, and fisheries science some of the most interesting problems emerge from the study of phenomena which are not immutable and may be historically and culturally specific, as are most problems in sociology. If my theory about why sociology does not develop core knowledge is correct, then we should expect to see differences in the ease of developing core knowledge among the various natural sciences according to their placement on the causal dimensions I have identified.

Defining Progress

If the purpose of this paper is to understand why sociology doesn't make progress in the same sense as fields like physics, we must have a clear definition of progress. A field is making progress if it has a core and is developing new knowledge which is being added to the core. This paper is based upon the assumption that although nature constrains what is at any time taken to be scientific "truth," the extent of this constraint can vary dramatically and it is therefore not useful to employ the concept of "absolute truth." Since so many theories which were once thought to represent truth, are now seen as incorrect, there is no reason to believe that what we currently see as truth will not later be seen as incorrect (Laudan, 1984). Many contemporary scholars in the social studies of science argue that it is necessary to engage in a whiggish type of history, in which the displaced knowledge is redefined in light of the new knowledge in order to make it appear as if there is a type of linear progress in science (Brannigan, 1981; Elkana, 1970; Kuhn ([1962] 1970). Thus, core knowledge is not knowledge which is "really" true but knowledge which the scientific community currently believes to be true.

It should also be clear that the content of the core of a discipline can change. The history of science reveals hundreds of cases where the core not only changes but sometimes in quite radical ways. Thus Priestely's notion of phlogiston in chemistry was replaced by Lavoisier's notion of oxygen. And in geology the notion of fixed continents was very quickly replaced by the concept of continental drift and the paradigm of plate tectonics. Because a contribution to science is ultimately displaced from the core does not mean that it did not represent progress at the time when it was in the core. Progress in science, as in other institutions, must be a time-specific concept.[1] Given the fact that science sometimes changes very rapidly, in some fields at times it would not be unusual to see new knowledge entering the core quickly and at times leaving the core quickly. In my view, though, the fact that knowledge is being produced which enters the core counts as evidence of progress. Quick and consensual displacement of core knowledge may indicate progress rather than stagnation. In fact, the "immediacy effect" or the extent to which a discipline depends upon new knowledge, has been used as a measure of progress in the past. (Cole, 1983; Price, 1970; Zuckerman and Merton, [1971] 1973).

Finally, my definition of progress does not depend at all upon the practical utility of scientific knowledge. Some natural science contributions turn out to have practical utility and others do not; but the latter does not necessarily represent any less intellectual progress. For example, in medical science, work which leads to a successful vaccine for AIDS does not necessarily represent a greater advance in science than fundamental knowledge about the immune system, which might not lead to any practical application for many years, if at all. It is my belief that sociological knowledge has had very little influence on the world in the past and even if it were to make more progress it is unlikely to have any significant influence.

Should Sociologists Act More Like Natural Scientists?

Now that I have defined progress, we can move to the primary purpose of this paper, which is to suggest some reasons why sociology does not develop a core. Some of these reasons are inherent in the subject matter of the discipline and are, therefore, not subject to change. Others are inherent in terms of how we have chosen to practice sociology and are theoretically subject to change— but the chances that they will be changed are very low.

Before going on to discuss these issues, however, there is one important answer proposed to the question of why the social sciences don't make progress like the natural sciences: the social sciences fail to follow the positivistic methods of the natural sciences. George Homans was a proponent of this view (1967), but the foremost contemporary proponent is the theorist Walter Wallace (1971, 1983, 1988). Wallace argues that sociology is a "natural" science but that it does not develop theory on which there is consensus because sociologists fail to follow procedures which the natural scientists follow. For example, sociologists do not define their concepts clearly so that all who utilize a concept will mean the same thing by it.

> Indeed, it is perhaps just this frequency with which we blithely go on using a term so utterly fundamental to our discipline without making a concerted effort to standardize its meaning that comes closest to justifying the charge that, scientifically speaking, we sociologists simply do not know (and may not care) what we are talking about. And never having established a common definition of "social structure" (and many other terms of similar centrality, including "culture," "status," "role," "value," "norm," and most important of all the term "social phenomenon" itself) *it is no wonder* that the catalog of sociological natural laws remains so empty. (Wallace, 1988, p. 24)

Wallace then goes on to give examples of how he would define some of these key terms. For example, he defines a "social phenomenon" as follows:

A social phenomenon may be generically defined as an *interorganism be-*
havior regularity - that is, a nonrandom coincidence in time and/or space of
two or more organisms' behaviors. (Wallace, 1988, p. 31).

Implicit in Wallace's critique is the conclusion that if sociologists were to
change their ways of proceeding, they would develop knowledge like that
in the natural sciences.

I don't believe that positivist critiques like those of Wallace provide an
adequate answer to our question. Consider only the question of defining
concepts. Wallace seems to think that if somehow we could impose uniform *definitions* of these terms we would have uniform treatment of the
concepts they represent. Think, for example, whether accepting Wallace's
definition of a *social phenomenon* is likely to change anything in sociology.
In order to get a definition that is innocuous enough for sociologists not to
object, Wallace is forced to ignore substance and be so general that almost
anything could be classified as a social phenomenon.

Although I agree with Wallace that it is annoying to have every sociologist define key terms in her/his own way, enforcing a standard wouldn't do
any good unless the consensus on the *meaning and significance* of the *con-*
cepts was real and natural. Of course, if all sociologists agreed that norms
were rules regulating social behavior, and that these norms determined large
areas of our behavior, sociology would be better off. But alas there are
many sociologists (ethnomethodologists and some symbolic interactionists)
who believe that norms, if they exist at all, have little influence on our
behavior. Agreeing on terminology won't get rid of the underlying lack of
consensus.

A problem with Wallace's positivistic views towards sociology is that
they tend to be based upon a distorted view of how the natural sciences are
actually conducted.[2] Wallace (1983, Ch. 14), for example, bases his account of how the natural sciences are conducted primarily on the normative
accounts of philosophers such as Popper, Hempel, Nagel, and Braithwaite
rather than on the more descriptive accounts of contemporary historians,
sociologists, and philosophers. In doing their work the natural scientists
simply don't follow the procedures described by the traditional philosophers. The natural scientists do not do science the way Wallace says that
sociologists should. For example, Wallace places a great emphasis on the
significance of replication; but work by Harry M. Collins (1985) and others
has suggested that replication is actually much rarer in the natural sciences
than one would expect from reading the normative accounts of positivist
philosophers.

My research on levels of consensus at the *research frontier* show that there are no significant differences between the natural and the social sciences (S. Cole, 1992, Ch. 5). For example, reviewers of National Science Foundation grants, or of manuscripts submitted for publication, are just as likely to disagree in natural science fields as in social science fields. This suggests that whatever differences there are in procedures followed by natural and social scientists, they do not influence the ability of the community to develop consensus on the frontier of knowledge.

If Wallace's prescription for the development of sociological knowledge is correct why haven't sociologists followed it? I believe that sociologists have not adopted these procedures because they don't work. In fact the natural scientists don't do science the way the positivist philosophers say they should because these prescriptions do not work in the natural sciences either.

I believe that the differences between fields like physics and sociology have considerably more to do with differences in the phenomena being studied than in the characteristics of the people who study them or the procedures that they employ. One difference in procedure which does make a difference is the ease of conducting experiments. Inability to conduct experiments is one impediment to the cumulation of knowledge; but as Wallace (1983) and others have pointed out, the theory of evolution in biology is not based upon experiment but is widely accepted as true and important.

There are two primary distinctions between the phenomena studied in a field like physics and those studied in sociology. The first is the mutability of the phenomena being studied, and the second is that sociologists — unlike physicists — study phenomena which they themselves are participants in.

Mutability of Phenomena Being Studied

Physicists study phenomena which as far as we know never change. The structure of an atom today is the same as it was a million years ago and the same as it will be a million years from today. Further, the structure of the atom doesn't change from one country to another or from one material substance to another. The phenomena of interest in physics are truly general. The phenomena that sociologists attempt to understand, frequently change faster than we are able adequately to describe them.

Wallace (1988) tries to counter this argument by switching from his general positivistic approach to a more relativistic one by claiming that "the search for 'fundamental...processes that are in principle stable' is 'ultimately destined to be futile' in all the sciences, and it seems both naive and facilely self-excusing to think this futility qualitatively distinguishes the social and behavioral sciences from the rest." (29) This isn't convincing, however, because Wallace is confusing stability of the phenomena with stability of the explanation. Because explanations have changed in the natural sciences does not mean that it is not more difficult to explain phenomena that change.

Consider the attempt by sociologists to develop a theory of gender inequality. The nature of gender inequality and its causes will differ from one society to another and can change rapidly within a given society. Consider, for example, why in a single society — the United States — there have been fewer women working in a high reward field like medicine. In a relatively brief period of time between 1970 and 1983 the phenomenon has changed dramatically. In 1970 only about 10 percent of all applicants to medical school were women and in 1983 one-third were women (today over 40 percent are women). In 1970 men were five times more likely than women to choose medicine as a career in their freshman year of college. In 1983 women were just as likely as men to choose medicine as a career in their freshman year (Fiorentine and S. Cole, 1992). In 1970 an explanation of inequality could have referred to gender norms which proscribed high commitment careers such as medicine as being incompatible with the family roles of women. In 1983 these proscriptive norms had all but disappeared and thus could not be an explanation of the still existing differences in the likelihood of men and women entering the field of medicine. In sociology by the time any theory is developed which might explain a particular phenomenon, it is possible that the phenomenon and the factors causing it will have changed. In short, sociologists are shooting at a moving target — a target which frequently has changed or disappeared by the time the bullet arrives.

The Difficulty of General Theory

Some might argue that rather than studying the changing and idiosyncratic elements of human society, sociologists *should* attempt to study the non-changing and constant elements in social organization and human behavior. We should study phenomena at a higher level of generality rather than a lower level. Perhaps this is a good ideal for some sociologists to pursue, but thus far attempts at developing high levels of generality sociological theories have not proven to be very useful in explaining social phenomena. In this paper I have space only to give the broadest outline of the reasons why I believe that sociologists have not, and will not, be able to develop useful general theory.

Some sociologists such as Parsons, Homans, Giddens, and Alexander have had very successful careers pursuing general theory, but their work has had very little impact on the vast majority of sociologists who are interested in empirical questions.[3] This does not mean that general theorists are not cited by sociologists who do empirical research; but these citations usually appear at the beginning of the article as a ceremonial citation and have little influence on the actual conduct of the work (Adatto and S. Cole, 1981; S. Cole, 1975).

Consider, for example, the attempt by Parsons (1950) to specify the functional requirements that all social systems must meet. In attempting to define functional requirements that were so general that they could apply to *all* social systems, Parsons was forced to develop a list of requirements which were so fuzzily-defined that sociologists could not frequently determine which functional requirements were being met. The AGIL typology did not prove to be a very useful descriptive taxonomy, and it is virtually impossible to identify how its development enabled us to understand any particular social phenomenon or outcome.

An interesting attempt to apply the Parsonian theory to analyze specific events was made by Smelser (1959) in his monograph, *Social Change in the Industrial Revolution*. The first part of this book consists of an elaborate development of Parsonian theory. The second part of the book is a historical description of how changes in the manufacturing economy of England served to disrupt traditional family patterns and motivated workers to participate in social change movements. The first part of the book could have been entirely deleted without affecting its value since the theory was not necessary in making Smelser's historical argument. Nor did the historical case study do anything to make the Parsonian general theory more credible. It should not be surprising that we cannot find empirical problems which were solved by utilizing the Parsonian analysis of functional requirements nor that today the Parsonian typology is not employed in sociology.

Likewise the attempt by Homans (1961) to develop a set of basic propositions that would explain all human behavior in all societies and at all times (for example, the greater the value of a reward to a person, the more likely he or she is to take action to get that reward) simply led to a type of psychological reductionism which has been widely rejected by sociology. This is because these types of behaviorist propositions tend to be tautological: what is of value is determined by how often it is done. Also, it is frequently difficult to explain macro level phenomena by simply aggregating the reward-driven behavior of individuals.

Frequently when sociology attempts to be very general it ends up reaching conclusions which tell us very little. In sociology it seems that the higher the level of generality of a sociological theory, the lower its explanatory power. Since most sociologists are interested in explaining some particular phenomenon in an interesting way, it is not surprising that very few sociologists engage in, or are concerned with, the attempt to develop general theory. In contrast to physics, the most interesting phenomena in sociology may not be general but outcomes of historically and culturally specific circumstances. Sociology may be closer to history than it is to physics because interesting sociological phenomena tend to be more nearly idiographic than nomothetic.

Consider the example used above of trying to explain gender inequality in the United States. There is some degree of gender inequality in all modern societies. Assume that for each society some of the causes are general — i.e. they would apply in all the societies. Other causes are idiosyncratic. What type of causes could be general? The only kind of answers that sociologists could give would be vague such as "culture," "social structure," "power," or "control of the means of production."[4] None of these answers would tell us very much about any particular case. If "culture" explains inequality we would want to know what aspects of culture do this, how did this culture develop, and how is it transmitted from one generation to the next? The answer to these questions would not be general but specific to each society. The general answers would tell us very little; the specific answers would tell us a lot about a particular case.

I have been doing research on gender inequality for about fifteen years (S. Cole, 1986; S. Cole and Fiorentine, 1991; Fiorentine and S. Cole, 1992). My research has led me to the conclusion that a key variable in understanding gender inequality is the content of gender culture. How does the society define what is appropriate or inappropriate for men and women? My research has suggested that internalized values and external social pressure based upon gender culture have a greater influence on inequality than direct discrimination.[5] One interesting question then is: what social, economic, and political forces influence the content of gender culture? I have found no general theory which adds anything to our understanding of this problem and that is because the answers seem to be historically and culturally specific. The only type of general answer to the question of gender inequality that would be interesting would be a biological one. If in the unlikely event it could be shown that gender inequality was "wired in" to the species, this would be intriguing — primarily because it would be so counterintuitive to the current beliefs of the great majority of social scientists.

Finally, I would like to look in some detail at one other attempt to develop a general theory — the theory of organizational ecology developed by Michael Hannan, John Freeman, Glenn Caroll (HFC), and others. The reason I pick this case is because it is one of the most successful and interesting attempts (that I am aware of) to develop a general theory with explanatory power. In other words, in my opinion, up until now this is about as good as general theory has done. The work of HFC is not simply a theory but it is accompanied by multiple empirical case studies which have been conducted utilizing the most up-to-date methods of both data collection and analysis. HFC are interested in populations of organizations. Thus, they have data on all labor unions founded in the United States, all semiconductor companies founded in the United States, all local newspapers begun in Argentina, all restaurants founded in a particular time period in particular places in the United States, etc. Perhaps the most detailed analysis has been done of the population of unions, and I will use this as my prime example in discussing this theory.

The theory has two dependent variables: the birth of organizations and the death of organizations. It has two primary independent variables: the legitimacy of the organization and the level of competition among organizations. Birth is primarily influenced by legitimacy; the more an organizational type like a union is legitimized the more new organizations of that type will be born. Death is primarily influenced by competition; the greater the competition the greater the likelihood that an organization of a given type will die. Both legitimacy and competition are measured by density or the number of existing organizations. The more organizations of a certain type exist the greater their legitimacy and the more organizations exist the greater the competition:

> Our modeling strategy begins with baseline models of the effect of density on vital rates, with density conceptualized as the number of organizations in the population. It assumes that processes of competition and legitimation can be usefully represented as functions of density. (Hannan and Freeman, 1989: 332)

> The consistent finding is that founding rates and mortality rates in the three populations depend on density in a non-monotonic fashion.
> (Hannan and Freeman, 1989: 333)

> We suggest that there are two opposing processes by which density affects life chance: first, growth in numbers in organizational populations provides legitimacy and political power; second, increasing density exhausts limited supplies of resources for building and maintaining organizations and thereby increases both direct and diffuse competition. Our theory holds that the first process dominates at low densities and the second (Michelsian) process dominates at high densities. (Hannan and Freeman, 1989: 275)

The data and models developed to test this theory are very complex and the authors have done a careful job in raising and attempting to answer a large variety of potential criticisms of their theory. My major criticism of the theory is that even assuming that the theory is true and that the authors have dealt successfully with the large number of measurement problems and other variables which might be influencing the result, the theory leads to obvious conclusions. To say that there is a greater chance of establishing a type of organization that has legitimacy than one that does not, and that organizations are less likely to survive when there is heavy competition, is not saying anything which intelligent non-sociologists would not know. It is not only the main points of the theory which seem obvious but most of the details. For example, the authors point out that unions which begin as secessions from other unions have a much higher chance of disbanding than unions which begin as a result of a merger with another union (Hannan and Freeman, 1989: 256). I am sure that this finding would surprise no union organizer or official.

Sociology has long been accused of coming up with obvious results. Whether or not this type of criticism is valid depends on the aim of the research. If the aim of the research is primarily descriptive, then to say that the results are obvious is an illegitimate critique. If we want to know what the facts are— and they turn out to be what we thought they would— then this is useful information. Because as Lazarsfeld (1949) has shown, many "facts" become obvious only after empirical data have shown them to be true. However, if the aim of the research is theoretical, that is to bring an understanding to the facts, then the critique of being obvious carries more weight. It carries more weight for two reasons. First, sociology is supposed to be a discipline that yields knowledge which is not simply common sense; otherwise, why the need for the expensive discipline? Second, a contribution to science is supposed to tell us something that we did not already know. To find what is already known (in this case even by non-sociologists) is not usually judged to be a significant contribution to new knowledge (Popper, [1963] 1972). Thus, in all sciences, theories which develop counterintuitive or unexpected results are more likely to be judged to be additions to knowledge.

The most important point I want to make about the type of general theory developed by HFC is that it is *impossible* to avoid being obvious. This becomes clear from the reply of Hannan and Carroll to the criticism that their density theory is a tautology. Hannan and Carroll (1992) clearly outline the criticism:

All organizational populations that we know begin small (initial density is low). If the population grows large enough to be a candidate for study, it must grow from the initial low level to some higher density. For some initial period, the founding rate must exceed the mortality rate. Conversely, the other side of the argument claims that because the populations that we studied have remained finite, mortality rates must eventually dominate (or at least balance) founding rates. The fact that founding rates dominate at low density and mortality rates dominate at high density suggests, according to this view, that the effects of density are not causal at all. Rather, the suspicion is that their patterns simply reflect the inevitabilities of finite growth. (67-68)

Hannan and Carroll then attempt to answer this critique:

Rates of founding and mortality presumably vary with external conditions facing organizational populations. These include abundances of resources, variations in political turmoil, and broad social, political, and economic structures. A truly simple account of population dynamics suggests that these conditions- not density- cause growth and decline in organizational populations. So, for example, one can obtain the observed patterns of growth, decline and stabilization by assuming that some condition favoring the organizational form arises, for some time persists, and then wanes before stabilizing. Many accounts of organizational evolution take exactly this perspective. Accounts of life cycles of industries, for instance, assume that technical innovations and industry learning curves account for the rise, stabilization, and eventual decline in numbers in populations of firms with particular technologies. We agree that external conditions affect rates of founding and mortality. When the data permit, we estimate stochastic models that incorporate the effects of social, economic, and political conditions as well as the effects of population dynamics. That is, we evaluate the effects of density on vital rates net of the effects of specified environmental conditions. (68)

In other words HFC do not deny that there are important non-general variables which influence the outcome in the various cases they study. In order to develop variables which fit all the cases it is necessary to make them so general that they lose— if not explanatory power— then interest. What we would really find interesting about the cases HFC analyze are the detailed particulars that they can't use as variables in their general theory because they do not characterize all the cases. For example, consider the question of under what conditions does a population of organizations begin to grow in the first place. Or under what conditions did teachers' unions begin to emerge; or under what conditions did semiconductor firms begin to emerge? Now think of the possible answers. The only general answers would be such obvious— and in this case— most definitely tautological statements as there was a "need" for this type of organization. Interesting answers to the questions would not be general for they clearly would differ for different populations of organizations mentioned.

The Choice of Topics

Thus far I have argued that sociology does not develop like physics because the most interesting phenomena of the former are mutable. Now I turn to the second primary way in which differences in the type of phenomena studied influence the type of core knowledge developed. Unlike physicists, sociologists study phenomena which they personally participate in — not as sociologists but as people. This means that the choice of topics and decisions made in the course of doing research are more likely for sociologists than for physicists to be influenced by non-cognitive concerns. My assumption is that research will advance and accumulate most rapidly when cognitive criteria are the most significant influence on the decisions made by scientists.[6] This point is made by Kuhn but has been underemphasized since. Kuhn ([1962] 1970: 37) argues that the reason there is progress during normal science is that the paradigm defines a set of problems that are doable. If the paradigm is "correct," the scientists know they can solve its problems. Inability to solve the paradigm problems will ultimately lead to a crisis and the replacement of the paradigm. A paradigm designates certain research problems as important simply because they are effective in demonstrating the power of the paradigm. *These problems may have no intrinsic significance other than their importance for the theory of the paradigm.* Kuhn stresses that if scientists select their problems for non-cognitive reasons they are less likely to be doable and there is less likely to be progress:

> Normal research, which is cumulative, owes its success to the ability of scientists regularly to select problems that can be solved with conceptual and instrumental techniques close to those already in existence. (*That is why an excessive concern with useful problems, regardless of their relation to existing knowledge and technique, can so easily inhibit scientific development.*) (1970: 96, emphasis added)

Kuhn then goes on to apply this reasoning to an examination of the differences between the natural and the social sciences:

> ...the insulation of the scientific community from society permits the individual scientist to concentrate his attention upon problems that he has good reason to believe he will be able to solve. Unlike the engineer, and many doctors, and most theologians, the scientist need not choose problems because they urgently need solution and without regard for the tools available to solve them. In this respect, also, the contrast between natural scientists and many social scientists proves instructive. The latter often tend, as the former

almost never do, to defend their choice of a research problem- e.g., the effects of racial discrimination or the causes of the business cycle- chiefly in terms of the social importance of achieving a solution. Which group would one then expect to solve problems at a more rapid rate? (Kuhn, 164)

This position is strongly rejected by constructivists such as Latour (1987, 1988) who argue that it is untrue that the scientific community is insulated from the larger society and that there is indeed no meaningful distinction between science and what goes on in the larger society. But Latour's position is unconvincing and Kuhn's position enables us to explain, in part, why sociology does not develop a core as does physics. In physics, problems raised by the paradigm are doable. In fields like sociology the choice of problems, and the decisions made in the course of doing research, are significantly more influenced by non-cognitive variables— such as political values— than they are in fields like physics. The usual argument made against this position (Wallace, 1983: 465) is that natural scientists are also influenced by values. I consider this an inadequate response because it does not consider the degree to which the various sciences are influenced by values and other non-cognitive concerns. To say that physicists are influenced by values should not lead to the conclusion that there is no difference in the ways and the extent to which physicists and sociologists are influenced by values.

Let us consider the variables which might influence the choice of research problems by physicists and sociologists (Zuckerman, 1979). In general, physicists will be more likely to work on those problems which are capable of garnering financial support. Decisions about what research to support made in some funding agencies utilizing peer review might be primarily influenced by cognitive considerations; but in others the value of the work for non-scientific concerns will be of greater importance. Thus, more funds might be available for work on superconductivity and nuclear fusion because of the economic and political implications of successful solutions to these problems. Young physicists might decide to work on those problems deemed important by their advisers or sponsors. The availability of equipment or apparatus could determine the problem selected. Scientists might decide to work on those problems which were currently fashionable so that any discovery would have higher visibility. The researcher might select a problem because he or she wanted to utilize certain skills or intellectual resources that he or she has developed (Giere, 1988: ch. 7). Or one might be selected because the researcher finds a problem of particular intellectual interest. What the individual physicist decides is "interesting," however, might be influenced by the other factors I have mentioned.

Now let us consider how a sociologist might select a research problem. All of the factors I have mentioned for the physicists would also apply to the sociologist. In addition to these considerations, however, the sociologist would be influenced by a large number of personal experiences and non-scientific values. A sociologist, for example, might select a problem because of the biographical experiences that he or she has had. Thus, I became interested in teachers' unions—the subject of my doctoral dissertation (S. Cole, 1969)— because my mother was a militant member of the union and had participated in the first strikes, not because the research site was a compelling one for answering urgent theoretical questions. Or a sociologist will decide to study marriages between blacks and whites because she is involved in an interracial marriage. Or a sociologist will decide to write a book about the Amana community because her relatives had lived there in the past.

Physicists don't decide to study quarks because they have experienced them. Sociologists study aspects of phenomena which they themselves participate in. The problem with selecting topics for research based upon non-cognitive criteria is that it reduces the chances that the results of the research will be important in answering any significant theoretical questions. There are literally an infinite number of empirical problems that a sociologist could choose to study; but only a small number of them may have any theoretical significance given the current state of the discipline.[7] The reason physicists can make progress is that they know what to study. Instead of dealing with an infinite variety of possible research sites, the paradigm defines a few sites which are important only because of the paradigm. Because sociologists actively participate in the phenomenon they study, personal experience is frequently more important than intellectual significance as a criterion in problem choice.[8] Personal experience *outside the realm* of science has little or no influence on how physicists select their topics for research.

Because physicists use primarily cognitive criteria and sociologists primarily non-cognitive criteria in selecting problems, this produces another significant difference between the two fields—i.e. the scope of the phenomena studied. High energy physicists concentrate their entire effort on understanding the nature of the elementary particles of the nucleus. At any given time the scientists are focusing on a relatively small number of problems. Thus, in the early 1980s in experimental particle physics, scientists concentrated their efforts heavily on experiments aimed at detecting the W and Z quarks predicted to exist by the Weinberg-Salam model of weak interactions but not yet discovered. This problem was important because the detection of these particles could substantially increase the credibility of the Weinberg-Salam model, an important part of the core of high energy physics. Failure to detect the particles would not necessarily have reduced the credibility of this theory as most would have believed that the designed experiments were not up to the task. If, however, more and more sophisticated experiments were conducted and the particles were not found, this could have caused theoretical physicists to think about a modification of the Weinberg-Salam model. In order to detect these particles, massive experiments were conducted, costing millions of dollars, and involving collaborative efforts of hundreds of the world's experimental high energy physicists. Several large laboratories around the world were working simultaneously on the problem. The problem's solution was known to be so important that it was believed that the team to solve it would receive the Nobel prize. Eventually the particles were discovered at CERN by a large group led by Carlo Rubia, who was awarded the Nobel Prize for the experiment (Taubes, 1986).

Contrast this mode of doing research with that usually followed in sociology. Instead of concentrating its efforts on a few problems, sociology spends its energy investigating a huge number of empirical problems. In general, there are so few people working on the same problem in sociology, that sociologists rarely worry about priority— one of the top concerns of the physicists. Another reason why sociologists are not as concerned with priority as are physicists, is that the problems they work on are more vague and less clearly defined. Thus, multiple solutions to a problem can receive equal recognition.[9] Instead of sociologists selecting their research problems to address pressing theoretical issues, most sociologists do descriptive work which is motivated by their personal interests and sometimes experience. Most of this research has virtually no impact on the growth of sociological knowledge because its results are not relevant for any important sociological problems. It is unusual to find sociological research in which an important empirical or theoretical problem is defined, the potential solutions to this problem described, and then an empirical study designed which will generate evidence capable of increasing the credibility of one possible solution and decreasing the credibility of another.

Because sociologists frequently choose their research sites as a result of non-cognitive influences they rarely do research on strategic research sites.[10] A strategic research site is a research venue in which the results have a high theoretical payoff by allowing us to distinguish which of two or more competing explanations is credible. As Kuhn points out, even in fields like physics it is very difficult to find such sites:

...there are seldom many areas in which a scientific theory, particularly if it is cast in a predominantly mathematical form, can be directly compared with nature. No more than three such areas are even yet accessible to Einstein's general theory of relativity. ([1962] 1970: 26)

But because such research sites are so important, a significant portion of the intellectual and material resources of the physics community is expended looking for them and investigating them.

To understand the importance of strategic research sites in sociology consider the analysis of altruistic suicide conducted by Durkheim ([1897]1951) in his classic study *Suicide*. Durkheim was arguing against the "happiness" theory which explained suicide by personal hardships faced by the individual. Durkheim's theory of altruistic suicide claimed that membership in social groups which emphasized the importance of the collectivity and deemphasized the importance of the individual would lead people to place a lower value on their own lives and be more likely to commit suicide. At first, Durkheim compared data on suicide rates of people in the military and people in civilian life. These data, however, would not tell us very much about which of the two theories is more credible. This is because both the altruistic suicide theory and the happiness theory would lead to the same expectation:that people in the military would commit suicide more than civilians. In this case the choice between the two theories was "underdetermined" by the data. But when Durkheim compared officers with enlisted men, volunteers with draftees, and reenlisters with first time enlisters, he was utilizing a strategic research site to study the two theories. In these cases the altruistic suicide theory would lead to one expectation and the happiness theory to the opposite expectation.[11] In this research site the data became useful in choosing between the two theories. The comparison substantially increases the credibility of the theory of altruistic suicide. A strategic research site is one in which the data help to reduce the extent of underdetermination.[12]

Because sociologists select their research problems on non-cognitive grounds they frequently work on problems which are almost by definition undoable (Lieberson, 1985). Natural scientists generally avoid problems, no matter how significant they may be, if they do not think there is a good probability that the problem can be solved. This point was made by the biologist Peter Medawar:

No scientist is admired for failing in the attempt to solve problems that lie beyond his competence.... If politics is the art of the possible, research is surely the art of the soluble... Good scientists study the most important problems they think they can solve. It is, after all, their professional business to solve problems, not merely to grapple with them.... That is why some of the most important biological problems have not yet appeared on the agenda of practical research. (Quoted in Zuckerman, 1979: 79-80)

Since sociologists are more motivated by interest in the subject matter for its own sake rather than by theoretical issues, sociologists frequently give more credit for working on an interesting topic than for effectively solving a sociological problem. This leads many sociologists — but few natural scientists — to pursue what must be considered to be currently undoable research programs.

Consider, for example, the attempt by comparative historical sociologists to develop a "theory" of revolutions. The best example of this work is Theda Skocpol's book, *States and Social Revolution* (1979). This book contains very interesting analyses of the French Revolution of 1789, the Russian Revolution of 1917, and the Chinese Revolution of 1911; but is it a successful theory of revolutions?[13] A better question would be: is it possible to have a successful sociological theory of *revolutions* as opposed to a specific revolution? The dependent variable for such a theory would be whether or not a revolution occurred in a given society at a given time. As well as having to explain why the French Revolution, for example, took place in 1789, it would have to explain why this revolution did not occur in 1788, 1787, etc. There would be a great deal of trouble in simply defining the dependent variable. Should the events which occurred in Eastern Europe in 1989 be classified as revolutions? Given the great diversity in the structure of various societies and in the historical circumstances they faced, there would be an almost endless list of independent variables to be considered.

One might argue that although it is impossible to explain all the variance, there may be some general independent variables or causes which will explain some of the variance. In trying to develop such a theory we would be faced with the problem of finding variables which are generalizable enough to apply to all the cases, and when we did this we would most likely lose the ability to explain any of the cases or end up with tautologies— e.g. a revolution will occur when the state loses its power (this is measured by the occurrence of the revolution). This is ultimately because each of the major revolutions is an idiosyncratic historical event and the causes which they have in common are likely to be less interesting than the specific conditions influencing any one.

Solving Problems

Thus far I have been discussing how sociologists are influenced by non-cognitive factors in selecting both their problems and their research sites. Despite the paucity of solutions to sociological problems I will conclude by showing how decisions made in achieving attempted solutions are also strongly influenced by non-cognitive factors. If we consider decisions that natural scientists make in the course of conducting a research project or what Knorr-Cetina (1981) calls "selections," we find similar differences between the natural and the social sciences. It is clear that "objective" cognitive criteria are frequently not the reason for decisions made by natural scientists. They might make a decision because one choice will support their intellectual interests, or for political reasons (to please an important colleague, for example), or simply because of chance. All these factors also influence decisions made by sociologists. But in addition, sociologists are influenced by their non-scientific values.

Let us consider the extent to which a scientist will be personally involved in having the results of a research project "come out" in a particular way. All scientists are anxious to have their research result in a way which they believe will enhance their professional reputation. This is true in the natural and the social sciences. But in the social sciences the researcher frequently has more than just a career interest in the substance of his or her research. Thus, suppose that Watson and Crick could have devised a different model of DNA — in fact, one which would have been in total contradiction to the one they actually published. Suppose that this different model had a better fit with existing data and was more useful in posing new and exciting research puzzles. In such a case it is likely that posing the "counter Watson-Crick" model would have enabled them to gain personal recognition at least equal to what they in fact earned for the Watson-Crick model. In such a case there would have been no reason for them not to have adopted the "counter" model, and we would have expected them to have done so.

Now, in contrast, suppose that a feminist sociologist had the option of putting forth a theory that claimed that overt sex discrimination plays only a minor role in the creation of gender inequality in contemporary American life. Even if such a theory fit the existing data better than the discrimination theory, the sociologist would be unlikely to propose it because of a personal — as opposed to intellectual — stake in the content of the theory. When feminists study the cause of gender inequality most are not doing so primarily because this topic is of theoretical significance but because they want to show that the inequality which is "bad" is a result of discrimination which "should" be eliminated. These political or social goals are very often more important to investigators and audiences in sociology than are cognitive goals.

In this case it is quite doubtful that the counter theory— no matter how well it fit the data— would result in professional recognition, because the majority of sociologists have feminist values. Thus, in sociology, both the choice of problems and the choice of solutions are heavily influenced by the personal experiences and the values of both the researcher and the audience.

In conclusion, sociology has not, and probably will not develop core knowledge similar to that of the natural sciences because of the inherent problems in studying highly mutable phenomena, and because of the impossibility of separating the sociologist-as-a-scientist from the sociologist-as-a-participant in the phenomena being studied. The first of these problems is not susceptible to change. Sociology will have to settle for developing theories of middle to lower levels of generality of historically and culturally specific phenomena. The second of these problems is conceivably susceptible to change. There is no necessary reason why sociologists must place such a high emphasis on non-cognitive factors in doing their research. It is possible, although unlikely in the near future, for the community to change the way in which problems are selected. For example, if every adviser to every Ph.D. student would require the student to justify a dissertation topic on the basis of its theoretical significance, there might be a more rapid accumulation of theoretically relevant knowledge in sociology. However, as Turner and Turner's (1990) review of the history of American sociology has made clear, from its inception the people attracted to study sociology have been motivated by a desire to bring about social reform not answer theoretical questions. Sometimes they have been seduced by charismatic professors into an interest in sociology as a science. But it is likely that recruits to sociology will continue to be primarily motivated by non-theoretical issues.

Acknowledgements

This paper was written while the author was a Visiting Member of the Institute for Advanced Study. The author thanks the Institute, the National Endowment for the Humanities, and the Andrew W. Mellon Foundation for support. Discussions with Nils Roll-Hansen, Larry Laudan and James B. Rule were of great value in the writing of this paper. The author thanks them for their help.

Notes

1. For a view which differs from that expressed here see James B. Rule, *Theory and Progress in Social Science*, 1997. Rule argues that in order for contributions to represent progress they must have lasting significance.

2. For a similar critique see Alexander (1988).

3. My critique of general theory should in no way be taken as a dismissal of the importance of the work of the general theorists. Each of the general theorists mentioned here has done work which has significant sociological interest.

4. See, for example, the theory developed by Blumberg (1984).

5. I have data to support this conclusion for the question of why women have been less likely than men to pursue careers in medicine in the post World War II period.

6. Stating that science is more likely to advance when cognitive criteria are employed does not mean that the use of cognitive criteria will necessarily lead to advance. Zuckerman (1979) points out how the use of cognitive criteria can cause delay in when a discovery is made or a fruitful topic investigated. It is also possible that the use of non-cognitive criteria may serendipitously lead to significant advance.

7. The concept "theoretical significance" is here being used as a black box. In fields which have developed paradigms the theoretical significance of a problem is defined by the paradigm. In fields like sociology which do not have highly developed paradigms it is much more difficult to define such significance. I am currently working on a paper in which I attempt to delineate the elements which make some problems more theoretically significant than others.

8. I do not intend to imply that research problems which are selected as a result of non-cognitive criteria cannot yield cognitively significant results; but just that the chances of obtaining such results are lower.

9. Also, as I point out below, sociologists are frequently not very concerned with whether or not a research project has succeeded in solving any problem.

10. Robert K. Merton developed the notion of strategic research sites in his theory lectures at Columbia University.

11. For the importance of such studies in sociology see Stinchcombe, 1968.

12. Lack of space prevents me from illustrating how much sociological research is of little value because its results do not enable one to distinguish between the credibility of competing explanations. For a detailed discussion of this problem in the field of gender inequality see S. Cole and Fiorentine (1991) where we show how many studies are inadequate because they fail to distinguish whether observed inequalities are the result of self-selection or discrimination.

13. Skocpol does not claim that she has developed a general theory of revolutions. But even for the revolutions (or failed revolutions) she claims to explain, she is not successful in demonstrating the influence of general causes.

References

Adatto, Kiku and Stephen Cole. 1981. "The Functions of Classical Theory in Contemporary Sociological Research: The Case of Max Weber." in Robert Alun Jones and Henrika Kuklick (eds.). *Knowledge and Society: Studies in the Sociology of Culture Past and Present*. Greenwich, CT.: JAI Press, pp. 137-162.

Alexander, Jeffrey C. 1988. "The New Theoretical Movement." Pp. 77-101 in Neil J. Smelser, ed. *The Handbook of Sociology*. Beverly Hills: Sage.

Blumberg, Rae Lesser. 1984. "A General Theory of Gender Stratification." Pp. 23-101 in Randall Collins, ed. *Sociological Theory* 1984. San Francisco: Jossey-Bass.

Brannigan, Augustin. 1981. *The Social Basis of Scientific Discovery*. Cambridge, England: Cambridge University Press.

Cole, Stephen. 1969. *The Unionization of Teachers: A Case Study of the UFT*. New York: Praeger Publishers.

———. 1975. "The Growth of Scientific Knowledge: Theories of Deviance as a Case Study." in Lewis A. Coser (ed.), *The Idea of Social Structure: Papers in Honor of Robert K. Merton*. New York: Harcourt Brace Jovanovich, pp. 175-220.

———. 1983. "The Hierarchy of the Sciences?" *American Journal of Sociology* 89: 111-39.

———.1986. "Sex Discrimination and Admission to Medical School: 1929-1984." *American Journal of Sociology* 92: 549-67.

———.1992. *Making Science: Between Nature and Society*. Cambridge, MA.: Harvard University Press.

Cole, Stephen, and Robert Fiorentine. 1991. "Discrimination Against Women in Science: The Confusion of Outcome with Process." Pp. 205-226 in H. Zuckerman, J. R. Cole and J. Bruer, eds., *The Outer Circle: Women in the Scientific Community*. New York: W. W. Norton.

Collins, Harry M. 1985. *Changing Order: Replication and Induction in Scientific Practice*. London and Beverly Hills, California.: Sage.

Durkheim, Emile. 1951 [1897]. *Suicide*. Glencoe, Ill.: The Free Press.

Elkana, Yehuda. 1970. "The Conservation of Energy: A Case of Simultaneous Discovery." *Archives Internationales d'Histoire des Sciences* 90-91:31-60.

Fiorentine, Robert, and Stephen Cole. 1992. "Why Fewer Women Become Physicians: Explaining the Premed Persistence Gap." *Sociological Forum* 7: 469-496.

Giere, Ronald N. 1988. *Explaining Science*. Chicago: The University of Chicago Press.

Hannan, Michael T. and Glenn R. Carroll. 1992. *Dynamics of Organizational Populations: Density, Legitimation, and Competition*. New York: Oxford University Press.

Hannan, Michael T. and John Freeman. 1989. *Organizational Ecology*. Cambridge, MA.: Harvard University Press.

Homans, George Casper. 1961. *Social Behavior: Its Elementary Forms*. New York: Harcourt Brace Jovanovich.

———. 1967. *The Nature of Social Science*. New York: Harcourt, Brace, World.

Knorr-Cetina, Karin. 1981. *The Manufacture of Knowledge: An Essay on the Constructivist and Contextual Nature of Science*. New York: Pergamon Press.

Kuhn, Thomas. 1970 [1962] *The Structure of Scientific Revolutions, Second Edition*. Chicago: The University of Chicago Press.

Latour, Bruno. 1987. *Science In Action*. Cambridge, MA.: Harvard University Press.

———. 1988. *The Pasteurization of France*. Translated by Alan Sheridan and John Law. Cambridge, Mass,: Harvard University Press.

Laudan, Larry. 1984. *Science and Values: The Aims of Science and Their Role in Scientific Debate*. Berkeley: University of California Press.

Lazarsfeld, Paul F. 1949. Review of Stouffer et al., *The American Soldier* in *Public Opinion Quarterly* 13: 377-404.

Lieberson, Stanley. 1985. *Making It Count: The Improvement of Social Research and Theory*. Berkeley, California.: University of California Press.

Parsons, Talcott. 1950 *The Social System*. Glencoe, IL: The Free Press.

Popper, Karl. 1972 [1963]. *Conjectures and Refutations*. London: Routledge and Kegan Paul.

Price, Derek J. de Solla. 1970. "Citation Measures of Hard Science, Soft Science, Technology, and Non-Science." Pp. 1-12 in *Communications among Scientists and Engineers*, edited by Carnot E. Nelson and Donald K. Pollock. Lexington, MA.: Heath.

Rule, James B. 1997. *Theory and Progress in Social Science*. Cambridge: Cambridge University Press.

Skocpol, Theda. 1979. *States and Social Revolutions*. New York: Cambridge University Press.

Smelser, Neil J. 1958. *Social Change in the Industrial Revolution*. Chicago: The University of Chicago Press.

Stinchcombe, Arthur L. 1968. *Constructing Social Theories*. New York: Harcourt, Brace and World.

Taubes, Gary. 1986. *Nobel Dreams*. New York: Random House.

Turner, Stephen Park, and Jonathan H. Turner. 1990. *The Impossible Science: An Institutional Analysis of American Sociology*. Sage Library of Social Research Newbury Park, California: Sage.

Wallace, Walter L. 1971. *The Logic of Science in Sociology*. Chicago: Aldine.

———. 1983. *Principles of Scientific Sociology*. Chicago: Aldine.

———. 1988. "Toward a Disciplinary Matrix in Sociology." Pp. 23-76 in Neil J. Smelser, ed. *The Handbook of Sociology*. Beverly Hills: Sage.

Zuckerman, Harriet. 1979. "Theory Choice and Problem Choice in Science." *Sociological Inquiry* 48: 65-95.

Zuckerman, Harriet, and Robert K. Merton. 1973. [1971] "Institutionalization and Patterns of Evaluation in Science." Pp. 46-96 in *The Sociology of Science*, by R. K. Merton. Edited by Norman Storer. Chicago: The University of Chicago Press.

2

Why the Social Sciences Won't Become High-Consensus, Rapid-Discovery Science

Randall Collins

Introduction

In the postmodernist atmosphere of the late 20th century, it has become unfashionable to ask about the scientific prospects of sociology and the other social disciplines. The natural sciences are regarded by many intellectuals as authoritarian and destructive; hence in the social disciplines we should not try to become a science even if we could. On the other side, science was once considered a liberalizing and enlightening movement in Western culture, and some persons continue to work at exploring the social realm in the same spirit. These contentions are moot, if there is no possibility that the social disciplines can be sciences in the same sense as the natural sciences. Let us step back from the polemics and consider the issue using the resources of the sociology of science.

I stress the social organization of intellectual fields in order to avoid the ideological and philosophical terms in which debates over the scientific character of the social "sciences" have often been carried out. Philosophical efforts at demarcation between science and nonscience have a long history of difficulties. The logical positivist program of reducing true scientific knowledge to observation statements plus the tautological calculus of mathematics foundered on the inability to make sense of its own metastatements, as well as on paradoxes in the foundations of mathematics. Historians of science and social ethnographers of laboratory life have shown that criteria such as precision, verifiability, and falsifiability are not often used in practice, that they are ideals or after-the-fact reconstructions.

Latter-day philosophers from the positivist tradition, such as Quine, hold that no theory is conclusively verified or defeated by any particular empirical observation or logical inconsistency. At best science is justified by a global pragmatism; some scientific theories work better than others, on the whole and in the long run, while others break down and undergo Kuhnian paradigm shifts. Why this is so continues to be debated by philosophers of science, thus far without definite conclusions.

Does this mean that all disciplines are the same, that physics and theology, literary criticism, and sociology are all on the same plane? Postmodernists revel in dissolving boundaries, and the failure of positivist philosophy seems to give grounds for regarding every discipline's knowledge claims as dubious and relativistic. Nevertheless, there is an appearance of sophistry in claiming that all the disciplines are the same. There are social facts to be accounted for: massive differences in their material equipment; sources of funding; social prestige; patterns of recruitment and training. Epistemology is not a good basis for understanding why such differences exist and how they have come about over the past few centuries. A more fruitful approach is to ask, What is distinctive about the social organization of the disciplines that we now take as natural science, and do the social disciplines have (or can they acquire) the conditions that make possible that kind of organization?

The Emergence of High Consensus and Rapid Discovery In Intellectual Communities

In Europe around 1600 emerged a form of scientific organization characterized by two distinctive traits: high *consensus* on what counts as secure knowledge and rapid-discovery of a train of new results.[1] These traits did not exist previously, even in the subject matter of natural sciences; it was not science in general that was created in this period, but the organization of high-consensus rapid-discovery science. (To avoid the clumsiness of this term, I will hereafter abbreviate it to rapid-discovery science.) The adaptation of this organization, usually known as the scientific revolution, was in fact not so sudden; from a few areas, notably mechanics and mathematics, it spread during the next 300 years to encompass most of the natural sciences.

High consensus contrasts not only with the pattern of the humanistic disciplines, which have remained outside the orbit of modern science, but with the typical mode of intellectual life throughout world history. In every civilization since the invention of writing, the undifferentiated intellectual role has been that of the philosopher. In this field, in China and India, in ancient Greece, and in the medieval and modern West, the pattern has been for major innovators in philosophy to appear in clumps: that is to say, rival positions are created at the same time, and opposing schools of thought maintain themselves over many generations without one of them establishing ascendancy. The basic pattern of intellectual life is not consensus, but disagreement. This does not mean that philosophy is totally unstructured; it is structured precisely by its rivalries, by its focus upon issues of contention. The rivalry is structured socially by the intergenerational networks that connect eminent individual philosophers with each other: in any period of creative life, there are typically between three and six such lineages or schools, a pattern that I have labeled the Law of Small Numbers. Times when the number of schools exceeds the upper limit of six are periods of structural instability and transition; during these times there is a sense of intellectual crisis, followed by restructuring in the following generations, which reduces the number of lineages to the normal ceiling. The dynamics of intellectual life in the philosophical mode have been driven by the struggle to appropriate a portion of this limited attention space, to be one of the small number of contending parties. Success does not consist in being a sole hegemon, but in finding a place within the action of a multisided conflict.

Prior to the scientific revolution and the adoption of the rapid-discovery mode, the fields of natural science also generally had this structure of disagreement. Often natural science was pursued by the general-purpose intellectual, the philosopher; thus there were Aristotelian and Stoic physics, various brands of Taoist and Confucian cosmology, and so forth. Even when there were specialists in a field that would be considered a natural science today, such as medicine or astronomy, there were typically rival schools: for example, in Greece between 300 BC and 200 AD a variety of systems of astronomy were used; there were five in medieval India; throughout ancient and medieval China, there were between three and five rival astronomies (Neugebauer, 1957; Jones, 1991; *Dictionary of Scientific Biography*, Vol. 15:533-632; Needham, 1959:171-436; Siven, 1969). Greek medicine was divided in a fluctuating alignment among as many as half a dozen schools; Chinese medicine was divided among a variety of Taoist and non-Taoist schools (Frede, 1987: 236-260; Welch and Seidel, 1979).

In this perspective, there is no abnormality in the proliferation of schools and the lack of consensus that characterizes 20th-century sociology or anthropology. These fields are much more typical of the form intellectual life has taken throughout history than are the rapid-discovery sciences of the last few centuries. Social scholars tend to regard their disagreements as a pathology of their discipline; but they are merely operating according to the dynamics of the Law of Small Numbers, dividing the attention space among factions who get their topics and their energies from mutual points of contention. Modern philosophy, too, continues to operate as it always did, through the clash of factional disagreement. That a large group of philosophers has taken as their topic the methods and epistemology of the natural sciences has not meant that philosophy itself has become a high-consensus, rapid-discovery science; the focus on science has given these philosophers a particular content but not a new social structure for their own field. One might say that the nonconsensus fields are in the normal condition of the intellectual world; only the rapid-discovery sciences have become deviant.

The modern natural sciences are unusual in their high consensus. Structurally, this means that they have found a mode of organization that evades the Law of Small Numbers, the focus of intellectual life upon rivalries and disagreements. How this has happened will become clearer when we examine the other key feature of modern science — rapid discovery.

In a field with a fast-moving research front, there is a chain of new results following one another with such regularity that innovation becomes expectable. This phenomenon became socially recognized in several fields by the mid-1600s. The speed of this research front has apparently not been constant. Data from the 20th century based on the obsolescence of the research literature suggests a turnover of attention in some fields of as little as five years or less.[2] But even in physics this extremely rapid turnover may have set in only in the 1920s (Griffith, 1988) and we lack good comparative studies of just how fast the foci of research changed in various fields (e.g., astronomy, biology, chemistry) during the past four centuries. Generally we can say that the rapidness of discovery became noticeably distinctive in some natural sciences in the 1600s, and that the rapid-discovery mode has speeded up since that time and spread to many scientific fields.

In contrast, the normal mode of intellectual life has not been characterized by rapid discovery. The natural sciences before the rapid discovery revolution, both in Europe and elsewhere, tended to maintain the same theories and bodies of recorded facts over long periods of time.[3] And in modern Europe as elsewhere, philosophy and the humanistic disciplines have not had a fast-moving research forefront. This is not to say there are never any changes in topics and conceptions in these fields; also there is the propensity to return repeatedly to the same issues -as in philosophy's classic epistemological questions, reinterpretations of the same authors by literary critics, or historians' repeated explanations of the same historical events-whereas the rapid-discovery sciences move on to find new topics about which to make their discoveries. The nonrapid discovery disciplines alone have revivals (bringing back Aristotle or Marx or Nietzsche, experiencing neo-Kantian or neo-Hegelian movements, reviving the reputation of past literary figures). Another facet is the study of the classic text, writing commentaries on Confucius, Hobbes, or Max Weber, whereas the researcher on the forefront of the rapid discovery science does not study Galileo or Newton, but leaves this to the humanistic discipline of historians of science.

The contrasts that Thomas Kuhn and Derek Price initially drew between high- and low-consensus disciplines (paradigm and nonparadigm fields), in the one case, and between fast-moving/high-immediacy and stagnant/classics-oriented research literatures, in the other, now appear overly simple. There are aspects of dissensus in the rapid-discovery sciences, and of consensus in the humanities; and there are various forms of innovation which take place in the nonsciences intermingled with the several aspects in, which their current publication forefront does not have a rapid discovery character. But the basic intuitions were on the right track; the high-consensus, rapid-discovery mode has made a crucial division in the social organization of the intellectual world.

Rapid discovery science does not escape the Law of Small Numbers that structures intellectual life. It too continues to be driven by rivalries and the energizing focus upon disagreements. But these disagreements are confined to the research frontier. As Latour (1987) points out, science has two cognitive aspects, and these correspond to two modes of social organization. At the research forefront, what Latour calls "science-in-the-making," there are disagreements among rival positions that are similar to those found in the humanistic disciplines. Just as in the pattern of rivalries found in philosophy, there is evidence of around five competing research groups in a scientific specialty (Price, 1986:130-133), similar to what would be expected under the Law of Small Numbers.

Here, too, studies of scientists' argumentative discourse show them using rhetorical tactics to elevate their own position and denigrate those of their opponents, not unlike clashes of humanistic ideologies (Mulkay, 1985). Once a topic is no longer on the research front, it passes into the area of consensus that Latour calls "science-already-made." Old results are taken for granted, elevated to the status of objective facts. One form of dissensus in science that has been widely researched is priority disputes. These do not reflect the rivalry and disagreement at the research frontier, but questions of assigning credit for discoveries that are regarded as having already been achieved. A priority dispute is possible because there is consensus on what counts as an item of knowledge. It is indicative of the difference in organization that disciplines that are not rapid-discovery sciences do not usually have priority disputes.

Rapid discovery science does not so much overthrow the Law of Small Numbers as dynamicize it, by abandoning old controversies in order to get on to new ones. It is the existence of the rapid discovery research front that makes consensus possible on old results. When scientists have confidence they have a reliable method of discovery, they are attracted by the greater payoff in moving to a new problem than in continuing to expound old positions. The research forefront upstages all older controversies in the struggle for attention. Because the field is moving rapidly, prestige goes to the group associated with a lineage of innovations, which carries the implicit promise of being able to produce still further discoveries in the future. Rapid discovery and consensus are part of the same complex; what makes something regarded as a discovery rather than as a phenomenon subject to multiple interpretations is that it soon passes into the realm of consensus, and that depends upon the social motivation to move onward to fresh phenomena.

Inadequate Explanations of Rapid Discovery Science

What is it in the activity of scientists, emerging at a particular time in history, that gave rise to this new mode of cognitive and social organization? Let us briefly review several traditional candidate causes of the scientific revolution; these turn out to be inadequate to explain rapid discovery science.

Empiricism

One explanation is to attribute the scientific revolution to a turning away from philosophical speculation and textual tradition, and toward the direct study of nature. This explanation was touted by many scientists themselves at the time, in attacking the scholastic and humanistic traditions that preceded them. But it fails to stand up to historical comparisons. There is a good deal of empirical observation in the sciences prior to and outside of Europe in 1600. The careful collection of astronomical observations had gone on for many centuries in Greece, China, India, and elsewhere, without giving rise to either consensus or rapid discovery. Medicine, biology, and mineralogy had long been studied empirically, and collections of naturalistic observations were incorporated in major works of the philosophical tradition ranging from Aristotle to Albertus Magnus. By itself, empiricism has no dynamism that leads either to a consensus on conceptual schemes and theoretical explanations or to a rapid-moving research front.

Measurement and Mathematization

Was the scientific revolution due to greater precision, or more particularly, to a new emphasis upon measurement, allowing the formulation of mathematical laws? Again the generalization does not hold. Some discoveries did take this form (Galileo's experiments with the inclined plane to formulate the law of acceleration of gravity); but much scientific work at the period of the scientific revolution, and even later, was not very precise (e.g., experiments with the mercury tube at various altitudes, or the pioneering air pump experiments); and many areas of discovery did not involve measurement at all (such as Galileo's best-known discovery of the moons of Jupiter by means of the telescope). If the scientific revolution was not necessarily measurement-oriented and mathematical, conversely there was a good deal of mathematical science in the period before rapid discovery science. A telling instance was Greek astronomy. One highly sophisticated version, Ptolemy's planetary system, was the classic exemplar of a non-moving research front. Moreover, in comparative perspective, mathematics is not intrinsically a rapid discovery discipline or even one necessarily characterized by high consensus. The ancient Greeks had rival forms of mathematics, oriented respectively toward geometric proofs and toward number theory carrying religious significance; in China, the official mathematical textbooks often disagreed with one another, and advanced methods discovered by particular individuals were often lost in subsequent periods (Ho, 1985). The introduction of mathematics into science does not guarantee a shift to the rapid-discovery mode.

Experimental Method

Positivist philosophers have often epitomized scientific method as the design of experimental tests, either in the form of direct manipulation of conditions or comparison of naturally produced variations. But this method is not the common denominator of rapid discovery scientific research, as we see by many examples of non-experimental and non-comparative findings, ranging from Galileo's telescopic observations to 19th-century physiology. Nor is the inductive logic of Mill's Canons unique to modern science; it has been used in the modern social sciences without making them into rapid-discovery sciences, and it was used on occasion in Greek and Chinese science. Again we find the explanation is neither necessary nor sufficient.

Rapid Discovery Science is Produced by Genealogies of Research Technologies

Modern rapid discovery science hinges on the mode in which scientists became organized around their research technologies. Galileo's discoveries in the early 1600s were often considered the takeoff of the scientific revolution. His crucial innovation was not so much a set of new ideas as the practice of adapting or inventing technologies for purposes of research (Price, 1986:237-253). Galileo tried out various combinations of lenses available as eyeglasses since the 1200s-to adapt them to astronomical observation; he made use of a pendulum for measuring time in calculations of motion; he adapted inclined planes not for traditional mechanics but as a way to make observations on the effects of gravity on balls rolling along them. Galileo's techniques may have had earlier precedents, but now they spread to constitute a research forefront. His followers invented barometers and thermometers, and modified the telescope into a different configuration of lenses, yielding the microscope and opening up further areas for investigation. Other researchers, away from Galileo's personal network, took up the example; Guericke and Boyle, for instance, recognized that pumps, which are already available from the technology of mining, could be modified for scientific experiments with pressure, temperature, and the vacuum. In the late 1700s, another wave of research techniques was set off by the invention of the electric battery, giving rise to far-flung research areas including the discovery of new chemical elements by electrolysis of fluids, and by techniques of electromagnetic and subatomic particle research in the following generations. In the same way, the history of modern nuclear physics hinges on a genealogy of accelerators, each evolved from the last; and the progress of astronomical discovery has been the production of new phenomena by the successive developments involving larger optical telescopes, their use in combination with spectroscopy, and the analogous development of radio telescopes. Instead of regarding these technologies as transparent media between scientists' brains and the phenomena that are discovered, we should see the main dynamic in the research technologies.

Genealogies of research technologies can be regarded as the core of the rapid discovery revolution because they produce the fast-moving research forefront as well as the tendencies to consensus and imputed objectivity of results. What Galileo and his followers hit upon was not so much the value of any particular technique, as the practical sense that manipulating the technologies that were already available would result in previously unobserved phenomena. Such a stream of new observables in turn gave rich materials for interpretation in scientific theories. What was discovered was a method of discovery; confidence soon built up that techniques could be modified and recombined endlessly, with new discoveries guaranteed continually along the way. And the research technologies gave a strong sense of the objectivity of the phenomena, since they were physically demonstrable. The practical activity of perfecting each technique consisted in modifying it until it would reliably repeat the phenomena at will. The theory of the phenomenon, and the research technology that produces the phenomenon, became socially objectified simultaneously, when enough practical manipulation had been built into the machinery so that its effects were routinized.

In the early years of the scientific revolution, the practice of making research equipment capable of repeating results took considerable time. Boyle's generation of air pumps produced consistent results only after about 15 years (Shapin and Shaffer, 1985:274-276). Even in the late 20th century too quick an announcement of findings leads to controversy and embarrassment when phenomena like cold fusion cannot be routinely evoked. In general, the speeding up of the rapid-discovery front has probably been due to the growing backlog of reliable equipment available to be tinkered with.

Research technologies are not necessarily the brain-children of scientific theorists -ideas embodied in physical apparatus. The Kuhnian paradigm, insofar as it is a cognitive model of the topic under investigation, gives a misleading sense of what scientists on a research forefront are doing. The scientists may have quite irrelevant ideas of how their equipment is operating. What guides them is on a nonintellectual level, a sense of what kinds of physical manipulations have resulted in interesting phenomena in the past, and of what sorts of modifications might be tried that will produce yet further phenomena. This is not to say that scientists' ideas are superfluous; scientists can bring their equipment-generated discoveries into the social community of scientists only by interpreting them in concepts related to the going currency of intellectual discussion. Research scientists lead a double life: as intellectuals in the game of argument for theoretical positions and as possessors of a genealogy of machines.

Just as the intellectual community consists in networks that pass ideas, problems and social validation along from one person to another, research technologies comprise a parallel set of networks. One machine gives rise to another in a genealogical succession: by modifying the past machine, or by cloning it from another in the same laboratory, or by a kind of sexual reproduction recombining parts from several existing pieces of equipment. Human and machine networks develop symbiotically; a machine embodies the results of the human activity that went into making it work in a particular way, while these human skills are typically tacit (H. Collins, 1974) and cannot be conveyed to another person except by hands-on experience at the machine. There is some evidence that research technologies on the active cutting edge can only be made to operate successfully by persons trained on the immediately preceding generation of machines. For instance, Boyle's vacuum pump diffused to other researchers only through a network of persons who had used an earlier exemplar (Shapin and Shaffer, 1985:229-230, 281). Sometimes there are bigger breaks in the genealogy of research equipment, as when one scientist recognizes that something may be made analogous to the kind of equipment used in another line of research, perhaps even the word of mouth that a particular kind of equipment has yielded interesting results.

Two implications of this genealogical structure of equipment are important for the social organization of rapid discovery science. One is that access to the forefront research technology tends to be socially concentrated; since new discoveries are produced by machines based on those that had made the previous discoveries, the new discoverers are likely to be persons who worked intimately with the previous round of equipment. It is not unusual for a person admitted to the scientific network as a laboratory technician to become a notable discoverer in his or her own right — as Hooke did by working with Boyle and his equipment, or the instrument maker Watt who developed a steam engine after working for the chemist Black. Limited access to forefront research equipment is one of the features that reduces competition among rival scientific theories and helps bring about consensus.

The other result is that research equipment, once routinized, may be exported from the laboratory, where they stand as physical reminders of the scientific theories that are associated with them. The triumphs of applied science are not necessarily the application of a scientific theory to a lay person's problem. They often consist in a practical activity developed in the laboratory and then reproduced in the field; for instance, the pasteurization of milk to eradicate disease consisted in transforming the dairy into a technological routine resembling that of the medical laboratory (Latour, 1988). We noted above that scientific research equipment may begin by being imported into the laboratory after existing, perhaps for hundreds of years, in the lay world. After modifications at the hands of scientists, the equipment may become commercially viable when reintroduced into the lay world. Thus the research device for producing and detecting electromagnetic waves could be adopted for lay use as the radio. Once this happens, the research, process is socially legitimized to a high degree: not merely on the level of ideology (which may wax and wane), but in the taken-for-granted practices of everyday life. Rapid-discovery science generates a strong sense of its objectivity and factuality because its research technology produces many allies.

In these ways, genealogies of research technologies play a key role in every aspect of modern rapid discovery science: making possible rapid movement along a research front, creating a sense that new discoveries are always possible, turning attention away from old controversies in order to get on with still newer discoveries, and promoting consensus and the sense of objectivity of past results.

Do the Social Disciplines Have
Rapid Discovery Research Technologies?

If this is correct, sociology and the other social disciplines have severe obstacles to being rapid-discovery sciences. The most glaring lack within social science is a self-generating lineage of research technologies. Let us briefly follow the preceding argument with a parallel consideration of the conditions of social research. In the interests of space, I will concentrate on sociology with occasional glances at the other social disciplines.

The problem of the social disciplines is not their youth. They have not lacked sizable bodies of practitioners and institutional bases of support during the past several centuries at least. Yet they have had neither much consensus — sociology in particular is famous for its battles among opposing schools of thought — nor a pattern of rapid discovery.

As long as we believed that the problem was in the area of theoretical approaches or methodological canons, it was possible to believe sociology might be made scientific. It should be necessary only for enough sociologists to adopt the right approach and to cease using unscientific methods. In fact, the latter part of the prescription would be redundant, since in a rapid discovery science those who clung to methods that did not bring new results would soon be unstaged by the achievements of those who were moving ahead.

Comparative evidence does not support the picture that a field becomes a rapid-discovery science by adopting particular ideas or methodological canons. That is not to say that these theories and methods are worthless; they may yield some good results without bringing about consensus and rapid discovery. It should be noted that if sociology is not a rapid-discovery science, it does not follow that it is not a science of any kind; it may well resemble the natural sciences before the rapid-discovery revolution, something like Chinese astronomy or Greek mathematics.

The usual prescriptions for scientific sociology are much the same as those that are erroneously credited with causing the scientific revolution.

Empiricism is not a panacea for sociology. Although some areas of the field are not empirical (or at any rate not very systematically empirical), increasing our degree of empiricism would have little effect in bringing about consensus or speeding up the rate of discovery. In sociology, there has been a good deal of systematic collection of data since the statistical compilations of Quetelet in the 1830s and the field studies of LePlay in 1850s, accelerating since the establishment of academic sociology departments from the 1890s onward. By itself, empirical research does not lead to consensus or rapid discovery; the results are just as likely to be sets of local descriptions repeated in other times or places, epitomized by the compilations of demographic data that have been made over many decades.

Nor does *quantitative precision* and *mathematization* result in rapid-discovery science. These were not responsible for that effect in the natural sciences. In the social sciences, there have been areas of considerable statistical precision and of mathematical treatment without bringing about a social scientific revolution. Economic theory became extensively mathematicized since the marginal utility paradigm was created in the 1870s; on the empirical side, econometrics dates from the 1920s. Nevertheless, it is not clear that economics has either a rapid-discovery forefront or a high degree of consensus, especially in macroeconomics. In many ways economics is a conservative, classics-oriented discipline, much like sociology, with neo-Smithian and other revivals and a continuing focus upon paradigms over 100 years old. It is true that large areas of economic theory have been mathematized to a degree that resembles the natural sciences much more closely than any other social science. But mathematical theory appears as an encapsulated specialty within economics; it generates its own lineage of technical refinements, but these are often regarded as an idealized world bearing little relation to empirical explanation (Whitley, 1984; Rosenberg, 1992). The mathematization of theory in economics has results paralleling the theory/data split in sociology, and contributing not to consensus but dissensus about the overall direction of the discipline.

In sociology, statistical and mathematical approaches have become specialties within the larger discipline, without transforming the whole into a rapid-discovery science. Mathematical modeling has taken its place as another branch of theory alongside the great variety of sociological theories. Although it contains some works of considerable creativity, it does not appear that mathematical sociology has generated any rapid-discovery lineages, nor achieved any consensus as to a dominating approach. Socio-logical statistics may have come closer to approximating the rapid-discovery mode, but only among its own specialists. Social statisticians have. created a progression of methods, building upon past forms, without much ten-dency to revive older methods or to engage in prolonged rivalries between opposing forms of statistics. But this characterizes not so much the average sociological researcher, the consumer of statistical methods, as the much smaller community of social statisticians who produce these methods. The distribution and historical changes of research methods actually used by sociologists are not known with much precision; but it seems clear that the progress of statistical methodology has not brought about a high degree of uniformity in the way sociologists do their research, and more generally has not generated consensus or a rapid discovery forefront on substantive matters.

If there is something like a rapid discovery science *within* the commu-nity of social statisticians, this may result from a process similar to the genealogy of research technologies described above. A given statistical method may be regarded as a kind of machinery, much in the same way that the algorithmic techniques of pure mathematics have provided sets of pro-cedures that can be manipulated to produce results in a new form. A takeoff of rapid discovery occurred within European mathematics in the period between Cardan and Tartaglia in the 1530s and Descartes in the 1630s. This development hinged upon the shift from verbal arguments and abbrevia-tions to the invention of standardized symbols and the formulation of rules for manipulating systems of equations. The invention of this mathematical "machinery" set in motion a series of investigations that paralleled the takeoff in physical science based on tinkering with research equipment. Succes-sive generations of symbolism were created and recombined in various ways, with new mathematical results produced at each step. Mathematics became a rapid-discovery science in its own realm, not as an adjunct to research in natural science; its chain of techniques and discoveries has proceeded by its own dynamics; conversely, the development of pure mathematics has not centrally determined the process of empirical discovery in natural science.

Much the same process of development may be seen in the history of statistical techniques. A genealogy of statistical methods is created by modifying earlier methods and trying out analogous procedures (as in the invention of ordinal statistics paralleling those based on interval measure-ment). There is progress within statistics, taking the form of a succession of methodological discoveries. The relationship between statistics and its application in social research, however, remains like that between pure mathematics and the empirical sciences. By itself, the pure statistical (or mathematical) side can far out run what is happening in empirical research, and the application of the pure technique to the empirical enterprise does not make the latter a rapid-discovery science. In sociology, it may even lead to a growing sense of divergence, between the refinement of the technique and the noncumulative quality of the substantive results.

Experimental method was not responsible for rapid-discovery science in the natural sciences, nor has it had that effect in social science. It is true that the experimental method lends itself to programs of research exploring a clearly delineated topic, and several such programs in sociology have accumulated series of results (e.g., Willer's Elementary Theory, 1987, and the Expectation States program of Wagner and Berger, 1984). Nevertheless, these experimental programs have not generated widespread consensus, but have become several more strands among the many rival positions within sociology. A broader analogue to the logic of experimental design has been used elsewhere in sociology, in the form of systematic comparison. Historical sociologists have often explicitly used the comparative method, with cumulative results on macroissues such as the theory of revolution (Moore, 1966; Paige, 1975; Skocpol, 1979; Goldstone, 1991; see Collins, 1993, for an overview of continuity in this area). Other comparative work has been done by accumulating available studies and synthesizing their findings into a larger system of generalizations. Such projects have gone on in sociology since the beginning of the 20th century. This method was the basis of Durkheim's project in the *Année Sociologique* and played a large part in Weber's encyclopedic treatment of economy and society; subsequent instances include Lipset (1960) and Etzioni (1975).

The comparative method is particularly useful for producing explanatory theory, since it focuses our attention upon generalizable conditions and on bringing to light the most central causal processes. These virtues are also shared by experimental research programs in the narrower sense. Why then has this work not transformed sociology into a rapid-discovery science? The paradox, I suggest, is that what can be found in the intellectual content of sociology clashes with the way the field is socially organized. Substantively, sociology has accumulated a good deal of knowledge on the causal and structural conditions explaining the major variations in social behavior and organization; in this sense sociology possesses a moderate amount of scientific knowledge. I have argued elsewhere that within sociology can be found fair approximations of the basic principles determining micro-interaction, the major forms of formal organization, the dynamics of conflicts and social movements, some aspects of stratification, and some macro-sociological patterns, especially in the realm of politics. In Collins (1975) 1 held, more optimistically than now, that sociology already had the basis of a science in the coherent patterns demonstrable by synthesis of previous researches. But this was an argument based on the cognitive content of sociology, ignoring its social organization as a discipline.

At the same time, the social organization of the discipline disperses attention onto a wide variety of theories and researches. Some of these have no social motivation for scientific consensus and cumulation, while others, which are consciously oriented toward scientific knowledge, do not generate a strong enough attraction to sustain a rapid-discovery forefront. The method of comparative research produces impressive results, but it does not give off a chain of such researches that cumulate in the way that research in the physical sciences gives off a research front.

The primary social tendency of intellectuals is to split into contending positions to fill the attention space, to follow the Law of Small Numbers. As we have seen, this tendency is overcome only by special circumstances in the rapid-discovery sciences; it is only because there are greater payoffs in plunging forward into new discoveries that these scientists forego the traditional intellectual mode of maximizing attention by making their positions distinctive from each other. Lacking genealogies of research technologies, sociology and the other social sciences are condemned to the endless contention of positions. Along with this goes the ideology that no scientific knowledge exists in these fields. The reality that is being reflected upon here is the social structure of the field, rather than a description of its cognitive contents. It is feasible, on the epistemological level, to apply canons of generalizability, explanatory power, and coherence, and to extract from the myriad sociological publications some materials that have a higher scientific quality than others. On the substantive level, there is no need to be a relativist. Some of the contents of sociology are scientific. But they do not become the focus of a social consensus, because they are not linked into rapid-discovery chains. Lacking that social support, they are merely one strand among many others.

Without this prize possession of the rapid-discovery sciences, sociology is unable to produce a stream of discoveries, or the forward-looking structure of intellectual competition that goes along with them. Social science thereby also lacks another major support enjoyed by the natural sciences. The practical applications of the natural sciences typically take the form of exporting laboratory equipment or its physical products into the lay world. Since social science does not invent a stream of new equipment, it is cut off from this form of applicability. When the social sciences offer practical application, it is in the form of information or advice: we give policymakers descriptions of a social problem, and sometimes (more common in economics than in most other social sciences) projections of what should happen if a given policy is followed. Beyond this, applied social science consists to a large extent of exhortation — e.g., the study of stratification is ammunition for social reform movements, and the study of revolution has been an encouragement to make one. Applied sociology frequently takes the form of intervening on a particular side in social conflicts, giving an ideological appeal for one interest and thereby alienating the other.

The natural sciences have acquired a deeper basis of legitimacy. Their ability to spin off physical products from their research equipment has made the exchange between scientific intellectuals and the lay community appear more even-sided. In return for support, laypersons receive material benefits, and often these take the form of equipment that can be individually owned and used, giving huge numbers of persons a visible stake in the scientific research enterprise. Television sets and electric lights are personal reminders of the payoffs of natural science, whereas the benefits of social science are typically collective, as well as remote and hypothetical. The concrete practicality of the natural science can be appreciated by laypersons without understanding the intellectual processes that produced it; in contrast, social science applications, even relatively popular ones such as psychotherapy, are embraced largely by persons who are committed to the underlying intellectual doctrines. Without the results that flow from a genealogy of rapid-discovery technologies, the social sciences are left with a weaker base of societal support.[4]

Prospects for Inventing Rapid-Discovery Research Technologies In the Social Sciences

Are there any signs that rapid-discovery research techniques for social science are on the horizon? Let us review how this has occurred in natural science. At the outset is a technique like Galileo's lenses. Assembled in one way they produce a telescope, in another way, a microscope; combined with mirrors and prisms, they give rise to the analysis of light spectra. This, in turn, combined with techniques of the chemical laboratory for heating and separating materials, results in spectral analysis of the elements. Recombined with the telescope, the result is the study of stellar spectra, and so on, apparently endlessly. The key characteristics are a machinery that produces some new observable phenomenon (thus giving material for theorizing), plus the capacity that by physically tinkering with the machinery, modifying or recombining its parts or applying it to new uses, it produces still further phenomena for study. It is a tinkerable research technology that gives rise to a stream of discoveries.

Do the social sciences have anything like this? We are looking for something quite specific, not merely general resemblance to the forms of presentation found in scientific papers. The use of statistics in social research, as I have argued above, is not a tinkerable research technology in this sense. It is part of the theoretical manipulation of the data, not a method of producing new data. In general, sociology's repertoire of techniques for data gathering has been quite slow moving. The basic empirical methods — field observation, questionnaires, experiments, and historical analysis — have not changed much over the past century. What has changed, in some cases, has been the kind of data that have been collected by such methods (e.g., questions about network ties) and the methods by which data are analyzed (e.g., the changing fashions for statistical analysis of questionnaire data). Occasionally we have turned up new phenomena (e.g., the micro-detail pioneered by Goffman and others), but there has been nothing like a stream of rapid discoveries driven by innovations in research methods. Our research techniques are not tinkerable and recombinable in the way that those of the natural sciences are. Ultimately we rest upon native human skills of making observations, and our discoveries are laboriously driven by theoretical acumen in where to look for data and in how to package it conceptually. What we lack is the key possession of the rapid-discovery sciences, their non-human machinery for generating previously unobservable phenomena. They have acquired a mechanical device that produces a rich stream of novel data as rapidly as the machinery can be manipulated.

The outstanding example of new hardware in social research was the introduction of the computer. But this has been used since the 1950s, without major effects on the rapidity of the research front. The computer does not produce data, but assists in analyzing it. Developments of computer hardware are extrinsic to social research, and for the most part have little bearing on the phenomena we study or our theoretical consensus in understanding them. On the other hand, social scientists have made some contributions in creating software — for instance, algorithms for social networks or simulation models for sociological theories. But such activity is essentially theory driven; not unexpectedly, it has thus far not given rise to rapid discovery.

There are some possibilities that social research hardware may move in this direction. In micro-sociology during the past 30 years, the introduction of audio and video recording has opened up the field of conversation analysis; new phenomena have become visible, such as the fine-grained coordination of persons in social interaction (Sacks *et al.,* 1974; Grimshaw, 1990; Clayman, 1993). Is it possible that such research technologies can turn into a self-sustaining genealogy of new technologies producing a stream of discoveries? There are some signs that a stream may be emerging. For example, by combining voice recording with a Fast Fourier Transform analyzer, a device that distinguishes the component frequencies of a sound, new social phenomena have been produced (Gregory, 1983; Gregory *el al.,* 1993). This equipment has brought the discovery of a low-frequency acoustic region where conversationalists' voices converge during an interaction, thus giving a nonverbal measurement of social solidarity. An offshoot of this technique gives an instrumentation for who is deferring to whom in an interaction. So far the pace of innovation from one technology of micro-conversational research to another has not been particularly rapid, but perhaps the field is in the early phases of an acceleration that will become more noticeable in the future. We lack comparison studies on the pace of technological innovation in research equipment in the early phases of the natural science revolution; for instance, how long did it take before Galileo's techniques, or those of the early air-pump experiments, were extended to new discovery-making techniques? It is possible that in sociology such technologies as those involved in micro-conversational research will encourage analogous developments outside the realm of conversation and micro-interaction that will lead to a wider stream of discoveries.

Another possibility exists in the field of artificial intelligence (AI). The software of AI is an application of theory, and hence would not be expected to be the source of rapid discovery. What raises a stronger possibility is that a series of hardware innovations may emerge that is directly connected to sociological research. Elsewhere (Collins, 1992) 1 have suggested that an AI that has human-like capacities can be built if it has the basic competencies of social interaction. The fundamental argument combines theoretical points from Mead, Durkheim, and conversation analysis. Human thinking is interiorized conversation; and verbal conversation operates on two levels: a cognitive level of symbols which are acquired in interactions and represent group membership; and a behavioral level of emotion-laden rituals, which establish membership. A sociological AI can be built by modeling these processes. An early prototype could be an "infant AI" which gradually builds up symbols through its history of social interactions. An important requirement is the capacity for emotional attunement with other persons. Along with software design, this requires building an AI robot with voice sensors (or sensors for other emotional signals) and also equipment that can communicate emotional gestures to others. Such a piece of socio-logical research hardware would be subject to tinkering, and thus to the production of new phenomena. These would not be limited to the nonver-bal properties of micro-interaction; for instance, it could become possible to simulate and experiment with various interactional situations and forms of social organization. In this scenario, a sociology-built robot could give rise to a stream of research techniques and to rapid discovery forefront.

It is beyond the scope of this paper to survey the research technologies of all the social sciences. In general, sociology, political science, and anthro-pology are methodologically in the same boat. Economics has been dis-cussed above in terms that suggest it too lacks the research technology of rapid-discovery science. An exception is the research technologies of ar-cheology and physical anthropology, which draw on those of the natural sciences in dating artefacts or establishing genetic links. There are indica-tions that the use of these techniques is splitting anthropology into noncommunicating factions (Morell, 1993). Whether they are giving rise to rapid-discovery science in the hardware-using branches is not clear.

A brief comment on psychology is in order. Psychology became a labo-ratory science in the 1870s. But it has remained a typical social science in key respects: long-standing dissensus among many competing theoretical programs (both in the period of introspection ism and during the heyday of behaviorism) and the lack of a rapid discovery front. In recent decades, part of psychology has closely allied with methods of biological research, espe-cially genetics and neurophysiology. The result has been a rift with the cognitive, behavioral, and social-motivational sides of psychology. It re-mains for the sociology of science to investigate whether any of these de-velopments shows signs of bringing a shift to the high-consensus, rapid-discovery mode. During the time when the battle goes on among biologically oriented, computational, and more traditional methods, the re-sult is lower rather than higher consensus. Whether one of these areas is becoming a rapid-discovery science, and what effect that will have on other parts of the field, needs investigation. One possibility is that the rapid-discovry sector will drive the others out of existence through the com-petition for attention and funding. Another is that the discipline may perma-nently split into separate enterprises.

Scenarios of Future Social Science

None of the above scenarios for sociology is certain, or perhaps even likely. The possibility cannot be ruled out that sociology will acquire a selfsustaining stream of research technologies in the future and thereby move into the rapid-discovery mode. If so, this will happen in the midst of many other kinds of sociology that continue to be pursued by traditional methods. What then will happen to all these other data-gathering techniques —historical comparisons, field observations, interviews — and to other modes of sociological discourse? Many of these would be unaffected by a research technology, say, for measuring nonverbal interaction. Nevertheless, we should bear in mind that the rapid-discovery sciences have developed not as individual technologies but as streams of research technologies. Earlier techniques give rise to new ones, sometimes by application to remote topics, sometimes by the creation of new research technologies by analogy or recombination from those existing in another area. In this case, one can imagine that sociology, with a first few pieces of research hardware, would resemble natural science in the early 1600s. There would be hundreds of years ahead of us during which research technologies would penetrate and transform the older branches of social research; and since a genealogy of research technologies produces new phenomena to be studied, we could expect that many new branches of social science would be created.

It may be that some areas of social science simply cannot be technologized, and hence cannot be turned into the rapid-discovery mode. It is hard to envision, for instance, how historical sociology would be turned into a hardware-driven research field. And doubtless huge areas of meta-theory and ideological controversy will remain. Social scientists, dealing intimately with human interests and conflicts, are intrinsically more active in promoting ideological disputes than are natural scientists, and this difference will remain no matter what happens to the conditions determining the rapidity of the research front. At most, one can expect that social sciences could become hybrids: part in the rapid-discovery, high-consensus mode, other parts much as they are today.

Perhaps the more likely scenario is that the social sciences, except perhaps in isolated pockets, will not develop streams of research technologies, and will never acquire the rapid-discovery mode. On the balance sheet of pluses and minuses, this may not be altogether a bad thing. What we forego is social prestige and material support, collective pride in what our field has accomplished, and the excitement of intellectual adventure that goes along with rapid discovery. What we preserve is the independence that goes with having a great variety of methods; for some scholars, the pleasures of pursuing humanistic scholarship, and the freedom to teach and theorize over the whole corpus of our disciplinary history rather than observing a consensus that tracks past movement of the research forefront. There are social advantages of living in an intellectual community with low consensus and slow movement. Oddly, despite the self-images of many sociologists today, this makes our field a conservative and traditionalistic one — in terms of its own history — whatever political position sociologists may hold in regard to the larger society. Precisely what we do not like about the rapid-discovery sciences is their incessant progressivism, their trampling on all other values in their march to new discoveries.

Ultimately, these value questions are moot. Whether the social sciences become rapid-discovery sciences or not depends upon whether they acquire streams of research technologies. And that contingency does not depend primarily upon whether we believe it ought to happen.

Notes

[1] Detailed documentation cannot be presented in this paper. The analysis derives from a comparative study of long-term intergenerational networks of philosophers, including their overlap with European scientists and mathematicians in the period between 1500 and 1900. Sources of data are given in my manuscript in progress, *The Sociology of Philosophies: A Global Theory of Intellectual Change*. Portions are available in Collins (1987, 1989). [Editors Note: This book has now been published: Collins, Randall. 2000. *The Sociology of Philosophies: A Global Theory of Intellectual Change*. Cambridge, MA.: Harvard University Press.

[2] Price (1986). Subsequent work (Cole, 1983; Cozzens, 1989; Leydesdorff and Amsterdamska, 1990) suggests citation analysis is not the best way to measure movement of a research front, since citations are used for a number of different purposes that vary across fields. Differences between the sciences and humanities continue to be found, especially in consensus (Cole el al. 1978; Hargens and Hagstrom, 1982). Rapidity of a research front may best be judged qualitatively, in terms of changing content of ideas and focus on new discoveries.

[3] We lack comparative studies of the rate of movement in particular periods when sciences were changing — e.g., in ancient Greek or Chinese astronomy-so we do not know just how the non-European sciences at their most innovative compared with the rates of change in Europe since the 1500s.

[4] Turner and Turner (1990) have called sociology an "impossible science" because the fragmentation of research specialties and theoretical positions in America during the late twentieth century is reinforced by decentralization of organizational resource bases. But this is an inalterable situation only to the extent that sociology does not develop streams of rapid discovery technologies.

References

Dictionary of Scientific Biography. New York: Scribner's, 1981.

Clayman, Stephen E. 1993 "Booing: the anatomy of a disaffiliative response." *American Sociological Review* 58:110-130.

Cole Stephen. 1983. "The hierarchy of the sciences." *American Journal of Sociology* 89:111-39

Cole, Stephen, Jonathan R. Cole, and J. Dietrich. 1978. "Measuring the cognitive state of a scientific discipline." In Y. Elkana *et. al.* (eds)., *Toward a Metric of Science*. New York: Wiley.

Collins, Harry M. 1974. "The TEA set: Tacit knowledge and scientific networks." *Science Studies* 4:165-186.

Collins, Randall. 1975. *Conflict Sociology: Toward an Explanatory Science*. New York: Academic Press.

————. 1987. "A micro-macro theory of creativity in intellectual careers: The case of German idealist philosophy." *Sociological Theory* 5:47-69.

————. 1989. "Toward a theory of intellectual change: The social causes of philosophies." *Science, Technology and Human Values* 14:107-140.

————. 1992. "Can sociology create an artificial intelligence?" In Randall Collins, *Sociological Insight, 2nd Edition*. New York: Oxford University Press.

————. 1993. "Maturation of the state-centered theory of revolution and ideology." *Sociological Theory* 11(March):117-128.

Cozens, Susan E. 1989. "What do citations count? The rhetoric-first model." *Scientometrics* 15:437-447.

Etzioni, Amitai. 1975. *A Comparative Analysis of Complex Organizations*. New York: Free Press.

Frede, Michael. 1987. *Essays in Ancient Philosophy*. Cambridge: Cambridge University Press.

Griffith, Belver C. 1988. "Derek Price's puzzles: Numerical metaphors for the operations of science." *Science, Technology and Human Values* 13:351-360.

Goldstone, Jack A. 1991. *Revolution and Rebellion in the Early Modern World*. Berkeley: University of California Press.

Gregory, Stanford. 1983. "A quantitative analysis of temporal symmetry in microsocial relations." *American Sociological Review* 48:129-135.

Gregory, Stanford, Stephen Webster, and Huang, Gang. 1993. "Voice pitch and amplitude convergence as a metric quality in dyadic interviews." *Language and Communication* 13:195-217.

Grimshaw, Allen D., ed. 1990. *Conflict Talk*. New York: Cambridge University Press.

Hargens, Lowell and Warren O. Hagstrom. 1982. "Scientific consensus and academic status attainment patterns." *Sociology of Education* 40:24-38.

Ho Peng, Yoke. 1985. *Li, Qi, and Shu: An Introduction to Science and Civilization in China*. Hong Kong: Hong Kong University Press.

Jones, Alexander. 1991. "The adaptation of Babylonian methods in Greek numerical astronomy." *Isis* 82:441-453.

Latour, Bruno. 1987. *Science in Action*. Cambridge, MA: Harvard University Press.

———. 1988. *The Pasteurization of France*. Cambridge, MA: Harvard University Press.

Ledesdorff, Loet and Olga Amsterdamska. 1990. "Dimensions of citation analysis." *Science, Technology and Human Values* 15: 305-335.

Lipset, Seymour Martin. 1960. *Political Man*. New York: Doubleday.

Moore, Barrington, Jr. 1966. *Social Origins of Dictatorship and Democracy*. Boston: Beacon Press.

Morell, Virginia. 1993. "Anthropology: Nature-culture battleground." *Science* 261 (24 September):1798-1802.

Mulkay, Michael. 1985. *The Word and the World*. London: Allen and Unwin.

Needham, Joseph. 1959. *Science and Civilization in China, Vol. 3*. Cambridge: Cambridge University Press.

Neugebauer, O. 1957. *The Exact Sciences in Antiquity*. New York: Dover.

Paige, Jeffery. 1975. *Agrarian Revolution*. New York: Free Press.

Price, Derek J. de Solla. 1986. *Little Science, Big Science, and Beyond*. New York: Columbia University Press.

Rosenberg, Alexander. 1992. *Economics: Mathematical Politics or Science of Diminishing Returns?* Chicago: University of Chicago Press.

Sacks, Harvey, Emanuel A.Schegloff, and Gail Jefferson. 1974. "A simplest systematics for the organization of turn-taking in conversation." *Language* 50:696-735.

Shapin, Steven and Simon Schaffer. 1985. *Leviathan and the Air-Pump: Hobbes, Boyle and the Experimental Life*. Princeton, NJ: Princeton University Press.

Sivin, Nathan. 1969. *Cosmos and Computation in Early Chinese Mathematical Astronomy*. Leiden: Brill.

Skocpol, Theda. 1979. *States and Social Revolutions*. New York: Cambridge University Press.

Turner, Stephen P. and Jonathan R. Turner. 1990. *The Impossible Science: An Institutional Analysis of American Sociology*. Newbury Park, CA: Sage.

Wagner, David G. and Joseph Berger. 1984. "Do sociological theories grow?" *American Journal of Sociology* 90:697-728.

Welch, Holmes and Anna Seidel. 1979. *Facets and Taoism: Essays in Chinese Religion*. New Haven, CT: Yale University Press.

Whitley, Richard. 1984 *The Intellectual and Social Organization of the Sciences*. Oxford: Clarendon Press.

Willer, David. 1987. *Theory and the Experimental Investigation of Social Structures*. New York: Gordon & Breach.

3

Disintegrated Disciplines
and the Future of Sociology

Arthur L. Stinchcombe

Introduction

The basic argument of this essay is that disintegrated disciplines with many different and incompatible standards for what is good work tend to be precarious in academic settings. Geography, speech or rhetoric, organizational behavior or management studies, comparative literature, fine arts, communication studies, urban studies, evolutionary biology, history, philosophy, and sociology seem to me to have similar problems in justifying their continued existence. (A justification for parts of this list of comparable cases, and of contrasting cases in the argument below, may be extracted from Whitley, 1984:90-94, 130-148, 155, 158, 168-208.) What is good in them does not depend on the disciplines' corporate existence; what is bad in them discredits the disciplines.

What is essential to a discipline is that it can tell whom a leading university should hire — lesser universities can follow by imitating them at a lower level. Disintegrated disciplines can sometimes solve the problems posed by their being broken up into more or less separable subparts by having a strong ordering of the subparts, so that although they do not agree at the bottom they can agree at the top. In mathematics this seems to be achieved by the fact that mathematical talent is strongly ordered, so that the great geniuses that fill great departments can do everything that their inferiors can do, and more besides. In economics and physics this seems to be achieved by the dominance of theorists, especially mathematical theorists, over empirical economics and "applied" physics (astronomy, geophysics, physical chemistry biophysics, etc.), and then the application of the mathematical talent principle among theorists to pick the elite that leading universities should hire.

Chemistry seems to solve the disintegration by the division of the world into "Pure substances" (elements and compounds). The convenient outcome of identifying such pure substances is that facts about a given pure substance from one chemist can be used by another chemist if they need a substance with those characteristics. The metric of chemical ability, finding out the most things about the reactions of the most substances, allows one to determine the academic chemistry elite in a moderately reliable way that will be recognized across subparts. Perhaps history has a system much like chemistry in this respect: although a history department hiring a Renaissance scholar may not know much about Venice in the 13th century, they know what good work on 13th-century Venice would look like.

The second crucial thing that a discipline has to be able to do is to agree on how to teach elementary courses. This involves being able to establish in the minds of the university community that the elementary course in (say) chemistry leads to recognizable advanced courses that are also in chemistry, and will help people to learn the material in those advanced courses. For example, elementary language courses are obviously connected to the literature written in that language (especially the poetry where translation does not really work as a substitute) and to the grammar and phonetics of that language, so a literary discipline that is split between linguists and literary historians at the top may be defensible at the bottom. Since many Americans or French are excluded from being able to teach the elementary courses in any language but their own, the discipline of literary analysis of a given literary tradition can defend its turf at the elementary level even if it has a disintegrated elite.

I argue in this essay that sociology has a dim future first because it is unlikely to develop much consensus on who best represents the sociologists' sociologist to be hired in elite departments. Second, it has a dim future because it is unlikely to be able to argue with one voice about what is "elementary," and how what is elementary is connected to what is first class, and so unlikely to be able to defend its freshman and sophomore courses with solid arguments. This will be true even if some leading sociologists will be recognized as clearly elite by many (never all) people from other disciplines, as for example Pierre Bourdieu or James S. Coleman would be. And it will still be true even if some sociologists teach elementary courses that are very popular with students, and some others teach courses that will be required as elementary by professional schools.

Partially Ordered Stratification Systems and Their Troubles

Our argument in this section will be that since disintegrated disciplines have partially ordered stratification systems, any particular department cannot convince deans that it is elite enough to be suitable for an elite university. We can illustrate what we mean by a partially ordered stratification system by considering three criteria that are central in the stratification of professors: seniority, personal research performance, and the reputation of the university. All three of these strongly affect wages and working conditions. But in the nature of the case, the correlation between seniority and personal research performance is near zero; as one generation succeeds another, the average quality does not go down. As a group powerful senior professors are equal to — half better and half worse than — the people they judge. This is one of the many sources of "error" in judgment in recruiting people to leading departments. Personal performance is correlated with prestige of department, but elite departments are by no means homogeneous and some of the best people are in obscure places. And that means that (especially but not exclusively in disintegrated disciplines) many of the senior professors at leading departments "have not fulfilled their promise," and so are mismatched with their high position on criteria of seniority and prestigious department because of recent poor performance on the third criterion.

The slang of the stratification system reflects this partially ordered character of the system as a whole. For example, the senior professors in leading universities who have "not done anything since . . . " are commonly called "deadwood." Those too distinguished for their age are "too big for their breeches." One who stays in a less prestigious department than his or her fame warrants likes to be "a big frog in a small pond." A distinguished older researcher in a leading department is "a 600 pound gorilla," or a "silverback." That two out of the four of these phrases describing senior distinguished professors assume the professor is male may show that slang discourse is more accurate than formal discourse.

The salience of the dimensions varies across the structural elements of the stratification system. For example, it would be outrageous to propose that only those who had published an annual average of two articles in refereed journals since their Ph.D. could vote on promotions (because one did not want high-seniority "deadwood" to have too much influence). But it is perfectly proper to have senior and junior scholars have equal access to the journals by blind refereeing. So the seniority rather than the merit principle is more salient in voting rights on promotions, merit rather than seniority on acceptance in the journals.

The salience of seniority, research, and department prestige also varies across individuals. There is always someone on the promotion and tenure committee who cannot see why we should promote anyone ahead of schedule; always someone on a recruitment committee who does not see why we bother with candidates from departments not in the top five; always someone who will introduce into foundation policy a provision that people under 40 will be preferred for grants and scholarships (though the behavior generally does not agree with the reversed seniority principle, except when that principle is absolutely restrictive, partly because the foundation advisory committee are likely to be senior, therefore less convinced that senior people's research is less valuable).

I have introduced the notion of partial ordering with an example that applies to all disciplines, in order not to confuse the introduction of the concept with empirical assertions about why disciplines like speech or rhetoric, organizational behavior or management science, or sociology tend to get into trouble with deans and other allocators of academic resources. My argument here is that a main reason why what I have called disintegrated disciplines have political trouble in universities is that their disciplinary stratification system has more than the average number of additional criteria besides seniority, distinction, and prestige of department. I hope I have already given reason to believe that political troubles arise through different saliency of the standard stratification principles of all disciplines. Now we want to extend that suggestion to disciplines that have partial orderings by other criteria than these three, especially multiple standards for judging research.

When salience of these other criteria varies between situations, between people, and between institutions such as grant-giving agencies and universities, deans do not know whom to hire in order to be sure that they remain in, or move up relative to, elite institutions. When they ask for peer review in disintegrated disciplines with partially ordered stratification systems, they get conflicting opinions. Young scholars in all disciplines who get more grants than they can manage because their topic is "hot" nevertheless cannot get past recruitment committees dominated by senior people who are not working in "hot" areas because there is no standard set of criteria for excellence. But this effect is intensified when in addition a sufficiently large random sample in the discipline will apply different standards in evaluating the research.

In more integrated disciplines with more standard criteria for excellence, areas that get a lot of grant money because they are important to production in the chemical industry (for example) can be discounted on an agreed basis. Senior people writing evaluations or staffing promotion committees can apply more standard measures of originality and fundamental character of the research, and can agree not to count industrial usefulness as a criterion.

Since deans are risk averse in hiring or promoting people, when disciplines disagree within themselves on the criteria for excellence, the recruitment process becomes more random. This in turn implies that the average distinguished department in a disintegrated discipline (by the nature of the regression effects of random error) will have more "deadwood." Distinguished departments will on the average have more senior professors who retrospectively look like hiring and promotion errors in disintegrated disciplines. Those few people who, by accident, had nothing damaging in their personnel file were not actually any better than those who had some trace of a reason for a negative dean's decision.

In sociology there are different valuations of research, training, prestige of departments, and so on. Those who study interaction qualitatively and those who study populations of individuals quantitatively, or "radicals" who think class and race conflict are a good thing (provided the right side wins) and "liberals" who think they are a bad thing (provided the power is properly pluralistically divided), or those who think social processes in a laboratory are much like those in real life and those who think one has to "get the beauty of it hot" from the field, or those who think sociological knowledge should be equally applicable to the 18th century as to the mid 20th century and those who think "prediction is the test of science," all will evaluate training programs and research prestige of departments differently. All of these differences in values to be applied to the judgment of work mean that one cannot easily agree on who is elite and what department really has it together in training graduate students. Since ideologies are more powerful in determining people's views of the future than of the past, even when people agree at a given time that (say) Columbia University has the most distinguished department in the sociology of science, they may well disagree about whether the type of training one gets there will prepare students for where the sociology of science is going.

Partial Ordering By Interestingness

In addition, the wide variety of substantive subject matter in disintegrated disciplines, and the strong boundaries around substantive specialties, means that people cannot get interested in each other's work. The best established generalizations about the late-marriage pattern of western Europe in early modern times and its breakdown in the industrial revolution among proletarian wage earners, especially in the cities, are "not interesting" to someone interested in teenage pregnancy in American central cities in the 20th century, because they are in different subdisciplines. Even the study of 20th-century prison life and prisoners' culture — which is of course disproportionately constituted by the fathers of some of these children — is not conceived of as relevant because it is in a different "section" of the American Sociological Association. Unfortunately, one shows one is a reputable family sociologist by agreeing to be ignorant of facts that come from the 18th century or from criminology.

Of course, that is partly because without consensus on methods, one has to be an expert on the 18th century in France and Britain, or on prisons, in order to judge whether the facts are good enough to use to judge a hypothesis about the mechanism of teenage pregnancy in modern central cities. A biochemist interested in the mechanism of lead poisoning can transfer knowledge from inorganic chemistry or physical chemistry (about how lead behaves) in a way impossible in the contact between historical sociology or criminology and family sociology.

But the upshot of all this is that "boring" is actually a word heard in the discourse of evaluation of sociologists. Judgments of "boring" very often have to do not with the quality of the explanation of the facts or the solidity of the facts themselves, but instead with whether the facts are interesting in themselves. In management science an editor-referee's report on a paper can actually say unashamedly that they reject a paper because they would like the paper to have "more punch" (it happened to me). And a book review editor can unashamedly say he or she is asking one to review because he or she "wants to get interesting reviews" and not because one is an expert on the matter at hand (it happened to me, and I agreed to do the review).

But varying valuations of what facts are "interesting" produces variations in what work is considered excellent, so sciences with wide variations in criteria of interest have wide variations in evaluations of the importance of work. Variations among scholars, research granting agencies, and departments in the salience of interestingness as a criterion, and about what facts are interesting if interestingness is salient, mean that it is very difficult to get agreement on whether a candidate is elite in any moderately heterogeneous department. And homogeneous departments are hardly ever considered distinguished. It is difficult to get agreement that, say, Harvard has an elite sociology department if there happens to be no one there who studies facts one happens to think interesting.

Much of the variation in interestingness of facts in sociology has to do with their moral value. Because much of sociology is interested in contemporary facts about things the government and the economy do not have under control, about "social problems" (if they were under control political scientists or economists would study them), a disproportionate share of the facts we study are matters of ideological import, especially facts about what conservative institutions are to be blamed for.

Race and gender differences in earnings are, for example, of about the same size as differences between workers in their late 20s and early 30s and those in their late 50s and early 60s. The seniority difference in the society as a whole is much smaller than the difference between professors and assistant professors in academic life, so academic life would be a good place to study the question of age discrimination. Most people in the society have no particular moral or ideological objection to seniority discrimination, but find racial and gender discrimination morally objectionable. One result is that we have almost no studies of how much of the extra reward for older people is discrimination, not explainable by the merits of the aged, but very many about how much of the gender and race difference is discrimination.

But more important for our problem here, it would be very difficult to appoint a person who did a brilliant job of statistically sorting out the seniority effect (into discrimination vs. merit) if the leading competitor had done a moderately good job on sorting out the gender or racial difference. The facts the former had found and explained would be of very little moral or ideological interest, and so would be boring.

Thus, adding multiple criteria for the epistemological value of socio-logical academic work, and further multiple criteria for the ideological and moral value of the facts explained at an equal level of epistemological excellence, to the standard three of seniority, research, and departmental prestige, create problems because they make the judgment task difficult. But I argue that they create trouble as well because the salience of those criteria varies among judges, among departments, among institutional are-nas. That means that those who get lots of grants are not necessarily highly evaluated by people who read their papers; that people on a recruitment committee who have never written about any country but the United States can complain that sinologists only write about China; that someone who analyzes historical data qualitatively can be considered a substitute for a fieldworker who just left by some department members but not by others. Those who think that class conflict is tending to get more peaceful cannot pass muster with those who wish it were not.

This variation in salience of interestingness then means that sociologists cannot reliably sort out who is elite for deans of leading universities, and that one can always get negative opinions from the discipline about the standing of an elite department. A dean at Yale may, then, not know whether or not he or she has a distinguished sociology department (or department of organizational behavior in the business school) and get conflicting advice on what to do about it if it is not. The dean in James G. March and Pierre J. Romelaer's study could not tell whether the popularity of the speech program with 20 faculty and 117 courses was due to its distinction (March and Romelaer, 1976/1979: 254-258) or to its lack of distinction, so abolished it to create another nondescript department of communication. The analysis here would suggest that if one went back to March and Romelaer's university now, the department of communication might well be in the same situation as the abolished speech department because it was equally disintegrated. And one will go back to Yale to observe the standing of organization behavior and sociology in another couple of decades with trepidation.

Similarly, what constitutes the elite of geography, comparative literature, history, urban studies, or evolutionary biology is also problematic, and so whether one has an elite department is problematic. We would expect that such departments would tend to disappear first from elite universities, and then by imitation from universities on their way up.

I believe that the solid political standing of history in all elite schools disproves the generality of this prediction, because history is fragmented strongly by place and period, and to some degree by variations in ideology and in the salience of morally significant facts. I am not sure why the prediction does not follow. It may be that across subdisciplines historians refuse to take the fact that they are not "interested in" other people's facts very seriously, and so refuse to give negative evaluations to people from other subdisciplines. The fight then may end up being over whether a university will have the subject of medieval China in its history department, rather than whether it will have a history department. Or it may be that because undergraduate history is regularly conceived to cover larger periods and areas than the specialty of the professor who teaches it, historians regularly show "interest" in other periods and places, and expect to have to have a quasi-expert knowledge of the things they teach, as well as expert knowledge of the things they do research on.

When Elementary Is Just Dumb

The link between elementary teaching and scholarship or research is different in different disciplines. The link is generally more precarious in the humanities than in the sciences. In the sciences one can teach elementary students the boring mechanisms (e.g., valences and electron sharing) whose exciting interactions with each other (e.g., in catalysis) one does research on five or six years later. In the humanities (except for elementary languages) one wants to take students' artistic taste, metaphysics, or political ideology where they are and introduce complexity of mind into them, using the interests already there to make even elementary courses exciting.

In elementary languages one has to deal with the fact that anything one can read or write in the first year leaves one functioning at an intellectual level a standard deviation or more below the average native speaker of the language-, hardly anything one can read or write in the new language is of interest to a college student. But with this exception, advanced scholarship in the humanities is a further complexification of mind on questions of taste, metaphysics, or ideology, of the same general kind as one is trying to teach at the elementary level.

A central teaching problem in the humanities is that some students are not far enough advanced to see why, say, the *Taming of the Shrew* is morally unacceptable in the modern world — so not advanced enough to find it an interesting question for discussion in a freshman seminar how a humane and sensible person like Shakespeare could write such stuff in his time and place. It is often hard for a senior humanities scholar to imagine how few facts about the world and its history and literature are of interest to 19-year-olds.

The social sciences are in the anomalous circumstance of teaching undergraduates as if their job was the humanities' job of complexification of students' oversimplified tastes, philosophies, and ideologies -and doing their research as if it were the search for simplified explanatory mechanisms rather than further complexification of mind. Thus in their research sociologists may routinely run across a humanities judgment of the paragraph at the beginning where the main argument is stated: "How can you imagine the world to be so simple?" But then in teaching they have to berate students for thinking racism in Mississippi in 1850 was essentially the same as in New York City in 1994, just as historians have to worry about how to relate Jefferson's racism to modern students' and professors' sensibilities. (Wood, 1993).

In sociology one cannot get away with the physical science strategy of teaching dull elementary mechanisms. One cannot teach sophomores the mechanisms by which some people are valued less highly than other people, and promise them, as chemists promise, that they will get to the inequality between men and women in the second year in graduate school when they are ready to understand complexities. So one is reduced to trying to catch the interest he or she hopes they might have in comparable worth, so that they can have their minds expanded by the possibility that comparable worth legislation and supportive union practice in Sweden may perhaps have functioned to keep women out of better jobs, because then women could not offer to do them cheaper. It is not clear why sociologists whose research is trying to simplify stratification processes to mechanisms that can be tested by research should be also the ones to introduce complexity into the budding feminist ideology of sophomores.

Political science has some of the same problems with this as sociology, but since the advanced undergraduate curriculum is still about the same topic area as the introductory courses, the complexification of mind can go on for a considerable time; the elementary treatment is mostly just a less complex form of what one studies in a senior honors seminar. Economists, on the other hand, take the high road of physics, teaching the elementary mechanisms without calculus, then with calculus, then with systems of simultaneous equations (linear and then differential). They save the complexification of mind for the dissertation, when it turns out that one really has to understand the details of the system of airline regulation before one can build a model of the impact of changing regulation on prices, costs, and services delivered by airlines. Economics only comes apart at the graduate level, rather than right there at the beginning of elementary instruction on the mechanisms as sociology does. Economists agree on the mechanisms, though not on how they apply to the world. Sociologists agree on neither.

Part of the problem in sociology elementary instruction is that since sociologists do not agree about what their science consists of, they do not agree about what would be important to educate people about in the introductory course even if the students were headed for advanced training. I, for example, used to teach a short unit of elementary statistics in introductory sociology, because I figured that in more advanced courses the students would have to read quantitative papers in sociology. This was somewhat utopian even at Johns Hopkins, but my point here is that a large share of my colleagues would not agree that quantitative research was what sort of reading they should do in advanced courses anyway, even if they were being prepared for graduate school. Johns Hopkins' students did not know this was not elementary sociology (nor did the dean) because sociology was new there, and statistics was not difficult compared with what these students (disproportionately premeds) had to learn in elementary chemistry. Most of my sociological readers will find my misjudgment ridiculous, and of those roughly half will wish that it were not. That half will wish that statistics really were elementary sociology, but the division illustrates our difficulty in defining the elementary course in terms of our scholarly practice.

The partially ordered nature of our stratification system that prevents us from being confident about who is the elite of sociology also adds to the troubles that come from having a humanities teaching mission for a scientific field: we would be incapable of defining what the basic and elementary mechanisms and research operations of our field were even if we had a science-like undergraduate mission. One measure of our trouble in defining what undergraduate instruction should be about is the great tendency for exams in the elementary courses — even in the special field component of the Graduate Record Examinations — to be a vocabulary test about sociological jargon. If the best we have to teach undergraduates is how sociologists use words, we should just give it up.

The Professional Association As An Ineffective Trade Union

I have been talking as if deans got to decide freely whether to abolish sociology, geography, or comparative literature, and that the discipline would end up not having anything much to say about it. But the relative effectiveness or ineffectiveness of disciplines as trade unions — preserving their positions and their place in the academic firmament — has to be explained. I believe disintegrated disciplines are less effective as trade unions. We are not surprised that the chemists' association can undertake to certify undergraduate chemistry programs and generally make it stick, while one can hardly imagine what would be certified in sociology, or where the power to impose certification of sociology on a college or university administration would come from.

It is impossible for sociology to dictate to colleges that want sociology what it is they need to have. But this incapacity extends to dictating whether they should want it. One can imagine Washington University in St. Louis remaining reputable, and San Diego State retaining its assigned place in the hierarchy of California public universities, both without sociology. One would be extremely loath to offer the hypothesis that Yale failed to abolish its sociology department because it did not want to lose status, but much less reluctant to hypothesize that their lack of enthusiasm for organizational behavior in the business school was due to their failure to turn it from a variety of sociology into a variety of economics with a mathematical elite.

But in all that speculation, it would never occur even to conflict-oriented sociologists that we might fight the university administration, use our trade union power at a national and local level, and win. One might choose such an approach to a fight over a medical school, or over a chemistry department, but not over speech, or evolutionary biology, or sociology.

I would argue that some part of this ineffectiveness of sociology as a trade union is due to the disintegration of sociology as a discipline. The argument in favor of sociology at San Diego State, for example, used as evidence that many of the scholars there had got large grants for their research, and some people no doubt thought that was a good argument. But some probably thought that it was a very doubtful argument until they knew where the grants came from and for what kind of research. And when the argument that undergraduates need sociology turns out to mean that they should have had at least one radical professor in their lives, some of us will be persuaded, and some of us will have a jaundiced view of our trade union. Thus even if there were powers concentrated in our trade union that could and would intimidate our bargaining partners, it is difficult to call on sociological solidarity when it is difficult to say what it consists of-what it is solidarity about.

What Is To Be Done?

My own belief is that this disintegrated state of sociology represents the optimum state of affairs, both for the advance of knowledge and for the expansion of mind of undergraduates. We do not have basic mechanisms even if we want them for our elementary course, nor basic and universal methods so that we can attach an appropriate laboratory experience to that elementary course. So it is better that I try teaching basic statistics, and someone else exposes them to *Street Corner Society* (Whyte, 1961; actually I have done that, too), and someone else sends them home to pretend they are a boarder so as to teach them to uncover the assumptions on which everyday life is predicated (Garfinkel [1964/1967]; I have not done that).

Similarly, I think it better to have disagreement about who is elite in sociology rather than to develop a single dimension of research contribution. It is in the nature of sociology at this time that in my father's house there are many mansions. This makes it hard to write to the Fellows of Harvard College or the relevant committee at Columbia about whether someone is really elite. It has happened to me that I have been asked to evaluate a candidate, and could not answer because I did not know the work of any one on the comparison list. This obviously meant that someone considered the candidate to be distinguished on some criterion that I might be expected to know something about, but also considered them to be distinguished on a criterion that I did not in fact know anything about, on which the others on the list were presumed to be elite.

I presume that the same thing would happen less often in economics or physics, because those near the top do pretty much the same sort of thing, and less often also in chemistry or history, because only those would be asked for an evaluation who would know the comparison group, because the evaluator, the candidate, and the competitors would be in a well-defined subdiscipline.

But it seems to me that an attempt to impose unified criteria near the top of sociology would have worse effects than in economics, physics, or chemistry because it would not reflect the fact that the advance of knwledge goes on with many different methods, many different theories, and with many different relations to ideological, granting agency, and theoretical objectives.

So nothing is to be done except to suffer from the fact that deans are not going to like us, and from the fact that inside our departments we will fight with each other about how to determine the merit of research and what our curriculum ought to be about. And if we want to find others who are as bad off as we are, we should look to comparative literature, geography, speech, and organization behavior for groups, compared to which we are relatively well off.

References

Garfinkel, Harold. 1967 [1964] "Studies of the routine grounds of everyday activities." In Harold Garfinkel (ed.), *Studies in Ethnomethodology*: 35-75. Englewood Cliffs NJ: Prentice-Hall.

March, James and Pierre J. Romelaer. 1979 [1976] "Positions and presence in the drift of decisions." In James G. March and Johan P. Olsen (eds.), *Ambiguity and Choice in Organizations*: 251-276. Oslo: Universitetsforlaget.

Whitley, Richard. 1984. *The Intellectual and Social Organization of the Sciences*. Oxford: Clarendon Press.

Whyte, William Foote. 1961. *Street Corner Society*. Chicago: University of Chicago Press.

Wood, Gordon S. 1993. "Jefferson at home [elsewhere labeled "Jefferson within limits"]." New York Review of Books, 40(9) (May 13):6-9.

4

What's Wrong With Sociology?

James A. Davis

I was asked to write on what's wrong. If I had been asked to write on what's right, I could have done that.[1] But I will do what I was asked to do. Rembember, however, I was not asked to be balanced, totally objective, or diplomatic.

I did do some research. My first reaction had been, "What's wrong with sociology? It's all embarrassing, pretentious, painfully obvious, turgid, humbug." (I had just returned from the annual meetings.) To document this notion I flipped through recent issues of three or four of the leading journals and was surprised. By and large the published articles in the major journals can stand anyone's test of academic/scientific quality. They are sober, carefully researched, well documented, and contain very little overt ideology, back scratching, self-promotion, or name calling. They are poorly written and the reader often feels the topic is not very exciting, but in terms of basic intellectual quality, mainstream academic sociology need not bow to any other social science.

On Incoherence

So what is wrong? What is wrong is that sociology is incoherent. It does not cohere ("to stick together, be united; hold fast, as parts of the same mass"). While each article/book/course may be well crafted, they have little or nothing to do with each other. They may share methods and even data sets (and grammatical voices so passive as to suggest a drug problem), but each is about a unique problem with a unique set of variables.

Try this test: list the key concepts/variables in each article in the last two or three issues of the *American Journal of Sociology, American Sociologi-*

cal Review, or *Social Forces*. I expect the number of different variables will be at least 20 times the number of articles and few variables (save for a handful of demographics such as age, sex, and race) will turn up in more than one article.

Another indicator: there are no intermediate level texts in sociology and no sequences of *substantive* courses. Everything is either an introductory melange of unconnected topics or an advanced monograph on an isolated topic.

And another: List the major subfields of sociology. Then try to arrange them in some pattern that has more intellectual bite than alphabetization. Hard, isn't it?

Yet another: Why are there no conflicts over priority in sociology? Because sociologists are nice? Nope, because no two sociologists ever study the same thing so such conflicts are impossible.

So far we are talking about incoherence at any particular time. This is untidy but we do study an enormous variety of topics and only a crank would argue that three or four variables explain anything and everything. But incoherence over time is a more serious problem. We may spew out ritual citations, but we do not build anything cumulative. Whenever we turn up something good we either drop it or we turn it into desiccated methodology. (See any recent article on mobility tables or trace the history of network studies from substantive theories about balance to substance-free computer packages.) Some examples:

Prestige. To my knowledge the *only* important empirical discovery of empirical sociology is the remarkable robustness of occupational prestige ratings. My experience has been that this is the only sociological finding one can try on a class knowing it will work and knowing they will not say they knew it already. One would think dozens of sociologists would build on this to study the causes and effects of occupational prestige and to develop measures of prestige of this, that, and the other. Nope, instead, all we have are a few crackpot articles trying to show it isn't true and a decision to use a different measure -one contaminated by education and income — because it gives bigger correlations.

Union Democracy. The Lipset-Trow-Coleman (1956) study of social structure and democracy in the International Typographical Union is acknowledged as a classic — provocative but not definitive. One would think it would have been followed up by studies of democracy in diverse groups cumulating into a documented set of principles based on broad research. Nope, the topic sank without a trace.

Authoritarianism. In its time the notion of "authoritarian personality" dominated attitude and opinion research. Methodological criticism pretty much killed it. But why didn't someone develop good measures, or if they did, why aren't they used? (As a matter of fact, in the General Social Survey authoritarian type items predict free speech items as well or better than more reputable items.) Does personality have a big influence on social attitudes? We'll probably never know since we lost interest in the question.

And so on, for ... small group process, opinion leaders, cultural lag, the principle of least interest, role conflict, anomie, presentation of self, etc., etc. All are old-fashioned and outmoded ideas. But why? Because they are wrong? I doubt it. The only sociological ideas that ever turned out to be demonstrably wrong are "status consistency" and "relative deprivation," and both pop up as regularly as true ideas. We neither refute nor confirm and expand ideas; we just become bored with them and move on to some "cutting edge" novelty.

Since I hear no one claiming that sociology really is coherent, there is no need to labor the case. But it may be worth asking whether incoherence is really bad. Consider, for example, newspapers. They are just as incoherent as sociology, but no one frets about it.[2] Maybe we should think of sociology as an extremely highbrow news gathering. But newspapers have readers (fewer every year) while there is no audience for highbrow news. Despite our pretensions, the world of affairs has zero interest in sociology except when snippets can be waved in the air for ideological reasons.[3] And our only real audience, college undergraduates, require it boiled down to syrup, before they will register in our classes. We are talking to ourselves and none of us is listening.

Even academia is unlikely to tolerate such waste indefinitely. In the lingo of our dear friends the economists, we need some comparative advantage. In plain English we have to be able to do something that somebody wants and do it better than our competitors.

The obvious candidate is subject matter. Alas, we share it with all the social sciences. Every topic we study is also studied by economists, psychologists, and political scientists, plus a few anthropologists and historians. Indeed, our competitors have virtually driven us out of important areas such as urban ecology, attitude studies, and demography, while our classic turfs, family and poverty, are hotly contested.

Alternatively, we might consider ourselves specialists in social research methods. That, actually, is what we are best at. Perhaps, but I'm doubtful. We use methods but we seldom invent them. Our methods are almost entirely derivative[4] and our undergraduate bread and butter audience is not gorged with young people attracted by the opportunity to learn about research methods.

Theory I discuss below. This leaves the "sociological imagination," a concept so vaporous (and tautological) it would be disdained by Shirley McLaine. I'm afraid there is no unique substantive turf for sociology; we must do something unique and valuable with the raw materials available to all the social science disciplines.

In sum, it behooves us to do something about the incoherence of sociology if only to show we have a claim on a niche in the academy. Before acting, however, it may be useful to speculate on the causes. There is no end to them and some may be symptoms rather than causes, but I shall comment on six anticoherent aspects of our intellectual culture: (1) terror of substance, (2) the millennial attitude toward theory, (3) mismatch between methods and problems, (4) a weak immune system, (5) confusion between importance and tractability, and (6) regressive progress in statistical analysis.

Terror of Substance

Unlike the humanities and economics, sociology places high value on empirical truth, perhaps too high a value. As in some religions where the sacred is so awesome one never mentions it but beats around the bush with euphemisms and indirect hints, sociologists have a hard time coming out and saying "Black voters prefer the Democrats." Instead, we say,

> It is not improbable that, *ceteris paribus*, races, to the extent that skin color is an indicator of race, which, of course, is to a considerable degree to be interpreted as a cultural, that is to say learned, trait, have, to a certain extent, differential presidential preference vectors — although the relationship probably does not hold prior to 1932.

Some of this is inevitable in statistical work, especially in the anti-intuitive language of statistical inference, but there's an enormous difference between qualifications stemming from scientific procedures and qualifications stemming from handwringing and pussyfooting.

There is more to it than the problems of technical writing. Howard Becker (1986) catches the problem brilliantly (if you have to choose, read his book rather than this essay; you'll learn the same things) when he says (8),

> Sociologists' inability or unwillingness to make causal statements similarly leads to bad writing. Sociologists have many ways of describing how elements covary, most of them vacuous expressions hinting at what we would like, but don't dare to say ... We write that way because we fear that others will catch us in obvious errors if we do anything else, and laugh at us.

Consequently, sociological writing has very little content because content could get you in trouble, while discussion of methods and conceptual frameworks gives the patina of scholarship. Both methods and concepts are necessary, but a structure that is all patina is seldom sturdy. If you read a sociological article on X, you will learn (a) the various sociological schools' disagreements about X, (b) the various methodological approaches to X, and (c) every single step in the author's statistical analysis though not much about the sampling or wording of the questionnaire. But you won't learn much about X.[5]

Item: In a recent issue of *Contemporary Sociology* there is a page-length review of a book that apparently summarizes family research from 1930 to 1990. Sounds like just what incoherence fighters need. But *nowhere* in the full-page (favorable) review is there even a hint as to what is actually in the book! And we all know such examples are hardly rare. Is there any other journal, aside from *The New York Review of Books*, that would routinely print book reviews that never mention the content of the book?

Item: Over the last 35 years I have participated in personnel decisions in several major departments. We have discussed the candidates' productivity, biopolitical credentials, specialization, research approach, and teaching skills. I have no recollection of any discussion (or any outside letters) mentioning the findings of their research and whether they were true or not.

Item: Consider the review of the literature section of any article in a major journal. The references there are the key to coherence over time. How many times do the citers refer to specific previous findings and how many times do the citations merely name a string of predecessors who (presumably) wrote on the same topic?

The point is effectively summarized in what I have come to call "Price's Paradox." James L. Price, in the introduction to a reader, puts it this way (1969: iii):

> The lack of comprehensive, comparative, and historical factual information in introductory sociology textbooks and anthologies obscures the real strength and weakness of contemporary sociology. Sociology lacks a common set of concepts, has very few verified propositions. and is totally devoid of systematically tested theory. However, sociology has a large amount of comprehensive, comparative, and historical factual information. The feature of contemporary sociology that is perhaps its point of greatest strength — its relatively solid factual base -is underrepresented in introductory sociology textbooks and anthologies, whereas the features of relative weakness — its concepts, propositions, and theory — are overrepresented.

Price was writing about introductory sociology 15 years ago but the conclusion is appallingly apt for the discipline today.

What does all this have to do with incoherence? It's simple: If you don't say anything, you can not be shown to be wrong. If you cannot be shown to be wrong, we cannot progress from there to a better answer.

A first step in building coherence into sociology would be to stop pussyfooting around about substance and start centering our research reports on what we learned rather than how and why we learned it.

Millennial Attitude Toward Theory

If sociologists live in terror of substance, our attitude toward theory is downright millennial ("a period of general righteousness and happiness, esp. in the indefinite future"). Nothing can be more damning than to say an otherwise commendable study "lacks theoretical relevance." But where is this theory that sanctifies our regression equations? Presumably it can be found in theory courses and theory textbooks. But scrutiny of them does not reveal anything like theory in any rigorous sense.[6] Instead, we find a goopy mess of (deceptive) intellectual history, a healthy dollop of ideology, and a Chinese menu of "schools," "approaches," and buzzwords. One of the least disappointing of these works is Ritzer's *Frontiers of Social Theory* (1990), but I'll give you a nickel for every falsifiable causal generalization in its 415 pages.[7] Could any other discipline come up with a comprehensive book on theory that was devoid of theory? Theology comes to mind, but not many others.

The blunt fact is this: today there is no such thing as sociological theory if you mean empirical relationships that are comfortably predictable and general enough to turn up across more than one topic.[8] That parrot is dead, regardless of what its salesperson claims.

Item: For 20 years the National Opinion Research Center (NORC) General Social Survey has solicited proposals for items and topics in its nonreplicating section. I'd estimate we have received more than one hundred ideas. No one has ever suggested a question or battery to test an hypothesis from sociological "theory."

Item: There is supposed to be a theory called "functionalism." To my knowledge, there has never, ever, been a refereed, published empirical study of a social function.

Will there ever be any sociological theory? I am not optimistic. We have been at it now for a century without much luck. Although the average talent in our discipline compares unfavorably with our competitors, theories are not developed by those at the median. We have recruited enough outliers so that somebody should have come up with something if it is possible. Why such bad luck despite hard work by talented people? I don't know, but my guess is this: successful theories in the life sciences (e.g., Darwinian evolution, learning theory, economics, Downs' 1957 theory of party competition) center on attempts by an actor to maximize some single something (gene survival, rewards, utility, votes). But groups, other than commodity traders and political parties, either maximize many things or just sit there and don't maximize anything. And if we downshift from groups to individuals, it is unlikely we can beat psychology or economics at the individual actor basic theory game.

I am not against trying; that's what made America great. But I am worried by our tendency, like religious sects, to withdraw from the present because we are obsessed with the immanent arrival of the rapture. To judge all current work in the light of nonexistent "theory" and to denigrate any scholarly work that is not in accord with the sociological equivalent of the Book of Revelations is self-defeating. Salvation may (or may not) be just around the corner, but in the meantime we have to put some bread on the table.

(A Digression on Economics)

Today's buzzword is not "plastics," it's "economics." On the empirical side, stratification research is becoming a satellite of labor economics. On the theory side we have sociologists drawing on economics (Coleman, 1990; Hechter 1987) and economists analyzing sociological topics (Becker, 1971, 1981; Grossbard-Shechtman, 1993; Posner, 1992). This is new. In my graduate school days (the 1950s), psychology was the alpha animal and economics was a "dismal science" vaguely associated with business. Today economics doth bestride the academic world like a Colossus and we petty persons walk about under his/her huge legs and peep about to find ourselves early retirement.

Should we give up and swear fealty? It is tempting. No doubt many Austrians felt better after the Anschluss. Economic theory is the most successful social science theory and sociologists lust for THEORY as pants the hart for cooling streams when heated in the chase.

But I have some reservations:

First, economic theory, when put to the test, doesn't work very well. From individual behavior (Sears and Funk, 1990) through firms (Cyert and March, 1963) to the macroeconomy (buy today's newspaper) the textbook predictions just don't work very well. This doesn't trouble economists in the least since a real economist simply rejects uncomfortable facts out of hand. It has been said that economics is the only field in which being wrong is no bar to distinction. But sociologists don't think that way.

Second, our devotion is unlikely to be reciprocated. We are bad at the things that economists value. While labor economics is our closest cousin, it is a low status specialty in the field, and I'm not sure it will be fun to become data bearers for a low-ranking caste.

Third, the current overlap between the fields is a good deal less than might appear. Those who claim to bring economics to sociology seldom treat topics that have been central to sociological research. The best example is the "free rider problem," the subject of endless sophisticated (i.e., convoluted and hypothetical) disquisitions. But the free rider problem is only a problem if you make the initial assumptions of economics. Sociologists have studied an incredible variety of human situations for decades without ever running into free riding as a serious problem for people on the hoof. More exactly, the theorists construe absence of the problem as evidence that some solution has been invented. Thus the discussions amount to "just-so stories." Ditto for the "prisoner's dilemma."

Fourth, since research resources come almost entirely from the applied area, nutrients for a discipline depend on the goodwill of politicians and bureaucrats. They are enamored of economics today, but I suspect in a decade or less it will become clear that economics is of no more (or less) help in solving social problems than we were. In the social problems areas, the two disciplines differ considerably more in their self-confidence than in their payoff. Do we want to be riding on economics' rug when it is pulled out from under?

Fifth, there is poor chemistry between the cultures of the disciplines. Economists are competitive, individualistic, conservative in their politics, smart, and arrogant. Sociologists are cooperative, group-minded, leftish in politics, sincere, and docile. Except as master and dog, these two psyches are not a promising combination.

Mismatch Between Theory and Methods

Scientific method, as taught in methods courses, involves a theory-data-theory-data cycle that has little to do with reality in science -social or antisocial. (If it is true, why are there never any specific examples of the complete cycle in the texts?). In the real world, science frequently advances through developments in instrumentation[9] and clever investigators capitalize on this to find hot research topics.

Controlled experimentation is seldom possible in sociology. After a flashy start, mathematical formalization doesn't seem to be getting anywhere because you can't formalize mush. This leaves the nonexperimental analysis of large data sets — OK I'll say it out loud, "survey analysis" — as our sharpest tool. The combination is not random: if we can't do experiments, we must invoke statistical controls. Since we have no theory to rule variables in or out a priori, we have to have a lot of variables; if we are going to have a lot of variables, we must have a large number of cases.

When one adds the necessity of sampling to support generalizations, one has a method perfectly adapted to problems of microsociology, aka social psychology, the study of how individuals' behaviors are influenced by their social settings. The method is poorly adapted to problems of macrosociology, the study of how very small numbers of very large groups develop.

Having honed this tool for microsociology, the discipline, with characteristic poor strategic judgment, has abandoned microsociology for the study of large organizations, societies, and epochs- precisely the topics most difficult to study with our best methods. Compare the sparse, naive, verbal (and not always useful) methodological literature on comparative sociology with the voluminous, sophisticated, high-tech (and not always useful) methodological literature on surveys.

I did not say macrosociology is unimportant or unsociological. I do say we do not make life easier for ourselves by doing things the hard way. Fighters with one hand tied behind their backs look brilliant when they win, but more often they drop to the canvas in the first round.

There is a statistical approach perfectly adapted to macrosociology for those brave enough to venture beyond the single case. It is "exploratory data analysis" (Tukey, 1977; Erickson and Nosanchuk, 1992) and its recent offspring "dynamic graphics" (Weisberg and Smith, 1993, Velleman, 1993). The approach has failed to penetrate sociology, perhaps because it seems insufficiently pretentious, and "they" might consider its users naive. (Anyone who thinks John Tukey is naive needs his/her naivety meter checked.)

A Weak Immune System

A healthy (coherent) organism has the ability to reject invading organisms that wish to thrive at its expense. An organism with a weak immune system must play hotel to whatever bugs seek a free lunch. Since sociology is incoherent, we have a hard time rejecting foreign objects. Until we know who we are, we can't tell who we aren't.

The problem is exacerbated because of our disciplinary culture. Sociologists tend to be nice people, tolerant, favorable to progressive ideas, sympathetic to downtrodden people and ideas. We have a hard time saying, "No!" Randall Jerell caught the tone perfectly in his academic novel, *Pictures From An Institution*, when he says of a sociologist,[10]

> If she had been told that (everyone in her family) and the furniture had been
> burned to ashes by the head of the American Federation of Labor, who had
> then sown salt over the ashes, she would have sobbed, and sobbed, and then
> said at last — she could do no other — I think we ought to hear his side of the
> case before we make up our minds.

Consequently, we have put up with an appalling amount of bunk
(postmodernism, ethnic "studies," "feminist methodology," "humanistic
sociology," "critical theory," ethnomethodology, "grounded theory," and
the like) simply because we cannot draw a firm line between what is legitimate academic sociology and what is not.

I should not flog dead horse feathers, but the case of sociological Marxism is instructive. If you are under 50 years old, you believe Karl Marx was
a founder of sociology and contemporary sociology can be traced back to
him in an unbroken chain of apocalyptic succession. The truth is quite different. Prior to World War II, American sociology had its roots in biological
theories of social evolution and (honest, I'm not kidding) Mainline Protestantism.[11] After the war, refugee scholars condescended to educate the na-
tives in correct European thought, but they were *anti-Marxists* who worked
busily to inoculate us against a virus to which we had never been exposed.
It was not until the post-Vietnam period that Marx loomed larger than, say,
Ibn-Khaldun. The Marxian infection came with the use of academia as a
sheltered workshop for intellectual refugees from the Vietnam turmoil.[12]

In sum, we have a dysfunctional loop. Lacking any coherent definition
of the field and blessed by a democratic attitude, our ark accepts animals,
plants, rocks, bicycles, junked cars — you name it — which, in turn, makes
it harder and harder to turn anything away.[13]

Confusion Between Importance and Tractability

What do poverty, homelessness, racial inequality, man/woman conflicts,
the fall of communism, aging, and third world development have in common? Answers: (1) They are all hot topics in contemporary sociology. (2)
They are about the only topics where research money is available. (3) They
are intractable, massive, convoluted social problems where it is extremely
unlikely that any progress can be made through policies and programs.

What do preferences for various candy bars,[14] short-range demographic
predictions, development of attitude scales, and election polling, have in
common? Answers: (1) They are all low status topics in contemporary sociology. (2) Billions of dollars are spent on such research but we don't get any
of it. (3) They are tractable problems where social research really works.
Painting with a rather broad brush one might argue that the two major im-

pacts of sociology/social psychology on modem society are (1) the survey method and (2) a doctrinaire denial of any biological influence on human behavior.

In short, we tend to be suckered into research problems where failure is inevitable while we disdain topics and methods where we could be successes.

We need to learn that getting on base by hitting singles is better than always striking out swinging for home runs.

Regressive Progress in Statistical Analysis

If you thumb through the leading journals you will see the vast majority of studies are documented by columns of logistic regression coefficients with standard errors stuck between to make it impossible to scan up and down the column to compare them. But it wouldn't help much to move the standard errors since no one knows what the coefficients mean. I'm not kidding. I do not mean one needs to brush up on one's statistics before interpreting the coefficients. I mean that extremely knowledgeable people flatly disagree about what the damn things tell us. See, for example, the not entirely pleasant exchange between Demaris (1993) and Roncek (1993) or any author quietly converting her results back to proportions when it is necessary to actually talk about them.

For a more general proof of my point, read the actual articles. You will find the authors never assess, compare, or evaluate the magnitudes of the actual coefficients. And for a good reason. Taken at face value, the coefficients are nonlinear functions that interact with each of the other variables. To "see" what's going on one must visualize curves moving through 10-20 dimensional spaces. I know of only one case where the author actually works out the curves (Zaller, 1992) and it takes him a full book to walk through a three-variable model. Exegesis of a routine ten-variable logit regression would tax the typing abilities of Anthony Giddens plus Andrew Greeley.

In short, despite the *trappings* of modeling, the analysts are not modeling or estimating anything; they are merely making glorified significance tests. Furthermore, they are usually making wrong or deceptive significance tests because (1) they ignore issues of multiple comparison despite the plethora of independent variables, (2) in multistage samples they ignore design effects and weights for household size, (3) in telephone samples they ignore the vast amounts of embalming fluid that must be injected to correct for sampling bias, and (4) they usually work with such large Ns that virtually anything is significant anyway.

I'm not opposed to significance tests. In prehistoric times I took on the famous "Bureau" at Columbia in a debate in which they argued against them. But every elementary statistics text labors the point that significance tests per se are only a crude first step, a necessary condition but no place to stop. Serious analyses go on to consider magnitudes, shapes, and causal structures.

As a technique, logistic regression is a pretentious way of doing a routine task awkwardly. If the decision really turned on concerns about statistical inference, dummy variables plus jackknifing or bootstrapping (Mooney and Duval, 1993) would solve the problem. But the situation is worse in terms of cumulation. Stripped of its glamour, logistic regression provides nothing more than a list of direct effects, given haphazardly chosen controls and an arbitrary sample size. There is no way to cumulate lists of variables save by alphabetizing. The way to cumulate findings is to show that the new variable has a larger effect than previous ones or, even better, incorporate the variables into a causal model. To repeat: statistical results cumulate when they allow one to add or subtract stronger/weaker relationships in a model, not when they simply provide lists of effects.

This leads us back to "path analysis." During the 1950s, 1960s, and 1970s, sociology developed a research approach one might call "causal network analysis." Path analysis is its best known application (Duncan, 1966) but the same ideas can be applied to regression as a whole (Heise, 1975), theory (Stinchcombe, 1968), percentage tables (Davis, 1985), and methodological principles (Alwin and Hauser, 1975). In a nutshell: when the data are construed as a network of linear relationships, it is possible to analyze variable means and pair relationships into exact components that can be tied to plausible causal structures. The approach has many assets: (1) the same principles span high-tech regression, theory construction, and simple Lazarsfeldian survey analysis; (2) the key principles are not obvious but they can be taught to beginners (Davis, 1995); and (3) success and failure are easy to measure (the correlation is or is not explained). We will return to point 3, we surely will.

How does this compare with logistic regression? First, the central mystery of causal network analysis- decomposition into path components simply does not work for nonlinear relationships (Davis, 1974). Second, the key principles of logistic regression remain obscure and controversial even for sophisticated practitioners. Third, there is no practical[15] measure of success or failure since significance tests are inherently "iffy." Given the mores of sociology, it is only surprising that this technique-which only mandarins can understand and where users cannot fail to get good results-has not taken over sooner.

In sum, I believe the seeming technical progress of logistic regression (and its cousins) is actually regressive since (1) it necessitates a retreat from thinking about magnitudes to thinking about significance tests and (2) it is inappropriate and clumsy for building multivariate causal models-about the only way serious empirical results can cumulate.

Paradigm As Shtick

Fans of Thomas Kuhn will have seen I have been ringing the changes on his concept, "paradigm." The word has been rubbed down to a highbrow cliché for "approach" or "school," but in Kuhn's oft-cited, though seldom read, book[16] the concept has a much narrower meaning. Chapter 4 treats paradigms as rules for "puzzle-solving":

> It is no criterion of goodness in a puzzle that its outcome be intrinsically interesting or important. On the contrary, the really pressing problems, e.g. a cure for cancer or the design of a lasting peace, are not puzzles at all, largely because they may not have a solution. Consider the jigsaw puzzle whose pieces are selected at random from each of *two different* puzzle boxes. Since the problem is likely to defy . . . even the most ingenious of men, it cannot serve as a test of skill in solution. In any usual sense it is not a puzzle at all. Though intrinsic value is no criterion for a puzzle, the assured existence of a solution is ... *One of the reasons why normal science seems to progress so rapidly is that its practitioners concentrate on problems that only their own lack of ingenuity should keep them from solving* (36-37, emphases added)

Shifting pastimes, as I said above, we should learn how to hit singles instead of striking out trying for home runs. Or in Yiddish, we need a shtick.

Moving from analogies to propositions, I believe a paradigm for cumulation in empirical sociology should have these properties: (1) definite criteria for success and failure, (2) problems of moderate difficulty such that not all will succeed and not all will fail, and (3) comparability such that one can tell whether the new solution is better than the old one.

Suggestions are welcome, but let me advance one based on the statistical discussion above. Consider the causal network task of "explaining correlations." I think it meets all three requirements: (1) It has clear cut criteria -the correlation will vanish, be reduced by a certain percentage, or will not be affected (the rare case of suppressor variables aside). (2) The task is moderately difficult. On occasion correlations are explained or at least vastly reduced; but as we all learn when we do research, these are not daily occasions. (3) Newer causal models will be unambiguously better if they give better explanations with the same or fewer explanatory variables.

Jumbo equation logit analysis does not fare so well: (1) Since significance tests are hostage to an arbitrary factor-sample size-there can be no
overall measure of success and failure save the referee's judgment that the
results are or are not interesting. (2) Success is too easy and failure almost
impossible since it would require perverse unconscious motivation to not
come up with some significant effects. (3) Who is to say a newer equation is
better than a previous one except in terms of R^2? (But see footnote 15).

Actually, we have seen a telling example of this paradigm difference in
the classic Blau-Duncan research. As discussed in note 15, their R^2 is not
impressive at all. What is impressive is that the intervening variable, educational attainment, (almost) explains the correlation between father's and
son's occupational prestiges. The result is not only technically cool, it has
important resonance for social policy and deepens our insight into how
modern societies work. (I am not totally mechanical in my thinking. All
other things equal, I'd prefer to explain interesting correlations with interesting variables, but before judging the seasoning in rabbit stew it is necessary to catch some rabbits.)

Let me take it one step further. I would like to see someone (who? see
below) post a list of interesting correlations and encourage the rest of us to
compete for the quickest and best research to explain them. With luck the
result could be the evolution of small causal models ala Blau and Duncan
and thus cumulative coherence.

In my opinion sociology could consider itself a coherent, cumulative
science if and when its core topics have at their core causal networks similar to Figure 5.1, page 179 in *The American Occupational Structure* (Blau
and Duncan, 1967).[17] I neither can nor should come up with the list, but let
me lay out a few to give the flavor:

1. It "stands to reason" that married women's labor force participation weakens marital bonds through increasing wives' independence,
but I'm not aware this has been demonstrated; and if it has, I suspect it
has not been done in a clean, straightforward fashion.

2. It is well established that in the United States, net of education, the
newer the cohort the lower the verbal skills. But is this due to something about schools, something about the new generation, or what?

3. There is a striking positive correlation between socioeconomic status and self-rated health. Can it be explained by objective medical
factors or is there a social variable at work too?

4. In the United States today there's a sharp race difference in marital status. There are dozens of books, zillions of conferences, and oodles of speculations on the reasons. But can anyone make the correlation actually go away?

5. Married people are distinctly happier than the nonmarried. And white people are distinctly happier than black people. But exactly why- and why is the marital status correlation declining?

I submit that concerted effort at explaining correlations like these with small causal models would be paradigmatic -feasible but challenging and the research necessary to do it will increase cumulation enormously.

Suggestions

While the culture of sociology may explain a lot of what's wrong, culture is a poor tool for reform. To produce change, one needs to operate on social structures. One can not be optimistic about authoritative social structures in our field. Sociology is like a class room where everyone's hand is up but there is no teacher in the room.

I doubt the formal organizations of the discipline -departments, The American Sociological Association, and funders — have much potential for effecting intellectual change.. Departments would be shocked by the idea of setting intellectual priorities and the role of the ASA is (quite properly I guess) to bless anything that generates memberships. Mission funders have no interest in advancing the discipline, leaving this to the slender resources of the National Science Foundation (NSF). Regarding cumulation, NSF has already "given at the office" through its wavering but unbroken support for the NORC General Social Survey. NSF does not need any further suggestions from me about how to spend its money.

But there is one arena where not every idea is considered equal and where those in authority have a definite effect on research -publications. If the major journals and publishers were to announce they favored articles in rhyming couplets, the journals would look like poetry anthologies within 18 months.

Book publishers are an intermediate case. They certainly do not consider every manuscript equal, but advancing the discipline is not their top priority. Commercial publishers (other than Sage) are oriented to the infamous "intro text," and university presses — led by Harvard's own — have shifted from scholarship to screeds about the fashionably oppressed. For what little effect it might have, here are some book suggestions:

1. We need intermediate level texts in areas such as stratification, family, urban, and collective behavior, especially texts that can talk about quantitative results in quantitative language, but that focus on what we know rather than how we found out about it.

2. We need an intellectually honest history of American academic sociology-as it actually evolved, not as a convenient origin myth to justify some "school." It should be based on what actually appeared in books and journals-what courses were actually taught, and what sociologists had actual influence. For a start in this direction, see Burton and Grusky (1992). Be warned though: predictably, the article is about the history of "approaches" and tells us almost nothing about what stratification researchers found out.

3. We need affirmative action for sociology in introductory sociology textbooks. Publishers should be forced to state the proportion of sociological material vs. political science, philosophy, newspaper clippings, general intellectual history, and movie stills. As with affirmative action for people, this should be put in the form of goals (aka quotas). I would propose that by 1995 we should boycott any introductory text unless 50% of the references are to sociologists born within the last 70 years. The target should be raised 5% every five years until it reaches 75. The shock of constructing a sociology text out of only sociology may be too much for many authors, but there is no shortage of ambitious textbook writers.

Effective leadership is more likely for journals (more likely, not likely). They each have a style sheet that sets out in mind-numbing detail picky conventions to satisfy antiquated production technologies. If they can force us to retype our footnotes and references from scratch after the higher prestige outfit turned us down, they can issue guidelines for the content. Is this authoritarian and un-American? Maybe, but one may argue these guidelines actually exist in unwritten form and are communicated to authors only in rejection letters. In the light of the discussion in this essay, I suggest at least the following:

1. Reviews of the literature should state previous specific findings (and samples) not just drop names. Priority should be given to reviews using the approach of meta-analysis (Thomas D. Cook et. al., 1993).

2. Each article must contain a one-paragraph summary of the major findings-free of statistical terms, ritual qualifications, and propitiations of the dead, written in terms of people or substantive variables. For a

fine model see Kelley and Evans (1993; 115-118). (Such paragraphs should be vetted by a committee of undergraduate sociology majors with the power to require revisions.)

3. Authors must report the bivariate coefficients with the dependent variable for all variables that appear in regression equations.

4. Editors, in consultation with advisory editors, should list half a dozen problem correlations (see above), announce that priority will be given to articles explaining them, and review progress on these fronts annually, dropping or adding problems as the discipline cumulates.

Summary and Conclusion

Sociology's problem is not the quality of its pieces but their incoherence. Terror of substance and worship of theory are inhibiting cumulation. Fashionable methods are seriously flawed as tools for cumulation. An older methodology, the explanation of interesting correlations as products of causal networks, can generate a paradigm -i.e., challenging but soluble problems. Only the major journals are in a structural position to steer sociology in a forward direction.

Sociology does not need a sharper cutting edge, it needs a sturdier handle.

Notes

1. What's right with sociology? (a) It has the most fascinating subject matter of all the academic disciplines. (b) It was open to women and minorities while the humanities were still discriminating against Jews. (c) Considering how little society invests in it, it produces a prodigious amount of scientifically respectable research.

2 Pace, Satchel Paige, we should probably view newspapers as true competitors. Today I suspect many more professional-quality surveys are conducted by newspapers and TV networks than by sociologists.

3. Trivia Question 1: How many sociologists were on the huge Clinton administration task force on health?

4. Trivia Question 2: Name an important social research tool, other than block modeling, that was actually invented by a Ph.D. in sociology? Warning: Leo Goodman is not a Ph.D. in sociology, Dudley Duncan did not invent path analysis, Louis Guttman was a psychologist.

5. Trivia Question 3: List the three or four leading sociologists in your general area. Now, for each, name two or three findings that advanced sociology. Yes, you can have extra time to complete the question.

6. A theory, by the way, is a network of falsifiable causal generalizations.

7. Your best hope for a nickel would be in the Friedman and Hechler chapter, but there is some question whether their 20 propositions are falsifiable and no question their theory is economic not sociological.

8. There have been some near misses. Putting aside applied economic theory for the moment, I would nominate Downs (1967), Homans (1950), Stark and Bainbridge (1987), and Stinchcombe (1968). Others might conceivably add Davis (1963).

9. You can get a Nobel prize in physics or chemistry for developing a better measure of something. In sociology you'd be lucky to get elected to the membership committee of a regional society.

10. Actually, the character is a sociologist's wife. but the two are described as much alike.

11. Trivia Question 4: Who funded the first Middletown study?

12. Do not misread my politics. During the Cambodian incursion I was a member of the student-faculty strike committee at my institution. It was one of the high points of my life.

13. I would not be surprised to sooner or later see a pedophile section in the ASA.

14. Trivia Question 5. Where did the candy bar example come from?

15. Yes, I've heard of R^2. How small an R^2 does it take to be embarrassed? They run as small as .02 in the most selective journals. The R^2 for the most famous regression equation in sociology (Blau and Duncan, 1967, p. 174) is .43 for current occupation, which is pumped up 10 points by including first job. Anyone who believes that sociological research is or should be judged by R^2 has been reading too many textbooks and too few journals. And logistic regressions don't seem to have any R^2s.

16. Some maintain that Kuhn is difficult reading. This is only true for those who are not very well informed on 18th-century chemistry.

17. I, myself, would add mother's education to the family background variables.

References

Alwin, Duane and Robert M. Hauser. 1975. "The decomposition of effects in path analysis." *American Sociological Review* 40:37-47.

Becker, Gary S. 1971. *The Economics of Discrimination.* Chicago: University of Chicago Press.

————.1981. *A Treatise on the Family.* Cambridge, MA: Harvard University Press.

Becker, Howard S. 1986. *Writing for Social Scientists: How to Start and Finish Your Thesis, Book, or Article.* Chicago: University of Chicago Press.

Blau, Peter M. and Otis D. Duncan. 1967. *The American Occupational Structure.* New York: John Wiley and Sons.

Burton, Mary Diane and David B. Grusky. 1992. "A quantitative history of comparative stratification research." *Contemporary Sociology* 21(5):623-631.

Coleman, James S. 1990. *Foundations of Social Theory.* Cambridge, MA: Harvard University Press.

Cook, Thomas et al. 1993. *Meta-Analysis for Explanation.* Newbury Park. CA: Russell Sage Publications.

Cyert, Richard M. and James G. March. 1963. *A Behavioral Theory of the Firm.* Englewood-Cliffs, NJ: Prentice-Hall.

Davis, James A. 1963. "Structural balance, mechanical solidarity, and interpersonal relations." *American Journal of Sociology* 68(4):444-462.

————. 1974. "Nonparametric path analysis-The multivariate structure of dichotomous data when using the odds ratio or Yule's Q." *Social Science Research* 3:267-297.

————. 1975. "Analyzing contingency tables with linear flow graphs: D systems." In David Heise (ed.). *Sociological Methodology* 1976: 111-145. Jossey-Bass.

————. 1985. *The Logic of Causal Order.* Newbury Park, CA: Russell Sage Publications.

DeMaris, Alfred. 1993. "Odds versus probabilities in logit equations: A reply to Roncek." *Social Forces* 71(4):1057-1065.

Downs, Anthony. 1957. *An Economic Theory of Democracy.* New York: Harper Collins.

————. 1967. *Inside Bureaucracy.* Boston: Little Brown and Company.

Duncan, Otis D. 1966. "Path analysis: Sociological examples." *American Journal of Sociology* 72:116.

Erickson, Bonnie H. and Terence A. Nosanchuk. 1992. *Understanding Data.
2nd ed.* Toronto: University of Toronto Press.

Grossbard-Shechtmen, Shoshana. 1993. *On the Economics of Marriage: A Theory
of Marriage, Labor, and Divorce.* Boulder, CO: Westview Press.

Hechter, Michael. 1987. *Principles of Group Solidarity.* University of California
Press.

Heise, David R. 1975. *Causal Analysis.* New York: Wiley-Interscience.

Humans, George C. 1950. *The Human Group.* New York: Harcourt Brace and
Company.

Kelley, Jonathan and M. D. R. Evans. 1993. "The legitimation of inequality:
Occupational earnings in nine nations." *American Journal of Sociology*
99:75-125.

Kuhn, Thomas S. 1962 [1970]. *The Structure or Scientific Revolutions.* Chicago:
University of Chicago Press.

Lipset, Seymour Martin, Martin A. Trow, and James S. Coleman. 1956.
*Union Democracy: The Internal Politics of the International Typographical
Union.* Glencoe, IL: Free Press.

Mooney, Christopher Z. and Robert D. Duval. 1993. *Bootstrapping: A
Nonparametric Approach to Statistical Inference.* Newbury Park, CA: Sage
Publications.

Price, James L. 1969. *Social Facts: Introductory Readings.* New York: MacMillan.

Posner, Richard A. 1969. *Sex and Reason.* Cambridge, MA: Harvard University
Press.

Ritzer, George. 1990. *Frontiers of Social Theory: The New Syntheses.* New York:
Columbia University Press.

Roncek, Dennis W. 1993. "When will they ever learn that first derivatives
identify the effects of continuous independent variables or 'officer, you can't
give me a ticket, I wasn't speeding for an entire hour." *Social Forces*
71(4):1067-1078.

Sears, David O. and Carolyn L. Funk. 1990. "Self interest in Americans' political
opinions." In Jane J. Mansbridge (ed.), *Beyond Self Interest.* Chicago:
University of Chicago Press.

Stark, Rodney and William Sims Bainbridge. 1987. *A Theory of Religion.*
Peter Lang.

Stinchcombe, Arthur L. 1968. *Constructing Social Theories.* New York: Harcourt,
Brace and World.

Tukey, John W. 1977. *Exploratory Data Analysis*. Reading, MA: Addison-Wesley.

Velleman, Paul F. 1993. *Learning Data Analysis With Data Desk*. San Francisco: W. H. Freeman.

Weisberg, Herbert F. and Charles E. Smith, Jr. 1993. "The advent of dynamic graphics statistical computing." *PS: Political Science & Politics*. 26:228-232.

Zaller, John R. 1992. *The Nature and Origins of Mass Opinion*. New York: Cambridge University Press.

5

Sociology in the 1990s*

Howard S. Becker & William C. Rau

Sociology in the 1990s is so hopelessly fragmented that it is increasingly difficult to define its subject matter and to find a common voice in the babel of competing theories and specialties. Not unrelated, it is also under attack by beleaguered administrators looking for vulnerable targets for budget cuts in this recessionary period.

Contemporary sociology has no theoretical, methodological, or institutional center. The field takes different organizational forms depending on the audience its members have to deal with. When sociologists act in their capacity as intellectuals and scientists, their collective action takes the form of a discipline; vis-à-vis their university, their action takes the form of a department; in relation to other professional groups, it takes the form of professional organizations.

Professional Specialties

Despite its struggles for logical coherence, intellectually sociology has always had an ad hoc character. Coming late to the academic table, it got the scraps, those forms of collective action not already taken over by earlier arrivals. History commanded the past and anthropology non-western exotica. Psychology had the individual, economics the market, and political science the state. Sociology got what was left: the family, crime, immigration, race, and all the other topics conceived of at the time as "social problems."

---

* Editor's Note: Originally published in *Society,* 1992. The authors wrote this article in a period of economic recession. During the last eight years of prosperity conditions in sociology have not improved although we have heard of fewer cases of retrenchment of sociology departments.

Because there were so few sociologists, they had to make common cause in the academic arena. So, whatever the differences in the actual subject matter, they looked for common themes. They created organizational and intellectual coherence, justifying the melange of topics that made up the field by creating abstract theories based on whatever it could be said that all these phenomena had in common. They summarized those features of social life as patterns of association which "explained" everything by reference to the collective character of human life. Early theorists such as Emile Durkheim made it their business to isolate the "social" in everything and to demonstrate its importance, thus demonstrating the right of a discipline that studies the social to a place in the academy.

As the number of sociologists grew, the specialties became more self-sufficient. Well before the middle of this century, such fields as demography, criminology, and marriage and the family had their own organizations, shared with scholars from neighboring and competing disciplines concerned with the same subject matter. Most of the other specialties, however, were still closely tied intellectually to a core of sociological thinking. When sociologists wrote about art or science or religion or stratification, they referred to a common body of ancestral materials, the works of Durkheim, Max Weber, Robert E. Park, George Herbert Mead, and (later) Karl Marx.

In the last twenty years, however, the number of sociologists reached the point where all those specialties could themselves support organizations and all the accompanying scholarly paraphernalia, particularly journals. The increased numbers of specialists buy books by their peers, recommend them to their libraries and, in general, provide the material base of a scholarly world. The scholars who work in these areas have less to do with other sociologists than they used to and less to do with a common disciplinary core. They no longer orient themselves to an overarching discipline of sociology, nor do they worry about what is going on in sociology generally. Their sub-area generates enough work and activity to occupy them.

The organization of intellectual work now rewards inter-disciplinary rather than intra-disciplinary border crossing. So sociologists invest their effort in work in disciplines with concerns that overlap theirs. Sociologists who study deviance, for instance, read and maintain a dialogue with work in law (itself increasingly influenced by social science), political science, and criminology. Sociologists of culture, a fast-growing group, read extensively in the contentious postmodern literature and talk to each other and to humanists about the writings of Baudrillard, Derrida, Lacan, and Lyotard, names that would puzzle most experts in deviance. Sociologists of science, another fast-growing specialty group, and one which is perhaps the most interesting new area of work intellectually, find common ground and more to debate and discuss with historians and philosophers of science than with sociologists who do comparative historical studies.

The result of this growth and differentiation is a discipline in name only, whose members have fewer common ancestors than they did twenty years ago, fewer common concepts, less to talk about and less language to talk about it with.

Professional Organizations

The numerous specialties and groups that make up sociology still find it convenient to come together periodically and to have a central office that gets out journals, coordinates meetings, and represents the discipline to whoever it needs representing to, most especially such sources of funds as the government and foundations, and such sources of trouble as financially squeezed college administrators who threaten to eliminate graduate programs or entire sociology departments. The convenience of these centralized functions convinces some sociologists that the discipline still has an intellectual core.

The American Sociological Association has often tried to speak for the entire profession, but is frequently challenged. Its officialdom, rather than representing the full variety of the discipline, favors the notions of specific choices of subgroups about what sociology should consist of and tries to make these appear as the "will of the membership." No one person or group can now claim to speak for the entire discipline. Fragmentation of the discipline has gone too far for that. Sociology now consists of a great variety in subject matter, political stance, theories, methods, and aspirations.

Academic Departments

The enduring organizational basis for the practice of sociology has been, and continues to be, the academic department. Academic departments of sociology consist of a selection of trained specialists from the available specialties, never (even in the largest departments) all the possibilities, and usually not just one practitioner per specialty. The typical department contains some clusters around convergent interests, coexisting more or less uneasily, their real unity arising from joint responsibility to provide an undergraduate program for majors, service courses for majors in other fields, and in research training centers, a graduate program.

They provide those services in the context of a continual competition with other departments for resources-money, space, positions-which are and never have been sufficient, even in the boom periods of academic growth, for all the dreams of everyone in the institution. This competition sets the limits on a department's growth, sometimes allowing for expansion, at other times (as now in the Bush recession) requiring limits or cutbacks. The internal workings of departments, and therefore their intellectual life, largely reflect the politics of the resulting budgetary and administrative situations they have to deal with as they confront trustees, legislators, and other governing bodies.

Departments try to present a defensible front to students, administrators, and the world by describing the mélange of interests represented by their faculty as intellectually orderly. In fact, for the reasons we have already mentioned, the order is adventitious and ad hoc, although department members often lose sight of that and believe that their "program" represents an order copied from nature. Departments earn their institutional positions in many ways. Some academics, notably those in the natural sciences, bring in large research grants, which pay a substantial portion of faculty salaries, provide support for graduate students, pay for equipment and support staff, and (through the payment of overhead) contribute to the school's operating budget. Some bring honor to the institution by collecting externally recognized distinction; an internationally renowned English department, for instance, will be supported despite its lack of "profitability." Many departments, however, make their chief contribution to the school's economy by teaching large numbers of undergraduates. Most American universities have many more undergraduates than graduate students. Those students must be taught, even though faculty almost always, given the chance, prefer to teach graduate students.

The Teaching Problem

Sociology supports itself by teaching undergraduates, justifying this role with the shaky assertion that nowhere else in the university do students learn about some of the major issues confronting their own society, such issues as race, sex, and poverty. Such assertions avoid a more basic issue, however: the caliber of students sociology attracts. Large schools, especially state-supported ones, and all universities and colleges where students are scarce, typically have intellectually diverse student bodies. The range of admissions test scores is great.

Some departments make it their business to provide demanding programs for the top portion of that distribution, and thus provide university administrators with programs of quality to point to when necessary. Others recommend themselves to administrators by taking care of the bottom half, those who are less ready to do the kind of school work most colleges demand, by providing "service" courses and majors which enable students who are not prepared to do college level work to get their credits and graduate. University administrators depend on this job being done, but have little respect for those who do it and do not reward departments that specialize in servicing the bottom half. Departments in that position are the ones now vulnerable to administrative raids.

Where does sociology fit in this picture? A little historical perspective is necessary. Briefly, the number of sociology majors grew enormously in the 1960s. Then, just as rapidly, it shrank just as enormously. During the flush times, faculties grew substantially in order to deal with the influx, but did not fall when the trend changed direction. Sociology had 35,491 graduates in 1973/74, its peak year, compared to 14,329 in 1988/89, a decline of 60 percent, which is greater than any other discipline in the sciences and humanities. As enrollment dropped, the intellectual ability of sociology undergraduates, at least as measured by Graduate Record Examination scores, fell to near the bottom of the academic ladder.

Overstaffing of sociology departments led to heavy reliance on service courses over which they have only partial control. The small number and low quality of the undergraduate majors in sociology combine to make the discipline vulnerable to the belt-tightening budget cuts which began in the 1980s and still continue. But sociology has become highly specialized, increasingly devoted to generating (at least in graduate training programs) people who do pure social science. This puts sociology on a collision course with reality.

At one time sociology may have been able to lay claim to providing training for several occupational niches to which graduates could aspire. Instead sociologists, in search of academic respectability, chose to become pure scientists and lost that potential constituency, mostly to social work and criminal justice. Sociology thus cast its lot with other disciplines whose graduates do not know what they will do once they graduate from college. This has made sociology vulnerable to fluctuations in undergraduate enrollments and made it difficult to recruit majors during uncertain economic times.

These difficulties are most obvious in the incoherence of undergraduate sociology offerings. In the divided state of the field, sociologists provide neither a sound training in the discipline nor a really good introduction to the field for non-majors, further increasing the discipline's institutional vulnerability. Sociology increasingly draws the least intellectual students and increasingly adapts to them, as opposed to, say, anthropology, which demands more and gets better, though fewer, students.

Undergraduate Curriculum

Specialization tends to produce scholars who prefer to teach courses in the area of their expertise. They usually get what they want. This then results in an undergraduate curriculum in the shape of an inverted pyramid: a few lower-division courses, a substantial increase in intermediate courses, where specialty topics can first be introduced, and an even greater number of advanced or senior-level courses. Few of the intermediate or advanced courses have any prerequisites other than introductory sociology, and this vast array of substantive courses has no structure. No theory of curriculum or intellectual development justifies this unstructured program; it results from a system of academic perquisites in which specialized scholars teach what they want.

Most departments limit course requirements for the major to introductory sociology and theory, methods, and statistics, so students can graduate in sociology without taking a core of substantive courses, another instance where specialization structures the undergraduate curriculum. The Sociology of Sport, Children with Special Needs, Attitude Theory and Change, the Ethnography of Local Cultures, Growth in Need and Demand for Health Care, the Sociology of X or Special Problems or Topics in Y (fill in the sub-specialty, area, or topic), and a long list of other courses tied to the specific research interests of individual faculty members are given equal footing. Everyone gets a piece of the curriculum.

Thus undergraduates in many departments can, just like their professors, specialize, taking all or nearly all of their elective hours in sociology in just one area. Researchers can shape undergraduate majors in their own image; not sociologists, but demographers, criminologists, gerontologists, social psychologists and so forth. Departments sell specialties as career options just as business schools sell their students on specialties in finance, marketing, or production management.

Sociologists are adept at selling specialties. What about introductory sociology, where they must sell the discipline as a whole? Instructors in that first course might give students a lucid, engaging, and integrated view of sociology. This requires a well-read instructor with unusual expository qualities, familiar not only with sociology but also with related fields, and the issues of the day. But the increasing specialization in graduate training, research, and publication weeds out graduate students with broad-gauged intellectual interests while failing to prepare new scholars to teach introductory courses, even though these courses are often among their first teaching assignments.

Commonly used reading materials make matters worse. Sociology has, and always has had, a small number of intellectually coherent texts, but the best-selling textbooks show how specialties dictate the structure and content of the curriculum. Texts that sell well, as Turner and Turner note, are "unintegrated summaries of major topic areas and subspecialties within sociology." Having chosen poor texts, many instructors then offer a smorgasbord which is, in the words of James Davis, "superficial, unscientific, unduly eclectic, moralistic, thin in substance, and boringly focused on antiquated concepts." Marketing sociology as a smorgasbord reaches its logical conclusion in texts that give the student several "theoretical paradigms" for interpreting the various specialties aggregated in each chapter.

Academic Standards

Such theoretical paradigms would make more sense to students if they were assigned an exemplary book from each paradigm, but sociologists seldom demand that much work from undergraduates. We examined a year's worth of undergraduate syllabi or book order requests for sociology and anthropology programs at two state universities, one with major PhD programs in both fields, the other with a small MA program in sociology and a BA program in anthropology. The amount of reading in the anthropology BA and PhD programs is virtually the same for introductory and intermediate courses. In addition, the BA program required fairly lengthy (fifteen pages) term papers in all its advanced courses. The library research required for such papers would increase the amount of reading to the level required for advanced courses in the PhD program.

In contrast, there was a noticeable difference between the MA and PhD programs in sociology where the PhD program assigns one more text in courses at the intermediate and advanced levels. Even so, the sociology PhD program still requires less reading than the BA program in anthropology. If these programs are, as seems likely, representative of the disciplines as a whole, then anthropologists require twice as much reading as sociologists.

Perhaps the most significant difference lies in intermediate courses, which are the courses in which disciplines are most likely to recruit majors. At this level sociologists typically use one or two texts, and possibly a packet of articles, while anthropologists require three to five books and readers. Anthropologists also rely more on original works and works published by scholarly presses.

Unlike sociologists, anthropologists understand that their comparative advantage rests in what they know about the peoples of the world-and their students receive a healthy dose of that knowledge through extensive, sustained exposure to the best works in anthropology. A majority of college students thus constitute a leisure class, an inevitable outcome of the small amount of reading required in such courses as the typical sociology course. Michael Moffatt's research at Rutgers University, and similar research done at Illinois State University, found that a quarter or more of the students living in residence halls at both universities do not study at all during a normal week. Even those who do claim to study average only ten hours a week, which is why slightly more than half of the students prepare for examinations primarily by cramming. In short, somewhere between 10 and 20 percent of the lower division students conform to conventional work norms while the balance put in an academic work week of no more than fifteen to twenty-five hours, if they actually attend all the classes they are enrolled in.

Serious students have little respect for indulgent instructors or gut courses. But they are a minority on most campuses, and their wishes seldom get much consideration. If too many students complain about a "difficult" text, or about the length of the reading list, instructors who want to avoid trouble, improve student ratings of their courses, or attract enough students for the course to "sell," drop the offending book and shorten the reading list. New faculty members often "dumb down" their courses during the first year or two of teaching, once they learn that enrollments and student ratings carry more weight than the quality or rigor of instruction.

Faculty must agree on minimal expectations for undergraduate courses to avoid such pressures. But specialization works against that. Since sociologists have trouble keeping up with even their own specialties, the increased emphasis on research and expertise paradoxically reduces knowledge of the most exemplary scholarship in sociology, be it generic or specialized. In the end, more and more faculty have a perverse tunnel vision. Members of the same department do not talk with each other about work because they share few interests and little or no reading in common. The lack of shared understandings minimizes the chance of agreeing on what courses students should take, and what or how much students should read. Thus, the drift toward a lowest common denominator is most likely in departments with highly specialized faculty, not only because of the lack of agreement about what is important in undergraduate instruction, but because specialists compete for available students to fill advanced courses.

So sociology programs recruit students committed to a life of leisure rather than those who pursue their studies methodically. Because sociologists make few intellectual demands on students, they also underdevelop the talents of the students they do attract. Put crudely, sociology curricula invite lazy, undisciplined, or just plain dumb students to drop in and sample a course or two, and possibly become a major in the process.

This analysis may seem harsh, but standardized national tests provide evidence for it. Between 1987 and 1990, the rank and mean scores of the Graduate Record Examinations for twenty-five college major fields indicate that sociology ranks twentieth on the verbal and twenty-second on the quantitative tests. These ranks are identical with those established by Paul Baker and William Rau for 1977 to 1982 test data. Social work and criminal justice majors end up at the very bottom in these rankings. Had sociologists kept these fields by vocationalizing sociology, its performance would be even worse.

The future of sociology thus rests on matters only partly in the hands of its practitioners. If the economy does not improve and academic budgets continue to be squeezed, the situation we have outlined- intellectual fragmentation and resulting organizational weakness will make things tough. A concerted effort to "raise standards" in undergraduate curricula across the discipline might make it less vulnerable by increasing its academic respectability. But it is not clear that today's highly specialized discipline would find that either palatable or possible.

Readings Suggested By The Authors

Baker, Paul J. and William C. Rau. 1990. "The Cultural Contradictions of Teaching Sociology," in *Sociology in America*. Edited by Herbert J. Gans. Newbury Park, California: Sage Publications.

Becker, Howard S. 1996. "What's Happening to Sociology," in *Doing Things Together*. Evanston, Illinois: Northwestern University Press.

Davis, James A. 1982. "Five Well-Established Research Results," *Teaching Sociology*, 10: 186, 209.

Turner, Stephen Park, and Jonathan H. Turner. 1990. *The Impossible Science: An Institutional Analysis of American Sociology*. Newbury Park, California: Sage Publications, *1990*.

6

Progress and Cumulation in the Human Sciences After the Fall

Mayer N. Zald

Introduction

The sciences rest their claims to superiority over other methods of revealing truth (e.g., philosophy, theology, literature) on two related bases — superior methods for accepting or rejecting truth claims (e.g., controlled observation, experimentation) and methods for cumulating and organizing truth claims (e.g., classification systems, theories, propositional inventories). The sciences are (were) thought to be progressive, systematically eliminating error or falsehood and cumulating knowledge. For much of this century, the social sciences, especially in the United States, attempted to emulate the physical and natural sciences. Positivistic methods in the social sciences were thought to be superior to interpretivistic, phenomenological, and text analytic approaches to arriving at the truth. Even when a discipline eschewed the generalizing (nomothetic) aims of theoretically driven science, practitioners thought they could progress by adhering to rigorous modes of data collection and data analysis.

While many physical scientists continue to believe in the positivistic view of progress and cumulation, with its attendant materialist and mechanistic ontologies and its epistemic coordination of theories, measurement, and observation, historians and philosophers of science have increasingly challenged that vision. The fall from foundationalism not only challenges the epistemological grounds of science, it also has implications for conceptions of progress and cumulation. On the one hand, post-Kuhn, few believe that theories are largely supplanted through critical tests, or through the formulation of more general encompassing frameworks. The language of paradigm succession or shift seemed much more ambiguous and open to social and cultural processes than the language of positivism and verificationism suggested. Although Kuhn (1977) has continued to believe in the progressive character of science, what progress means has become ambiguous. Science is a more disorderly and disunified enterprise than some philosophies of science had suggested.

Post-Rorty, philosophers and historians of science tend to believe that the act of observing the world is deeply influenced by the language system — the linguistic categories, embedded metaphors, and rules for using language. There is a world out there, but we only know it through a socially constructed language system. An epistemology that assumes a mapping is in some sense a logical impossibility, because as we speak about it, the world as we know it is already language and theory prefigured. Indeed, even this phrasing artificially separates language/practice from its constitutive role in human-world embeddedness (Rouse, 1987).

Not only is positivism a misleading doctrine for the natural sciences, but, say interpretivists, for the social and human sciences it is doubly misleading. What is to be observed and understood is a meaning system and its implications. Most of the "brute facts" that are subject to enumeration in positivistic social science gain their force because of the cultural/social meanings in which the subjects of social science participate (Taylor, 1971). Explanation in the causal sense must give way to, or be embedded in, hermeneutic unveiling and interpretation.

Now, how might we think of progress and cumulation after the fall? If older verificationist and/or logical positivist models seem less useful, what can we substitute for them? Specifically, how might we think of progress and cumulation in the human and social sciences? Beginning from an anti-foundationalist and anti-unificationist set of assumptions (Dupré, 1993), I want to argue, first, that some notion of progress (advance) is a central ordering or control device in the community of scholars. It is a criterion we use in evaluating scholarly products, in judging dissertation proposals, in evaluating journal articles, in praising or condemning studies. It is part of local practice. Second, the notions of progress and cumulation are themselves social and rhetorical constructs that vary among disciplines and sub-disciplines. Moreover, there may well be a difference between the evaluation and conception of progress within a discipline or subdiscipline and relevant external audiences — which may include other communities of scholars. This disjunction may have grave implications for the reputation and economic status of the subdiscipline. Third, the conception of progress and cumulation is tied to the structure and epistemic assumptions of scholarly communities; thus we must ask what are these communities' relevant dimensions for understanding conceptions of progress? Fourth, what are the implications of this discussion for progress and cumulation in sociology and for the human sciences as a whole?

To foreshadow the argument, I will argue the following: (a) Progress and cumulation are separate or separable issues. Moreover, progress and cumulation are subject to rhetorics of stylization or modelling and rhetorics of use or practice. (b) The operative epistemic and methodological assumptions or commitments of sociological subdisciplines vary enormously; these epistemic/methodological assumptions structure the criteria for progress in subdisciplines and shape the linguistic form of truth claims and the "architectonics" of the system of truth claims. (c) In many subdisciplines in sociology there has been great progress, but, paradoxically, in some of the same areas where there has been great progress, there has been little cumulation. (d) Finally, because some of the human sciences are deeply connected to the political and social concerns of the day, the changing agenda of society reshapes the animating concerns of scholarly disciplines. Again paradoxically, cumulation may occur most in subdisciplines least tied to the intellectual currents of the day, as scholars are tied to a more limited range of concerns; however, great leaps of progress, in the sense of innovative ways of looking at issues, may occur in those subdisciplines most attuned to the larger currents of society.

Rhetorics and Usages

Reflect on everyday usage. To make progress is to advance, to move forward. To progress is not just movement, but forward movement. Movement backward, or energy expended to stay in place, is less often considered progress; it has to be argued for, justified. Progress has a temporal and/ or spatial component. It implies some comparison with a previous state or a potential future state. Progress usually implies a goal, either an objective, however loosely defined, or a comparison of states of knowledge on some implicit or explicit criterion; it is measured against a stylized or idealized state of being, or is a comparison of two or more alternatives, including the current state of knowledge.

Although it is common to think of progress, especially in science, as a good, progress can be tied to dark ends, witness Hogarth's *The Rake's Progress*. In scholarship a dark sense of progress, a path toward the abyss, is sometimes attributed to work that appears to be nihilistic and to have a destructive edge without promoting alternatives. Ethically, a dark side of progress is found in the release of destructive and uncontrollable consequences of scientific advance.

The word "progress" can be associated with modernity and the enlightenment program linking rationality and improvement. A lively debate in contemporary philosophy of science revolves around exactly how much scholars such as Kuhn actually depart from a modernist, progressive view of scientific achievement (Rouse, 1991). For our purposes, without privileging science over everyday and practical knowledge, and without making claims for science in its overall contribution to human welfare, we will start from an assumption that the human sciences and its practitioners are organized around, are oriented toward, some notion of advance, better understanding or superior truth claims.

Progress or advance in intellectual matters implies doing things better along some dimension relevant to the task. Better methods, new observations or observation methods, greater certainty, more aesthetically pleasing ways of representing, more satisfying interpretations of events, all qualify as making progress. So too does discarding falsehoods and rejecting theories. Notions of creative destruction suggest progress by elimination, or by eliminating residuals, to make way for new advances in knowledge or competencies.

Pre-Kuhn, cumulation and progress were seen as in some sense linear. There was little room for backsliding, for losing knowledge. Facts cumulated as more studies were done; theories cumulated as successive formulations became more general and encompassing. The truths of an early theory were contained within the new formulation. Post-Kuhn and post-Rorty matters are more complicated, since facts are not independent of theory laden language and since both depend upon often unexplicated assumptions and frames. When paradigms shift there may be losses of knowledge and knowledge creating potential since the older paradigms may be better for pursuing certain kinds of questions than the newer paradigms, even though the newer paradigms are better for the problems at hand.

Philosopher Larry Laudan (1977) avoids some of these issues by focusing on progress as problem solution. Admitting that there may be losses as well, he takes progress to be the resolution of problems — in the formation of concepts and in their linkage in explanatory and mathematical systems, in measurement, in data collection and data analysis, as perceived by the working community of scholars.

Increasingly scholars have seen progress as a process in which a community of scholars working with a set of (often implicit) consensus practices comes to accept new practices and ideas. Both the history of those practices and ideas, and the organization of the community, play a large role in what is on the table at any point in time and how new ideas and solutions will be evaluated (Kitcher, 1993; Rouse, 1990). The state of a field is socially and historically constructed; what is on the table is to some large extent the residue or result of prior siftings, debates, and discourse. Consensus is not easily won. Indeed, as Gilbert and Mulkay (1984) demonstrate for the case of the chemiosmotic rationale in the field of photosynthetic phosphorylation, even when a consensus emerges that a once renegade theory is in fact important and valuable, the meaning of the theory and its fit in the field of knowledge may still be open to debate.

Modernist philosophies of science argued not only that science advances, but that it leads to more encompassing and unified systems of explanation. In this way of thinking, advance leads to cumulation through the successive retention of superior theories and the assimilation of facts to those theories. Yet advance and cumulation are separable processes. Possibly because philosophy of science had on its agenda issues of epistemology and the establishment of truth, it had less to say about the retention or cumulation of "truths" once they were established. Even today, discussions of scientific advance tend to say less about the problem of cumulation than about the problem of progress. Cumulation is somehow seen as automatic. Yet Stephen Cole (1992, 1994), a leading sociologist of science out of the Mertonian framework, argues that it is precisely the difference in communities' abilities to agree on what is the core (the retained knowledge handed on to the next generation as accepted practices and ideas) and to assimilate knowledge to the core that distinguishes "real sciences" from the protosciences. For Cole, all scientific fields have dissension at the "frontier," but some do not appear to be organized to adjudicate, decide, and retain important findings, theories, and concepts.

Just as progress might come in several guises, so too may cumulation occur in several forms. One form of cumulation, accumulation, registers observations, preferably replicable observations. In its most empiricistic form, cumulation is the systematic registering of facts. But, say the more theoretically inclined, empiricistic cumulation is a kind of random cumulation — a growing mountain of assorted tidbits organized only around agreed upon categories of observation; what is needed is a mechanism for selecting important observations, or selecting important and precisely explained or predicted observations. Classification systems, theories, and related mathematical formulations become more explicit guides for organizing the retention of knowledge and guiding future research.

Cole (1994) argues that agreeing on the core depends upon having stable objects to explain; general theory and their elementary components in sociology are vacuous and nongeneral phenomena are too subject to changes (e.g., gender relations). One might also argue that the agenda of some parts of sociology is tied to recent political and morally charged events and trends in society; thus, it is not just change within the objects of concern that creates instability for social scientists, but changes in the focal problems of concern. Here the lack of cumulation is caused not by changes within the object of analysis, but by which objects come, and stay, on the table (Zald, 1991). In the natural and physical sciences, findings, facts, and generalizations become assimilated to the background assumptions of the problems that are on the table. However, in some parts of the social sciences, shifts within objects or in the topics of concern, make irrelevant those findings or generalizations from what was once the frontier.

The distinction between core and frontier hides the possibility that even among disciplines that have relatively stable objects, the architectonics of cumulation may differ. Ernst Mayr (1982) argues that the growth of biological thought has occurred not through the development of universal laws, but through the articulation of major concepts. The scaffolding of cumulation is created by the addition of new concepts that bracket fields of investigation and explanations. While it is possible to attempt to formulate laws, that is not how biologists have actually proceeded. Extending Mayr's argument, and without prejudging whether succeeding theories, systems or facts are in an absolute sense truer than earlier ones, different fields organize their truth claims about, and their representations of, their objects of analysis by different modes. Musicologists, literary theorists, anthropologists, physicists, and sociologists differently privilege classification systems, theories, concepts, notation systems, and so on. In some sense, all use texts to communicate and cumulate, but the organization of textual representation and the link of the texts to communities of practice will vary.

So far I have treated the issue of progress and cumulation as a kind of natural category or language used by a community of scholars to guide research decisions and to present and organize discourse. But progress and cumulation are also subject to abstract discussion, emulation, and stylization, as scholars within a community reflect on and discuss their own practices and interact with scholars from other disciplines, as well as the interpreters and translators of those disciplines — philosophers, historians, sociologists, who render the logics and practices of disciplines. Stylized rhetorics develop such that practitioners who do not use them are treated as less advanced than those who do. At an earlier time, physicists who did not use mathematics were seen as less competent than those who did. Today, all do. Over the last century, the mathematicization of economics, called "physics envy" by some, has proceeded whether or not it was appropriate to the more important problems in the field (McCloskey, 1985). In sociology, the belief in formal deductive theorization led to a style of presentation that required the formal statement of axioms and hypotheses, even if the logic of the argument was really contained in the explanatory paragraphs accompanying the propositions and derived hypotheses (cf. Zetterberg, 1963). The rhetorics of cumulation sometimes showed in the publication of propositional inventories (Berelson and Steiner, 1964).

It is probably inherent in the human condition for people who happen to be scholars to reflect on their own practices and to compare them with past practices, with the practices of others, and with abstracted models of practice. Yet, more self-confident and autonomous groups of scholars are less likely to take seriously what others are doing or saying about what disciplinary practice should be. They may have an internal debate about what progress is, but the debate will be drawn largely from an internal logic of practice and aspirations within a discipline or community, rather than organized by and contrasted with abstracted views of science and scholarship or other disciplines' practices. This is an aspect of the internalization of disciplines (Shapere, 1984).

Moreover, explicit concern with progress and cumulation may vary by disciplines and context. The collective project of legitimizing the natural and physical sciences, especially in England and the United States, led them to contrast themselves with the humanistic disciplines on the criteria of progress and cumulation. In turn, the social sciences, once called moral sciences, attempted to nestle close to the physical and natural sciences. Scholars in the humanistic disciplines surely make judgments about advances in their disciplines. New modes of annotation, classification, and interpretation are judged superior in explaining, illuminating, and gathering together observations about the objects of humanistic understanding. They may be less likely to articulate a research or theoretical frontier, because some are organized around interpretative topics, not "problems." That does not mean, however, that better interpretations — interpretations that are more coherent, more illuminating, more closely tied to evidence — cannot be judged and handed down to successive generations.

To summarize the thrust of the argument so far, progress and cumulation are interconnected but separable concepts; progress has more to do with advance, and cumulation has to do with the storage, transmission, and recycling of advances for further research and knowledge building. Both concepts are "fuzzy," and forms of advance and cumulation may be multiple. Stylized rhetorics about progress and cumulation may be borrowed from other disciplines and imposed on subject matters, just as techniques of investigation or concepts may be borrowed. Finally, since disciplines vary in how they organize knowledge and make advances, progress and cumulation must be understood in the context of disciplinary practices and commitments, and in the context of the texture of scholarship.

The Texture of Scholarship and Epistemic Communities

Anthropologist Roy D'Andrade (1985) argues that it is useful to think about three models of scientific disciplines — physical science, natural science, and semiotic science. He argues that the physical sciences — physics, astronomy, and chemistry — can be well described by the covering law model and are most appropriately mathematicized. The natural sciences, which include the biological sciences and some of the social and earth sciences, have a different texture. They describe adaptive systems, typically components of systems and their interaction with other components. Functioning systems' mechanisms of adaptation are important elements. Semiotic sciences — cultural anthropology, much of social psychology, and components of linguistics — deal with systems of meaning. Following the psychologist Thomas Lauduaer, d'Andrade argues that experimental social psychology is often a special way of doing American ethnography. The social sciences, he says, often require both natural system and semiotic approaches. It is, for instance, possible to describe capitalist societies as systems of interconnecting parts. However, for many purposes semiotic analysis of the (changing) meaning of the system and its components will be required.

He does not argue that mathematicization is restricted to the physical sciences, only that it is less prominently featured in the others and will often be subsidiary to the description of components. D'Andrade uses his threefold categorization to argue that form of argument, the nature of generalization and, by implication, the logic of progress and cumulation, will look very different from discipline to discipline. However, aside from arguing against the usefulness of a covering law formula, and distinguishing system like disciplines from semiotic ones, he does not spend much time discussing how texture of scholarship might vary by disciplines and subdisciplines. Moreover, the broad sweep of his categorization conceals large differences within scientific/scholarly fields. It also fails to explore the complex linkages between parts of fields (subdisciplines, or invisible colleges) and to subdisciplines nominally located in other disciplines.

Texture is a global term for the ways in which discourse in a community is conducted. It is rhetorics in its most inclusive and nonpejorative sense. It refers to the mix of linguistic/symbolic representations and the conventions governing their use in a community. Everything from mathematical formulae, to the presentation of graphics, to footnote conventions are part of the texture of a community's discourse. Different textures lead to different modes of reporting advances and summarizing whole fields. A review article in history will look very different from a review article in physics. Textures or rhetorics are both products and creators of epistemic communities.

Scholarly communities are epistemic communities. They have what Margaret Somers (forthcoming) calls "knowledge cultures" or what Ian Hacking (1984) calls "styles of reasoning." Earlier, Fleck (1935/1979) even used the term "thought collective" to refer to the shared communal understandings.

How might we describe epistemic communities? First, they are organized around topics. Second, the scholarly community has a repository of more or less organized findings, and claims about findings, in its accumulated and retrievable stock of writings and oral claims about the topic. Third, the community has a set of methodological commitments and claims about how findings are to be obtained. Fourth, the community has a set of implicit and explicit assumptions about what the repertoire of constituting ideas, interpretations, and explanations that can be entertained to order research, to choose among renderings and readings, and to focus activity.

To talk about progress and cumulation, then, is to talk about change in the stock of knowledge, methods, and assumptions in particular communities of scholars. Since these communities may have different and deep methodological commitments, orientations toward data collection and analysis, etc., it might be possible, though beyond my scope here, to develop a comparative analysis of epistemic commitments. Central are a description of the kinds of observations and readings made on objects (natural or human made), the forms of summarization (quantitative, graphic, visual), and the language structure (mathematical, statistical, propositional, universal extension, etc.), used to interpret and order the observations.

Any particular scholar may be part of several communities. For instance, a scholar may be a student of Marxism in American social history studying mining towns and working with quantitative indicators of collective action. Or, a rational choice Marxist working on collective action in mining communities. Depending on the scholar's own capacities and predilections, she might be more or less attuned to debates and issues in adjoining or overlapping fields of study (e.g., psychoanalytic studies of 19th-century child-rearing practices in the working classes). Donald T. Campbell (1969) describes this overlap, or interlink, of communities of scholars as the "fish scale model" of interdisciplinary overlap. One form of progress is constituted by forming new communities. Over time, scholars may discover topics untreated by, and disjunctive with, the stock of problems within a community. The very recognition of the separateness of the problem set is a form of progress.

Over time the epistemic community produces a set of problems to be solved. One of the differences among communities is, of course, the amount of agreement about when a problem is solved or what constitutes a solution. The problem set may be relatively stable, and indeed so called solutions may represent interpretations that only crowd in on earlier interpretations, forcing them to the background without in any sense vanquishing them. However, the problem set may be changing rapidly, with or without consensus on solution. This juxtaposition of problem stability and change and consensus on the meaning of change is especially important for thinking about cumulation and progress. Where there is rapid change in problems studied or solutions suggested for those problems, and little consensus about either the importance of the problems or the solutions being offered, charges of faddism, as opposed to advance, are likely to be made.

Communities of scholars are not only epistemic communities. They participate in a social organization that rewards and punishes behavior. Communities of scholars are organized around communications about the central topic(s) — through journals, books, conferences, and scholarly societies. They are not the same as, though they overlap with, disciplines. They are made up of members — those people who are "credentialled" to speak on the topic. Credentialing can be formal or informal, but the uncredentialed have a tough time getting a hearing in the community. Credentialing occurs through complex processes. It is especially important for the warranting of findings and perspectives that break from the established repertoire. It may be that membership within the community is heavily dependent upon certification of methodological competence, e.g., the ability to do fieldwork, to use archives, to use mathematics, to do laboratory work, and to have command of relevant rhetorical forms (e.g., footnotes and footnote practice, modes of argumentation, and presentation of data forms). Many disciplines may have multiple certification routes. Moreover, in an era of blurred disciplinary/community boundaries, scholars may be at home in and received by multiple communities.

Communities of scholars allocate prestige and have an internal stratification system that links contributions to the community to material and symbolic rewards, including jobs. Communities may vary in the uniformity and coherence of their stratificational/allocational systems. Those high in the system act as gatekeepers by evaluating contributions to the community. They may not be the first to recognize the contribution to progress in the community, and over time they may be replaced, but because the gatekeepers control access to journals, jobs, awards, career movement, and acceptance of dissertations, at some point progress is validated within the prestige system of the community. Stinchcombe (this volume) argues that the fragmented nature of sociology leads to many errors in the evaluation of work and the placement of sociologists in the academy, presumably in contrast to more unified, coherent disciplines.

Communities of scholars vary enormously in their density and size, the number of scholars at any one time working on a set of related topics, or indeed, on the same problem within a topic field. The number of scholars working on the same problem and related topics creates both a validation and replication ground for the "truth" or "interpretative truth" claim, and a user field for demonstrating the value of the claim over time. The distinction is not sharp, of course. Nevertheless, in many fields there may be a debate in which scholars address their work largely to peers thinking at the same level of abstraction and discourse (the validation and replication ground) and a group who use the arguments, concepts, and findings to illuminate their own extensions and applications of the argument. In other fields, few scholars may actually work on the same problem, but may share a discursive field and orientation.

In many parts of the social and human sciences, exact replication and similar problem focus may be rare, though a sense of participating in a larger common topical area or orientation may be common. For instance, many scholars are now concerned with the emergence, maintenance, and force of nationalism in social structure and ideology, though few with nationalism in 18th-century Bosnia, or some other specific locale. They share a general discursive field and may rely on classic and contemporary texts that compare nationalist movements or discuss nationalism more generally.

Finally, communities of scholars differ substantially in their "nodality," the extent to which scholars are clustered around organizational settings, such as research institutions — astronomy labs, survey research centers, or schools and publication outlets of like-minded scholars. As Whitley (1984) shows, the institutional/organizational nodality of a community affects the acceptance of truth claims and the orientation of research, at least in the short run.

This discussion of the epistemic texture and social organization of communities has been developed in order to get purchase on the variation among communities as they develop a discourse about superior and inferior scholarship, claims about truth, and the value of findings and their reporting. Given that communities differ in their epistemic commitments and the stability of their problem sets, we should get purchase on how advance and cumulation are registered. Let us now ask, How does progress and cumulation occur in sociology?

Progress and Cumulation in Sociology, A Fragmented Field

Disciplines may contain many subdisciplines. To the extent that a community of scholars is coterminous with a subdiscipline, as often happens, the analysis of disciplinary structure illuminates progress and cumulation in the constitutive communities. Where there are many topics and subdisciplines, where there are few specifications of connections among the topics, and where there are strong disagreements about methods that help create non-communicating communities, the discipline resembles an "adhocracy." Whitley (1984), drawing on the organizational theorist Henry Mintzberg (1979), sees sociology as an adhocracy with little integration across subdisciplines. An "adhocracy" is an organization in which the various units have little to do with each other and have different views of what the enterprise is about, but each makes claims about its own contribution to the overall organization — there is at least that much awareness that the units are part of the larger organization and gain legitimacy, status, and resources from participating in it. To understand progress and cumulation in sociology, then, is to examine the texture of knowledge in the many communities contained in whole or in part within the discipline.

Sociology has been a brawling, inchoate discipline. In *The Impossible Science*, Stephen and Jonathan Turner (1990) treat the cycles and trends that have occurred in American sociology over its history. One cycle has been the oscillation between what might be called knowledge for its own sake and social problem and civilizational concern. A related cycle is an oscillation in concern with scientific methodological purity. Depending upon both external and internal issues, these axes of orientation may combine or conflict in a variety of ways. For instance, methodological purity emphases may be combined with applied concerns, leading to an emphasis on evaluation research. Or, methodological purity may be combined with a knowledge for its own sake emphasis, leading to what C. Wright Mills called "abstract empiricism."

Trends include a continuing growth of substantive specializations and methodological techniques. Although the American Sociological Association's membership has not grown much in absolute numbers over the last two decades, the number of organized sections has more than doubled — there are now over 25. New specializations, represented by sections, may overlap considerably with older ones; nevertheless, each new section represents some focus of attention on a redefined or new central topic and defines a somewhat new community.

Turner and Turner do not draw out the implications of their analysis for progress and cumulation, or the perception of progress and cumulation. However, they tend to be pessimists: Because sociology is inchoate and various groups cannot (will not) agree on core problems and methods, sociology is doomed to wander in the wilderness. Progress and cumulation are unlikely. Although they do not explicitly discuss their epistemological commitments, I suspect that they tend to be foundationalists. But if one rejects foundationalism and accepts a community-based definition of knowledge, quite a different set of conclusions emerges.

If sociology had an overarching paradigmatic consensus, progress would be examined in terms of solving and posing questions related to the paradigmatic agreements and assumptions. Since it lacks that consensus, progress, and cumulation are measured against the problems and topics being debated, studied, disposed of, and succeeded in particular communities of scholars. In disciplines with strong paradigmatic consensus, introductory texts are likely to cover similar topics, have a shared language, and exhibit a consensus on the core. In an adhocracy such as sociology, however, cumulation occurs in the subdisciplines and introductory texts will vary because few writers will agree on the core topics, concepts, and communities that need to be represented.

Moreover, in the human sciences in general, and sociology in particular, communities vary in the extent to which their core problems are affected by large societal events and/or broad intellectual currents. Thus, the subdisciplines of sociology may well vary in the extent to which their orientations and concerns are shaped by the larger moral and political milieu.

Let me give a somewhat cursory overview of progress and cumulation in four communities within sociology — ethnomethodology, historical sociology, demography, and collective behavior/social movements. These four were chosen because they manifest a variety of epistemic commitments and trajectories of advance and cumulation. In the first instance, I attempt to represent progress and cumulation as it might be seen from within the community.

Ethnomethodology

Ethnomethodology has comprised a community of scholars committed to analyzing the core problem of how intersubjectivity is reached among interactants in a local setting. Whether the local setting is the negotiation of sexual identity, cab drivers and their dispatchers, young doctors learning to be gynecologists from other gynecologists and related practitioners, or welfare workers in a welfare bureaucracy, the task is to examine the devices of interrogation, the markers of agreement (indexicality), and the mechanisms for sustaining social understandings and cognitive order of micro-interaction and changing interactional directions. Although not opposed to experimental intervention, for instance presenting subjects with someone with a false identity, the community disavowed quantitative analysis of interaction. Close logical analysis of the implications of verbal signing has been the core method. Although, it has been deeply committed to close analysis of language and conversation, ethnomethodologists are different from sociolinguists, who often have had a more descriptive and processual orientation, and semioticians, who are concerned with substantive meaning. The community of ethnomethodologists overlaps several other communities — it has boundaries (and disagreements) with phenomenologists, students of occupations and organizations, and socio-linguists.

The community took large steps in the late 1960s and 1970s. Progress occurred when the community agreed to conceptual distinctions and statements about when interactants can be thought to have achieved intersubjectivity or when intersubjectivity was defeated. Since the community disavowed the logic of covering law models, it neither developed general propositions, nor statements of variance. Progress was contained in a set of interlinked papers that most members of the community read and discussed (Heritage, 1984). A review of the paradigmatic papers would reveal a succession of debates in which the later papers built on the earlier ones, sharpening distinctions and adding new ones. A taut and tightly reasoned style dominated. By the mid-1980s, the core problems may have been exhausted (but see Pollner, 1991), yet the methods of close analysis of language turns and referentiality could be applied to a wide variety of problems. As attention shifted from the core problems, the community became less distinctive in its concern. In some regard it merged with sociolinguistics and conversation analysis, on the one hand, and substantive sociological topics like political sociology, gender relations and analysis, medical sociology, etc., on the other (Drew and Heritage, 1992). Today recruitment to the community has slowed and fewer sociologists call themselves ethnomethodologists.

Historical Sociology

An interest in large-scale historical change has been part of sociology since its inception, and scholars such as Weber were lauded for their historically based studies of societies. Yet prior to the 1950s, few in American sociology carried out detailed historical analyses in a sociological mode. Beginning in the 1950s, expanding rapidly in the 1960s and continuing since there has been a massive expansion and transformation of the community of historical sociologists (Abbott, 1994; Smith, 1991). One might argue that historical sociology is a field, not a community, since so many topics can in fact be treated with an historical, over time, orientation. After all, every societal institution, category, or process can be given an historical dimension. Conceivably equal attention could be paid to such topics as the history of schooling, the transformation of cities, the history of administration, etc. Moreover, as Abbott (1994) argues, all studies of social process, no matter how micro, have an implicit overtime orientation, and are thus historical. However, the agenda of historical sociology was heavily shaped by its ties to and emergence from political sociology with a left-liberal slant. The core problems grew out of an attempt to understand the social response to industrialization and the transformation of capitalism. Two interlaced topics dominated when the focus was on the internal developments of nations — first and foremost, a materialist class based analysis of the relationships of types of workers and types of elites, and second, and tied to external relations, the growth and transformation of the state. Later sociologists with a strong interest in less developed countries reacted to contemporaneous economic and political trends to redefine older topics such as imperialism in terms of dependency and world systems theory.

Methodologically, the community, especially the first generation, focused on secondary data and interpretation, rarely venturing into archives. Moreover, even when they used archival material, their ties to the larger sociological community led them to transform archival information into quantitative indicators of conflict or industrial structure.

From Barrington Moore, to Tilly, Skocpol, Wallerstein, and beyond, enormous progress has been made. Sharp controversies about the interplay of class formation, state formation, state autonomy, and world system theory generated serious and detailed analyses. Reuschemeyer et al. (1992) represent a culmination of the tradition energized by Moore. Obviously, the study of revolution and societal transformation remains viable. Thus, one can see continuity of problems, new perspectives brought to bear on older problems, evidence assembled, and some sense of advance.

Yet there have been changes in epistemic assumptions and in core problems. For one, the larger meta-narratives have been questioned. Moreover, positivistic epistemic assumptions have been shaken, leading to a healthy debate about methods and an opening toward culture and narrative analysis. Second, the growth of feminist theory has transformed the problem agenda. Historical sociology more than many other areas has moved to make gender a central problematic. Finally, as a focus on context and local study emerged, and as the dominant political/macro focus of analysis receded, the unity of the community may have disappeared. The demise of grand meta-narratives and their clashes may appear to mean a decrease in intellectual breakthroughs, while a process of accumulation on many fronts goes on.

The historical sociology community is much larger than the ethno-methodological one. It is deeply interconnected to a national and international community of historians and other social-scientists with interests in varieties of social history. However, it is still the case that historians and historical sociologists often view each other over a divide: With a few exceptions, sociologists, their theories, and their findings, have only a small audience among more traditional historians, even while a new generation of historians is more closely linked to the social sciences than their progenitors.

Demography

Both ethnomethodology and historical sociology have ties to fields and approaches long considered part of the humanities. Demography separated earlier from natural and moral philosophy and has its roots in social statistics. In some ways linked to human biology and in other ways to the needs of the administrative state, demography is "big science" compared to the other communities we have considered. Its location within sociology is somewhat accidental and it has sometimes made claims for autonomy from sociology and location elsewhere in the academy.

Either it uses the data bases of the administrative state — national censuses, epidemiological surveys, morbidity and mortality data — or it collects data on large samples, in many nations. Philanthropic foundations and government agencies fund these data collection efforts and, indeed, have played a large role in promoting and expanding the domain of demography around the world. Although demographic events and processes have large implications for many aspects of social life — from community integration and socialization, to the health and welfare of populations, to economic growth and change, to party politics — the agenda of demography is set to a larger extent than in most social science disciplines by the agenda of the state and major funding agencies. When family planning and birth control is perceived as a large problem, funds are committed to relevant studies. When societal interest switches to migration and immigration, a different part of the demographic equation is examined.

The demographic community, more than any of the others discussed, has made a wholesale commitment to positivism, especially of an empiricist kind. There is a large commitment to data quality and data sets. Theoretical ideas are close to the ground. Although Marxist or neo-Marxist theories of the relationship of households to production systems play a role in demographic thinking, demographic theories tend to have clear indicators and testable propositions. Although gender issues have become important in demography, especially the relationship of the changing status of women to a host of household compositional issues, feminist theory more generally has not.

The commitment to precise measurement ties demography to advances in statistics that are fairly precise and clear in their consequences for estimation. Advance in statistical techniques tied to computer processing capacity allows for more complex modeling of larger data sets, with a greater range of variables. Within the community of demographers, the reasons why earlier methods have been superseded is clear, even though debate often is quite fierce and some social statisticians argue that the application of more "sophisticated" tools often leads to difficult-to-interpret findings and a violation of statistical assumptions (see Davis in this volume).

In American sociology population studies were tied to ecology. Over the last two decades the field has changed significantly in its dominant interests and connections. For a while, roughly from the mid-1950s until the mid-1970s, the statistical focus upon aggregate changes in large samples was applied to studying the distribution of status and prestige in the stratification order. In more recent times, ecological and stratificational interests have declined, while social epidemiological issues have come to the fore.

The core may be represented by mathematical demography and stable population theory, which provides accounting identities around which the field is organized (Preston, 1993). Thus, even though topics recede from the agenda and others come to the fore, a sense of continuity and cumulation is achieved. More is known about birth rates, death rates, and migration and their interpenetration with social and economic processes. Demographers can cite area after area where empirical findings have clarified our knowledge of such matters as the cost of divorce, or the relationship of social indicators to mortality and morbidity, or the relationship of birth control programs to birth rates, or to the causes and consequences of single-headed families.

At the same time, the larger intellectual currents sweeping the social sciences and the humanities often have been marginalized. It is not that demographers are unaware of the importance of societal definitions for either their own research agenda or for the definitions of their key terms. Demographers know, for instance, that racial categories are social constructs, that natalist and immigration policies are the result of political-social processes. In recent times, the impact of culture on demographic processes has become an important topic. But these larger currents do not challenge the core commitments of the epistemic community. They may nuance the discussion, or denaturalize and deuniversalize some concepts, or introduce new variables for analysis, but the discourse proceeds within the commitments to large data sets, statistical estimation and core population variables.

Collective Action/Social Movements (CA/SM)

In contrast to demography, whose core topics were strongly linked to specific statistical modes of analysis, and concepts, such as cohorts, that had clear methodological implications, CA/SM has been driven more by theoretical and conceptual developments and has been quite eclectic in its methodological commitments. Originally, CA/SM largely organized around descriptive case studies, but increasingly a variety of methods have been employed — experimental studies of collective action in small groups, computer simulations, detailed observational studies of collective action events, such as protests and riots, codings and quantitative analysis of CA/SM activities as reported in the media, event-history analyses of the births and deaths of Social Movement Organizations, and so on.

The study of social movements and collective behavior was transformed by the political events of the 1960s and the intellectual currents of the social sciences of the 1960s, first, and then the 1970s and 1980s. The political events — the rise of the civil rights movement and the student and anti-war movements — normalized social movements. Where the Chicago School approach tended to lump social movements with collective behavior (riots, panics, fads, public opinion), the irrationalist assumptions sometimes assumed to undergird that clustering were challenged by those who saw political movements as politics by other means.

The newer resource mobilization approaches explored the implications of assuming that social movement and collective action activity was in some sense rational, responding to a sometimes implicit, sometimes explicit, calculation of costs and benefits. One of the great achievements of social science, and social movement theory in particular, was to problematize "interests." Most political scientists and sociologists had assumed an automatic link between interest and action. Although he was not the only one to raise the issue, Mancur Olson's (1965) important *Logic of Collective Action* cast starkly the free rider, mobilization, and collective action dilemma. The Resource Mobilization/Collective Action paradigm became the dominant paradigm (Morris and Herring, 1987; Zald, 1992). The Political Process approach was a major restatement and extension for political movements. Even though these approaches became dominant, many social movement scholars did not and do not buy into these approaches and older traditions retain vitality.

By the end of the 1970s, the growth of the new social movements (the women's, gay rights, and environmental movements), with their focus on social redefinition, consciousness-raising, and identity, presented a challenge to these earlier approaches, which assumed agreed upon social categories and definitions of injustice. In a sense, New Social Movement theorists problematized interests in a different way: Where CA/SM scholars problematized mobilization, New Social Movement scholars problematized identities that lead to interests.

Moreover, in the United States, borrowing from Goffman, analytic and methodological approaches to the study of frames (i.e., the way symbols and phrases define problems and potential solutions), cognitive constructs, and symbolic packages provided tools for the examination of discourse. Matters of ideology and culture are more prominent in this community today than they were 15 years ago, yet the turn to discourse and culture is often treated without historical and cultural depth, in part because the community focuses mainly on contemporaneous movements and recent battles. Currently the "hot" end of the field is focusing on political process models and framing, yet the mobilization/collective action approach retains a fair degree of viability.

This area reveals an almost Lakatosian process of research program development and change. More influenced by events in the larger society than many areas in social science or sociology, and open to intellectual currents in the humanities as well, it is less open than historical sociology to these latter currents.

Although within the community there is a great sense of advance and cumulation, not all who work in this area see the process so benignly. Piven and Cloward (1991), for instance, believe that the normalization of protest in social movement theory leads to an underestimation of the importance and value of disruptive and less organized protest. From a different slant, James Rule (1988, and this volume) argues the choice of approaches has been more a function of expressive taste than logic and observation, and that the shift from older approaches has led to important losses of topics from the research domain. Thus, he thinks, we may only be seeing a faddish shift in focus. While there have been losses, such as scholars' tendency to underestimate the role of hot emotions in fueling movements and collective action, losses occur in many fields when paradigms shift. The gains from the newer work have been substantial.

These communities differ quite substantially in their ability to generate cumulative knowledge and to progress over their recent histories. Arguably, the demographic community, because it agrees on a core set of population components with measurable dimensions, is well structured for cumulation, not around a hierarchically ordered set of theoretical propositions, but around a set of topics with well-defined parameters. But the intellectual strategy tends to be incremental and is not conducive to large steps forward. Historical sociology, which made large progress as it blocked in major explanatory schemes for major social processes, may be in the process of splintering. As meta-narratives are brought into disrepute, strong unifying themes, tying researchers together, vanish. Alternately, since historical sociology inherited political sociology's emphasis on moral and political concerns — it has attracted the left within the discipline — those same concerns may structure the agenda. But without unifying meta-narratives, progress may come more by examining new areas than by developing encompassing explanations (see Lloyd, 1993, who argues for the enduring value of a macrostructuralist agenda). It may be that cumulation will occur around narrower topics. I should add, however, that the fact that historical sociology bridges to intellectual history and the humanities makes it more open than some other sociological communities to broader intellectual currents. Ethnomethodology made enormous progress early, but has been diffused into conversation analysis and applied concerns. There is some reason to believe that a market for ethnomethodology, narrowly conceived, never developed. It is difficult to separate the political economy of the field, which then limits the possibilities of research, from a fading intellectual agenda. However, ethnomethodology was cumulative, in the sense that later work was based on earlier work, but because of a narrow agenda, around sharper analytic distinctions. Empirical generalizations were never its goals. Finally, the study of social movements made large strides, but is now in a period of consolidation. There are large sets of problems that have not been well investigated; for instance, only recently has the transnational nature of collective action and social movements come onto the agenda, but the contours for major advance may be past — for now.

Other fields or communities in sociology would reveal quite different patterns. Cultural sociology, for instance, has been on the upswing, with a heightened sense of controversy and progress. For almost two decades the sociology of organizations has been shaped by two or three large theoretical agendas, although other approaches have continued to flourish. What appears to be clear is that progress has been rapid in some subcommunities, incremental in others, and barely happening in still others. What we cannot do is draw conclusions about progress and cumulation in the discipline as a whole.

Problems, Progress, and Cumulation in Interpretative Communities

It is likely that this approach can be applied to many of the communities that make up the social sciences. In some of them we may even be able to speak of progress and cumulation in a discipline, if the discipline has an overarching paradigm that guides subdisciplines and communities that comprise it. Economics is the most likely current candidate. But can this approach work in disciplines and communities less organized around research problems, more oriented to a community discussion and interpretation of shared objects of attention? Does it work in communities where the language of truth claims seems alien to the community? Where there is little attempt to disprove or validate others claims? Where in fact only a very few people identify a common problem, even though they share broad intellectual orientations and commitments to modes of argument and evidence?

With some qualifications, I think the main contours of the argument hold. First, interpretative communities vary among themselves in their methodological commitments. Although most give primacy to texts, the use of texts varies considerably. In some the text is the basis for a conversation. In much of contemporary Anglo-American philosophy, for instance, footnotes are lightly used, argument is logical, and great attention is given to definitions and consequences of alternative definitions. In others, the text is heavily footnoted and the footnotes refer not to other scholars' interpretations but to historical/linguistic evidentiary claims. The dialogue with other contemporaneous scholars is minimized.

In many interpretative communities a clear succession of problem topics can be seen, or new topics coming on, and old topics leaving. Moreover, a similar transformation of communities can be seen, as the utility of older ways of studying subjects is found to be wanting. For instance, the philosophy of science has been radically reconfigured, opening up to the history and, possibly, the sociology of science in ways in which the older philosophy of science did not. (Some philosophers of science still operate in a pure analytic/epistemological mode attempting to preserve an uncontaminated realm.) Other areas of philosophy proceed in the same analytic mode that they have for decades. Similarly, it is obvious that over the last 70 years there have been significant shifts in literary theory, which many practitioners would evaluate in terms of progress or advance, even though outsiders might not validate those claims; I am sure that criteria of goodness and badness, or betterness, will be found in almost all communities. I am less clear about the question of cumulation in interpretative communities and leave it for further discussion. It may be that there is progress in problem definition, and cumulation of facts, but that changes in problem definition operate more to rule out interpretations than provide scaffolding for inclusion and cumulation. To the extent that interpretative glosses are not lost, possibly we can speak of interpretative cumulation. At the very least, the reigning interpretative glosses set the stage for the next generation as they use evidence and logic in a community dialogue.

Conclusions

The core of my argument is that the collapse of foundationalism and linear models of scholarly progress has created a gap in our self-understanding of what we as scholars are about. Older notions of progress and cumulation have to be revisited. Here progress, or advance, has been at least partially separated from cumulation, the processes of retention, transmittal, and recycling. Different fields of knowledge will vary in the stability of their problem sets, in the degree of consensus about what is an advance, in the recognition of and recycling of those advances by neighboring communities of scholars, even in the extent to which their fields are organized around problems or broader discursive topics.

I have chosen to think of progress and cumulation in terms of community practice, epistemic commitments, and organization. Since sociology is a fragmented discipline, progress and cumulation have to be seen in the contexts of the subdisciplines/communities that compose it. Here we have sketched progress and cumulation in four communities, ethnomethodology, historical sociology, social movements and collective action, and demography. In the first instance, advance and cumulation is internally viewed and used, even though the importance and valuation of those advances may largely depend upon the judgments and valuation of external audiences, and the relevance of findings and interpretations to others' life-worlds. After all, scholarship becomes largely an avocational affair, if deans, students, other scholars, funding agencies, and the broader public cannot connect to the scholarship in some way. Still, amateur scholarship can pursue truth, and amateur communities can be epistemic communities.

I do not rule out other, more holistic critiques of the very enterprise, which emphasize the political constitution of communities (Rouse, 1987). There are no transcendent truths in this approach — it is communities all the way down. In this paper, I have only alluded to the political economy of scholarly communities. The sociology of science has at least two large, though interconnected, agendas — one accounting for the intellectual constitution of communities, the other tying it to the flow of resources and rewards. In recent years, the former has received more attention. Moreover, the sociology of the human and social sciences is much less developed than the sociology of the natural and physical sciences. If we do develop the sociology of the human sciences, we have to pay attention to a key resource flow rarely mentioned in the sociology of science, the flow of students and the interplay with publishers, mass media, and audiences. Many of the human sciences are less internalized than the natural and physical sciences; their ideas arise from and are more easily assimilated to the larger cultural milieu. Understanding these processes represents a real opportunity. My sense is that an exciting field remains to be explored.

Acknowledgments

A large number of colleagues have helped me think through the issues of this paper. I owe a debt of gratitude to Renee Anspach, Gerry Bruns, Stephen Cole, Phil Converse, Lowell Hargens, Michael Kennedy, Arthur Kleinman, Silvia Pedraza, Kim Scheppele, Mark Schneider, Howard Schuman, and Margaret Somers. Several of these conversations took place while I was a Fellow at the Center for Advanced Studies in the Behavioral Sciences, Palo Alto, in the winter of 1994. Once again, the Center proved to be an extraordinary environment for reflection.

References

Abbott, Andrew. 1994. "History and sociology: The lost synthesis."
In E. Monkkonen (ed.), *Engaging the Past: The Uses of History Across the Social Sciences*: 77-112. Durham, N.C.: Duke University Press.

Berelson, Bernard and Gary A. Steiner. 1964. *Human Behavior: An Inventory of Scientific Findings*. New York: Harcourt, Brace.

Campbell, Donald. 1969. "Ethnocentrism of disciplines and the fish scale model of omni-science." In M. Sherif (ed.), *Interdisciplinary Relationships in the Social Sciences:* 328-348. Chicago: Aldine.

Cole, Stephen. 1992. *Making Science: Between Nature and Society*. Cambridge, MA.:Harvard University Press.

———.1994. "Why sociology doesn't make progress like the natural sciences." *Sociological Forum* 9:133-154.

D'Andrade, Roy. 1985. "Three scientific world views and the covering law model." In D.W. Fiske and R. A. Shweder (eds.), *Metatheory in Social Science: Pluralisms and Subjectivities*: 19-41. Chicago: University of Chicago Press.

Drew, Paul and John Heritage, eds. 1992. Talk at Work: *Interaction in Institutional Settings*. Cambridge, U.K.: Cambridge University Press.

Dupré, John. 1993 *The Disorder of Things: Metaphysical Foundations of the Disunity of Science*. Cambridge, Mass.: Harvard University Press.

Fleck, Ludwig. 1935 [1979]. *Genesis and Development of a Scientific Fact*. Chicago: University of Chicago Press.

Giddens, Anthony. 1978. "Positivism and its critics." In T. Bottomore and R. Nesbit (eds.), *A History of Sociological Analysis*: 237-286. New York: Basic Books.

Gilbert, G. Nigel and Michael Mulkay. 1984. *Opening Pandora's Box: A Sociological Analysis of Scientists' Discourse*. Cambridge, U.K.: Cambridge University Press.

Hacking, Ian. 1984. "Five parables." In R. Rorty, J. B. Schneewind, and Q. Skinner (eds.), *Philosophy in History: Essays on the Historiography of Philosophy*: 103-124. Cambridge, U.K.: Cambridge University Press.

Heritage, John. 1984. *Garfinkel and Ethnomethodology*. Cambridge, U.K.: Polity Press.

Horwich, Paul. 1993. *World Changes: Thomas Kuhn and the Nature of Science*. Cambridge, Mass.: MIT Press.

Kitcher, Philip. 1993. *The Advancement of Science*. New York: Oxford University Press.

Kuhn, Thomas. 1977. *The Essential Tension*. Chicago: University of Chicago Press.

Laudan, Larry. 1977. *Progress and its Problems*. Berkeley: University of California Press.

Lloyd, Christopher. 1993. *The Structures of History*. Oxford, U.K.: Blackwell.

Mayr, Ernst. 1982. *The Growth of Biological Thought: Diversity, Evolution and Inheritance*. Cambridge, MA.: Harvard University Press.

McCloskey, Donald N. 1985. *The Rhetorics of Economics*. Madison: University of Wisconsin Press.

Mintzberg, Henry. 1979. *The Structuring of Organizations: A Synthesis of Research*. Englewood Cliffs, N.J.: Prentice-Hall.

Morris, Aldon and Cedric Herring. 1987. "Theory and research on social movements: A critical review." In Samuel Long (ed.), *Political Behavior Annual*. Norwood, N.J.: Ablex.

Olson, Mancur. 1965. *The Logic of Collective Action*. Cambridge, MA.: Harvard University Press.

Pollner, Melvin. 1991. "Left of ethnomethodology: The rise and decline of radical reflexivity." *American Sociological Review* 56:70-80.

Piven, Frances Fox and Richard A. Cloward. 1991. "Collective protest: A critique of resource mobilization theory." *International Journal of Politics, Culture and Society* 4:435-458.

Preston, Samuel. 1993. "The contours of demography: Estimates and projections." *Demography* 30:593-606.

Rorty, Richard. 1980. Philosophy and the Mirror of Nature. Princeton, N.J.: Princeton University Press.

Rouse, Joseph. 1987. *Knowledge and Power: Towards a Political Philosophy of Science*. Ithaca, N.Y.: Cornell University Press.

———. 1990. "Narrative Reconstruction of Science." *Inquiry* 33:179-196.

———. 1991. "Philosophy of science and the persistent narratives of modernity." *Studies in History and Philosophy of Science* 22:141-162.

Rueschemeyer, Dietrich, E. H. Stephens, and J. D. Stephens. 1992. *Capitalist Development and Democracy*. Chicago: University of Chicago Press.

Rule, James B. 1988. *Theories of Civil Violence*. Berkeley: University of

California Press.
———. 1994. "Dilemmas of theoretical progress." *Sociological Forum* 9:241-258.

Shapere, Dudley. 1984. "Reason and the search for knowledge: Investigations in the philosophy of science." In Robert S. Cohen and Marx W. Wartofsky (eds.), Vol. 78 in *Boston Studies in the Philosophy of Science.* Boston: D. Reidel Publishing Co.

Smith, Dennis. 1991. *The Rise of Historical Sociology.* Cambridge, U.K.: Polity Press.

Somers, Margaret. 1996. "Where is social theory after the historic turn? Knowledge cultures and historical epistemologies in social analysis." In T. McDonald (ed.), *The Historic Turn in the Social Sciences.* Ann Arbor: University of Michigan Press.

Stinchcombe, Arthur. 1994. "Disintegrated disciplines and the future of sociology." *Sociological Forum* 9:279-292.

Taylor, Charles. 1971 [1979]. "Interpretation and the sciences of man." Review of Metaphysics 25:1. Reprinted in P Rabinow and W. M. Sullivan (eds.), *Interpretive Social Science: A Reader*: 27-72. Berkeley: University of California Press.

Turner, Jonathan and Stephen Turner. 1990. The Impossible Science: *An Institutional Analysis of American Sociology.* Newbury Park, CA.: Sage Publications.

Whitley, Richard. 1984. *The Intellectual and Social Organization of the Sciences.* Oxford, U.K.: Clarendon Press.

Zald, Mayer N. 1991. "Sociology as a discipline: Quasi-science and quasi-humanities." *American Sociologist* 22:165-187.

———. 1992. "Looking backward to look forward: Reflections on the past and future of the resource mobilization research program." In A. D. Morris and C. M. Mueller (eds.), *Frontiers in Social Movement Theory*: 326-350. New Haven, CT.: Yale University Press.

7

Dilemmas of Theoretical Progress

James B. Rule

Introduction

Anyone who delves deeply into the literatures of theoretical sociology must eventually come to feel that the reach of our discipline exceeds its grasp.

On one hand, the relevance of many sociological concerns to key human values is unmistakable. Our work, at its best, aims at questions central to any rationale for the conduct of social life. Why do we have social stratification? What accounts for variation in its forms and extent? How much of it is strictly necessary, or desirable? Where does deviance come from, and what are the best possibilities for coping with it? What makes organizations work, or fail to work, and how can we help them realize their best potentials? What causes civil upheaval – riot, rebellion, civil war, and the like – and how might the destruction caused by such things be minimized? These questions are not just analytically profound. They are basic to any attempt to make sense of social experience, and to act intelligently in response to such interpretations. Answers to such questions, from the profound to the inane, play a pivotal role in everyday social practice. Most of us would like to imagine that we are helping, in some small way, to improve the quality of such answers – both for the benefit of sociological discourse, and ultimately for that of some greater public.

But the trouble is, it is hard to identify widely accepted solutions to such questions, or *a fortiori* to demonstrate any uncontested line of progress in our understanding of them. The various literatures offer many provocative points of departure for reflection. But it would be hard to produce a list of authoritative answers to such theoretical puzzles--answers that one could claim to represent a consensus of sociological wisdom. I scarcely mean that sociologists, individually, lack convictions on such important issues. The situation is more the opposite: a cacophony of rich but often mutually antipathetic responses. Indeed, on politically charged theoretical issues like those cited above, the doctrines of social scientists often sound suspiciously like abstracted versions of the conflicting prejudices of nonspecialists.

What is worse, nonspecialists turning to current social science literatures for insight on questions of stratification, deviance, civil upheaval, or the like risk disappointment. For "state-of-the-art" discussion on these and other specialisms is often so arcane as to mystify outsiders. And disappointment will be all the more acute should the uninitiated reader stray into the domain of "pure theory" – arguments on behalf of discourse analysis, or network theory, or ethnomethodology, or other generic ways of knowing social reality. To be sure, other disciplines foster internal debates no less arcane. Few of us would profess surprise at finding communication among specialists in molecular biology or systems analysis or seismology to some degree opaque to the uninitiated.

But there is a difference. In many fields, arcane scientific speculation is ultimately constrained by results of interventions in the natural world. A space satellite is sent aloft, and attains (or fails to attain) its expected orbit; a vaccine is developed that successfully creates immunity in a previously vulnerable population; or (someday, we hope) seismologists learn to predict earthquakes with accuracy. Such outcomes may generate or reduce support for one theoretical position or another, no matter how obscure the debates en route may have been.

In the study of social life, instances of such vindication are, let us say, elusive. Indeed, I would hazard that participants in many key theoretical debates would find it difficult to agree what would constitute vindication — empirical or otherwise — for their theoretical systems. True, theoretical "breakthroughs," "new syntheses," "reorientations," and above all, "revolutions" are proclaimed with stunning frequency in our disciplines. But it is difficult to show how such changes are constrained, before or after the fact, by any systematic encounter between theory and evidence from empirical investigators – in the way that other theories have sometimes been subverted or supported by the success of a vaccine, or the detonation of the first atomic explosion, or the successful transfer of genetic material.

Nevertheless, change is a constant feature of our theoretical landscape. And if these changes are not constrained by new empirical inputs of one kind or another, we must ask, What in fact does explain them? Consider the succession of theoretical visions that have preoccupied sociology in the English-speaking world in the second half of the 20th century: structural-functionalism, symbolic interaction, rational choice thinking, discourse analysis, and countless varieties of Marxism, to note just a few of the more prominent. And within the subdisciplines focusing on organizations, religion, deviance, stratification, the family, or the like, one could identify many other theoretical twists, most of them short-lived.

Contemplating the array of such innovations, one cannot shake the impression that they reflect nothing other than a constantly varying intellectual taste. Insofar as this is true, one might conclude that durable answers to basic theoretical questions are a utopian prospect. Theoretical movement in the study of social life might then better be characterized in terms reserved for pure fashion: always changing, but never improving.

Such a conclusion would be less disturbing were it not for the relentlessly progressive self-image of our discipline. To affirm the *raison d'etre* of books, articles, dissertations, or other sociological work, we insist that they constitute "contributions" to knowledge – as though each new creation somehow moved the intellectual enterprise forward, however imperceptibly, in some identifiable direction. Perhaps the most sought-after accolade to any work is that it occupies "the cutting edge," that it "breaks new ground," that it represents the "state-of-the-art." And the ultimate dismissal is that it "leads nowhere," that it represents a "dead end."

But the longer the historical view one adopts, the more ironic such extravagant claims seem. The half-life of theoretical projects in social science, it would appear, is considerably shorter than most academic careers. What is heralded today as the "state-of-the-art" or "the leading edge" is apt to appear tomorrow as unremarkable, banal, or even embarrassing.

Nor have the salient virtues of yesterday's theoretical obsessions been assimilated into any sort of unified body of knowledge. Most often, these once-incandescent inspirations simply lose their claim on the sociological imagination, disappearing from our intellectual landscape with scarcely a trace. The lucubrations of the ethnomethodologists of the 1960s, the sententious conceptual embroideries of Parsons and his followers of the 1950s, or the maunderings of the Althusserian structuralists in the 1970s, now appear utterly dated. Some present-day thinkers may claim to find virtue in these writiings. But the numbers of those actively pursuing these intellectual agenda today are few. For most of us, such projects now seem as remote from current analytical concerns as the art of creating Mayan pyramids or Gregorian chants.

And in light of such transience, is anyone safe in imagining that the theoretical preoccupations of today — including one's own — will prove more enduring than earlier ones? Is it reasonable to expect that the next 50 years of intellectual history will describe clearer lines of intellectual progress than the last? Or will future theoretical history in our discipline simply resemble what we are familiar with to date: a succession of short-lived visions, each satisfying a specific and ephemeral theoretical taste? If so, I hold, the implications for what sociology has to offer to those on the outside are severe and limiting.

Questions like these have to be perplexing to any candid observer of our discipline. But they also offer us an opportunity for reflection and self-criticism that could ultimately prove useful. If, as I believe, the gap between our professed expectations for theoretical work and the realities of the historical record is marked, we might logically do one of two things: change our expectations, or change our way of going at our work. The following pages provide some elements of my own response to this choice.

Criteria for Theoretical Success

The perplexities of which I write here have to do with theoretical knowledge, as distinct from the techniques of social inquiry. The distinction is crucial for these purposes. In the strictly technical aspects of our work — indeed, as in the technical side of art, music, and literature — progress is unmistakable. By almost any standard, today's means for assembling, organizing, and analyzing sociologically relevant information are far more effective than those of earlier periods — indeed, even than those of a few decades ago.

By technical improvements, I mean something more than just increased sophistication in electronic data processing and statistical analysis, as important as these things are. I also have in mind such things as compilations of comparative ethnographic data, techniques for transcribing and analyzing conversations, methods of content analysis, and a host of other ways of bringing analytical attention to bear on relevant data.

These successes count to the enduring credit of our disciplines. They provide bases, for example, for varieties of practically useful activities – from public opinion polling to demographic planning. But technique is not theory. Today we have statistical and survey techniques far superior to Durkheim's for analyzing such things as suicide, crime, and divorce. But a definitive judgment of Durkheim's broad doctrines, say, on the relationship between moral authority and deviance, and on their relative import in any overall view of that subject, is more elusive. I do not mean by this that Durkheim's position is forgotten, or should be; on the contrary, it has shown far more staying power than most theoretical doctrines in our discipline. I simply mean that dissensus reigns among informed analysts as to how right Durkheim was on key theoretical points – for example, on the relative weight of moral authority vs. other social forces in ensuring adherence to social strictures.

When I speak of theoretical work, I mean analytical ideas of applicability extending beyond any single case — not just the cause of a single strike, but the causes of a wave of strikes, or a category of similar strikes; not just an account of the social forces underlying Hitler's rise to power, but an analysis of shifts from pluralist to extremist politics in a variety of settings. And to this list one must add all the questions of conceptual organization and intellectual strategy implicated in the pursuit of such questions.

Strictly one-of-a-kind, idiographic investigations may hold much interest. The effort to understand the chain of events that brought Hitler to power, after all, has a claim on our imagination quite independent of any parallels to similar processes elsewhere. Moreover, many utterly non-theoretical investigations lead to insight of enormous practical value — for example, by charting the spread of an infectious disease or showing how to reach voters susceptible to particular electoral appeal.

But few students of social life, I suspect, can altogether resist what I call the theoretical yearning – that is, the temptation to draw from analyses of specific situations implications for the understanding of others. What does an analysis of the transmission of AIDS in a particular population, for example, suggest about the spread of the same disease elsewhere, or about that of other diseases altogether? Like many another tempting yearning, the appetite for theoretical inquiry is hard to suppress, once aroused.

Moreover, it seems clear that such theoretical appetites are what have drawn most of us to the study of social life in the first place — and what accounts for the interest in our work among those outside the discipline. One does not have to be a social scientist to wonder about the causes of wealth and poverty, or the origins of civil strife, or the future of the family in the world's affluent societies, or the possibilities and limits of change in gender roles. So far-reaching are any judgments on such questions, so central are such judgments to any rationale for the conduct of human affairs, that one can hardly imagine any social order that does not produce efforts to answer them. If social science is to have any enduring claim on the interest of those on the outside – to whom we look, after *all*, to fund the institutions and activities that create a context for our work — we need to produce convincing and durable answers to such questions.

Clearly any judgment of the potential for our work to produce such answers is utterly implicated with questions of the progressive character of metric to specify what should count as one unit of explanatory success. And some would argue that no such objective criteria exist, apart from the interests and predilections of the analyst.

Certainties Imperiled

The widespread willingness to entertain such relativistic views of the accomplishments and potentials of social inquiry is of recent origin. Until perhaps a generation ago, the potential of sociological understanding for progressive development was taken as axiomatic. The study of social life, it was assumed, like all the rest of science, was bound to "build up" over time. As the state of the art "improved" and rigorous empirical investigation "broke new ground," more and more long-standing theoretical questions about the workings of the social world would be answered. By this token, the history of the discipline should resemble an expanding map of once-unfamiliar territories, more and more fully charted with the passage of time. To be sure, there was soul searching and recrimination about what form of inquiry was most promising to this end. But the consensus position was probably close to the view given by Shils in 1948:

> Sociology has indeed not yet ascended to the heights of science .... There is little cumulative growth, relatively little deliberate concentration of effort on major problems; and those who demand a finished science or definitive answers are justified in their dissatisfaction .... [nevertheless] There are elements in sociology which show distinct promise of development toward the domain of reliable scientific knowledge on problems of fundamental scientific and moral or political importance. (1948: 3-4)

Note the unreflective reference to "major problems" and "problems of fundamental scientific and moral or political importance." Like his readers at the time, Shils seems to have felt that these things had some objective status, that they were not simply matters of transient theoretical taste or appetite. Hence, when success finally occurred, its status as such should presumably be clear to all concerned.

But if the history of theoretical sociology since Shils' statement demonstrates anything, it is that notions of "success" in these connections are anything but transparent. Indeed, a self-conscious effort of many of the innovative approaches to theoretical sociology over the last generation has been to redefine analytical "success" — that is about what constitutes the most authentic, most meaningful way of knowing social reality. Considered as a whole, these developments surely offer grounds for viewing theoretical change in our disciplines as a series of fluctuating intellectual tastes.

Adherents of views like Shils' have not found it easy to assimilate these new perspectives, especially given the latter's untroubled devaluation of orthodox visions of progressive social science. Consider the words of the late sociologist of science Joseph Ben-David, who spent his career articulating the progressive, universalistic view of science inspired by Robert K. Merton. At the end of that career, Ben-David became rudely aware of theoretical insurgencies in social science emanating from the political and intellectual effervescence of the 1960s. It became increasingly difficult for him to reconcile these activities with his view of social science as part of a progressive process of scientific enlightenment.

Particularly allergic were Ben-David's reactions to theorists viewing the intellectual content of mainstream science as manifestations of prevailing political or economic interests. Of these "subordinationists," he wrote,

> they can accept science as some kind of specialized knowledge but not as a philosophical method to establish what is false and what is (under specified conditions) true. From all this stem the attempts to show that there is no connection between scientific research and scientific ethos and the insistence that there is no such thing as science in general but only a multitude of discrete historically determined scientific traditions. (1991: 498)

He finally reads such thinkers out of the church of science altogether; writing (perhaps wishfully) in the past tense, he charges,

> These anti-scientistic critics of science were not concerned with improving science ....These critics drew on arguments elaborated by the rational critics of science but they used these arguments for a different purpose. For instance, the difficulty in establishing epistemological criteria for a clear-cut demarcation of scientific from nonscientific knowledge was used to support the argument that science was not at all different from religion, magic, or ideology....Underlying this new science criticism was the assumption that science as such could be replaced with a new, radically different type of science. (1991:554)

That is, of course, just what proponents of many insurgent theoretical programs aim at.

The first of these quotations is from an article originally published in 1980; the second is from a posthumously published essay apparently written in 1984 or 1985. One wonders what Ben-David would make of the view articulated by Donna Haraway in an article published in 1988. Proposing an alternate to establishment science, she writes:

> Feminism loves another science: the sciences and politics of interpretation,
> translation, stuttering, and the partly understood. Feminism is about the sci-
> ence of the multiple subject with (at least) double vision. Feminism is about a
> critical vision consequent upon a critical position in homogeneous gendered
> social space. Translation is always interpretive, critical, and partial...Above
> all, rational knowledge does not pretend to disengagement: to be from every-
> where and so nowhere, to be free from interpretation, from being represented,
> to be fully formalizable. Rational knowledge is a process of ongoing critical
> interpretation among "fields" of interpreters and decoders. Rational knowl-
> edge is power-sensitive conversation. (1988:589-590)

Does the quest for scientific knowledge pursued by Ben-David have
any ends in common with that described by Haraway? Or does each
worldview involve its own *sui generis* criteria for success such that insight
formulated in one set of terms cannot be expected to matter to those outside
the relevant theoretical community? From all indications, one imagines that
these authors would embrace the second alternative as an account of their
differences.

Yet the implications of strictly relativist views are troubling — both for
one's understanding of one's own work and for one's expectations of the
public role of the discipline as a whole. If the virtues of any particular way
of understanding the social world, of any specific analytical program, are
simply matters of taste, we have no compelling grounds to adjudicate clashes
of understanding. Few theorists, I suspect, are ultimately satisfied to leave
matters at this, because such thoroughgoing relativism undermines the credibility of any theoretical position. Indeed, the essay of Haraway's quoted
above seems to represent an effort to develop some overarching standard
for theoretical veridicality — at least for the subcommunity that she ad-
dresses. The alternative is a world where every single way of seeing things
is equally worthy, but only "in its own terms."

Expression and Coping

Thus, a question that is essentially simple, yet subtle and far-reaching in
its implications: Can one identify any set of common ends or standards for
theoretical work in our discipline? Can we point to any problems or goals,
however abstract, that might be defended as the ultimate standard of
success or progress, even across the intellectual chasms separating
theoretical worldviews? To ask such questions is obviously to ask whether
what one might call the various intellectual interests driving social inquiry
have significant commonalities. Any judgments on these subjects must obviously be framed in very abstract terms, yet we cannot escape the need to

make them.

Such judgments require consideration of the relationship of two quite different principles for the guidance of theoretical work. One could call these expressive and coping models of theory — theory as expression of social experience vs. theory as an account of external constraints imposed by social forces and processes. These two views, I hold, offer deeply different implications for the organization of theoretical work.

No one should be surprised that a single slice of reality may successfully be portrayed in two or more different ways. We simply expect something different in an artist's rendering, say, of a building from what we expect in an engineer's drawing of "the same" building. The former succeeds by capturing the inner experience of the viewer — or at least, by capturing one version of such experience, among a variety of possibilities. The criteria of success or failure of the artist's work is aesthetic, like those applicable to poetry, fiction, music, or drama.

By contrast, the engineer's drawing may aim to capture the experience of no one; indeed, such a drawing may not even resemble a building to any but the well-tutored eye. It succeeds by providing a guide to characteristics of the building likely to matter for one human purpose or another, but that have nothing to do with aesthetics — the strength of the beams supporting the structures, for example, or the materials used inside the walls, or the points of connection to electrical, water, and sewer lines. The virtues of this second kind of representation lie in the ability to identify constraints on human action that may form part of no one person's experience of the building when the drawing is made. Insofar as our quest to understand the social world obliges us to reckon with external realities that exercise constraint over us, regardless of how we perceive them, we cannot get along without such coping representations.

Insofar as social analysis is governed by expressive criteria, it would appear unreasonable to expect progress of other than a technical sort. For in this view, the intellectual standards for evaluating theoretical accounts of the social world are bound to change — as is true of all standards governing works of the imagination. No one would imagine that American abstract expressionism represents an effort to improve upon, say, German social expressionism — any more than Shakespeare's tragedies should be judged as attempts to improve on those of classic Greece. Such different aesthetic forms simply seek to realize fundamentally different expressive ends. The aesthetic visions underlying Dixieland-jazz or Elizabethan sonnets may be better or worse realized in specific works. But success and failure can only be reckoned, in such cases, by rules internal to the guiding vision itself.

Aesthetic worldviews also do more than just satisfy preexisting intellectual or perceptual yearnings. They ultimately create the perceptual appetites that only they can satisfy. Early impressionist painting (or free verse or Bauhaus architecture) may strike the uninitiated public as jarring, if not repellent. But when such insurgent principles win out, they shape our expectations to such an extent as to seem "natural." The greatest victory that a school of painting or fiction can have is to create a public who want, and ultimately "need" perceptions that only that school can satisfy.

Much theoretical change in social science clearly fits the aesthetic model. What sociologists want out of theoretical work changes from period to period, and from constituency to constituency — as in the shifting expectations of theoretical accounts of militant phenomena discussed above. And as the analytical needs of "consumers" change, one might note, theoretical forms are bound to change in turn. Moreover, successful theoretical visions in our disciplines clearly do succeed in instilling intellectual "needs" that set a new standard for successful analysis. When this occurs, no analysis can be deemed theoretically satisfactory unless it takes account of the "deep structures" or "underlying principles" identified by the theory in question— whether these be the insights of dialectical materialism, or indexical nature of everyday concepts, or the implications of analysis for women's interests. The experience of embracing new theoretical visions of this kind is apt to resemble religious conversion more than intellectual persuasion.

In the extreme case, fidelity to the demands of a theoretical aesthetic may be all that is considered necessary for successful analysis of a particular subject. In such a case, there can be no analysis that is true to the logic of the theory but wrong — wrong, that is, in terms of failure to fit some objective, transcendent criterion of accuracy. Instead, the theoretical "aesthetic" is an end in itself—much as in art or literature. Thus analytical success would be defined solely in terms set by the theoretical worldview itself.

By contrast, consider the notion of theory as a coping, rather than aesthetic activity. Here success is governed by criteria that are comprehensible, and significant, from outside the theoretical worldview, as well as from within. For a pure case, one might think of the search for a needle in a haystack-or to make the example more exact, an effort to develop a theory for locating needles in haystacks in general. Differences there may be as to which, among contending approaches to such a problem appears most elegant or intellectually exciting. In the absence of solutions of an objective sort, aesthetic considerations may have everything to do with which approach attracts more followers. But ultimate success — a formula that enables any competent analyst to locate any needle in any haystack — is unmistakable to all concerned, and supports the credibility of the theoretical approach that produces. Such successes, if all concerned indeed agree in identifying them as such, could surely imply a case for progressive development of knowledge. For if reliable formula did in fact exist for locating needles in haystacks, any reasonable person would want to employ it in any such search.

At issue here is the distinction between theories of social life as means (or dealing with objective social constraints) vs. theories as expressive ends in themselves. Such assessments confront us with the question of what, ultimately, we expect of theories. Is it the ability to highlight, emphasize, or dramatize those aspects of social reality that matter most to a particular public at a particular moment? Or the ability to represent the subject matter according to some more broadly based criterion of analytical usefulness? Should we expect theory to capture a particular perception of a particular slice of social reality, or to provide an intellectual map for any and all who might wish to deal with that reality?

A little of each, many readers will respond. The response is empirically accurate, as far as it goes. But it does not take us very far. For the demands of expressive vs. coping strategies in theory making are often antipathetic, and the organization of our intellectual work often requires choice between them. We cannot avoid committing ourselves, consciously or by default, as to what sorts of theoretical payoffs we aim for. Such choices have everything to do with the kind of work we produce.

Foreign Relations

Perhaps this moment in the history of social science offers a special incentive to consider this choice. Sociology, especially, seems at a low ebb in public esteem in the last decade of the 20th century. One reason appears to be precisely the lack of persuasive conclusions on theoretical issues emanating from sociological work — conclusions that are both persuasive and important to those outside the inward-looking communities of social theorists themselves. For many, it would appear, sociology and its sister disciplines have failed to yield long-awaited "answers" — however vaguely such answers are conceived.

These disappointments have to be understood in contrast to the widely heralded public promise of social science in the late 1960s and early 1970s. The prestige of our disciplines was then at its crest. University enrollments in social science were high, money for research was plentiful and —perhaps most important — the interpretations of public issues offered by social scientists were taken seriously by the broader public of citizens and policymakers. Much of this acceptance involved the perception that public life was afflicted with "social problems," and that social scientists were uniquely qualified to propose authoritative solutions to such problems. As one can imagine, few social scientists went out of their way publicly to contest such views.

Thus the report of a blue-ribbon committee of eminent social scientists, issued in 1969, could state:

> Our society cannot delay dealing with its major social problems ....The social sciences . . . . are our best hope, in the long run, for understanding our problems in depth and for providing new means of lessening tensions and improving our common life. (National Academy of Science, 1969: 17)

The moment when such pronouncements could be widely accepted— and perhaps even the moment when sociologists are prepared to make them—has obviously passed. Today, the public attitude toward both the academic teaching of sociology and the pronouncements of sociologists on public issues is far more skeptical. And one theme of the skepticism is unmistakable: the "answers" to questions of public interest generated by our disciplines, it is held, are indistinguishable from the partisan prejudices and special theoretical tastes of their proponents.

Note that the charges of the critics have certain by-no-means trivial commonalities with the views of theory put forward by many social scientists themselves—provided only that one subtracts the disparaging tone. The idea has grown widespread, I have argued, that the role of theoretical work is ultimately to formulate and convey representations of social life that gain their validity from congruence with the frame of mind of the analyst. By these lights, one would hardly expect our insights to be persuasive to those who do not begin by sharing the same theoretical mind-set.

Thus it seems to me that many social scientists — perhaps like Haraway in the quotation above — would be happy to renounce any claims to produce "answers" to questions about social life that have validity outside their own theoretical communities. In other words, the expectation that theoretical work in our discipline should yield conclusions to puzzles or problems that just anyone might entertain is misguided and foredoomed. Instead, people may insist, different theoretical projects define their own ends — and their own standards for "progress" in those directions.

There is nothing logically inconsistent about such positions. That is, one can imagine perfectly self-sufficient programs of social inquiry predicated on the most diverse aesthetics for representing social reality. The history of our discipline demonstrates the extraordinary range of such programs that may win a following among the community of professional sociologists — at least for a time. For some observers, success of this kind is the most that one can hope for in our discipline. Much as in art or literature, it might be said, one does not expect any one theoretical aesthetic to endure. Each theoretical vision lasts just as long as it continues to offer expressive satisfactions to those who embrace it, and no longer. Progress, in the sense of incremental movement toward some stable goal, however abstractly defined, is thus as irrelevant to our work as to the tasks of the poet, composer, or dramatist.

But whatever else one might say on its behalf, I do not think that such a rationale can suffice to ensure public support for our work. After all, sociology does not pay for itself. Unlike art, music, drama, poetry, and architecture, theoretical sociology has rarely given much inherent satisfaction to non-sociologists. There are exceptions, but for the most part, the intellectual "tastes" inculcated by exposure to our theoretical tradition do not extend much beyond membership in the discipline. For professional sociologists, there may be constituencies that find ethnomethodology, or Althusserian structuralism, or rational choice theory inherently satisfying lenses for making sense of everyday life. But for the most part, these and other theoretical specialisms are just not engaging enough to attract constituencies outside the discipline itself.

Conclusion

I, of course, understand that many readers will find the vision of sociological inquiry as oriented to what I have called coping interests unattractive. But I hope that no one will mistake the importance of what is at stake. Whether one prefers to pursue theoretical work as an expressive end in itself, or as a means to some highly abstract, shared, practical end, matters profoundly for how we go about our work. The demands and constraints imposed on sociological work by either of these two models differs profoundly from those implied by the other.

But assume, if only for a moment, that one does embrace some version of the coping model as a guiding orientation for sociological work. Are there grounds for believing that such a strategy could produce results consistent with its aspirations? Can one point to any insights generated in the long history of social inquiry that appear to meet this criterion? Could one go so far as to argue that such successes constitute progress in the overall work would offer the best hope of maximizing such results?

Systematic answers to such questions are far beyond my scope in a statement like this. Let me nevertheless at least indicate the broad directions that my response would take.

One thing that should be clear is that any broad strategy for social inquiry emanating from the position I have taken has to be more subtle and pluralistic than a call for frontal attack on "social problems." One grave difficulty with such an idea is that our notions of what constitutes a social problem, and what might represent a solution, are themselves endlessly contested and transient. Perhaps even more important is the fact that theoretical work that initially appears irrelevant, or even obscure, may ultimately prove useful to a broad and enduring range of human interests. Thus it makes no sense to forswear any and all theoretical inquiry that does not yield immediate gains in addressing what are construed, at any particular moment, as pressing issues for social practice.

Yet it is equally unacceptable to take what one might consider the polar opposite to this position — the notion that all theoretical programs have an equal claim on our attentions, if only we find them agreeable to pursue. We would not accord the same attention, or the same resources, to a quest to develop a comprehensive theory of bottlecap-dispersion on American streets, for example, that we would to efforts to document and explain the allocation of jobs between men and women. Much as we can never absolutely exclude the possibility that the distribution of bottlecaps might hold the key to matters of compelling human interest, we have reason for skepticism on this point. By contrast, any thorough and persuasive analysis of how gender affects job allocation will be fraught with interest for concerned observers of public affairs — sociologists and non-sociologists alike.

Much theoretical work in our discipline, I am afraid, has little more hope of resulting in insights with enduring claims on our attention than do programs for analyzing bottlecap dispersion. Consider some dreary but familiar examples: The efforts to enumerate every last intellectual "presupposition" underlying every theoretical statement (regardless of any justifiable analytical need to do so), or the self-obsessed conceptual refinements of Althusserian structuralism (in the absence of any apparent need to employ such categories), or the efforts of rational choice theorists to generate explanations based on long-term calculation to actions much more readily understood as consummatory than instrumental. Such efforts may clearly yield aesthetic rewards for those who embrace the theories in question. But we have little reason to believe that they will generate insights of enduring interest, once the vogue of these theoretical tastes has passed.

But here and there, very occasionally, our theoretical work yields results of a different kind. Consider a few examples: Durkheim's insights on affiliation and suicide, Spencer's formulation on the linkage between the scale of social structures and the specialization of their organization, the insights of social psychologists on the role of reference groups in shaping ideas of what constitutes acceptable circumstances, Granovetter's analyses of the role of acquaintance networks as channels of critical information in labor markets. The theoretical traditions that yield these insights are utterly heterogeneous. But they share a quality of enormous significance: they matter to anyone who needs to deal with the domains of human behavior in question, regardless of whether that person has any aesthetic investment in the theory involved. They are things that we need to know about the social processes in question, rather than images of social life that we find agreeable to contemplate. And to this extent, the insights involved show promise of continuing to matter to analysts yet to come. Surely it is not too much to count such insights as one significant form of intellectual progress.

References

Ben-David, Joseph. 1991. *Scientific Growth: Essays in the Social Organization and Ethos of Science*. Berkeley. University of California Press.

Gamson, William and James McEvoy. 1972. "Police violence and its public support." In James Short and Marvin Wolfgang (eds.), *Collective Violence*. Chicago: Aldine Atherton.

Haraway, Donna. 1988. "Situated knowledges: The science question in feminism and the privilege of partial perspective." *Feminist Studies* 14(3).

Morris, Aldon and Cedric Herring. 1987. "Theory and research in social movements: A critical review." In Samuel Long (ed.), *Annual Review of Political Science II*.

National Academy of Sciences. 1969. *The Behavioral Sciences: Outlook and Needs*. Englewood Cliffs, NJ: Prentice Hall.

Rule, James. 1988. *Theories of Civil Violence*. Berkeley: University of California Press.

——. 1989. "Rationality and non-rationality in militant mobilization." *Sociological Theory* 7(2).

Shils, Edward. 1948. *The Present State of American Sociology*. Glencoe, IL: The Free Press.

8

Going Out

Harvey Molotch

We are misfits. The most developed sociology in the world exists in a country inhospitable to it. The related US traits of individualism, jingoistic arrogance, and lack of a labor party tradition, combine to make sociology a suspect endeavor. There is little incentive to understand our underlying assumptions nor attend to the progress of our work. The ideas of social structure, of social facts, of situated behavior are hard sells in a land where the way to get elected, to become head of the PTA, or make a living in consulting is by pushing wars on drugs and locking people up. Our national traditions support forms of making sense that run counter to ours. Absent a strong hunch that social conditions affect individual behavior, you get a blameful and dangerous society and certainly one with little use for sociology.

The symptoms appear with a glance at the media, high or low, or down the corridors of power. Magazines like *The New Yorker* and the *New York Review* seldom review the work of sociologists, nor use us as commentators or reviewers. Few bookstores, even in academic environments, stock much real sociology on their shelves. While in France, a blink in a theorist's nervous system snaps neurons down the Paris boulevards, we can throw public fits and nobody much cares. Our ASA passes resolutions on the most important problems of our time (some endlessly debated in-house), and the press ignores them. Confused with social work, socialism, or perhaps the putatively failed programs of the '60's, our work is unknown or utterly trivialized.

There have been no sociologists in the cabinets of any president (political scientist Moynihan was the closest call) and our current leader, policy

wonk though he be, would be politically fool-hardy to treat the credential of
a Ph.D. in sociology as anything but a confirmation bearing liability. Some
sociologists have taken to obscuring their disciplinary connection by calling themselves "social scientist" or using some other self-deforming sub-
terfuge to pass. In the Scandinavian countries, to take a strong contrasting
case, the policy world turns heavily on sociological concepts and the craft
of empirical research connects to receptive government agencies and supportive publics. In the Czech Republic, President Havel makes speeches
and writes essays rich in sociological substance, without apology. The other
social sciences fare somewhat better image-wise in the US: economics putatively makes people rich, psychology helps with angst or at least a nicer
day, and anthropology amuses with exotic tales. Our attentive public, at
any level, is thin. All of this has major consequences, many of them negative, for the way we conduct ourselves. One of the things wrong with sociology, in our country, is that we need a better country — a point to which to
return.

The interdependence of sociology and its society is an old story. In some
sense all societies have a sociology in that there are shared ideas of social
boundaries and some notions of how the group can influence the individual
and roles shape attitudes and behavior. Aristotle said "Poverty is the parent
of revolution and crime" (Politics, Book II); Mme Cornuel (1605-1694)
observed "no man is a hero to his valet" and Shakespeare, of course, wrote
that "all the world's a stage..." and so much more that is grist for the sociological mill. There are homilies from around the globe, all elements of folk
sociologies, micro and macro, and some as sharp as tacks. The popular
circulation of these proto-sociologies affected, more or less, the societies
they purported to describe, just as those same social conditions shaped the
"work" of the analysts. Sociology and society are deeply "in" one another,
mutual in their determination. Society and its sociology, of whatever form,
are not two "things," but an evolving process of knowledge, action, and
substance.

In the modern context, the sociology-society process has speeded up, as
description and analysis more rapidly feed back into the social order from
which they come. That professional sociology is a part of this two-way
enterprise is one of the reasons why it (or any of the social sciences as
Stephen Toulmin has pointed out) can never be normal science. If we report divorce rates are up, divorce rates may go down as folks and government become concerned about "the family." Or the same information may
cause divorce rates to rise still higher because, after all, "everyone is doing
it." Survey results alter the behavior of those polled, not just the sample but

the universe. The Heisenberg principle is radically in play; our very talk
alters the object under our microscope. Our work is never done, not just
because there are always new realms to conquer and "history" marches on;
our work is never done because it self-destructs, if it is any good. Only if
we do our sociology competently — if we learn new things and communicate them quickly and effectively — will they have a chance of entering
other discourses and lead to the changes that undermine their adequacy. We
need to be able to say things well enough to make them untrue.

Rather than capturing a fixed reality, the goal of a substantive sociology
necessarily becomes participation — as fully and as responsibly as possible through description-alteration. We are professional structurators, paid
to observe, study, report and, even if only inadvertently, change the context
that changes us. This is just what most everyone else does too, but we do it
as occupation rather than as byproduct of other activities. What a deal,
what a privilege!

Sociology's initial rise after World War II as another positivist endeavor
was part of the heady American optimism that a "science of man" could
solve our social problems just as a science of matter could solve our defense
and health problems. That was our doing and our undoing. Sociology, of
course, could never deliver the goods, something most everyone now knows.
Rather than lament that we fail by the lights of science or, much worse,
play at being one, we should competently embrace the creative task at hand:
buzz around like gadflies, gathering up bits of news from here and there,
developing systematic techniques for looking at one thing intensively or
many things extensively. Putting aside scientific magic, we need to be the
shamen who act as clearing house for what everyone is up to and how it's
turning out. Many feel parts of the elephant, together we feel more of it.
We are society's kibbitzers, moving from table to table, watching the hands
in play. By not ourselves having a hand to play, we have the time and
inclination to reflect on how the game itself is conducted. This is not "mere
journalism," but deep journalism.

Some others will be just as good as we at the task and indeed more than
a few of the most important contributors to "our" field are free-lance, people
like Betty Friedan, Jane Jacobs, and Harry Braverman — individuals we
need to celebrate in our circle and in the disposition of our awards. We will
never have a monopoly, but we can aspire to be reliable and useful. Timing
is of the essence or our message will come when everyone knows it or, what
may be the same thing, when it is too late to do any good. We needed (and
eventually got) a good notion of cultural lag before nuclear Armageddon,
not after; we needed (and eventually got) data on the social networks of

AIDS transmission to save millions from the fatal theory that the disease spread through gay "lifestyle" rather than a virus (Silence = Death, and so does No Data).

World events have given new life to the sociological project, even if sociologists play only small roles in them. While clever entrepreneurs are celebrated, markets are understood to thrive through state intervention and productivity to turn on specific kinds of "corporate culture." Increasing recognition within the economics discipline, including the Nobel prize, goes for work that demonstrates the sociological elements of markets — like transaction costs, neighborhood effects, and organizational behavior. Rather than "sociological factors," the economists call them "market failures." But a sociological framing is their key, no matter what they call it. The country's social problems do not go away with policies of revenge. By listening to the sociologists the nation could learn why its anti-drug repression won't work, why more cops won't stop crime, or why tax breaks for industries won't improve communities or build the commonwealth. The irony, once again, is that our professional fate, and the use of our learning, is strongly influenced not just by what we know or how much the problems of the day require our skills, but by ideological currents that discourage an explicitly sociological approach. We really have to change America to change us.

No small task, as I am not the first to indicate. But we can, in this forum, constructively address how elements of our current sociological practice are a response to these conditions and how they function vis a vis such a grandiose goal. In other words, we can start by understanding how as misfits we are led into practices that don't help our cause of building discipline and country. We are caught within a classic sociological tension that is a recipe for deviant outcomes: a disparity between aspirations and opportunities. It is stressful and, to borrow from a somewhat discredited tool box, dysfunctional. More than most professionals, we got into this business not just to make a living, but to make a mark — a contribution to the greater good. Frustrated with our lot, some retreat, some innovate, many get mad or rebel in various ways.

Suffering does not make people pretty; operating from an oppositional stance may not encourage the most effective practices. I take up some of the traits within sociology that I think come from living in a wrong country. It's not our fault but only we can lift our own bootstraps. Avoiding the pitfalls that follow may make the process less gawky.

Totalistic Claims

Although our journals are full of pro forma caveats and humble pie modifiers, when it comes to the role of sociology, we are megalomanic. Even Comte's designation of sociology as "queen" of the sciences pales next to our assertiveness. We hurl the word "psychological" as damning epithet for a colleague's work. Any mention of "personality" is a "reduction" or in the more loaded lingo of today, "essentialist." These are easy scores. At the other social science border, economists provide an alternative negative marker of crimes against humanity; an argument that turns on folks' engaging in ordinary market behavior (like buying at the lowest price) is obviously backward because it does not consider the social relations of production or the embedded quality of economy in society. Biological difference is clearly beyond the pale.

Our goal often becomes not to solve the problem, but rather to prove that only sociology can solve the problem. Even when we allow that sociology "is one of the important factors," we do not show how the other factors might count in light of the sociological contribution. Instead, we commit sociology and run. As I heard Eric Wright say at the 1993 Miami meetings, the real scientists don't act that way, or at least not so brazenly. I've watched marine biologists, for example, greet their counterparts in geology and chemistry with welcome arms. While competitive with other research teams, they understand they need other disciplines to solve their problem. Not us. As a result, we learn less from other disciplines and those in other disciplines learn less from us. This is one source of our general difficulty: since no one but the sociologists are interested in our Advance-the-Discipline agenda, outsiders lose interest or find us ridiculous.

It would be better if we could relax a bit into a multidisciplinary imagination and grant psychology, the market, and even biology their due, or something closer to their due. This does not mean, for one moment, giving up the importance of sociology or accepting the imperialistic forays into our field by the sociobiologists or Beckerite vandals from economics. We need to keep our sociological imagination and our pride. But we can enhance the standing, the utility, and even the thrill of sociology by understanding how the social intersects with other aspects of human systems. It would make the world come alive to confront it in its full complexity rather than worrying, as we look at a problem, whether our answer will be good for sociology.

Like ethnic studies, women's studies, and gay studies, sociology has perhaps needed the breathing space to construct its own agenda and solidarities, insulated from the depredations of the more established fields. Even now the other disciplines may devour us if we allow their nose under our tent. The Chicago economists proclaim their "imperialism" with the kind of crude gusto that their tall standing in the hierarchy makes dangerous. Risking for psychology may invite the crowds to charge past us for the individualistic explanations they seem to love. Calm and gracious sharing of the stage does not come easy to those struggling for bit parts. But moving forward as though we were self-confident may be the best form of aggression and it certainly would be a learning experience.

Literature Disease

Among the secondary adjustments we have made to our plight is retreat into our own paraphernalia, including the consecration of our literatures into the stuff of science. The best retreat is always an invisible one and our literature cocoons keep many of us safely out of view. The Literature becomes topic, *sui generis*, and "progress" in refining, testing, elaborating what the last journal article refined, tested, or elaborated becomes a sign of salvation, or at least tenure. In too much of our writing, authors' names perform the role of narrative tension: Jones was wrong but Schwartz is right, rather than education counts more than father's income. The plot line revolves around which scholar holds the trump, rather than which version of the world holds the wisdom. This allows underlying substance to be lost; after a while, somebody has to ask "what was that we were talking about?"

Journal referees act as insatiable citation cops— demanding more, more, more ("feed me, feed me") and never saying there are too many. As with other cops they sometimes go bad, corrupted by their desire to make sure their own names or those of their pals are among the references. Seldom do they have a sense that many different bodies of thought could be the relevant literature, and that their own version is idiosyncratic to a specific intellectual-biographic niche. The author has the challenge to cater to the citation world of the reviewers they draw, and hope a revise and resubmit won't switch the manuscript into still other citation firmaments.

Emphasis on citations rather than substance pushes the literature itself into ever more abstract and formal realms. With successive iterations through the journals, veins of scholarship lose whatever practical or theoretical thrust they might once have had. Besides Type I and Type II error, there is Type III error: that nobody cares about the null hypothesis anyway. No matter how quantitative or rigorous the presentation, work can cease to be empirical at all, taking the word "empirical" back to its root (as psychologist David Bakan once proposed) to mean "experience." Empirical knowledge relies on direct observation of the real world, as opposed to armchair reflection, intuition, or logical deduction. A clean observation of two people eating dinner is surely more empirical than indexes of affinity, dependence, or prestige run as regressions with dozens of other variables, some surrogate measures for still other measures, dubiously scaled and weighted. With disengagement from the real world, but armed with statistical machinery (however bogus its application sometimes may be), the literature is undisciplined by ordinary human sense-making and print-out rules.

The justification for citations and related sounds of science is a cumulative knowledge base in which one's own work could not have been done without the prior labors of specific, namable others. But our citations often do not indicate the work upon which we relied; they show we "know the literature." Rather than display the route to our findings, they pay homage. I often cite people who other people think should have been important to my work, but in fact I had never read. And the free lancers who have made powerful contributions probably didn't even know we had literatures.

That we can do our work without using others' conceptions of the literature we "need," signals how idiosyncratic our routes to knowledge actually are. Despite the existence of ASA sections, named "specialties," abstracting services, key word searches, and consortia data storage, we can't find what we need in any mechanistic way — even when we try. Fields are not distinct; findings in one specialty drift into another, and reshuffle in light of new knowledge or fashion, perhaps disappearing for a decade only to be later rediscovered. Key words that can be used in searches do not correspond to any agreed upon system of notation or hierarchy. It's hard to be cumulative if there is really no practical way to know what has been done before or what the trajectories of development have been.

Even some of the easiest challenges don't get met. I offer the career of one of my own little lost findings as a case illustration, chosen because it falls so squarely within a well-worked empirical tradition and because I have no particular passion about it (I swear). I learned, based on a case study, that neighborhood racial segregation is not due to white flight. This kind of thing is important to the human ecology types as well as for urban and racial studies. It was reported 20 years ago in one of the most mainstream, abstracted, indexed, assigned, and reprinted sources. More methodologically sophisticated scholars replicated the finding on large data sets, again well reported. But not only has this finding made no dent on the popular view, even the most important scholars in the field ignore it, because they don't know it. I bring this up not out of sour grapes (maybe just a tad), but because it is the kind of finding with which our system should have been best able to deal. That it doesn't even get in shows the crudeness of our retrieval system and the extraordinary noise, indeed cacophony, that surrounds any one element in what we "know."

While we can not retrieve an ordinary finding, the science model encourages us nevertheless to mark each published observation with support from authority and past studies. We sort of spray on citations like the white stuff that makes snow on indoor Christmas trees. Thus our literature is full of statements that begin "As x has shown..." or "as has been demonstrated by...". Tracing back, one too often finds only an assertion in the first place, or the results of a casual empirical inquiry — but cited like it was from Blau and Duncan, Incorporated. More status anxious than even their mentors, graduate students create their own citation mayhems, beginning dissertations with a summary of "the literature," moving through a review of "findings" — as though back in chem lab happily solving for unknowns. Whether in theses or journals, our system limits ways to read (or portray) the difference between vague assertion and well-reinforced documentation. Our adoption of the scientific notation system (Author, year), as opposed to substantive footnotes, communicates verification like a kosher stamp on a piece of meat, with no mister-in-between. The standing ban on use of first- person voice, on saying "I think but I'm not sure" or the use of similarly human qualifiers, promotes spiraling scientistic overstatement.

All these findings do cumulate, but as debris on the shop floor. We trip over our own stuff because, just as our departments have few ways to fail graduate students, the discipline has few ways to purge findings — either because they are wrong or, more importantly, because they have been replaced by more evolved formulations. The end of a line of sociological work does not result in a punch line ("it is a virus"), settling a long line of inquiries and thus embalming them as fixed on the shelf and out of the way. That would allow researchers to go on to their next stage (e.g. identifying the virus) without having to deal with an army of genies that keep coming out of the old bottles. But for us so little gets settled, even as practical consensus: we can learn 60 or so years after Durkheim that we were working with an "over socialized conception of man" or that, with Marx dead even longer, it was time to "let the state back in."

Symptoms of the same awkward incoherence play out at the undergraduate teaching level, where departments generate curricula and systems of prerequisites that presume "building blocks" and interchangeablility from one sociology department to another. But apart from certain subfields (like statistics), such assumptions are illusory. Courses in, say "urban," are totally different if the approach is political economy versus demography-ecol-

ogy versus community studies. "Stratification" can build on the Blau-
Duncan mobility approach, a Marxian-Braverman sociology of work orientation, or a world-scale comparative and/or feminist outlook. The sociology of culture can be akin to literary studies and discourse analysis, or can
treat culture as an industry, or as a problem in formal organization. These
are not different spins on the same topic, but as different from one another
as each is from courses with completely different titles. So how can there
be hierarchical curricula within a department, much less across departments
when what a student knows by taking the course depends not on its name
but on who taught it? The curricula quandary reflects the essential nature of
the discipline, not the need for another series of committee meetings to
shape a shared conformity — that's a cult, not a science.

The real divisions in the discipline are based in cultural and biographic
communalities: where people went to school, their politics, and general
intellectual sensibilities. So many people today can be "into culture," just
as so many in the past were "urban" or "critical," because the terms delimit
so little — mostly a mood shift and the willingness to put up four bucks for
section dues. If we organized ourselves as cultures, we would do better —
e.g. "Sociologists Active in the Sixties 'n' Such" or The Journal of Wisconsin Quantoids (as opposed to *American Sociological Review*). Naming this
way might really unite people who approach research and teaching in a
similar manner and link those who need each other to advance their work.
It would look bad for the gentiles, but it would capture something real.

Writing Mount Everest

Howard Becker, in his "how to write" book for social scientists gives
many good reasons for clear exposition. It makes our work accessible to
colleagues, students, and outsiders; it has a better chance to influence the
world. The advice is simple: use small and easy words and first person. He
doesn't say to write "in a more professional tone" — advice I've seen from
a journal editor.

Becker is not an enforcer, so let it be me who says that the profession
needs to guard itself and its students against obscurantist and difficult writing. Precisely because the boundaries of our various literatures are so indis-
tinct and because we must read what our subjects read to understand their
world, we have to read a lot of stuff. Its a zero-sum game out there.   I
greatly admire Harold Garfinkel, but he cost me. If it takes seven hours to
read an article by scholar x, we may never read three articles by other
scholars (or learn something in a bar). It may be that x is wonderful, but is
x three times as wonderful? Parsons was very smart, but was he 10 times

smarter than Mills? or Goffman? or Merton? Maybe "yes" and maybe "no." It's a question to ask.

It isn't just that we need clear writing so that we can better express knowledge; the accomplishment of clarity is the accomplishment of knowledge. Even if something is already "known" in some sense, finding the words that concisely formulate it, and make it memorable adds to the stock of what can be manipulated in the mind and made part of working sociology and of the culture. Notions like Merton's "self-fulfilling prophecy" or Giddens' "structuration" were, in some sense, already there but making the underlying thought available advances what we actually "know." "Problems with no name," to borrow from Betty Friedan, are known in a radically different way "merely" through naming them (sort of "perfomatives," in the linguistic lingo: utterances that accomplish something just by saying them).

Sometimes this process results in specialized terms and a distinctive conceptual apparatus. I am not preaching a know-nothing ridicule of scholarship, in the manner of Senator Proximire. Some very worthwhile sociology can appear, especially to the uninformed, trivial and empty. Two very different fields in which I am not a practitioner but a user, demography and conversation analysis, come closer to the model of cumulative science than most others in sociology and they utilize an arcane set of terms and methods. They make their gains through papers with titles that can seem ridiculous. The urgent goal for sociologists (and the outside world) is to know the difference between specialized language entailed by an authentic problem, rather than entailed by a retreat from one.

To help others make the distinction, we can begin by not treating "hard to read" as benign challenge, like climbing Mount Everest, with honor going to those with the temerity to take it on. We should not defer to exotic creatures who create Mount Everests of needless jargon and complex sentence structures that others will have to scale. It does not build our character, it only takes our time and tests our patience. The gatekeepers should treat bad writing as threat; it better be terrific to be let through. The guardians of journals, yours truly included, need extra gumption to warn against a paper that while full of citations and other marks of the trade may be using bad writing to obscure the fact that it has no important problem at its core. Like others, I suspect, I do my peer reviewing in off-hours (usually at night when I'm half dead). How can I be certain that it isn't fatigue that keeps me from "getting it" rather than the weakness of what is before me? How can I urge rejection for a paper that drugs with such rich professional paraphernalia. To these pushers of such downers I must, we all must, just say "no."

Staying Inside

In explaining the arcane writing style of professors, the historian Patricia Limerick says the key is that academics are the people nobody would dance with in high school (or choose-up early for gym class ball teams, I would add to her girlish remembrance). Nobody, the therapists will tell you, gets over that so easy. Limerick may be wrong in her blanket characterization, but it is certainly less threatening to come out only under full protection. For professors, that means the classroom and scholarly meetings, where vulnerability to real life can be kept at a minimum. For experimental physicists this probably does no harm and indeed protects against skin cancer. For sociology, its not good.

My first image of sociology was through the writing of C. Wright Mills, whom I also imagined as an album cover. He merged with Jack Kerouac, Lenny Bruce, and Henry Miller in my mind; they were all heroes who knew the world through its edges — deviant, strident, and/or dirty-mouthed. I figured all sociologists were something like that, all the names between the parentheses in the journals I gobbled up. The only way to know the society that surrounds us is by understanding its margins, it seemed to me. But that means going outside: the taxi-dance hall, the housing projects, the protest march, the youth gang and the dark places that most of us know only as haunting hints of the possible.

Staying in conventional settings (or as properly adjusted into an academic lifestyle of spicy food and ethnic clothing accessories) has substantive implications. Gouldner warned against the "congenial sentiment" (quoted in Jacoby, look up Gouldner/sociology) through which comfortable sociologists come to see the world, tenured with families and health care coverage, not too rich but not poor either. It isn't just that they aren't Kerouacs, they aren't Louis Wirths or Herbert Gans, or others who can sustain a pattern of taking on even the ordinary outside settings. Sociologists often know no world outside their own academic and family daily round; they don't hang around commodity trading floors, or holy roller churches, or exclusive golf clubs. Committee meetings, teaching loads, peer reviews and writing essays like this are the occupation, leaving little space for walking through the world. Going outside means for extramural funding, not for extraordinary experience. Russell Jacoby blames the university system for coopting the "public intellectual," enervating the country's civic life, and he devotes several pages to the specific case of sociology.

My point is more narrowly methodological. The sociologists' taken for granted world, like everyone else's, is partial. That's why it is important what that taken for granted world might be. Our ranks, more so than the other disciplines, must be diverse — not just to satisfy affirmative action requirements or moral urgings, but to have common sense that encompasses a broader range of senses. Our point of departure for a study comes overwhelmingly from our own lives. A thin slice of human experience weakens the sociologists' crucial first order of data, the thickness of one's own biography. If what the sociologists know best is what is also commonly known to the rest of the educated public, they are naive to all other settings — both substantively and methodologically — tabula rosa all over again. We are not ahead of the game, as we are paid to be.

In a written research report, every assertion, indeed every word, potentially "needs" evidence. The most thoroughly documented article contains infinitely more unsupported assumptions than it is possible to back up. The action turns on just which assertions are noticed as "not generally accepted" or because they just lack the "ring of truth" — the vastly important arbiter of what can pass, unexamined, through the gate of sociological custom. The looseness of our subfields and ambiguity of just which literatures ought to be cited for what, makes for a murky situation. Given that the more ambiguous the stimulus, the more that social factors intervene in perception (there's a lot of citation for that), the stage is set for the subjective folk knowledge of the gate keeper to operate, invisibly and hence irresponsibly, as the basis for discriminating. This again brings up the conventionalized yet idiosyncratic "literatures" which are invoked, in part as rationales, for determining which little items need the science regalia and which we can, as Garfinkel says, simply "let pass" so that there can be literatures at all.

So now we're back to the biographical ranch. Unless sociologists really do live rich lives, engage the world, or at least read widely, our research and writing are emaciated by misplaced demands for evidence — misplaced compared to what other folks further along the learning curve would demand. Without a broad sensibility, those who do have distinctive knowledge are held back by those who do not. Not knowing what "everybody" knows in the world of a specific study (on the streets, in the Army, at the boardroom), the gate-keeper turns into a judgmental dope who can't distinguish between what needs documenting compared to what should be self-evident. Does an assertion that big cities are rife with corruption require, in the halls of social science, "evidence" before it can be used in formulating an argument. Does corruption just pass or is the baseline one of civics course "democracy"? Do we presume that campaign contributions fix politicians or is the reverse the working common sense? Or are we supposed to have no brain whatever until the data comes in and comes in on everything?

Just as we can not rely on the literature of sociology to tool us up for knowing what to doubt, neither can the adages of political correctness do the job — no matter how strongly they take hold among progressive academics. They are as conventionalized (and detached) in their way as the Broom and Selznick table of contents was in its. People in real life know, even if it's hard to acknowledge, that when it comes to sex and romance, the young have power over the old, and that women sometimes indeed say "no" when they mean "yes" — just to bite a few harsh bullets. It is all part of the dance that makes life tense and interesting and, yes, sometimes criminally brutal. Sociologists disarm common sense knowledge of the embedded idiom of daily life to assert, as principle, that matters are more simple.

Again, the antidote is going out — not as leader but earnest listener and to stay awhile. The academic calendar and routine push us to draw more and more of our cultural knowledge from within our workplace. Many of us blow our sabbaticals by writing up what we've been doing, rather than immersing ourselves in new worlds. The anthropologists have a richer tradition of going into the field with body and soul. They used to be helped by an absence of phones and the presence of an ocean surrounding their little islands. For us, and increasingly for them, the temptations of e-mail and good fax conspire to keep things normal. Sociology would be better off if we, at least for sustained periods, could get out of it.

Staying Shy

Many sociologists are shy. Some of my best colleagues and my best parts are shy. It is not a sin and shy people make important contributions to sociology. But it takes nerve to hang out in a strange field work setting (one's own therapy group, housing coop, or political movement is at least a start). It is moxie to interview people (arrogance, we are now told), especially ones who lead different lives than we, whether because they lack the marks of middle class identity or have the trappings of power and wealth. Sociology does not select for fieldwork verve: I have rarely seen it mentioned as a criterion for admitting a graduate student, hiring an assistant professor, or granting tenure. Most people who do good interviews are people for whom it is an easy social maneuver; they go confidently forward and their subjects love to tell them what's going on. Being able to go with ease is important to our knowledge base and should count. Instead, personality is prized more for what it can do within the department (as friendly colleague) than for what it can mean for scholarship. A certain pushiness, perhaps even crudeness, can — depending upon the research setting — make for effective work. But we use the same basis for judging personnel as in any other field, adjusted a bit for the moral stance and interactive style we mostly share. Colleagues reproduce the "congenial sentiment" that Gouldner (who did not always suffer from this ailment) warned us against.

That many of us are shy is another one of the dirty little secrets in sociology, somewhat obscured by our routine contentiousness and assertiveness in hotel lobbies. All of us were not meant for public roaming, but more of us could be made ready with a little help from our friends for interaction beyond the department and the Hilton. Perhaps even a bit of training that recognized shyness as a life-long challenge would be in order. No matter what kind of sociology we do, whether number-crunching or comparative historical, there is nothing like varied life to launch ideas, facilitate interpretations, and help us speak well to others. We need to lessen our shyness if we are to get our act together and take it on the road.

Methods: One Size Fits All

While the science model, crudely applied, holds back all varieties of sociology, it is especially deleterious for qualitative sociology. It takes away the very advantages that such methods permit: the ability to change one's mind, learn as it goes, turn on a dime. Design and its accoutrements (hypotheses, operationalizations, etc.) count with survey research and small groups experiments because they involve so much up- front investment. The wrong wording on a question that will be asked of 300 people, failure to include what later turns out to be an important variable — these are costly errors. Funding agencies and graduate mentors are wise to ask for a lot of advance specification.

But the same idea carried into qualitative sociology, where there are few sunk costs, undermines empirical accomplishment. In qualitative work, design is disaster: The researcher will not notice the serendipity bouncing all around and stay the course through a field experience that shifts with new possibilities. NSF says it wants to support qualitative work, but insists on the instrumentation of sunk-cost sociology in the proposal (hypotheses, operationalizations, falsifiables). If they can get that kind of stuff, they can accept the lack of hard numbers they associate with real science. In effect, they want the positivist method laid on "bad data." Because qualitative data is not really appreciated, the research process that would best lead to it is also not appreciated.

The humanities have a different way of forecasting good outcomes. In the arts, the way you get a gig, a grant, a professorship is to do a little of it; show your art by opening your portfolio, dance across the stage, think a bit on paper. Grant applications in the humanities read like bits of finished articles and books; applicants provide a sampling of the quality of their mind by what they write. The granting agency says, in effect, we want more of this. But in sociology, the weight is on how one states what will be done, not on displaying an instance of doing it. There is a strong tendency on social science juries — and I've felt it — to reward the craft of proposal writing itself. By convention, the best qualitative proposals simulate the quantitative research method for the sake of gaining resources for qualitative work. But good simulation (deception?) is not an adequate predictor of a quality outcome, and certainly not of the kind of dedicated intellectual honesty that good field work does require.

The meaninglessness of much quantitative sociology has been well vetted, by some of its most distinguished contributors (Stanley Lieberson, for example, and most demanding of all, Otis Dudley Duncan). Number sociologists may screw up their own thing by the way they themselves mimic science, but they also damage, almost as side-effect, the rest of sociology. Their influence over the main journals, prestige systems, and foundation grants deforms qualitative work by forcing it into the same procrustean bed. Qualitative sociologists imitate the imitators, yielding a version of faux science that goes one step farther along the road of caricature.

Sociologists Eat Each Other

Sociologists at NSF have told me that sociology has trouble justifying higher funding levels to the higher-ups because our proposals are of "low quality" compared to those in other disciplines. Because "science" is their organization's middle name, the high-up NSF folks apparently count up the numerical scores from peer reviews to measure overall quality. Because the sociology scores are worse than others', sociology proposals are seen as weak. But those of us on the scene are right to suspect that these relative scores probably measure contentiousness. Sociologists, critics by disposition and occupation, freely take issue with one another, often ungenerously. If you combine this with the science-rigor criteria, add in the reality of ambiguity and diversity, and spice with the personal frustrations of thwarted ambitions, you have a recipe for peer cannibalism.

Qualitative workers have enough trouble to give one another, without the added liability of holding up the science canon as test mechanism (usually a science hit man will be on the job anyway). Add in the strong moral and political concerns of many qualitative sociologists and the threshold of acceptability becomes difficult to meet indeed.

Reaction Formation: Screams and Misdemeanors

Some sociologists, not entering the science mimicry business, take their frustration into other modes of expression, rebelling with all heart. This takes a number of forms. One is the aversion to numbers; since science sociology, real and ersatz, tends to come with numbers, numbers no good. The more avant garde departments, especially their graduate students, get caught up in this number-hating game. Positivism sucks and so does counting up anything. Silly.

Others in rebellion, push their politics, not as a method for changing the world or as heuristic device for sensing a problem and developing evidence, but as template for judging the outcome of any data manipulation, concept, or turn of phrase. Such sociologists overstate conclusions and patrol the discourses; they inhibit the open empirical or theoretic wondering that really could be a ticket to effective political action. Although their language is rich in critique, they too are often lost in their own discourse, reluctant to go out. They have trouble actually observing in the field, whether among the oppressed, in the demimonde, or — most unfortunately — the settings of deep power where privilege and wealth are actually centered. Few, from my experience, engage in off-campus political struggle where a natural laboratory of applied social change never ends. The social movements of the last decades and the sociological movements that have been both their cause and consequence have done an enormous amount to invigorate the discipline (feminist studies, gay studies, race and ethnic analysis). But the payoff for sociology and society can only continue with clear talk and, even when the results are disquieting, analytic openness.

Alternative epistemologies, such as versions of post-structuralism, urge new voice for the oppressed and encourage self-reflexivity that makes the scholars' role as observer an important topic of investigation. In embracing such doctrines, I believe, the sociologists are not leaving sociology, but buying into it via the sociological insights that have come into literary theory in the last decades. Many of these ideas have been around for quite awhile in non-mainstream versions of sociological practice — invited by Mannheim's sociology of knowledge and in the whole social construction school and ethnomethodology (where reflexivity, indexicality, intersubjectivity, have long been topic). The contemporary proponents seem unaware of this heritage, its richness as well as how it handled (or could not handle) some of the blind alleys that stymie the current thinkers.

Discourse analysis does usefully invite attention to the linkages among different expositional forms: talk, writing, and physical objects of architecture, clothing, furniture, and the body — all treated as interwoven texts. But the practitioners push out babies with bath water. The inanimate texts (writings and physical objects) are rightly seen as fateful means of communication, "liminal" in what they "give off," as Erving Goffman might have said. But in the zeal to see "life" in what used to be treated as passive detritus (mere fetishes, for Marx), the new scholarship gives short shrift to the humans who make these products and who manage to interact with and through them. "Agency," to be sure is featured, but through assertion, rather than precise study. If the sociologist is going to add anything to what the literature people already do, it is through empirical study of just how humans operate as the thinking, behaving, interacting intermediaries that link texts to one another and give them their power in behavior.

We need to learn just how all the various modes of expressivity, animate and inanimate, manage to cohere, how a message, an ethos, a hegemon operate through their social settings. The temptation to stay inside often triumphs under the rationale (unstated to be sure) that since there is life in the inanimate, we can just "address" or "interrogate" it. Today's pioneers of a new professional orthodoxy, for all their self-conscious marginality and solidarity with the masses, recapitulate the esoteric stance of their most inaccessible predecessors. In addition to the newer terms (simulacrum, liminal, subaltern), specialized use comes to old terms, like Other. Each scholar has the habit of dismembering terms to portray the etymology of words (not a new discovery) and their re-markable capacity to display their nefarious or richly complex social origins. Given that its hard enough to make oneself understood when just working with garden variety prose, these dashing little tripwires make comprehending any sentence a difficult move. When the obstreperous sociologists of the 60's denounced their elders, whether in print or in person, it was ugly and sometimes wrong, but at least they could be understood. Today, it's more like a premise for a Monty Python skit.

The insight that gives rise to much of this twisting in empty space, the fundamental reflexivity of all human accounts, must be honored in a different way. Reflexivity must concern itself not just with a tortured self examination of the privilege of the observer compared to the observed, but of the more general system bias imposed by not going out. Universities valorize something other than simple privilege; they represent a specific cultural niche that exists in contradistinction to both rich and poor, and most elements of the middle class. Those on our valued avant garde must not churn fundamental insights of phenomenology, communication theory, and literary criticism into a solipsistic nightmare that alienates sociology both from empirical reality and any potential public.

Solution

The diversity of sociology should be respected, not just through lip service but through the discipline's judgmental infrastructure. We need to retreat from the idea of professional literatures that adhere, just so, to a given project and adopt a more open sense of making use of whatever can advance an interesting and informing narrative. Writing "in a professional manner" should not consist of a particular style — such as associated with the traditional ASR format. Different kinds of sociology should read and sound differently. If we could climb out of the science trap, we could acknowledge different modes and write in many voices. Indeed the very computer that so helped sociology's science mania can now be used to express textures of truth, beyond the mechanics of validity tests. Fonts, formatting, and character size invite new manipulation of text to connote differing degrees of authorial certitude, evidence base, alternative means of knowing, and varying emotional sensibilities that correspond to specific words, sentences and paragraphs. This is a way to nuance our writing with the kind of interactional thickness present in face-to-face talk, whether in everyday life or at conference hob-nobbing. Whether through the computer or use of the first-person voice, this is a kind of mimicry worth striving for.

Striving is what it's all about. I have been guilty, increasingly over the years, of most all the sins and find a need to urge myself toward clear disclosure. The struggle is also social and political, given that our professional stresses come, in part, from the kind of country in which we live and the folk theories of human behavior that capture its peoples. It's never clear how one can simultaneously shape self and society when both are in reflexive relation to one another. But that is the way all change works and is as much the condition of sociological work as that of any other. There is a saying that if what we change does not change us, we are playing in a sandbox. How profound an anticipation of late modern insights into the construction of reality. To seriously engage in such efforts frightens precisely because success comes back, like karma, as part of one's being.

There are simple principles with which to start. There was another slogan I used to go by a lot, in part because it made me so fashionably obnoxious: "Speak truth to power." Increasingly I realize that can only work if we can speak clearly to anybody and about matters important on their face, or for which we can at least lay a trail of relevance. This is the only way we can, as sociologists, help better the society and the conditions of our own work.

The risks are those of self-revelation, of acknowledging the role of other disciplines, other parts of our own, as well as of the social movements and folk wisdoms that have shaped almost all our agendas, personal and scholarly. It is the way to win the allegiance of those who want what we really have to offer as opposed to what we can manage to concoct. Dangerous and thrilling, we need to pitch to those who will like us for what we are. Isn't that always both the risk and reward of integrity?

Acknowledgments

Avery Gordon and Don Zimmerman gave helpful reads.

9

Sociology: A Disinvitation?

Peter L. Berger

At this stage of my life I find that I have little stake in my identity as a sociologist. If asked for my academic discipline, I will routinely come up with this identification, but it has little to do with what I do or what I consider myself to be. I pay scant attention to what people in the discipline are engaged in, and I daresay that they return the compliment. This is quite all right. But I am sometimes reminded of the fact that, in my impetuous youth, I rather passionately invited others to this discipline, both in published writings (which, to boot, are still in print) and in my teaching. Should I repent this action? Should I perhaps issue a solemn disinvitation, so as not to be responsible for yet more innocent students being seduced into what may well be a bankrupt enterprise? I think that the answer to both questions is a less than hearty no-no, because I continue to think that the sort of sociology I once advocated is as valid today as it ever was — less than hearty, because I am aware of the fact that this is not what most people who call themselves sociologists are actually doing. Is there any chance of changing this state of affairs? Probably not, and for good sociological reasons. However, before one assesses the prospects for therapy, one should have some clarity regarding the diagnosis.

It is a truism to say that we live in a time of massive and rapid change. This is only an accelerated phase of the vast transformation brought on by the process of modernization first in Europe and then increasingly throughout the world. It is instructive to recall that sociology as a discipline arose precisely as an effort to understand, and if possible to gain greater control over, this huge transformation. This was clearly the case in the three countries in which distinctive sociological traditions first arose — France,

Germany, and the United States. To understand, perhaps even to control, modernity — an awesome proposition! It is no wonder, then, that the early masters of sociology were individuals of impressive intellectual and, in most cases, personal powers. It would be misguided to expect their successors, several academic generations down the line, to possess comparable characteristics. But one would expect a certain continuity of intellectual stance, a continuity in form if not in substance. It would be difficult to argue that this is the case. Sociology in its classical period — roughly between 1890 and 1930 — dealt with the "big questions" of the time; sociology today seems largely to avoid these questions and, when not avoiding them, dealing with them in exceedingly abstract fashion.

The classical sociologists were careful to look at social reality objectively, without regard to their own biases or wishes (what Max Weber summed up in the much-maligned notion of "value-freeness "); large numbers of sociologists now proudly announce their non-objectivity, their partisan advocacy. Sociology in America at one time was intent on cultivating a robust empiricism, which Louis Wirth summed up as "getting one's hands dirty with research" and which one could also call the cultivation of a sociological nose. Today many sociologists take pride in the abstract, antiseptic quality of their work, comparable to the fine model building of theoretical economists. One wonders whether these people have ever interviewed a live human being or participated with curiosity in a live social event.

What has gone wrong? And is there anything that can be done about it? I am not at all sure that I can authoritatively deliver either diagnosis or therapy. Nor can I claim to have been immune all along to whatever it is that ails the discipline. But I shall take a stab, if not at a comprehensive diagnosis, let alone a promising therapy, at least at describing some of the symptomatic failings. And I shall do it in light of four important developments that have taken place since the Second World War. Each of these developments completely surprised most, if not all sociologists. What is more, even after these developments had come sharply into view, sociologists found themselves unable to explain them or to make sense of them within a frame of sociological theory. Given the importance of these developments, the failure of sociology to either predict, or at least to apprehend, them indicates that something is seriously wrong here.

Case one: In the late 1960s and early 1970s a cultural and political upheaval took place in the major Western industrial societies. It was a total surprise. Looked at through the spectacles of conventional sociology, it posed a tantalizing question: How could it be that some of the most privileged people on earth, indeed in history, turned violently against the very society that had made them thus privileged? If one turns to American sociology, as it was taught then and still is in numerous college courses, one finds the proposition that people become more conservative as they become more affluent. This proposition may have been quite valid up to the aforementioned event. It certainly was not valid as the politico-cultural cataclysm occurred, and it is no longer valid today. On the contrary, both in politics and in culture the "progressive" movements have been socially located in the affluent upper middle class — the New Left and the New Politics, the anti-war movements, feminism, environmentalism and the Greens, and so on. Conversely, the newer conservative movements —whether led by Ronald Reagan, Margaret Thatcher, or Helmut Kohl — found their constituencies in the lower middle and working classes, dragging along a reluctant older conservative establishment. In the United States (very similar reactions occurred in Britain and what was then West Germany) old-style country-club Republicans held their noses while they shook the hands and kissed the babies of back-country evangelicals, culturally outraged ethnics, anti-abortion activists, and various other unmentionable social types. Conversely, radical middle-class intellectuals found themselves in bed, politically if not culturally, not with the "working masses" with whom their ideology identified, but with alleged representatives of the underclass and other marginal groupings.

I vividly recall a scene in the Brooklyn neighborhood where we lived from the mid-1960s to the late 1970s. The neighborhood was in the process of rapid gentrification (we were part of the process), changing from ethnic working class to professional upper middle class. On one street almost every house displayed what were then the politically correct peace placards in the windows "U.S. out of Vietnam," "Make love, not war," "Save the whales," and the like. With one exception: One house sported messages such as "Support our troops in Vietnam," "Support your local police" and "Register Communists, not guns." In this house lived an elderly invalid, a widowed veteran. One day, this man was evicted. Marshalls came and put his belongings on the street. Then they put him on the street, sitting in his wheelchair, wearing an American Legion cap. Some buddies of his drove up and took him away, and then his belongings were carted off to somewhere. The very next week new people moved into the house. Promptly, the peace signs went up in all the windows.

Today the conventional view has it that the "late sixties" are past history, recently re-evoked in a mood of nostalgia. This is a serious misinterpretation: The "late sixties" have not disappeared; they have become institution-

alized, both culturally and politically. The only halfway persuasive sociological explanation of this development was the so-called "new class theory,"
which surfaced briefly in the 1970s and has not been heard of much since.
Interestingly, this explanation had both a leftist and a rightist version, articulated respectively by Alvin Gouldner and Irving Kristol. Neither version fully meets the facts, and the formidable task remains of reformulating
a sociological theory of class in advanced industrial societies. But this is
not my concern here. The question is why have sociologists been so inept
in dealing with as massive a phenomenon? To some extent, perhaps, it is
reluctance   to   modify   accepted   theoretical   paradigms.

Sociologists of the left have tried, very unsuccessfully, to squeeze the
phenomenon into Marxist categories like the "proletarianization of the
middle class." More "bourgeois" colleagues have mumbled something about
"status politics." But the best interpretation is probably that most sociologists were very much a part of the phenomenon. The generation that entered the profession in those years, now tottering through tenured middle
age, had all the peace signs emblazoned on their hearts. To them, this was a
conflict between the good guys and the bad guys, and it still is-though the
politically correct markers have shifted somewhat. People are reluctant to
accept sociological explanations of their own commitments — even if they
are professional sociologists. In other words, the failure of sociology to
apprehend this development is largely due to ideological blinders.

Second case: One of the fundamental transformations in the contemporary world has been the rapid economic ascendancy of Japan and other East
Asian countries. What is happening here is not just an economic miracle of
enormous proportions, occurring at breathtaking speed, but the first
instance of successful modernization in a non-Western cultural context that
should be of special interest to sociologists. As I have argued for some time,
here is a second case of capitalist modernity, obviously of great interest in
and of itself, but of even greater interest from the standpoint of a theory of
modem society. Put simply, Japan is important for our understanding, not
so much of it, but of ourselves. Again, no one expected this. If any of its
proponents had been asked in the 1950s, the time when so-called modernization theory developed, which Asian country was most likely to succeed
in terms of economic development, chances are the answer would have
been the Philippines, now the one economic disaster in the capitalist sector
of the region. At a conference that took place at the time and which some
participants still recall uncomfortably, there was widespread agreement that
Confucianism was one of the most formidable obstacles to development in
Korea and in the Chinese societies. Today, this cultural heritage is

commonly cited as one of the causes of the East Asian economic success stories.

Modernization theory faltered in the wake of the late sixties, when it was widely derogated as an ideology of Western imperialism. Leftist sociologists meanwhile were busy giving birth to so-called dependency theory, according to which capitalism necessarily perpetuates underdevelopment; the solution, of course, was to be socialism. There is a bizarre synchronicity between empirical and theoretical developments. Just as capitalist East Asia was bursting into astonishing economic growth and prosperity while all the socialist societies, from Indochina to the Caribbean, were sinking into hopeless stagnation, more and more sociologists were proclaiming their allegiance to a theory according to which the opposite was bound to occur. One of the funniest events I attended a few years ago was a conference in Taiwan, home of one of the great economic miracles of the modern age. It was a conference about Taiwan and how to understand it. For reasons that were never quite clear, most American academics invited were dependency theorists who had previously done work on Latin America. They tried valiantly to fit what they could see happening all around them in Taiwan into their theory. The great theoretical achievement of the conference was the concept of "dependent development" which supposedly accounted for the Taiwan case. That neo-Marxists with no previous field experience outside Latin America should find this notion plausible may be understandable. Harder to credit was that several Taiwanese social scientists in attendance nodded approvingly as this orientalist translation of *dependencia* was trotted out before them. A possible explanation is this: While dependency theory has been massively falsified in terms of the world economy, it may have some predictive value in terms of world culture; the intellectuals of the "first world" with greatly superior resources and patronage at their disposal, do indeed have a "comprador class" in less developed countries.

In all fairness, my second case is not quite like the first, in that there has indeed been a considerable effort by sociologists to understand the phenomenon, even if they did not anticipate it. The aforementioned post-Confucian hypothesis, though first formulated by nonsociologists, has been the subject of intense and sophisticated discussion among sociologists both in the region itself and outside it. The left has obviously not been able to participate in this for ideological reasons. But non-leftist sociologists have not been prominent in the discussion either, except for those with a specialization in the region. Another formidable task is one of modifying the concept of modern society, as it developed from, say, Max Weber to Talcott Parsons.

This is a very "big question" indeed. It is uncongenial to people whose perspective is parochially ethnocentric and who are committed to methods that do not lend themselves to "big questions." What is called for is a sociology in the classical vein, grounded in a knowledge of history, methodologically flexible, and imbued with a cosmopolitan spirit endlessly curious about every manifestation of human life. Needless to say, sociologists practicing their craft in such a vein are rather difficult to find. Worse, one may say that both the training and the reward system of the profession is cleverly (if, probably, unintentionally) designed to prevent such people from emerging.

Third case: Another body of theory that seemed well-established in the 1950s and 1960s was so-called secularization theory. Briefly put, it posits the notion that modernization necessarily brings with it a decline of religion in human life, both in terms of social institutions and of individual consciousness. This notion has a long history in Western thought, going back at least to the Enlightenment of the eighteenth century, if not farther. But, in all fairness, it gained strength through the findings of sociologists of religion, especially in Europe. Good reasons were given for the linkage alleged between growth in the GNP and the demise of the gods. Modernity, built on the foundations of science and technology, brought with it an increasingly rational mindset that no longer found plausible the presumably irrational religious interpretations of the world.

Leave aside here the questionable presumption as to the irrationality of religion — a presumption certainly grounded in Enlightenment philosophy. The theory seemed grounded in empirical evidence and was consequently open to empirical falsification. By the late 1970s it had been falsified with a vengeance. As it turned out, the theory never had much empirical substance to begin with. It was valid, and continues to be valid, for one region of the world, Europe, a few scattered territories, such as Quebec, which underwent an amazing process of secularization after the Second World War, and a fairly thin stratum of Western-educated intellectuals everywhere. The rest of the world is as fervently religious as it ever was, and arguably more so than it was earlier in this century.

Two events in the late 1970s forced this fact on the public's attention. In the United States the validity of the theory had already been put in question by the so-called religious revival of the 1950s and the counterculture of the 1960s, though sociologists of religion tended to see the former as only dubiously religious and the latter as only marginally religious. What made the theory altogether untenable was the evangelical resurgence, first brought to widespread attention by the presidential candidacy of Jimmy Carter and a little later by the noisy appearance of the "moral majority" and similar groups. Suddenly it became obvious that, though little noticed intellectual milieus, American society contained millions of born-again Christians and, alarmingly, they kept growing and growing, while mainline churches went into a fairly steep demographic decline. The evangelical phenomenon served to underline a more fundamental fact: America differed from Europe precisely in its religious character.

Beyond the United States, though, the event that rattled the theory linking modernization to secularity was the Iranian revolution. Once again, a momentous event came into view that, theoretically, should not have occurred at all. Since then, religious upsurges of every sort have been erupting all over the world. Neo-traditionalist, or fundamentalist, Protestantism and Islam are the two biggest games in town, on a global scale, but almost every religious tradition in the world has evinced similar revitalization movements. And sociologists of every coloration continue to be baffled.

My only visit to Iran took place about two years before this revolution. Naturally, I spoke mainly to intellectuals, most of whom cordially disliked the regime of the Shah and looked forward to its removal. No one expected this to happen under Islamic auspices. Nowhere did I hear the name Khomeini. At about the time of my visit to Iran, Brigitte Berger was on a lecture tour in Turkey, a place she had never visited before and whose language she did not speak. In Istanbul, she noticed many cars with green flags and what looked like storefront mosques also marked with green flags which she recognized as Islamic symbols. When she mentioned her observation to her Turkish hosts, they were very much surprised. They either maintained that she was mistaken in her idea that something religious was going on or they discounted the phenomenon as quite unimportant. The people she talked with, mostly social scientists and all secularized intellectuals, literally did not see what was before their eyes — again, because none of this was supposed to be happening.

Sociologists have had a hard time coming to terms with the intensely religious character of the contemporary world. Whether politically on the left or not, they suffer from ideological blinders when it comes to religion, and the tendency is then to explain away what cannot be explained. But ideology apart, parochialism is an important factor here too. Sociologists live in truly secularized milieus — academia and other institutions of the professional knowledge industry — and it appears that they are no more immune than the sociologically untrained to the common misconception that one can generalize about the world from one's own little corner.

Finally, the fourth case: This is the momentous collapse of the Soviet empire, and what seems, at least for now, the worldwide collapse of socialism both as a reality and as an idea. Even the beginnings of this world-historical event are very recent, and the consequences are still unfolding with undiminished rapidity. Thus it would be unfair to blame anyone for not having at hand a theory to explain it all. It would be equally unfair to single out sociologists; just about nobody anticipated this (including regiments of certified sovietologists) and everybody is having great difficulty grasping it within any theoretical frame that makes sense. Still, it is worth stating that sociologists, even those with the relevant regional expertise, were no better than anyone else in predicting the event nor are they better in accounting for it. One must wonder how they will do in the years to come.

Those on the left, of course, will share in the general confusion (may one call it "cognitive anomie"?) of others in this ideological community. Leave aside those on the left who, despite everything, thought that the Soviet Union and its imitators were engaged in a noble experiment. Mistakes were made, and all that, but there was still the assumption that even a flawed socialism carried more hope than a capitalist system alleged to be hopelessly corrupt. But even those on the left who had long ago shed all illusions about the Soviet experiment were endlessly scanning the horizons for the "true socialism" that had to come, sometime, because the logic of history willed it. It was not just a matter of *le coeur à la gauche;* it was the mind that was on the left, in its basic cognitive assumptions. And the most basic assumption of all was that the historical process moved from capitalism to socialism. How to deal now with the transition from socialism to capitalism? Current leftist journals are full of tortured attempts to interpret the developments of the last few years in Europe and elsewhere, most of them attempts to deny the obvious. I have every expectation that sociologists will be whole-hearted participants in this enterprise, bravely led by the old cohorts of dependency theory. May we look forward to yet another brilliant concept, say of "independent underdevelopment", that will somehow rescue the theory?

The collapse of the Soviet empire and the worldwide crisis of socialism poses an enormous challenge to sociological understanding of modernity. And it is not just sociologists on the left who are unprepared to meet this challenge, who were no more prescient about these developments than their left-leaning colleagues. What is called for is a thorough rethinking of the relation between economic, political and social institutions in a modern society. I am reminded of the old witticism, sometimes still to be seen on signs in friendly neighborhood stores, "If you're good for nothing else, you can still serve as a bad example." For sociological theory, "bad" examples are just as useful as "good" ones. The more interesting question is not why "they" have collapsed, but why "we" have not. This is a basic theoretical point that much sociologizing has routinely overlooked: The "problem" is not social disorganization, but social organization — marriage rather than divorce, law-abidingness rather than crime, racial harmony rather than racial strife, and so on. We may safely assume that in Jan Romein's handy phrase- the "common human pattern" is faithlessness, violence and hate. These manifestations of human nature hardly need explanation, except perhaps by zoologists. What needs explaining is those instances in which, amazingly, societies manage to curb and civilize these propensities.

What do these cases disclose about what ails sociology today? One can point to four symptoms: parochialism, triviality, rationalism, and ideology. Each one is crippling. Their combination has been deadly. If one looks at the opus of the great classical sociologists, with Max Weber and Emile Durkheim in the lead, one is reminded of Wesley's dictum, "The world is my parish." Few sociologists could say this today, and those who do very often betray an embarrassing lack of historical depth.

At issue is much more than a bias in favor of some sort of sophisticated cosmopolitanism. One can be an excellent physicist without ever having stepped outside one's own society; I know that this is not so for a sociologist. And the reason for this is simple. Modernization is the great transforming force in the world today, but it is not a uniform, mechanical process. It takes different forms, evokes different reactions. This is why sociology, the discipline par excellence for seeking to understand modernity, must of necessity be comparative.

This, of course, was one of Weber's root insights; it is more relevant today than ever. Thus sociologists must look at Japan in order to understand the West, at socialism in order to understand capitalism, at India so as to understand Brazil, and so on. Parochialism in sociology is much more than a cultural deficiency; it is the source of crippling failures of perception. It should be part and parcel of the training of every sociologist to gain detailed knowledge of at least one society that differs greatly from his own-a feat that, needless to say, involves something many students shy away from: learning of foreign languages.

Triviality too is a fruit of parochialism, but in the case of sociology the more important root is methodological. This ailment of the discipline goes back at the least as far as the 1950s. In a futile and theoretically misguided effort to ape the natural sciences, sociologists developed ever more refined quantitative methods of research. There is nothing wrong with this in and of itself, sociology contains a good many questions that necessitate survey-type research; the better the quantitative methods, the more reliable will be the findings. But not all sociological questions require this approach, and some are of a character so as to require very different, qualitative approaches. Identification of scientific rigor with quantification has greatly limited the scope of sociology, often to narrowly circumscribed topics that best lend themselves to quantitative methods. The resultant triviality should not come as a surprise.

Sociology, as a science, will necessarily be an exercise in rationality. This is a far cry from assuming that ordinary social action is guided by rationality. This had been well understood in classical sociology, perhaps most dramatically by Vilfredo Pareto, a mathematically oriented economist who turned to sociology precisely because he discovered that most human actions are what he called non-logical. The discipline of economics, alas, has refused to share this insight and continues to operate with a highly rational model of *homo economicus*. As a consequence, it fails spectacularly, over and over again, to understand, let alone predict, the dynamics of the marketplace.

A good many sociologists seek to emulate economics, adapting theoretical models based on the "rational action paradigm" to their own discipline. We may confidently predict that the intellectual results of this approach will closely resemble those in economics. Yes, sociology is a rational discipline; every empirical science is. But it must not fall into the fatal error of confusing its own rationality with the rationality of the world.

To some extent these criticisms correspond to those of C. Wright Mills in *The Sociological Imagination*. Mills wrote before the ideological sea-change of the late 1960s overtook the field. We cannot know what Mills would have done, had he lived through this period. We do know what large numbers of his readers did, especially those who were most impressed by his criticisms; they plunged into an ideological delirium, mostly shaped by Marxist and quasi-Marxist assumptions, which seemed to provide remedies for all ailments of the field. It provided a theoretical orientation that certainly dealt with "big questions", did so in an international frame of reference ("world-systems," no less), was not greatly enthused about quantitative methods, and finally, while considering itself to be thoroughly scientific, also assumed that most everyone else was running around afflicted with "false consciousness."

Unfortunately, the answers to the "big questions" turned out to be wrong and the world refused to behave in the way the theory predicted. It is premature to proclaim the demise of Marxism, let alone that of "marxisant" doctrines that have been quite successfully detached from the total Marxist corpus. The worst consequence of the ideologization of the discipline that took place in the 1960s and 1970s is the persistent belief that objectivity and "value-freeness" are impossible, and that sociologists, understanding this, should expressly operate as advocates.

This stance need not be restricted to the left at all. In the great methodological disputes during the classical period of sociology, especially in Germany, it was thinkers on the right who took this position most forcefully. The antidote to the "false ideal" of objectivity was a "German science" and the most elegant formulation of advocacy science came from no less a personage than the late Dr. Goebbels:"Truth is what serves the German people."

As the left declines in American intellectual life, if it is declining, other ideologies can be observed adopting the same stance. It is a stance that transforms science into propaganda; it marks the end of science wherever it is adopted. Feminists and multiculturalists are the leading representatives of this stance in the American social sciences today, but we may confidently expect others to appear. Some may well be on the right.

In diagnosing the condition of sociology, one should not view it in isolation. Its symptoms tend to be those afflicting the intellectual life in general. Other human sciences are in no better shape. Most economists are captive to their rationalist assumptions, large numbers of political scientists seem to fall, *mutatis mutandis* into the same trap. Anthropologists are probably more ideologized than any other social science discipline, and people in history and the humanities seem to fall for every doctrinal fashion, that comes flying over the Atlantic, usually via Air France, each more obscurantist and intellectually barbaric than its predecessor.

Perhaps it is expecting too much of sociologists to do better. But sociologists have a particular problem no one else (with the possible exception of anthropologists) in the human sciences shares. Sociology is not so much a field as a perspective and if this perspective fails, nothing is left. Thus one can study the economy, or the political system, or the mating habits of the Samoans from perspectives that are quite different, one of which is sociology. The sociological perspective has entered into the cognitive instrumentarium of most of the human sciences with great success. Few historians have not somewhere incorporated a sociological perspective into their work. Unlike most other human scientists, sociologists cannot claim a specific empirical territory as their own. It is mostly their perspective that they have to offer. The ailments described above precisely effect the dissolution of this perspective, thereby making sociology obsolete.

One could argue that such obsolescence is not a great intellectual disaster, since what sociology originally had to offer has been incorporated into the corpus of other fields. But, when one looks at these fields, one can only reach the conclusion that they are badly in need of a good dose of sociology, as the discipline was understood in its classical period, and not just bits and pieces of sociological lore that have been assimilated. In other words, there are good intellectual reasons why one should not applaud the possible demise of the discipline.

But can this fate be averted? I am not at all sure. The pathology now goes very deep indeed. It is possible to suggest some conditions for such a reversal of fortunes. Substantively, the above observations have already outlined the necessary contours: We are talking about a sociology that has returned to the big questions of the classical era, a sociology that is cosmopolitan and methodologically flexible, and is emphatically and militantly anti-ideological. But what of the institutional requirements for such a reversal? Clearly it could not be effected by conferences, manifestos, and other fugitive intellectual endeavors. The revival of the discipline must be based in one or more of the academic programs in which sociologists are trained, probably (if regrettably) in elite universities. And the process has to be in the hands of younger people, those with two or more decades of active professional life ahead of them — because this is what it will take. Is any of this likely? Probably not. But one of the root insights of classical sociology is that human actions can be surprising.

10

Is Sociology of
Gender Stratification Parochial?
The Case of Women and Warfare

Maria Cole

> *Parochialism in sociology is much more than a cultural deficiency; it is the source of crippling failures of perception.* (Berger, this volume)

There have been many attempts to analyze the weaknesses of contemporary sociology (see for example Alexander 1982; Connell 1991; Becker and Rau 1992; Berger 1992). Peter Berger believes that contemporary sociology does not measure up to its past achievements marked by the great works of Durkheim and Weber. He identifies four symptoms which trouble the discipline: parochialism, triviality, rationalism and ideology. As he writes: 'Each one is crippling. Their combination has been deadly' (Berger 1992: 16).

Sociology of gender, like any subdiscipline of sociology, is open to the above criticism. One has to stress, however, that not all the studies in sociology of gender suffer from the problems mentioned by Berger to the same extent. Research on gender stratification, or occupational sex segregation, asks new questions which are no less important than those dealt with by the great sociologists of the past. Unfortunately, the 'big questions' often do not receive the big answers they deserve. The reasons given by Berger — parochialism, triviality, rationalism and ideology — provide much of the answer.

In this article, I focus on the factor of parochialism, which I illustrate in detail with reference to studies on gender stratification. Parochialism or '...the common misconception that one can generalize about the world from one's own little corner' (Berger 1992: 16) is particularly striking in that aspect of gender-stratification research which deals with war and its influence on gender relations. In general, wars have been treated in abstraction and with an intellectual distance which reflects the influence of American geography, history and culture, but grasps neither the historical detail nor the real human experience of war.

According to Berger:

> One can be an excellent physicist without ever having stepped outside one's own society; I know that it is not so for a sociologist... [S]ociology, the discipline par excellence for seeking to understand modernity, must of necessity be comparative... [S]ociologists must look at Japan in order to understand the West, at socialism in order to understand capitalism, at India so as to understand Brazil, and so on ... It should be part and parcel of the training of every sociologist to gain detailed knowledge of at least one society that differs greatly from his own — a feat that, needless to say, involves something many students shy away from: learning of foreign languages (1992: 16-7).

Unfortunately, the problem seems to lie deeper than a lack of knowledge of foreign languages. Information on the status of women which confronts the generalizations one finds in the American sociological literature is available in English (Hoffman 1989, 1993; Lorence-Kot 1992). The journalist and writer Eva Hoffman (1989) provides interesting information comparing the feminine role in Poland with that in the United States. She develops the subject in her second (1993) book on the basis of a few interviews with women in Poland and in Hungary.

In this article, I will look at Poland to demonstrate the limits of the theorizing on warfare and gender in American sociology. I begin by quoting two interviews with Polish women, published by Hoffman (1993). These interviews testify to cultural differences as well as to differences in the degree of gender stratification in Poland and in the United States. The interpretation by the interviewer points out the historical causes of these differences, which stem mainly from the wars which have taken place on Polish territories, in which women, along with men, were involved. The participation of women in warfare on Polish territories goes back at least to the November Uprising of 1831. Bruchnalska (1933) mentions the names of eleven women in combat whose role in the armed conflict she calls 'outstanding.' One of them was Emilia Plater[1] who became a personification of women in combat and a role model for those taking part in military activity in other uprisings and in both world wars. She was commemorated in a poem by one of Poland's greatest poets, Adam Mickiewicz, and in several poems written in German and French (Straszewicz 1835). In short, the participation of women in warfare in Poland since the 1830s (Straszewicz 1833-34; Dobaczewska 1922; Caban 1984; Bielecki 1995) provides many facts that are at odds with generalizations by American sociologists of gender, and indeed prove that these generalizations are false.

Journalism and History vs. Sociological Theory: Are General Laws on Gender Stratification Possible?

Hoffman (1993) reports an encounter with Helena Łuczywo, the co-editor (with Adam Michnik) of *Gazeta Wyborcza* — one of the most widely read newspapers in Eastern Europe — with a circulation of more than half a million. She was asked whether she felt that there are difficulties in being a woman in a position of such power and responsibility. Her answer was: 'No, that's not any kind of problem.' Łuczywo continued:

> 'That's why I couldn't understand American feminists when I spent a year in the US. But you see, in Poland it's different for women. On one hand, they're in a worse situation ... but on the other hand, they're better off.' They're better off, she thinks, because of the Polish tradition, which includes a long lineage of female activism and authority. Women took part in the many uprisings and conspiracies when Poland was an endangered nation; they participated in the resistance and later in the underground. It's possible that the commonality that came from fighting for the same fragile cause was a stronger force than the polarizing stereotypes of gender; it accounts in part for the formidable examples of feminine strength I've encountered in Helena and others.
> (Hoffman 1993: 48-9)

In Poland women have been 'better off' because their lives have not been limited to the private, but have extended into the public sphere. In the past the struggles for independence, in which women took part with men, created part of the public sphere; or more precisely, led to the blurring of the two spheres — private and public (Żarnowska 1994).

Hoffman (1993) reports another conversation with Polish women — members of feminist organizations who were protesting against a bill to outlaw abortion in front of the Sejm (Parliament). And she concludes:

> Indeed, in public life and in private, I keep encountering women whose spark and strength and personal authority seem quite formidable. Altogether, in the elusive realm of cultural values, there seems to be less of a division between 'male' and 'female' virtues here — and female valor, intelligence, and strength of personality are as highly prized as the male versions. Perhaps that, too, harks back to the political tradition, and all *the uprisings, rebellions, and insurrections in which women strove side by side with men as their comrades-in-arms.*
> (Hoffman 1993: 80-81, emphasis mine)

Hoffman also writes: 'Women strove side by side with men as their comrades-in-arms,' which indicates not only that women participated in warfare but also that there is, to some extent, equality between the sexes in Poland. These remarks by a journalist are consistent with those by a historian who writes about the 'partnership' between the sexes in the struggles for the independence of Poland. According to his account, 'Women had been admitted with equal rights to men' to the clandestine Polish army since its beginning in 1909 (Nalęcz 1994: 76). The ideas expressed by this historian are at variance, indeed, with generalizations by sociologists of gender such as the following: 'Women ... are subordinate everywhere to men in their own social group' (Lipman-Blumen 1984: 48).

In the quotations from Eva Hoffman, the similarity of characteristics considered desirable for both men and women, or the lack of a clearly defined ideal of femininity, is linked to the common struggles of men and women in wars and insurrections. A similar argument is presented by the historian Anna Żarnowska (1994), in her article on the public and private spheres in Poland at the end of the nineteenth and the beginning of the twentieth centuries. The facts from Polish history and their interpretations by journalists and historians are, however, at odds with generalizations by sociologists of gender.

Some of the sociological literature offers generalizations on the total exclusion of women from warfare (Dunn, Almquist, and Chafetz 1993). The exclusion of women from, and the engagament of men in wars are linked to the increase in gender stratification. As Dunn *et al.* write:

> In all types of societies, *women tend to be excluded from* (or seen as not fit for) work requiring (geographic) mobility. Examples include business roles that require traveling, large-animal hunting forays, claiming new land in horticultural or agrarian societies, and *warfare in all types of societies*. Each of these activities gives men access to other important resources and rewards ... men who successfully claim land can then acquire rights to control its use which exclude women. Military service may not always lead directly to property ownership as it frequently did in feudal society, but military veterans can claim a variety of services, benefits, and exemptions not open to non-veterans.
> (1993: 79, emphasis mine)

In the above quotation, different epochs (those characterized by claiming land and acquiring rights to control it, and those distinguished by business traveling), different types of societies (horticultural or agrarian societies and modern society), and different activities are all mixed together and compared with respect to male profit and the exclusion of women. A general theory of this kind violates historical and sociological perspective, because it looks for similarities in situations laden with differences and, basically, ignores concrete people, real-life situations, and historical variations in social conditions. Such a one-sided perception of history is influenced by ideological bias — one of the ills of contemporary sociology, as pointed out by Berger (1992).

At the same time, Dunn *et al.* (1993) provide an excellent example of generalizing 'about the world from one's own little corner.' The fact that 'the little corner' has been a geographically isolated superpower does not improve the situation. Dunn *et al.* (1993) talk about wars as if they were fought by winners only, and as if most wars took place thousands of miles away from the people who are not lucky enough to participate in them and to cash in on benefits later, as victors and veterans.

It is true that participation in wars might have given some males an access to 'resources and rewards' (the US, along with France, were the first states to provide welfare benefits to veterans and their families [Mann 1993: 501; Orloff 1988]). Wars, however, also lead to death, injury, misery, and general poverty. Military service has often led to property losses. For example, the Russians confiscated estates belonging to the participants of national uprisings in Poland and in Lithuania during the nineteenth century (Davis 1982;

Bruchnalska 1933). These confiscations caused the financial ruin of many families and contributed to the decline of a whole social class: the nobility. The resulting decrease in the power of men made their social position closer to that of women, and contributed to a decrease in gender stratification (Cole 1997).

Contrary to the generalization by Dunn *et al.* (1993) which holds that women are excluded from work requiring geographical mobility, women served as couriers and liaison-personnel during the January Uprising of 1863. Women couriers carried the commands and decrees of the military commanders to the guerrilla units, and often warned the leaders of the latter about the moves of the Russian army and coming danger (Bruchnalska 1933: 205). Some female couriers served in the foreign service, providing links between the national Government and the Polish emigration in Western Europe; most of them served, however, as domestic couriers. The historian Caban (1994: 68-9) mentions the names of 10 women couriers but also writes about hundreds of those whose names remain unknown.

Neither the Polish uprisings of the nineteenth century nor the world wars correspond, then, to the picture of war that emerges from the theorizing on gender and war by Dunn *et al.* (1993). Women had not been excluded from warfare and the participation of men did not give them access to 'important resources and rewards.' Both world wars led to enormous destruction on Polish territory. The destruction caused by World War I was so great that the national income of Poland in 1936 was still lower than that in 1914.

Both world wars were mass wars, which means that whole populations were involved, in one way or another, in the war which took place on their territories. As Mann (1993: 504) writes: 'Indeed, in Europe in the two world wars, mass-mobilization war actually became total war, involving all citizens.' One may find a similar opinion in the recent article by Higonnet (1995: 87) which explicitly deals with gender and warfare: 'The argument about men's "inclusion" in war and women's "exclusion" tacitly relies on and reproduces the schematic view of the battlefront as a place where women and other civilians are not ... This tidy division of the landscape into battlefront and home front serves military strategy. It does not serve history very well, although trench warfare may have reinforced the illusion that such a division could be made.'

While Higonnet (1995) writes mainly about World War I, the argument about the exclusion of women from warfare is even less justified with relation to World War II. Russian women were soldiers in World War II (Cottam 1980; Alexievich 1995); so were some Polish women (Drzewiecka 1965; Rudomin 1977; Praga 1986; Sobczak 1986). In occupied Poland hardly anybody was excluded: both men and women were involved in the struggles with the Nazis; and both men and women, if they survived, became veterans — virtually all of them with big losses and relatively small 'benefits and exemptions.'

In Poland one does not have to look for historical sources or monographs about World War II in order to realize that generalizations about the exclusion of women from warfare are false. Today documentation of this fact may be found on the streets of Warsaw, as well as in newspapers, in the form of short obituaries of women who are dying in their seventies and eighties. The information that they have been *soldiers* in the Warsaw Insurrection of 1944 is often included in a few sentences which describe their lives. In just one newspaper, Życie Warszawy, from December 1, 1995 to January 20, 1996 — I found 23 short obituaries in which women were characterised as soldiers, combatants, members of the resistance, and nursing personnel. One — with the rank of officer — had received the highest military honors; all the others had many awards and medals; four had been imprisoned by the Nazis in concentration camps.

Unlike Dunn *et al.* (1993), Chafetz (1990) admits that women participated in wars. She attempts to minimize the importance of that involvement, however, as she writes (1990, p. 120; emphasis mine): 'Although women have often been involved in wars, revolutions, and other violent political contests in which their nation, political party, or subcultural group (racial, religious, ethnic) was engaged, by and large they have *never* constituted more than a handful of the actual fighters.'

Although it is not clear what 'a handful of actual fighters' means, whether these are individual women, or tens, dozens, hundreds or thousands of them, I contend that the importance of this involvement may go far beyond numbers. It may influence gender culture in a way presented by Hoffman (1993) and it may serve to deflate gender stratification. The reasoning behind Chafetz's conclusion about the minor importance of women's involvement in warfare involves some elements of logic but very little understanding. She writes: 'During times of conflict, those roles most central to winning the conflict become most highly valued, and by extension the people who play those roles likewise experience enhanced evaluation.' She goes further: 'In situations of armed or violent conflict, men do almost all of the fighting; at most, women serve as support personnel in a variety of ways' (Chafetz 1990: 120); the simple conclusion is that these are men who experience 'enhanced evaluation,' and that wars generally lead to an increase in gender stratification.

However, when one moves away from the abstract war dealt with by Chafetz towards an actual war, it is not so easy to point out who experiences enhanced evaluation. As an author of an article on the participation of Polish women in World War II writes:

> Women had been everywhere: they fought the battle for survival behind the wires of the Nazi concentration camps ... [T]hey fought with arms in their hand both in the regular military forces in the East and in the West of Europe and in guerrilla units in the country. Many dangerous tasks they performed, although far away from the noise of the battle field, required more will power than a bravado attack with a rifle and grenade in the hand (Sobczak 1986: 165).[2]

Sometimes, it may not be easy to demonstrate whose roles are central to winning the conflict; and the division between the 'actual fighters' and 'support personnel' is not clear. Are actual fighters classified as only those shooting at the enemy, or would they include a sanitary instructor of the First Infantry Regiment, Irena Adamaszek, who carried 28 heavy injured soldiers from the battle field before she got injured herself? (Praga 1986: 181). Or another army nurse who crawled in trenches among the flying bullets, trying to help a seriously injured Nazi officer? She put bandages on his injured side and, while reaching for more bandages, she saw the officer trying to draw a pistol from his pocket (Drzewiecka 1965: 61-2). This nurse wanted to help the enemy, so she was not 'an actual fighter,' although the Nazi officer seemed to define her in these terms. He would have killed her as he had been killing other soldiers in the battle field minutes before, had he had enough strength. And what about the women who were couriers or who distributed clandestine literarure in occupied Poland? The first — as, for example, the champion skier Helena Marusarzówna — when caught by the Nazis, were sentenced to death. The others were

under constant threat of being caught during the street searches —
of being interrogated, tortured and, eventually, murdered by the
Nazis. Many of them carried poison since 'they preferred death to
treason' (Sobczak 1986: 143, 153). Were these women 'actual
fighters' or 'support personnel'?

The next theme in sociological literature dealing with gender and
war concerns gender ideology, and is reflected in the following
universal law : 'The more a society engages in warfare, the greater
its ideological/religious support for sex inequality will tend to be'
(Chafetz 1984: 41). To support this statement Chafetz mentions
'the great empire-building societies (e.g., classical Rome, Great
Britain in the nineteenth century, and China),' Nazi Germany,
'Islam,' feudal Japan, Cheyenne and Comanche and 119 other
'technologically simple' societies studied by Sanday (1981). The
list might look impressive but it is not very convincing and does not
constitute any 'proof' of the generalization.

First, the formulation 'the more ... the greater' implies some way
of assessing both the extent of a society's involvement in warfare
and that of its support for gender inequality. Chafetz does not,
however, specify the empirical meaning of either aspect of the
above generalization. We do not know, then, how the extent of a
society's involvement in warfare is understood and how it can be
measured. Does Chafetz refer to the number of years a war lasts, to
the number of battles fought, to the number of the dead on either
side, or to the very fact of initiating a war as opposed to being
attacked? The reference to 'empire-building societies' suggests that
instigating a war, rather than being attacked and occupied by a
foreign army, means being more involved in warfare. It is not clear,
however, and we do not know whether Nazi Germany, for example,
should be considered to have been more engaged in World War II
than was the Soviet Union. If the answer is positive, we do not know
whether the difference is large enough to explain the ideology of
'kitchen, children and church' for women in the first case and the
ideology of gender equality in the second. Was the Soviet Union an
empire-building society and, if the answer is positive, was it an
exception to the universal law quoted above? If yes, why is this
exception not mentioned? Is warfare always, or only sometimes
connected to an increase in the religious/ideological support for
gender inequality? If only sometimes, can we arrive at a universal
law to deal with this relationship?

And what about the meaning of 'society'? This concept, although not clear (Tilly 1984; Mann 1986), usually includes both men and women. If both men and women are involved in wars, which was the case in continental Europe during both world wars, why would the extent of their involvement lead to an increase in an ideological/religious support for gender inequality? Does Chafetz reduce the meaning of 'society' to men only? Presumably, women are included but somehow in different terms than men are. The most plausible guess is that they belong to different spheres. This, however, should be an empirical question, rather than an assumption. If it is assumed, it reflects the extension of knowledge of a society or societies that share a similar historical experience and gender culture, to the rest of the world — parochialism according to the definition of Peter Berger.

Chafetz is more cautious in her recent book where she reformulates the universal law, discussed above, in the following way: 'The more intense and prolonged a political struggle or war, the greater the likelihood that traditional gender social definitions will be strengthened' (Chafetz 1990: 140). This statement — devoid of empirical content — is as devoid of meaning as her earlier one. It is neither theoretical nor empirical, it is merely ideological. Despite the disciplinary jargon, it says no more than a proverb, 'The wind is always blowing into the eyes of the poor.' In sociological literature on gender stratification, the winds of war tend to blow in the eyes of the women, like all other winds.

Contrary to sociological theory (Chafetz 1990), in the Polish case traditional gender social definitions have been weakened, rather than strengthened during prolonged military conflict. Many authors indicate that the participation of women in the military struggles along with men, as well as the help and moral support given in these struggles, caused 'male' virtues — such as strength, persistance, stubbornness, courage, leadership, and insensitivity to the cruelties of war — to be seen as acceptable and even desirable for women (Boberska 1893; Dobaczewska 1922; Bia_okur 1928; Hoffman 1993).

Chafetz needs about four pages to solve the problem of wars and gender stratification. She does not have to analyze any real war, because abstract wars have been assumed to fulfil the purpose she has assigned to them: to elevate men at the expense of women. Chafetz's generalizations about gender and warfare reflect 'the militarized version of the doctrine of separate spheres' (Higonnet 1995, p. 88). As Higonnet writes (1995: 88-9): 'One reason for the perpetuation of the separate spheres doctrine in analyses of World War I literature, I would suggest, has been the reliance on evidence from the English-speaking world ... If we look at a more diverse and transnational population of women, especially those lacking material ease, which would permit flight into exile, we frequently find a clear-cut rejection of a binary geography of war.' In much of continental Europe, in short, the distinction between battlefront and home front had been blurred during both world wars.

Dunn *et al.* (1993) believe that macrostructural theories of gender stratification should be 'panhistorical' and 'universally applicable.' The American 'little corner' makes it difficult, however, to understand war in a way which is available to sociologists of European background. Attempts at developing theories of this kind are characterized by parochialism or, to use Archer's expression (1989), they often result in 'creeping ethnocentrism.'

A statement by Wippler and Lindenberg (1987) may serve as a summary of the above discussion of the general laws referring to gender and warfare, formulated within macrostructural theories of gender stratification:

> First the search for general *sociological* laws that are meant to hold independent of institutional and under structural changes is fruitless (a similar point is made by Boudon 1984). It only leads to ill-conceived problem of levels. Second, background knowledge (whatever its source) is of crucial importance for solving the bridge problem and the problem of transformation in nontrivial cases. Generally, descriptive studies are thus much more relevant for sociology as an explanatory enterprise than current journals and university curricula would have us believe.
> (1987: 149-50, emphasis in original)

More sociological research is necessary to provide background knowledge which supplements the above discussion. I provide an overview of the participation of women in the uprisings and wars on Polish territories from the 1830s until World War II in another article (identifying reference).

Conclusion

Sociological literature on gender stratification includes several generalizations about gender and warfare but there are serious doubts about their accuracy. First, the participation of women in warfare is sometimes denied altogether. Second, if this participation is admitted, its social meaning is minimized or denied. Third, the situation of war is linked to an increase in actual gender inequality. Fourth, the situation of war is linked to an increase in ideological support for gender inequality.

These generalizations have been analyzed above as examples of parochialism in the literature on gender stratification. Both world wars were too remote from the American 'little corner,' for American sociologists to recognize that a distinction between the battlefront and the home front did not hold in continental Europe. Moreover, since the wars were mainly experienced through the participation of male soldiers, sociologists fail to recognize that more than a handful of women served as regular soldiers, and that the concept of soldier was much extended in the East European context.

The sociological account of gender and warfare does not go much beyond the studies of 'primitive' societies on the one hand, and the stereotypical picture of the 'kuche, kinder, kirche' in Nazi Germany, on the other. If sociologists do not probe much beyond the stereotypes in their scholarly work, it may mean that they do not want to probe more or they do not need to probe more. The first situation reflects the ideological bias in their work — choosing those examples which confirm the picture of war as an exclusively male domain, leading to an increase in the power of men, and a corresponding decrease in the power of women, and, therefore, to an increase in gender stratification.

The second situation reflects politics — a problem in sociology which has not been mentioned by Berger (1992). Political power of a faction within sociology seems to underlie both supply and demand for sociological products. The political situation in the US in the 1970s gave a green light for gender studies including the 'development of theories at a pace faster than the rate at which empirical data became available' (Blumberg 1984). These theories appear too often to be generalizations based on an insufficient empirical base, developed under a heavy burden of positivistic tradition without the positivistic emphasis on the 'facts. 'The technocratic fetishism,' to use an expression by Alexander (1982), is carried on by the language of variables in the analysis of macrostructures (Folbre 1993) and by the faith that numbers are the only measure of the importance of social processes. The importance attached to numbers often leads to trivial answers given to questions that, in themselves, are not trivial.

'A handful of the actual fighters' or perhaps even one fighter, such as Emilia Plater in 1830, may be of enormous social and cultural significance. Emilia Plater in Poland, like Jeanne d'Arc in France, has been a symbol of women in combat — an embodiment of heroism and a role model for future generations of women. Small numbers of women in combat may have great symbolic meaning (Drzewiecka 1965). Women in warfare may influence gender ideology and undercut the ideological basis of gender stratification.

In Poland, the various forms of participation of women in warfare seem to contribute to an increase, not a decrease (as sociologists of gender maintain) in the status of women vis a vis men. It also seemed to contribute to a decrease, not an increase, in ideological support for gender inequality. In other cases warfare might have influenced gender relations differently. As Mann (1993: 152) pointed out: 'Mass-mobilization warfare has had variable effects on domestic power structure.'

A general theory of gender stratification should, perhaps, be less general. It should abandon the search for false similarities with only one aim: to show the advantage of men and the disadvantage of women. The formulating of universal laws about the increase or decrease in women's relative status in a situation of war or crisis seems to be futile. Rather, the increase, or decrease, in the status of women in the situation of war should be examined in a historical context. In other words, as pointed out by Tilly (1984), careful historical studies should serve as a basis for sound generalizations in sociology.

Notes

1. The name of Emilia Plater appears in *Grand Dictionnaire Universel* (Larousse 1878, p.1149), where she is described as a Polish heroine. The note includes a description of her military activities as well as some information on her childhood. As a young girl she was interested in Polish history, and desired to follow the example of the Polish heroines of the past. Despite her great femininity, horse-riding and target-firing were among her favorite activities.

2. All translations from the Polish unless otherwise stated are the author's own.

References

Alexander, J. C. 1982. *Theoretical Logic in Sociology. Positivism, Presuppositions, and Current Controversies*, vol. I. Berkeley: University of California Press.

Alexievich, S. 1995. 'I am loath to recall: Russian women soldiers in World War II.' *Women's Studies Quarterly*, No 3 and 4: 78-84.

Archer, M. S. 1989. 'Cross-national research and the analysis of educational systems.' In M.L. Kohn (ed.), *Cross-National Research in Sociology*: 242-262. Newbury Park: Sage.

Becker, H. S. and W. C. Rau. 1992. 'Sociology in the 1990s.' *Society*, November: 70-74.

Berger, P. 1992. 'Sociology: a disinvitation?'. *Society*, November: 10-18.

Bialokur, F. 1928. *Praca Samarytańska i Spoleczna Kobiet Polskich w Powstaniu Styczniowym 1863-1864 Roku* (Samarytanian and Social Work of Polish Women in the January Insurrection of 1863-1864). Warsaw: The Polish Red Cross Publishers.

Bielecki, R. 1995. *Źolnierze Powstania Warszawskiego* (The Soldiers of the Warsaw Insurrection). Warsaw: Directory of the State Archives.

Blumberg, R. L. 1984 'A general theory of gender stratification.' In R. Collins (ed.), *Sociological Theory, 1984*: 23-101. San Francisco: Jossey-Bass.

Boberska, F. 1893. *O Polkach Które się Szczególnie Zasluzyly Ojczyźnie w Powstaniu Listopadowym* (On Polish Women who Served the Fatherland Exceptionally Well in the November Insurrection). Lvov: Piller and Ska.

Bruchnalska, M. 1933. *Ciche Bochaterki. Udzial Kobiet w Powstaniu Styczniowym* (The Silent Heroines. The Participation of Women in the January Uprising). Miejsce Piastowe: The Publishing House of the Association of St. Michael Archangel.

Caban, W. 1994. 'Kobiety i powstanie styczniowe,' (Women and the January Insurrection). In A. Żarnowska and A. Szwarc (eds), *Kobieta I Świat Polityki* (Women and the World of Politics): 59-72. Warsaw: Historical Institute of the University of Warsaw.

Chafetz, J. S. 1984. *Sex and Advantage. A Comparative, Macro-Structural Theory of Sex Stratification*. NJ: Rowmanand Allanheld.

―――. 1990. *Gender Equity: An Integrated Theory of Stability and Change*. Newbury Park, CA: Sage.

Cole, M. 1997. 'Gender and power: sex segregation in American and Polish higher education as a case study.' *Sociological Forum* 12, 2: 205-232.

Connell, R.W. 1991. 'A thumbnail dipped in tar. Or: can we write sociology from the fringe of the world?' *Meanjin* 50, 1: 37-47.

Cottam, J. 1980. 'Soviet women in combat in World War 2: The ground forces and the navy.' *International Journal of Women Studies* 3.

Davis, N. 1982. *God's Playground. A History of Poland. 1795 to the Present*, vol. II. New York: Columbia University Press.

Dobaczewska, W. 1922. *Rycerki Polskie* (Polish Women ― Knights). Warsaw: Library of Selected Works.

Drzewiecka, S. 1965. *Szłyśmy znad Oki* (We Had Gone From the Oka). Warsaw: Ministry of National Defense Publishers.

Dunn, D., E. M. Almquist and J. S. Chafetz. 1993. 'Macrostructural perspectives on gender inequality.' In Paula England (ed.), *Theory on Gender/Feminism on Theory*: 69-90. New York: Aldine De Gruyter.

Folbre, N. 1993. 'Micro, macro, choice, and structure.' In P. England (ed.), *Theory of Gender/Feminism on Theory*: 323-31. New York: Aldine & Gruyter.

Higonnet, M. R. 1995. 'Another record: a different war.' *Women's Studies Quarterly* 3 and 4: 85-96

Hoffman, E. 1989. *Lost in Translation. A Life in a New Language*. New York: E. P. Dutton.

―――. 1993. *Exit into History. A Journey through the New Eastern Europe*. New York: Viking Penguin.

Larousse, P. 1878. *Grand Dictionaire Universel*, vol. 12.2. Paris: Administration du Grand Dictionaire Universel.

Lipman-Blumen, J. 1984. *Gender Roles and Power*. Englewood Cliffs, NJ: Prentice-Hall.

Lorence-Kot, B. 1992. 'Konspiracja: Probing the topography of women's underground activities. The Kingdom of Poland in the second half of the nineteenth century.' In R. Jaworski and B. Pietrow-Ennker (eds.), *Women in Polish Society*: 31-51. Bouldner CO: East European Monographs, no 344.

Mann, M. 1986. *The Sources of Social Power: A history of power from the beginning to A.D. 1760*, vol.I. Cambridge: Cambridge University Press.

———— .1993. *The Sources of Social Power: The rise of classes and nation states*, 1760-1914, vol. II. Cambridge: Cambridge University Press.

Nalęcz, T. 1994. 'Kobiety w walce o niepodległość w czasie pierwszej wojny światowej' (Women in the struggle for independence during World War I). In A. Îarnowska and A. Szwarc (eds), *Kobieta I Świat Polityki* (Women and the World of Politics): 73-9. Warsaw: Historical Institute of the University of Warsaw.

Orloff, A. 1988. 'The Political Origins of America's Belated Welfare State.' In M. Weir, A.S. Orloff, and T. Skocpol (eds.), *The Politics of Social Policy in the United States*. Princeton, N.J.: Princeton University Press.

Praga, J. 1986. 'Kobiety w regularnych jednostkach Wojska Polskiego na frontach II Wojny Światowej.' (Women in the Regular Units of the Polish Military at the Fronts of World War II). In *Kobiety Polskie* (Polish Women) collected work: 166-183. Warsaw: Książka I Wiedza.

Rudomin, F. 1977. *Z 'Drucikami' od Oki do Warszawy* (With the "Wires" from the Oka to Warsaw). Warsaw: Ministry of National Defense Publishers.

Sanday, P. R. 1981. *Female Power and Male Dominance*. Cambridge: Cambridge University Press.

Sobczak, K. 1986. 'Kobiety polskie w drugiej wojnie światowej' (Polish Women in World War II). In *Kobiety Polskie* (Polish Women) collected work: 136-165. Warsaw: Książka I Wiedza.

Straszewicz, G. 1833-34. *I Polacchi Della Rivoluzione Del 29 Novembre 1830*. Vol. I, II. Capolago: Tipografia E Libreria Elvetica.

————. 1835. *Emilie Plater; Sa Vie et Sa Mort*. Paris: Bourgogne et Martine.

Tilly, CH. 1984. *Big Structures, Large Processes, Huge Comparisons*. New York: Russell Sage Foundation.

Wippler, R. and S. Lindberg. 1987. 'Collective phenomena and rational choice.' In J.C. Alexander, B. Giesen, R. Munch, and N.J. Smelser (eds.), *The Micro-Macro Link*: 135-152. Berkeley: University of California Press.

Żarnowska, A. 1994. 'Prywatna sfera życia rodzinnego I
zewnętrzny świat z ycia publicznego — bariery i przenikanie
(przełom XIX i XX wieku)' (The private sphere of the family life and the external world of public life — barriers and penetration (the turn of the centuries). In A. Żarnowska and A. Szwarc (eds.), *Kobieta I Świat Polityki* (Women and the World of Politics): 5-28. Warsaw: Historical Institute of the University of Warsaw.

Życie Warszawy, December 1, 1995 - January 20, 1996.

11

Blame Analysis: Accounting for the Behavior of Protected Groups

Richard B. Felson

A group that is not doing as well as other groups is sometimes blamed for its predicament. Those who are prejudiced against the group, and those who seek to legitimate the inequality, attribute the problem to negative characteristics of the group rather than to external factors (Caplan and Nelson, 1973). In common parlance they "blame the victim" (Ryan, 1971). Historically, social scientists have sometimes participated in this ideological enterprise. However, at the present time, sociologists and others who study "oppressed groups" tend to be sympathetic to them. In many cases, they openly reject explanations of the behavior of these groups that might blame them.

In this paper I examine how the sympathies of sociologists and other social scientists for "protected groups" affect the way they interpret group differences in behavior.[1] The method they use to evaluate causal theories will be referred to as "blame analysis" in order to distinguish it from causal analysis. This method treats cause and blame as equivalent and evaluates theories according to the level of blame they attribute to protected groups. The use of social science to legitimate inequalities will only be mentioned in passing, since it has already been described (e.g., Ryan, 1971; Caplan and Nelson, 1973).

I begin by discussing the protective role of accounts in social interaction among individuals and then apply this reasoning to groups. I then discuss the role of blame analysis in social science, and its relationship to causal analysis and the issue of value-neutrality. Finally, I give illustrations of blame analysis from the literature on group differences in economic outcomes, academic and athletic performance, and crime and deviance.

Accounts and External Causality

Accounting for Individual Predicaments

When people believe that their performances may be perceived as inappropriate or substandard, they find themselves in a predicament (Schlenker, 1980). Worried that the audience may blame them for their failings, they usually provide an account. Accounts are the explanations people give when they think they have done something that might elicit disapproval from others (Scott and Lyman, 1968). People use them to avoid blame for their behavior and thus protect their identity or public image. While accounts are usually considered a form of impression management for the benefit of an external audience, they may also be used to protect self-esteem.

In spite of the connotation of these terms this literature does not assume that accounts are false. Rather, the focus is on the role that accounts play in social interaction, not on their validity. For example, someone who is delayed by traffic is careful to let the audience know that this was the reason that he or she is late. The issue is not whether this was the real cause of the tardiness, but rather the role of this account in excusing actions that could elicit disapproval and blame.

When people give accounts their strategy is to attribute what they have done to external rather than internal causes.[2] This is because people are not likely to be held responsible for actions that are externally caused (Heider, 1958). The issue of blame is more complex once causality is assigned to the person. From a rational perspective, cause is a necessary but not sufficient condition for blame to be assigned. To deserve blame, a person must also have either intended to do wrong, or to have acted carelessly (Ferguson and Rule, 1983). However, people often fail to distinguish between cause and blame. Thus, Heider (1958) suggests that people are sometimes blamed for events they cause even when carelessness and intentionality are not involved. In these instances, the assignment of cause is sufficient for the assignment of blame.[3] While the confusion of cause and blame is common among young children (Piaget, 1932), it also occurs among adults. Therefore, the safest way to avoid blame when giving an account is to deny any internal causality.

Heider's (1958) model of causal attribution implies that people perceive a fixed quantity of causal force. Thus, for a given outcome, the greater the level of external causality the lower the level of internal causality. Since attributions of blame are largely based on causality, this implies an important characteristic of blame (and credit) that, to my knowledge, has not received attention: blame tends to be treated as a fixed quantity. People can share blame for what happens, but the more blame assigned to one person the less assigned to another. In other words, there tends to be a zero-sum treatment of blame, where a fixed amount of blame is parceled out to various parties. For example, if we say that a crime victim has made a mistake (e.g., "he shouldn't have jogged in that park at night"), it implies that we are assigning less blame to the offender. Therefore, those who wish to assign a high level of blame to the offender—perhaps because they feel aggrieved— will prefer to deny any sort of blame for the victim.

In sum, mistakes, misbehavior, and failure are common in social life, and people feel it necessary to explain them. The accounts they give are attempts to attribute the cause of their predicament to external factors, and thereby avoid blame. The tendency to confuse cause and blame, and to treat them as a fixed quantity to be parcelled out, leads them to deny any role for internal causes in explaining their misbehavior. Because people are so concerned about protecting their identities, they are careful to provide accounts whenever they think negative identities might otherwise result.

Accounting for Group Differences

The literature on accounts focuses on individuals. The possibility that accounts can also be given to explain the performance of groups or social categories has, to my knowledge, never been examined. If people identify with a group, and if they believe others think the performance of that group is substandard, their situation can also be described as a predicament. They feel obliged to account for the performance, to attribute it to external factors rather than internal factors, in order to avoid blame for the group.

There are three reasons why those who identify with groups are so concerned with the avoidance of any blame or causal agency for their predicament. First, there is likely to be concern that negative identities will be attributed to the group. Using language more common in the discussion of groups, there is concern about prejudice. As is the case with individuals, a group that anticipates a negative reaction from an audience is particularly likely to give accounts. Second, these accounts often have implications for policy issues. The assignment of causality to characteristics of the group may lead to efforts to change the group rather than the larger society (Ryan, 1971). Further, demands for remedial action, such as affirmative action, are less likely to be honored. Finally, group members often feel they have a grievance against their "oppressors". Therefore, they wish to assign as high a level of blame to them as possible. Since blame is often treated as a fixed quantity to be parceled out, they wish to avoid any blame for their predicament because it might reduce the blame attributed to the oppressor.

Not all group members attempt to avoid blame for the group. However, it is likely that those who assign some blame to their own group tend to hide these opinions, particularly from outsiders. Following Goffman (1959), one might describe it as a type of team performance. Further, as indicated above, one does not have to be a member of the group to attempt to avoid group blame. Outsiders who are sympathetic with the group may be just as likely to provide accounts that minimize blame. Political beliefs, prejudice, and exposure to social science may all affect one's tendency to blame one group or another.

Members of groups that are doing well may also give accounts, if others accuse them of being responsible for inequalities. This moral challenge places members of the more successful group in a predicament, and they may feel a need to give accounts that relieve them of blame, and legitimate their position. For example, whites may have developed racial theories about the ability of blacks to justify slavery, colonialism, and other forms of exploitation and discrimination (e.g., Wilhelm, 1980).

Blame Analysis

Blame Analysis Versus Causal Analysis

In causal analysis, a theory is converted into a system of variables, and causal relationships among the variables are examined. Most social scientists assume that external (exogenous) social variables are the original source of human behavior in their causal models. However, causal analysis also emphasizes the examination of mediating variables in order to reveal the exact causal process through which these external variables affect behavior. Decisions on causal models are supposed to be based on such criteria as empirical evidence and parsimony, but never on the group identity implied by the model. In other words, attributions of blame are not viewed as a legitimate scientific concern.

Causal analysis of group differences presents a problem if the analyst is attempting to protect the identities of certain groups. The problem arises because cause is confused with blame. Since one is attempting to avoid blame for the protected group, only causal variables external to the group can be considered. This results in "blame analysis" rather than causal analysis. In blame analysis, a theory or explanation is evaluated according to the identity or image it projects for certain groups. Since there is a desire among many sociologists to protect groups who are identified as victims, there is a tendency for theories to be rejected unless they absolve the protected group of any blame. A theory must be avoided if it leads to "the unrealistic praise

of 'successful groups' and the condemnation of the less successful..."
(Tomaskovic-Devey and Tomaskovic-Devey (1988, p. 653).

Of course blame analysis can also be used by those who wish to blame
groups not doing as well. When blame analysis is used to attack these
groups, there is likely to be a focus on proximate causes of the groups'
behavior and a failure to recognize that these proximate variables mediate
the effect of more distal factors, such as social structure. Those who are
engaged in blame analysis in protection of these groups do the opposite.
They focus on distal causes and avoid any discussion of proximate causes.
The greater the distance between the explanatory variable and the behavior
of the victim, the better. The result is an avoidance of variables that mediate
the relationship between external factors and the behavior of the protected
groups since these are likely to be internal factors.[4] For example, Ryan
(1971) attacks the ideology of the new type of victim-blamer who, unlike
the old-fashioned conservative, recognizes environmental causation. For
these victim-blamers "... the stigma, the defect, the fatal difference — though
derived in the past from environmental forces — is still located within the
victim, inside his skin (p. 7)." As I will discuss below, Ryan prefers to think
that discrimination and the larger social structure are only direct causes of
group differences, and does not wish to examine characteristics of the protected group's culture or community as mediating variables.

The Issue of Value Neutrality

It is now generally recognized that complete value neutrality is impossible in social science. Political values can affect the choice of topics to
study, the formulation of theories, and policy recommendations, although
there is some dispute over whether they must. Dahrendorf (1968) argues
that these effects are not troublesome as long as theories refer to statements
that can be tested by observation because it is possible to be unbiased in the
evaluation of empirical evidence. Thus, it is perfectly acceptable that the
political values of researchers affect whether they choose to focus on internal or external explanations for group differences. It is therefore of no great
import if the present author's political values (which happen to be liberal)
affect the writing of this piece. On the other hand, to evaluate theories
based on the extent to which they conform to political values is both
unacceptable and avoidable (see Lieberson, 1989).

The issue of value neutrality creates a dilemma in blame analysis. On
the one hand, researchers lose credibility if they admit that their ideology is
influencing their presentation of evidence. This may be particularly costly
if they want to influence policy makers. On the other hand, the claim that

values have pervasive effects on social science is critical to blame analysis. Ideological bias is not denied, but attributed to everyone. Since we are all expressing our values— we are all blame analysts —the only choice is between blaming the victim and blaming the oppressor. Those who are blaming the oppressors are only defending against the victim blamers. This thinking has led to what Horowitz (1987) calls a "celebration of bias". Since values inevitably affect social science, why not give them full rein? At least those who blame the oppressor admit their bias, whereas those who wish to legitimate inequality hide behind the facade of scientific objectivity (Gouldner, 1962).

Individual Motives vs. Social Control

The use of blame analysis by those attempting to legitimate the status quo is never admitted, and so it is difficult to detect. For example, no one admits favoring a theory because it blames blacks or women or because it protects the wealthy. On the other hand, sympathy for protected groups is normative in sociology, and many sociologists openly acknowledge that they are rejecting certain theories because they blame the victim (e.g.,Ryan 1971; Pagelow, 1984; Dobash and Dobash, 1984; Eitzen, 1989). As a result, blame analysis on behalf of protected groups is often easy to document.

However, the use of blame analysis in sociology is not necessarily based on the motivation of authors. It can also reflect censorship and other forms of social control. Nonconformists may face difficulties getting tenure or promotion, or they become the subject of rumor. However, social control operates primarily through the review process. Since the scholars in politically sensitive areas are often sympathetic to blame analysis, and since reviewers are usually chosen from people working in those areas, studies that assign any causal role to protected groups are likely to get negative reviews. Those who do work in these areas understand that they had better take into account issues of blame if they want to see their work in print. Authors must contend with the "double standard" — where results are evaluated more critically if they are not "politically correct" — in order to get their work published (Lieberson, 1989). In sum, conformity to the rules of blame analysis, then, does not depend on internalization.

The use of blame analysis may also reflect the social scientists' concern for socializing the public. Even if social scientists are themselves aware of the difference between cause and blame, they may be worried that the public will confuse them and then assign blame to the protected group, using causal arguments. There is probably good reason for this concern since those who are prejudiced against the protected group are looking for causal ammunition for their own blame analysis. Because of these concerns blame analysis is conspicuous in textbooks and in sociology written for the general public. A common technique in these outlets is to present a list of stereotypes about a protected group, label them "myths" and then present "facts" to refute them (e.g.,Eitzen, 1989). For example, one list in a prominent social problems text includes the myth "welfare people are cheats" (Kornblum and Julian, 1989). In refuting this myth, the authors cite the rarity of prosecutions for welfare fraud. The obvious purpose of this exercise is to combat prejudice against a protected group. This may also be the main purpose of the "diversity" or "multi-cultural courses" that are now being required in some colleges and universities. For example, the "Afro-centric" viewpoint expressed in some of these courses may in part reflect an attempt by blacks to reduce prejudice by warding off blame for their predicament.

Weber (1958) described the relationship between ideas and interests in terms of their "affinity". Ideas are not as likely to be favored in society unless they converge with some interest. While the original development of ideas is not necessarily based on interests, ideas not aligned with interests are not as likely to survive. My purpose, then, is to demonstrate the affinity between an interest in protecting certain groups, and various causal arguments that are prevalent in sociology.[5]

Illustrations

I will now present some prominent examples of accounts of group differences that reflect blame analysis. I argue that receptiveness to these accounts in sociology is at least partially a function of the extent to which they protect certain groups from blame. Receptiveness to the accounts may also be based on completely reasonable interpretations of the available evidence.

I will not discuss empirical evidence that bears on the validity of the accounts presented below, since their validity is not the issue. Sometimes the empirical evidence is consistent with blame analysis; a causal argument can be both valid and "politically correct" just as an account can be both truthful and strategic. Sometimes the evidence suggests that the arguments favored by blame analysis provide only part of the answer, which should not be surprising given that human behavior has multiple causes. However, in most cases the evidence is ambiguous, which is the rule rather than the exception in social science. The ambiguity of evidence facilitates blame analysis, since it is much easier to believe what one wants to believe when information is ambiguous (e.g., Felson, 1981).

Economic Outcomes

Blame analysis results in sympathy for a "structural" approach and re-jection of a "cultural" approach in the explanation of the persistence of poverty.[6] A structural approach focuses on current constraints faced by the poor (House, 1981). Poverty persists because of restricted opportunities that result from discrimination. A cultural approach, on the other hand, suggests that cultural factors mediate the effects of past social structures. For example, Lewis (1966) argued that a subculture has developed among some of the poor as an adaptation to their economic deprivation. This sub-culture has been passed on from generation to generation. Characteristics such as present-time orientation, lack of self-control, and female-centered families all operate to hinder the mobility of the poor. Note that these char-acteristics are mediating variables in Lewis's theory.

Blame analysis leads one to avoid explanations that posit any causal role for poor people, or groups that are more likely to be poor. This leads some to argue that a structural approach completely explains any group differ-ences (Valentine, 1968; Ryan, 1971). Discrimination and lack of opportu-nity have only direct effects. They reject the possibility that discrimination in previous generations can affect the present culture (or internal structure) of the group, which in turn affects the behavior of group members. If past discrimination has an effect it would have to be mediated by characteristics of the protected group. Such an explanation is to be avoided because it assigns a causal role to the protected group, and this could imply some level of blame. Of course, present discrimination may in fact be the sole cause of poverty; this is an empirical question. Recall that the validity of an account is irrelevant in the accounts literature.

The argument that poverty reflects present discrimination by the domi-nant group implies high levels of prejudice and discrimination in society. This leads to a focus on subtle forms of discrimination and on recent inci-dents of racial violence, and to skepticism about survey evidence indicating strong declines in prejudice (e.g., Willie, 1983; Eitzen, 1989; Benokraitis and Feagan, 1987). It is also reflected in statements that "everyone is rac-ist" or "sexist." Sometimes the way group differences are discussed im-plies that all members of the protected group lack opportunity and that the relationship between group membership and opportunity is a perfect one (e.g., French, 1985). Causal analysis, on the other hand, leads to probabilis-tic statements about class and race effects on opportunity, as reflected in status attainment models.

Cultural arguments are not always objectionable from the point of view of blame analysis. Cultural diversity is emphasized when it focuses on positive aspects of the protected groups' culture, as it is in the diversity courses now being instituted on college campuses. A cultural argument is also acceptable for explaining why certain groups, such as Jews or Chinese-Americans, are economically well-off (e.g., Schaefer, 1990). Finally, a cultural argument is acceptable in explaining why offending groups engage in discrimination (e.g., Weitzman, 1979). To say that prejudice is the result of culture and learning implies that prejudice reflects ignorance, which assigns racists and sexists the blame they deserve. Here blame analysis relies on an offensive rather than a defensive strategy.

On the other hand, to say that the offending group's behavior is a response to the behavior of protected groups is not acceptable. For example, from the perspective of blame analysis "statistical discrimination" is not an appealing explanation of discrimination against workers from protected groups (e.g., Feiner and Roberts, 1990). According to this argument, for example, discrimination against females in hiring is based on valid generalizations about sex differences in continuous employment. The policy is discriminatory because it assumes individual females conform to the group stereotype when they often do not. Blame analysis would also lead one to reject the argument that prejudice against blacks may be affected by their high rates of violent crime. Even if the black crime rate is caused by external factors, such as discrimination, the argument could imply shared blame. This is another example of the avoidance of mediating variables when they reflect on the behavior of the protected group.

Blame analysis helps explain the controversy generated by Wilson's (1978; 1987) well-known discussion of the underclass. Wilson emphasizes three factors in his explanation of the increase in poverty among blacks: (1) economic changes; (2) the flight of middle class blacks from ghetto areas; and (3) increases in illegitimacy and female-headed households. On the other hand, he de-emphasizes the role of current racial prejudice. These arguments are objectionable from the perspective of blame analysis for a variety of reasons. First, such arguments assert that current discrimination is not the predominant factor explaining race differences in economic outcomes; this is the key external factor usually cited to avoid blaming blacks. Second, Wilson's argument attributes a mediating causal role to variables associated with the black community. Thus, the black middle class plays a causal role by leaving the inner city. This has the further implication of justifying white flight, suggesting it is a response to characteristics of black communities rather than a function of prejudice. It also implies a causal role for the black family, and blame analysis is uncomfortable with the idea that family variables might have effects on poverty. Since family members belong to the protected group, their causal influence must be minimized. This helps explain the extremely negative reaction to Moynihan's (1965) arguments about the role of family dissolution in black poverty.

The impact of individual characteristics on economic outcomes is minimized in blame analysis. Those who wish to protect the poor will emphasize opportunity—an external factor—over ability—an internal factor, in explaining class differences. In addition, they will emphasize structural factors rather than alcoholism or mental illness in explaining homelessness (Lee, Jones and Lewis, 1990). Finally, when correlations are observed between socioeconomic status and individual behavior, the former will be assumed to be the cause and the latter the effect. For example, poverty will be viewed as a cause rather than a consequence of emotional problems (e.g., Lauer, 1989).

Blame analysis deals with sex differences in income in a similar way. It is consistent with explanations that emphasize discrimination by male employers against female employees in hiring, promotion, and job segregation. Blame analysis is not compatible with the human capital approach, which emphasizes sex differences in factors such as continuous employment which affect the value of female labor (Marini, 1989; Feiner and Roberts, 1990). To suggest that women's behavior plays a mediating role might imply blame for women. Blame analysis is also incompatible with explanations that emphasize socialization of females to a career-orientation. An argument that males are more career-oriented or ambitious than women could imply some blame for women.

This raises the more general issue of the relationship between socialization arguments and blame analysis. Socialization arguments are certainly acceptable for explaining the oppressor's behavior, from the perspective of blame analysis. However, they are problematic for explaining the behavior of the protected group. On one hand, they locate an external cause of the group's behavior: the socializing agent's discriminatory behavior. On the other hand, socialization suggests internalization which implies that there are internal mediating variables.[7] Recall that this was the basis of Ryan's objection to the culture of poverty thesis, cited above. Therefore, it is not surprising that socialization arguments are out of favor as explanations for sex differences in income. On the other hand, the discussion that follows will show that socialization arguments are used to explain group differences in academic performance. However, these arguments do not mention the role of internal mediators.

Academic and Athletic Performance

Blame analysis emphasizes three external factors in accounting for group differences in academic performance: (1) test bias, (2) the self-fulfilling prophecy, and (3) role models. On the other hand, internal factors, such as ability, effort, and preparation are objectionable.

Group differences in performance on standardized tests, such as the Scholastic Aptitude Test, are sometimes attributed to test biases. From the perspective of blame analysis, test bias is an appealing explanation of group differences in test performance because it involves an external cause. On the other hand, group differences in preparation is not as appealing an explanation because preparation is an internal factor. While preparation mediates the relationship between external factors (e.g., poor schools) and test performance, some internal causality is implied.[8]

According to the notion of the self-fulfilling prophecy, the academic performance of children in protected groups suffers because adults do not expect much from them (e.g., Rosenthal and Jacobson, 1968). For example, girls are taught that math is a male domain or that females are not as competent in math (e.g., Eccles and Jacobs, 1986). From the perspective of blame analysis, these expectations or stereotypes are based on culturally learned prejudices rather than the past performance of individuals or groups. In other words, expectations affect performance, but not the reverse. Again, cultural arguments are useful in explaining the oppressors' behavior. The concept of a self-fulfilling prophecy has appeal not only because it posits an external cause of group differences, but also because it attributes prejudice and discrimination to the oppressor. Again, those who feel they have a grievance against oppressors prefer to assign as high a level of blame to them as possible.

Another account for group differences in academic and job performance focuses on role models (e.g., Weitzman, 1979). The basic idea is that youth model the behavior of other group members. Because of discrimination there is a shortage of role models in the protected groups, and young people become discouraged. For example, it is argued that girls are more likely to pursue careers if their mothers work, and minorities and women do better in college if there are minority and women faculty. It has also been argued that mentoring is more effective when students and their role models are from the same group. These arguments are often used to justify affirmative action programs.

The effects of self-fulfilling prophecies and role models involve socialization. As indicated above, socialization explanations are problematic from the point of view of blame analysis. However, in the discussion of these processes, internal mediators are rarely discussed. For example, the most likely internal mediating variable in an academic model is effort. That is, if successful role models and high expectations lead children to think they can succeed, then they will pursue an activity more vigorously. However, since effort is an internal factor, accounts of group differences in performance do not mention it (e.g., Weitzman, 1979).

Discomfort with accounts involving effort also plays a role in the explanation of race differences in athletic performance. The strong presence of blacks in many professional sports is well known. In blame analysis this difference is attributed to lack of opportunity in other areas rather than to race differences in physique. Genetic differences are rejected, in part, because they imply that blacks display less effort than whites. This is based on the attribution principle that if two persons are equally successful, and if one has more ability, the other must have displayed more effort (Heider, 1958).[9] In addition, discussion of race differences in any ability is offensive because it might open the door for discussions of race differences in intelligence.[10]

Affirmative action policies may increase the frequency of blame analysis. First, if these policies place less qualified people in contexts in which they find it difficult to compete, they are more likely to find themselves in a predicament; this leads to account giving. Second, when members of unprotected groups are unsuccessful in their competition with members of protected groups, they can claim reverse discrimination; affirmative action policies give them a ready excuse for their predicament. In general, social policies that increase the frequency of predicaments are likely to increase the frequency of account giving. Claims of discrimination assign blame to external factors and can be used by anyone in a predicament to avoid blame. To reiterate, this argument does not deny the validity of any claims of discrimination.

Crime and Deviance

Traditionally, sociologists have tended to be relatively sympathetic with criminals, except those who commit white-collar crime (Toby, 1980; Hirschi, 1973).[11] Criminals of lower socioeconomic status are victims of society — the victims of labeling and lack of opportunity. This leads to advocacy of the lenient treatment of offenders, since punishment can lead to stigmatization and criminal careers. In fact, many sociologists have avoided calling offenders "criminals" since they believe that a conviction for a single criminal act does not justify a pejorative label that engulfs the person (e.g., Lofland, 1969). Raiman (1979) goes further in suggesting that blaming criminal offenders automatically reduces the blame attributed to society—the truly guilty party. Finally, some have questioned whether there are class and race differences in criminal behavior, arguing that differences in official crime rates reflect discrimination by legal authorities (e.g., Eitzen, 1989). However, in the 1980s, political changes resulted in attention to the criminal victimization of members of protected groups. In particular, there was an increase in attention to rape, to "wife battering", and to crimes reflecting racial bias.[12]

This produced a dilemma for the blame analysis of crime, given the earlier sympathies. Now, in crimes against members of protected groups, more severe treatment of the offender is sometimes advocated, for example, in the form of special penalties for "bias crimes." The phenomenon is also reflected in the pejorative label "rapist", which seems more appropriate than the words "robber" and "murderer". Since a rapist attacks members of a protected group, one should not worry that a pejorative label engulfs his person.

The problem is also revealed in approaches to violence that stress social interaction (e.g., Black, 1983; Felson, 1984; Luckenbill, 1977; Tedeschi, Gates, and Rivera, 1977). These approaches emphasize the interaction between antagonists and the role of third parties in predicting violent behavior. They look at violence as a form of informal social control and impression management, a method people use to express grievances and influence others. However, a grievance implies that the victim may have done something wrong, at least from the offender's point of view. The claim that violence reflects grievances is fine until the victim of the aggression is a member of a protected group. In this case, a phenomenological emphasis creates ideological problems. Further, to describe the interaction preceding violence might lead to a discussion of the victim's misbehavior. Any approach that focuses on social interaction "muddies the water" in terms of blame, rendering the offender less evil and the victim less virtuous. Thus, the blame analysis of violence between men and women openly rejects any causal role for women because it blames the victim (e.g., Burke, Stets, and Pirog-Good, 1988; Pagelow, 1984; Dobash and Dobash, 1984; Kurz, 1989; Fine, 1989). This may be the source of the strong negative reaction to evidence that women are as likely to physically attack their husbands as husbands are to attack their wives (e.g., Brush, 1990; Kurz, 1989). One of the researchers who reported this result was the target of a demonstration during a speech, while another, a woman, was the target of a bomb threat (Murray Straus, personal communication). This occurred even though they also reported that the violence of husbands is likely to be much more severe.

The confusion over cause and blame is important in the controversy over the term "victim precipitation" (see Karmen, 1984 for a review). The controversy occurs because the literature is unclear about whether the term means that the victim played a causal role or that the victim was blameworthy. For example, if a husband assaults his wife because he objects to her behavior, her behavior surely plays a causal role in the assault. However, since cause is confused with blame, the concept of victim precipitation is objectionable. On the other hand, it is acceptable to analyze homicides committed by battered women against their husbands in terms of victim precipitation (e.g., Browne, 1987).

The application of blame analysis to the study of rape is more complex. "Rape is a violent crime, not a sex crime," according to conventional wisdom. This slogan is based on the idea that rape is motivated by hatred for women or by an attempt to control them, and not by sexual desire. For example, the most influential book in this area states that rape is "a conscious process of intimidation by which all men keep all women in a state of fear" (Brownmiller, 1975; italics added). While it is usually assumed that the major goal of robbery is money (and violence the means), similar reasoning is not applied to rape.

From a blame analysis perspective, there are at least three reasons why there are such strong feelings about the motivation of rapists. First, one image of sexual motivation is that it involves an uncontrollable urge. Such an image might be used to reduce the offender's level of personal causality or intent. Second, the key issue in conviction for rape is lack of consent. Since sexual intercourse is usually a consensual activity it is useful to separate rape from sex to avoid any connotation that there might have been anything consensual. Of course, it is the threat of force that changes the legitimate and consensual exchange of money into robbery. But robbery is not a crime specifically targeting members of a protected group, so blame analysis does not apply. Third, the rapist seems more blameworthy if he is motivated by power and hatred. This is related to the general tendency to view ends and means as consistently positive or negative. To fully condemn an act, one prefers to view goals as negatively as possible when illegitimate means are used.[13] In contrast, when criminals are viewed as victims, it is acceptable to view their goals as legitimate. This may help explain the appeal of Merton's theory of criminal behavior as an innovative pursuit of legitimate goals when legitimate opportunities are restricted.

Finally, blame analysis influences the interpretation of homosexuality. Homosexuality has sometimes been treated as a sickness and sometimes as immoral behavior. The "medical model" reduces the level of blame attributed to homosexuals for their stigmatized behavior, since sickness is an excuse that implies a lower level of personal causality. However, mental illness is still a pejorative label implying some blame, and in the 1970s, homosexuals, with the support of sociologists, fought successfully to convince psychiatrists not to treat homosexuality as a sickness (Gagnon, 1977). A persuasive scientific argument was made that the medical model was inappropriate when applied to sexual orientation and simply reflected anti-homosexual attitudes.

At the present time, blame analysis has moved from a defensive to an offensive position. Those who are opposed to homosexuality are called "homophobic". This label implies that those who object to homosexuality have a pathological fear of homosexuals. Now, it is the anti-homosexuals not the homosexuals who have an illness.[14] This suggests that for some sociologists, the issue is blame, and not the medical model. They have no objection to the medical model when it is used to stigmatize a group with whom they have a grievance.

The medical model of sexual orientation was rejected because it implied that homosexuality was abnormal. However, it is interesting that the homosexual community prefers a biological to an environmental explanation for sexual orientation. One could interpret this as an exception to the rule that groups prefer to attribute their stigmatized behavior to external factors. However, unlike other groups, homosexuals cannot attribute their sexual orientation to discrimination and external constraints.[15] If homosexuality is biologically determined, at least there is no element of choice. As indicated earlier, people are less likely to be blamed for actions that are unintended (Heider, 1958). Therefore the biological explanation may be the best one available to homosexuals wishing to avoid blame, since it reduces the level of personal causality without the pejorative implications of the medical model.[16] This concern with personal causality is also revealed in discussions over whether homosexuality reflects a sexual "preference" or a sexual "orientation".

Labeling Issues

Blame analysis affects the way groups and their actions are labeled. For example, there is a preference for the term "oppressed" over "disadvantaged" in describing the protected group (e.g., Ryan, 1971). Those who favor the sexual division of labor are described as "sexist" rather than as "traditional". And only males can be described as sexist and only whites can be described as racist. Recently, the term "underclass" has come under attack for its pejorative connotations (e.g., Gans,1990). There is also likely to be some uneasiness about descriptions of group differences as differences in "performance" or "achievement" since the terms might imply some level of internal causality.[17]

Even when the protected group is given preferential treatment, the actions of the dominant group may be described in a pejorative way. For example, when females receive lighter sentences for their crimes, the oppressor is described as "paternalistic" (e.g., Kruttschnitt and Green, 1984). The special assignment of protected group members to jobs and committees is referred to as "tokenism." These labels imply a higher level of prejudice and discrimination, and thus greater external causality in explaining group differences. While they are accurate descriptors in some contexts, these terminological preferences also reflect blame analysis.

Williams (1990) relabels internal variables as external variables when it is impossible to deny their role. The evidence is apparently clear, according to his review of the literature, that life-style variables (e.g., smoking, drinking, obesity) are the key mediators of the relationship between socioeconomic status and physical health. However, Williams worries that some health authorities are using this evidence "to blame the victim for their failure to follow healthier lifestyles" (p. 95). They want to "...launch national educational campaigns that would persuade the poor to give up their high-risk life-style" rather than "...alter the socioeconomic conditions of the disadvantaged in America" (p.95). Therefore he prefers to view smoking and other behaviors associated with social class "not as individual characteristics but as the patterned response of social groups to the realities and constraints of the external environment" (p. 81). Further, he argues that these life-style variables are not real causal variables, and that changing them would not affect the health of the poor since "new factors would emerge to perpetuate inequality in health status as long as social stratification remained" (p.91). Evidently, smoking is not harmful if you are poor.

Conclusion

The charge in the 1970s that certain causal arguments imply blame for victims was extremely influential in sociology. However, the unmasking of ideological underpinnings works both ways. Perhaps those who make that charge can be hoist with their own petard. Thus I have attempted to show how well-known causal arguments in the field imply a sympathy for protected groups and that sometimes this sympathy is openly acknowledged as the basis for a particular causal argument. To make my case I have borrowed from the interrelated literatures on account-giving and attribution theory. The paper also contributes to the development of those theories by applying them to group predicaments, and by showing how the zero-sum treatment of causality, and the confusion between cause and blame, affects attributions of blame.

I have argued that the central defensive strategy in blame analysis is to focus on external factors and to ignore internal factors in explaining the behavior of the protected group. This leads to an emphasis on distal variables rather than proximate variables, and an avoidance of the discussion of mediating processes.[18] It also results in an emphasis on the effects of constraints and mistreatment on protected groups, and an ambivalence about socialization arguments. While group differences in performance are minimized, the strength of group effects on oppressors (i.e., discrimination) is maximized.

The best defense is sometimes a good offense. The offensive strategy in blame analysis is to use internal rather than external variables to explain the behavior of the oppressor. Thus, explanations of the behavior of the oppressor emphasize proximate variables over distal variables. There is a preference for pejorative labels for oppressors and a tendency to view their behavior as reflecting illegitimate goals as well as illegitimate means. A phenomenological approach to the oppressor is avoided since oppressors are likely to identify causal factors associated with the protected group when they give their point of view.

Another offensive strategy is to accuse those who assign any causal role to the protected group of being racist, sexist, or reactionary.[19] Ad hominem attacks encourage causal analysts to consider the identities of protected groups in their research, thus complying with the principles of blame analysis. It also discourages many causal analysts from tackling these controversial issues, particularly if they are not members of the protected group. For example, Wilson (1987) suggests that many liberal scholars abandoned research on race as a result of the negative response to Moynihan's book on the black family. And I have no doubt that this paper will be misunderstood and that my motives will be questioned.

In conclusion, I am advocating an open discussion of the ideological impact on sociology of political views from the left as well as the right. Causal arguments have implications for group identities and the impact this has on the field should be addressed. While ideological influence is un-avoidable, it can be minimized. The use of blame analysis in the evaluation of evidence is avoidable. The rejection of internal factors as mediating variables can and should be based on empirical evidence rather than on the implication of causal arguments for group identities. The causal arguments favored by those doing blame analysis on behalf of protected groups may turn out to be correct. Internal mediating variables will not necessarily survive to the final model, but they should be considered in the opening model.

I recognize the dilemma that social scientists face when their results are misinterpreted. When dealing with the public (including undergraduates), it may sometimes be necessary for us to play a protective role. At the least, we should emphasize that cause and blame are different, and that proximate variables are mediating variables.

In general, however, judgments of blame should be the province of agents of social control not social scientists. We should avoid the polemic between those who wish to blame these groups, and those who wish to defend them. When sociologists and other social scientists participate in this ideological battle they sacrifice scientific principles and become propagandists for one side or another. More importantly, the threat of charges of prejudice, and the negative response of reviewers, discourages those who value these principles from working in some controversial areas of research. The result is the domination of blame analysis over scientific analysis in the examination of some of the most important issues of our day.

Acknowledgements

I wish to thank Steve Felson, George Gmelch, Sharon Gmelch, Marv Krohn, Allen Liska, John Logan, Steve Messner, Stew Tolnay, and Kathy Trent for comments on earlier drafts.

Notes

1. I have borrowed the term "protected group" from the affirmative action literature. The term does not deny that these groups are the victims of discrimination in the larger society.

2. Excuses (e.g., drunkenness) refer to accounts in which people deny or minimize their causal role, while justifications (e.g., self-defense) refer to account in which they admit their causal role but claim that there was a good reason for it (Scott and Lyman, 1968; Felson, 1981). While people admit an internal causal role when they justify their behavior, they view their behavior as a legitimate response to some external factor.

3. Heider also suggests the possibility that responsibility can be attributed to people for actions they are associated with in some way but did not cause. An example is when people are held responsible for the actions of other members of their group.

4. Actually, there appears to be some ambivalence about conceptualizing groups as victims, because it implies they are weak and ineffectual. For example, Smith-Rosenberg (1985), a prominent feminist historian, prefers to view women (and other oppressed groups) as active agents reacting to their oppression, rather than as passive victims.

5. I am using the term "interest" broadly so as to include people who are not group members but who sympathize with the group.

6. Sociologists also tend to favor structural arguments in order to differentiate themselves from psychologists, as pointed out by an anonymous reviewer. However, this does not explain discomfort with arguments that posit cultural variables as mediators of structural effects.

7. Perhaps blame analysis has contributed to the decline in status of social psychology in the field of sociology. Blame analysis is more compatible with an emphasis on more distal, structural causes of the protected group's behavior, as opposed to an emphasis on socialization.

8. Test bias and differential preparation are difficult to distinguish since both imply that the test requires knowledge that one group is more likely to have than another. The difference is that bias implies that the knowledge being tested is irrelevant for the purposes of the test.

9. Actually, blacks tend to outperform whites in many sports, and therefore this principle should not apply. The superior performance of blacks could be the result of both greater ability and greater effort.

10. Worry about claims of group differences in ability may have contributed to a deemphasis of innate ability as a factor in explaining individual performance in blame analysis. Actually, observations of group differences in performance and individual differences in ability do not imply that there are group differences in ability.

11. I am not claiming that criminals are, or ever were, a protected group in sociology. Rather, my claim is that sociologists tend to be much more sympathetic to

criminals than is the general public. Writing in 1973, Hirschi went so far as to claim that the appreciation of deviance was a "procedural rule" in the sociological study of deviance. I would describe "avoid blaming the victim" as a procedural rule in sociology today.

12. Since much crime is intraracial, and victimizes the poor, one could argue that the dilemma exists for many types of crime. However, this fact is not well known to the public. Actually, the fact that victims are often minorities has been used to justify acknowledgements of high rates of crime among some minorities, and examining causes of crime located in minority communities. It can then be claimed that the purpose of the inquiry is to protect minorities rather than blame them.

13. Thus, the phrase "the end justifies the means" has a negative connotation and is not usually an acceptable account. In this case we prefer to think that if the goal is legitimate, so is our means. This requires a relabeling of the means. For example, people avoid calling an act violent when they favor the goal of the act. Thus, Blumenthal (1972) showed that those who were sympathetic with the Vietnam war did not view police attacks on demonstrators as violent. Instead of saying that the police attacks were violent but justified, they denied that the actions themselves were violent. Such thinking frequently affects social scientists when they allow value judgements to influence what they define as aggressive, violent, abusive, or terrorist.

14. According to a reviewer, the term was actually coined by a psychologist. At the present time, there is a growing preference for the term "heterosexism."

15. The only alternative environmental explanation available is early childhood socialization. As I argued above, socialization explanations are problematic from the point of view of blame analysis because they imply some level of internal causation.

16. Unlike the other predicaments mentioned in this paper (e.g.,low socioeconomic status; low academic achievement; high crime rates) homosexuals usually do not view their behavior as inadequate or morally wrong. However, homosexuality is socially stigmatized, and people are likely to give accounts when they anticipate negative reactions from an audience, no matter how they view their own behavior.

17. Another problem with these terms is that the public sometimes confuses them with natural ability. I use the term "performance" in this paper because it helps explain the use of accounts.

18. I am not criticizing researchers for focusing in their empirical work on one type of variable (e.g., discrimination or culture) and not another; a division of labor is often necessary in science.

19. For an excellent discussion of ad hominem arguments against researchers with unpopular results, as well as other issues related to this paper, see Lieberson (1989). One anonymous reviewer of this paper insisted that I was a conservative despite my claims otherwise.

References

Becker, Howard S. 1964. (ed.) *The Other Side*. New York: Free Press.

Benokraitis, Nijole and Joe R. Feagan. 1987. *Modern Sexism: Blatant, Subtle and Covert Discrimination*. New Jersey: Prentice-Hall.

Black, Donald. 1983. "Crime as Social Control" *American Sociological Review*. 48: 34-45.

Blumenthal, M.D., R.L. Kahn, F.M. Andrews and K.B. Head. 1972. *Justifying Violence: Attitudes of American Men*. Ann Arbor: Institute for Social Research.

Browne, Angela. 1987. *When Battered Women Kill*. New York: Macmillian.

Brownmiller, Susan. 1975. *Against Our Will: Men, Women and Rape*. New York: Simon and Schuster.

Brush, Lisa. 1990. "Violent acts and injurious outcomes in married couples: Methodological issues in the National Survey of Families and Households" *Gender and Society* 4:56-67.

Burke, Peter J., Jan E. Stets, and Maureen A. Pirog-Good. 1988. "Gender Identity, Self-esteem, and Physical and Sexual Abuse in Dating Relationships". *Social Psychology Quarterly* 51: 272-285.

Caplan and Nelson. 1973. "On Being Useful: The Nature an Consequences of Psychological Research on Social Problems." *American Psychologist* (March) 199-211.

Dahrendorf, Ralf. 1968. "Values and Social Science: The Value Dispute in Perspective." in *Essays in the Theory of Society*, edited by Ralf Dahrendorf. Stanford: Stanford University Press.

Dobash, E. Emerson and Russell P. Dobash. 1984. "The Nature and Antecedents of Violent Events." British Journal of Criminology. 24: 269-288.

Eccles, J.S., and Jacobs, J.E. 1986. "Social Forces Shape Math Attitudes and Performance." *Signs* 11: 367-380.

Eitzen, D. Stanley. 1989. *Social Problems*. (fourth edition) Boston: Allyn & Bacon.

Feiner, Susan F. and Bruce B. Roberts. 1990. "Hidden by the invisable hand: Neoclassical economic thoery and the textbook treatment of race and gender." *Gender and Society* 4:159-181.

Felson, Richard B. 1981. "Ambiguity and Bias in the Self Concept."
Social Psychology Quarterly 44: 64-69.

———. 1984. "Patterns of Aggressive Social Interaction" in *Social Psychology of Aggression: From Individual Behavior to Social Interaction*, edited by Amelie Mummendey. Berlin:Springer-Verlag.

Felson, Richard B. and Steve Ribner. 1981. "An Attributional Approach to Accounts and Sanctions for Criminal Violence." *Social Psychology Quarterly* 44:137-142.

Fine, Michelle. 1989. "The politics of research and activisim: Violence against women." *Gender and Society* 3:549-558.

French, Marilyn. 1985. *Beyond Power.* New York: Summit Books.

Gagnon, John H. 1977. *Human Sexualities.* Glenview, Il: Scott, Foresman.

Gans, Herbert J. 1990. "Deconstructing the underclass: The term's dangers as a planning concept." *Journal of the American Planning Association* 56: 271-277.

Hirschi, Travis. 1973. "Procedural Rules and the Study of Deviant Behavior". *Social Problems* 21: 159-173.

Horowitz, Irving Louis. 1987. "Disenthralling sociology." *Society.* January/February 48-54.

House, James. 1981. "Social Structure and Personality" Pp. 525-561 in *Social Psychology: Sociological Perspectives* edited by Morris Rosenberg and Ralph H. Turner. New York: Basic Books.

Karmen, Andrew. 1984. *Crime Victims: An Introduction to Victomology.* Belmont, CA: Cole.

Kornblum, William and Joseph Julian. 1989. *Social Problems.* (6th edition.) Englewood Cliffs: New Jersey.

Kruttschnitt, Candace and Donald E. Green. 1984. "The sex-sanctioning issue: Is it history?" *American Sociological Review* 49: 541-551.

Kurz, Denise. 1989. "Social science perspectives on wife abuse: Current debates and future directions." *Gender and Society* 3:489-505.

Lauer, Robert H. 1989. *Social Problems and the Quality of Life* (Fourth edition). Dubuque: W.C. Brown

Lee, Barrett A., Sue Hinze Jones, And David W. Lewis. 1990. "Public beliefs about the causes of homelessness." *Social Forces* 69: 253-266.

Lewis, Oscar. 1966. *La Vida.* New York. Random House.

Lieberson, Stanley. 1989. "When right results are wrong." *Society* 26: 60-66.

Lofland, John.
  1969. Deviance and Identity. Englewood Cliffs: New Jersey.
Luckenbill, David F.
  1977. "Criminal Homicide as a Situated Transaction." Social Problems.
  25:176-186.
Marini, Margaret M.
  1989. "Sex Differences in Earnings in the United States." In Annual Review of
  Sociology, edited by W. Richard Scott and Judith Blake (Vol. 15). Palo Alto:
  Annual Reviews,Inc.
Moynihan, Daniel P.
  1965. The Negro Family: The Case for National Action. Washington, D.C.,
  Office of Policy Planning and Research, U. S. Dept. of Labor.
Pagelow, Mildred Page.
  1984. Family Violence. New York: Praeger.
Piaget, Jean.
  1932. The Moral Judgement of the Child. New York: Harcourt, Brace.
Raiman, Jeffrey H.
  1979. The Rich Get Richer and the Poor Get Prison: Ideology, Class and
  Criminal Justice. New York: John Wiley & Sons.
Rosenthal, Robert. and Jacobson, Lenore.
  1968. Pygmalion in the Classroom: Teacher Expectation and Pupil Intellectual
  Development. New York: Holt, Rinehart & Winston.
Ryan, Willian
  1971. Blaming the Victim. New York: Random House.
Schaefer, Richard T.
  1990. Racial and Ethnic Groups (fourth edition) Glenview, Ill.: Scott,
  Foresman.
Schlenker, Barry R.
  1980. Impression Management: The Self-concept, Social Identity, and
  Interpersonal Relations. Monterey, CA: Brooks/Cole.
Scott, Marvin and S. M. Lyman.
  1968. "Accounts". American Sociological Review 33:46-62.
Smith-Rosenberg, Carroll.
  1985. Disorderly Conduct: Visions of Gender in Victorian America
  New York: Oxford University Press.
Tedeschi, James T., Gates, J., and Rivera, A. N.
  1977. "Aggression and the Use of Coercive Power." Journal of Social
  Issues 33:101-125.

Toby, Jackson. 1980. "The new criminology is the old baloney." In Radical Criminology: *The Coming Crises* edited by James A. Inciardi. Beverly Hills: Sage.

Tomaskovic-Devey, Barbara and Donald Tomaskovic-Devey. 1988. "The social structural determinants of ethnic group behavior: Single ancestry rates among four white American ethnic groups." *American Sociological Review* 53:650-659.

Valentine, Charles A. 1968. *Culture and Poverty: Critique & Counter Proposals*. Chicago: University of Chicago Press.

Weber, Max. 1958. *From Max Weber: Essays in Sociology*. Edited by H. H. Gerth and C. Wright Mills. New York: Oxford University Press.

Weitzman, Lenore J. 1979. *Sex-role Socialization: A Focus on Women*. Palo Alto: Mayfield.

Wilhelm, Sidney M. 1980. "Can Marxism explain American's racism?" *Social Problems* 28: 98-112.

Williams, David R. 1990. "Socioeconomic differentials in health: A review and redirection." *Social Psychology Quarterly* 53:81-99.

Willie, Charles V. 1978. "The Inclining Significance of Race" *Society* 15 (5).

Wilson William J. 1978. *The Declining Significance of Race: Blacks and Changing American Institutions*. Chicago: University of Chicago Press.

——. 1987. *The Truly Disadvantaged: The inner city, the underclass, and public policy*. Chicago: University of Chicago Press.

12

The State of American Sociology[1]

Seymour Martin Lipset

Introduction

This article has a thesis: that the parlous state of sociology-the changes that have produced serious divisiveness -are related to its vulnerability to politicization. Concern for societal reform, to be accomplished politically, has drawn students to the field. This is not a scientific paper, it is largely one sociologist's reactions and memories, although I report on relevant qualitative and quantitative data as well.

As noted, what brought me and many others of my cohort-those who entered in the post World War II decade, as well as many of our predecessors — into sociology was political interests — reformist, even radical concerns. Before the war, the field attracted many religiously motivated reformers. I was associated politically in socialist movements prior to entering sociology with Daniel Bell, Lew and Rose Coser, Nathan Glazer, William Peterson, Peter Rossi, and Phil Selznick.[2] We linked our sociology with our politics. But unlike many activist students and leftist faculty from the late 1960s on, we, and the field generally, tried to keep our politics and our scholarship separate. Though some of us worked on political topics, we felt duty bound to be as objective as possible, to report results that contradicted our ideological concerns, following, unknowingly, the advice of Max Weber. Weber had written that every scholar had a "Party line," in terms of his academic concerns, if not external politics. Given this, researchers should be extremely careful not to easily accept and propagate findings that agreed with their line. If the results disagreed with their basic views, then, they were probably valid, but if they coincided, he recommended having the analysis redone, just to make sure it was correct.

My dissertation, a study of the social democratic movement and government in Saskatchewan, Canada-Agrarian Socialism-was motivated by the desire to understand the weakness of socialism in the United States (Lipset, 1950). My next book, Union Democracy (Lipset et al., 1956), was inspired by Robert Michels' classic work on oligarchy in socialist parties, Political Parties (1962). Phil Selznick's TVA and the Grassroots (1949) also stemmed from Michels. Bell's dissertation was his book on American socialism (Bell, 1967). Glazer's dealt with ethnicity and American communism (Glazer, 1961).

The 1940s and 1950s: A Scientific Revolution

I would like to start with the state of sociology after the war, in fact, from the mid-1940s to the mid-1960s. It is hard to reproduce the sense of revolutionary excitement that marked what the American Sociological Association (ASA) historian, Lawrence Rhoades (1981:42-53), called the "Golden Era." I report mainly about the Columbia-Harvard tradition. I must apologize to Chicago people for knowing much less about their department, but I have never spent more than a two- or three-day stretch in Chicago. Careerwise, I have been bi-coastal, from the East Coast to the West and back again. Columbia, in my day, meant Lynd, the prophet; Merton, the theorist; Lazarsfeld, the methodologist and survey analyst, supported by Herb Hyman; while Dan Bell and C. Wright Mills were the major figures in the undergraduate program. Harvard, of course, was Parsons, the theorist and teacher of Merton; Stouffer, the methodologist; Homans, the network theorist, but until quite late an isolated figure; Inkeles, the comparativist; Bellah, the radical moralist; with Riesman as the prophet.

Berkeley, which rose to greatness in the 1950s as an almost totally new department, recruited from Harvard, Columbia, and Chicago some of the subsequently most successful people. It was the most catholic, intellectually diverse department in the field. Stanford, which I joined in 1975, was then predominantly composed of social psychologists and small group analysts led by Joe Berger and Sandy Dornbusch. But it became much more diversified in the late 1970s and onward, eventually including major emphases in organizational and comparative analyses.

As I have already mentioned, the early period was marked by an enormous surge of intellectual creativity and energy. We literally believed that we, or rather our elders, were creating, for the first time, a scientific sociology based on a functional and conceptual scheme derived from Marx,

Weber, and Durkheim as elaborated by Parsons and Merton, and rigorous analytical statistical methodology, as developed by Lazarsfeld and Stouffer.

Much later, the critics who arose within the field in the mid-1960s were to turn on the sociology of the 1940s and 1950s, attacking it as conservative, reactionary, if not worse. I think they were wrong and that the record should be clarified. Not only were many of the students attracted to sociology on the left, often on the far left politically, but the bulk of the faculty certainly also were considerably left of center, and, as noted, had themselves moved into sociology from left-wing and reformist interests. Thus, Talcott Parsons had been an active student socialist as an undergraduate. He figures in an official history of the SLID-the Student League for Industrial Democracy-the predecessor organization to the Students for a Democratic Society (SDS) of the 1960s.[3] While Parsons was not a political activist as a faculty member, he expressed his social concerns and interests in analytical articles dealing with prejudice, fascism, and McCarthyism (Parsons, 1954, 1956). His principal collaborator at Harvard, Samuel Stouffer, undertook the first major survey analysis of the sources of anti-Communist and McCarthyite attitudes in the American population, which was published in his well-known book, Communism, Conformity and Civil Liberties (1954). He was under attack during this period for "harboring commies like Pete Rossi" (Strodtbeck, 1994). Robert Bellah had been a Young Communist, and Orlando Patterson a Marxist in Jamaica and the London School of Economics.

There were conservative members of the Harvard department, but they were not Parsons and Stouffer. They included George Homans-a life-long Republican and supporter of conservative views in economics, and even to some extent, in social policy — and Pitirim Sorokin, the founding chair of the Harvard department, who, like Homans, was a strong antagonist of Parsons within the faculty, and was also quite conservative. One of Sorokin's claims to fame was that he had been personally denounced by Lenin, and had left the Soviet Union in the early 1920s as an anti-Bolshevik émigré Ironically, Sorokin, though a major figure in the discipline, was not elected to the presidency of the American Sociological Association until 1965, when he was in his 80s. He was then nominated and strongly supported by left-wing, antiwar activists. They did this because Sorokin was a public opponent of the Vietnam war. The radicals obviously knew little about his views or earlier political activities, which included for a time showing visitors a revolver in his desk that he kept because he believed that the Bolsheviks were interested in killing him. David Riesman, who came to Harvard at the end of the 1950s, was, of course, a strong political activist from his early concerns about civil liberties. At Harvard, he played a major role in supporting student peace and antiwar activities, both before and during the Vietnam War. He was, however, firm in his views that political and academic concerns must be kept separate -that activists, whether faculty or students, must do their job. He strongly criticized antiwar militants who asked for delays in turning in papers or in taking exams because of their political activities.

At Columbia, all the major figures — Lynd, Merton, and Lazarsfeld - were on the left. Lynd, of course, was a radical and severe critic of capitalism for many years. He strongly supported left-wing socialist principles. He played a major role in bringing Paul Lazarsfeld to Columbia, in part because he had been impressed by Lazarsfeld's commitment to working on problems that were linked to left political objectives. Lazarsfeld's major claim to fame, prior to his immigrating to the United States in the early 1930s, was his direction of and involvement in a major study of -the unemployed in his native country Austria, which appeared as Die Arbeitslosen von Marienthal (Lazarsfeld-Jahoda and Zeisel, 1932). It was undertaken to analyze what it would take to make social democratic workers revolutionary. He planned to return to the subject in the United States after World War II, but the long period of postwar prosperity undermined his plans.

Lazarsfeld, of course, became better known as a strong proponent of quantitative analysis and even mathematical models in sociology. He pressed for rigorous methodology. This emphasis, plus the fact that much of his research activity at Columbia involved market research financed by corporations, led some students to think of him as an apolitical or conservative figure. Nothing could be further from the truth. Lazarsfeld, like Stouffer, had carried out a major study of the effects of McCarthyism, in his case, the book, The Academic Mind (Lazarsfeld and Thielens, 1958). The study-for those who have not read it-is a comprehensive survey of a sample of 2500 social scientists completed in the mid-1950s. Interestingly — and perhaps frustratingly, for traditional left stereotypical views of the academy at that time, Lazarsfeld and Thielens, his co-author, were unable to report that McCarthyism had been successful in repressing the left views or political activities of social scientists. Rather, they found that the minority of conservatives were more likely to be in trouble on campuses from their predominately liberal colleagues than were leftists, including Communists. I will come back to the issue of the politics of academe and of sociologists later on. Lazarsfeld, I would note, continued to be a life-long socialist or social democrat until his death.

Bob Merton was less publicly identified politically, although he was included in 1952 in a group of seven Columbia academics who were attacked by then vice-presidential nominee, Richard Nixon, as leftists. During his days on the Harvard faculty, he belonged to the teachers' union and was part of a left-wing faculty social network. He edited a book by Marxist economist Paul Sweezy and published in Science and Society, a Marxist journal. It is obvious where his sympathies lay. As is evident in his great work on Social Theory and Social Structure (1968), Merton explicitly attempted to mesh Marxist analysis with classic structural functional approaches, derived from Durkheim and Parsons. As he and others have emphasized, Marxism is in fact a variant of functional theory. Kingsley Davis, another major student of Parsons, who later served on the Princeton, Columbia, and Berkeley faculties, also was a supporter of socialism in the early days. As I recall, he publicly endorsed Norman Thomas in the 1948 election. Davis, however, was to become much more conservative and, more unconventionally, even backed Republicans in his later years. The leftist political views of C. Wright Mills, nor the lifelong commitment of Dan Bell to social democracy, obviously need not be elaborated on.

Robert Lynd, the strong mentor and supporter of both Lazarsfeld and Merton, considered himself, as I have noted, a revolutionary socialist. He was also an extremely moralistic individual, behavior that flowed from his Protestant sectarian religious origins. Lynd would express strong political views in class, but hesitated publishing his conclusions unless he was absolutely certain that what he believed could be supported by empirical data. In effect, Lynd took the same position on such matters as Max Weber. Lynd's position led him to be extremely critical of work by some other radicals when he found reason to believe that they were distorting their data and findings to justify their party line. He was greatly offended by some left social scientists, including, to my knowledge, at least two colleagues who, he thought, were not as committed to scientific integrity to reporting data that contradicted their beliefs, as he was. He brought that sense of rectitude to his evaluation of students and refused to support at least one subsequently prominent student, because he changed his position on academic issues in tandem with reversals in the Communist Party line. Lynd argued with other members of the department that they should not recommend this individual for an academic position, since he had demonstrated to their knowledge that he allowed his conclusions on academic matters to be affected by a political party membership.

The Chicago department also was severely divided for much of its history between the scientistic, demographic, and statistically oriented people vs. the qualitative "others." The others were themselves fragmented, with

Herb Blumer and Everett Hughes detesting each other. Ed Shils was off in a separate structure, the Committee on Social Thought, while Dave Riesman practiced his own type of macrosociology. Blumer was to leave for Berkeley, in large part because his salary was held down to a pittance, presumably with the complicity of many of his colleagues. Erving Goffman, a Hughes student, never made it at Chicago because of opposition to his mentor. Riesman was told by one of his scientistic associates that since he was not really a sociologist, graduate students should not work with him. The rumor mill suggests this played a role in his departing for Harvard. Janowitz, who replaced Riesman in the department configuration and eventually became a powerful chair, was soon at odds with Rossi, who headed the National Opinion Research Center (NORC). Janowitz worked hard and successfully to stop efforts to tenure Andrew Greeley. Larger ideological issues had little to do with these divisions, although as in other departments, the major figures were liberal Democrats or leftists and antiwar activists.

The Berkeley department -which was of course younger on average than the other two -also contained a number of people (like my close friend Reinhard Bendix) whose academic origins and intellectual concerns were linked to left-wing movements and who continued to adhere to different forms of liberal left politics as professors during the 1950s and early 1960s, i.e., before the rise of student activism. Blumer, who came as chair in the early 1950s, was determined to show up Chicago by hiring the best of every type of sociology. He did so, in spite of the fact that he had strong opinions and was contemptuous of every brand but his own. The atmosphere in this department -with Goffman, Kornhauser, the Selznicks, Gertrude and Philip, Bendix, Glazer, Skolnick, Matza, Blauner, Trow, the Davises, Judith and Kingsley, Wilensky, Lowenthal, Smelser, Glock, Selvin, Clausen, Swanson- was electrifying. That roster of names obviously includes people who varied considerably in their theoretical and methodological orientations, as well as in their political leanings, but who were all committed to and excited about sociology. We had little difficulty in making personnel decisions, although I would be lying if I said there were none.

We attracted interesting and politically aware students. To give just a slight indication, my research assistants and students at Berkeley included Juan Linz (who had accompanied me from Columbia), Robert Alford, Robert Blauner, Amitai Etzioni, Arthur Stinchcombe, and Maurice Zeitlin, to list a few, who have attained prominence. The semester before the Free Speech Movement (FSM) started in the fall of 1964, many of the subsequent leaders of the FSM were in a course on American society, jointly taught by Nat Glazer and myself. Some years later, I happened to read an autobiographical article by Jerry Rubin, a key FSM leader, in Esquire. It contained the line, "I decided to go to Berkeley to study with Lipset." In September, when a police car was trapped on campus by the demonstrators, Glazer and I were among those who stood on top of the car (it never was operative again). Only we were disagreeing with the protestors, arguing that the occasion did not warrant civil disobedience -closing down the university. Obviously many, perhaps most, of our students, disagreed. We did not know it but among the many changes in the country, and at Berkeley, which began that fateful night was the breakup of the Sociology Department and of consensus in the field generally. But I am getting ahead of the story. I must still deal with the earlier period.

Although the principal figures in sociology in the 1940s and 1950s strongly espoused what might be called a scientistic orientation, they, like their predecessors, believed that methodologically rigorous social science research was a prerequisite for effective social reform, often radical change. This meant that basic research and theory had to come first, they should take priority over activism -although most were reformist, if not radical, politically. The analogy was made to biology, that the effort to overcome cancer first requires basic research and knowledge, as in molecular and cell biology -work that never mentions or deals with cancer per se. The same logic should apply to efforts to do away with unemployment, or to enhance the education of underprivileged children. To simply have a worthy goal, to say that we have to get rid of what we do not like, will be ineffective, in lieu of scientific knowledge about the underlying factors that bring about the negative effects. The major departments concentrated, therefore, much more on basic theoretical and methodological issues than on substantive social problems.

The then existing Behavioral Science Division of the Ford Foundation followed this approach in its grant programs. Ironically, this orientation was rejected by Henry Ford 11, who played a major role in the foundation during the 1950s. He wanted it to deal directly with social problems, e.g., with problems of poverty, inadequate education, crime, delinquency, and the like. The head of the Division, Bernard Berelson — a close friend and former colleague of Lazarsfeld and Merton, reflecting the Columbia-Harvard orientation -said no, that we really did not know how to deal with these problems, that the Foundation should support basic research, not reforms. Henry Ford eventually was instrumental in closing down the Behavioral Sciences Division, precisely because it was not sufficiently concerned with reformist issues.

Some of the leading figures were great teachers. Talcott Parsons, although

alienating readers because he wrote in a complicated fashion, was personally easily available, kept his office door open, even to the lowliest freshman. Students (and senior sociologists) who wandered in were immediately subjected to a discussion of the latest "break through." He sometimes
would talk for an hour or two. This egalitarian treatment by the great man
produced converts. My image of Parsons is of a humble man in the robes of
a king. Parsons had no doubt that he was the king, that his theory was the
theory, but as a person, he was modest and available. Reflecting his convictions, Alex Inkeles reports that while at a social gathering at the Parsons',
their young son Charles, now a distinguished philosopher, marched through
beating a drum and proclaiming, "Sociology is about to begin."

Bob Merton is the best lecturer I have ever heard. His courses were
superbly organized and delivered. Sociology in his voice seemed able to
answer all questions. He was, and still is so brilliant, that many students,
including me, were intimidated, were afraid to go in to speak to him in his
office -trembled when they turned in papers. I admired Merton profusely,
and he liked and supported me. But my fear of him was so strong that I felt
I could not do my dissertation with him. Instead, I worked with Bob Lynd,
who though not as intellectually challenging, was extremely easy to relate
to and very supportive psychologically. He would keep your morale up and
edit your writing.

Paul Lazarsfeld was another genius. Whatever research problem you
presented him with, he immediately came up with sharp questions, did you
look at this . . . at that ... ? His seminar, Logic of Social Research, analyzed
the research decision process in major studies from Durkheim's Suicide on.
They were a delight; I learned much. Essentially Lazarsfeld thought in
multivariate terms and taught us how to do the same.

The Center for Advanced Study in the Behavioral Sciences, located at
Stanford and founded in 1954, had its origins in the belief of this postwar
social science generation that they were making a scientific revolution. In
the early 1950s, Lazarsfeld and Merton proposed to establish what they
called the "Professional School," an institution that would train people who
already had their Ph.D. in the new social theory and methodology, which
they believed would revolutionize the social sciences. Berelson, at the Ford
Foundation, put up money for a detailed prospectus of what a professional
school should be like. He subsequently was able to get the foundation to
commit ten million dollars to set up such an institution. The new institution,
however, never became a professional school. Its first director, Ralph Tyler,
believed in nondirective administration -that inmates of academic institutions should be allowed to do whatever they want to do, including not

listening to their seniors. This was the way he ran the Center for Advanced Study from the start. As a result, it became an institution to support scholars to do whatever their hearts desired during their year there. Lazarsfeld, though not Merton, had hoped it would also be a school with senior fellows teaching younger ones from all the social science disciplines. This never happened. But the force behind the creation of the center was the idea of a new methodological revolution in the social sciences, one that would produce the basic knowledge needed to make major social change happen.

The Politics of Sociology in the 1960s

The 1960s brought an end to the dominance of the emphasis on objectivity. The civil rights and antiwar movements strengthened radical activism among students, graduate students and junior faculty, even involved some older figures. They wanted to see sociology and the other social sciences become activist and openly radical and political.[4] And many of the graduate students and young faculty felt that the senior faculty in sociology had become more conservative because they were not politically active. A sharply critical literature emerged from scholars like C. Wright Mills and Alvin Gouldner. Gouldner laid out a complex and sophisticated argument that the leading figures, the most successful researchers in the discipline, had "sold out" to the established interests (Mills basically agreed with him). They were at the major universities and received large grants from the government as well as large incomes from consulting. His book, The Coming Crisis of Western Sociology (1970), purportedly documents the point by making occasional reference to data from a questionnaire study that he had conducted based on a large random sample of members of the ASA. Without presenting much statistical evidence to document his point,- he wrote that the study and other information validated his assumptions.

When I read Gouldner's Coming Crisis, I was somewhat puzzled by his claims to have empirical warrant for this analysis. His results seemingly contradicted my own findings drawn from reviewing some fairly comprehensive studies of the political behavior and attitudes of academe in general, including secondary analysis of earlier studies, like that of Lazarsfeld and Thielens (1958) in the mid-1950s, and the analysis of a very large sample of the academic profession taken by the Carnegie Commission on Higher Education in the late 1960s (Ladd and Lipset, 1976). I knew from my examination of the considerable amount of empirical data that the evidence indicated the more successful scholars-as reflected by the status of the university or department they were in, awards they received, publication records, and other indicators of prestige -were the most liberal-to-left politically. The data indicated that consultants to government and industry were much more left than those who had not been so involved not because they were consultants but because they were drawn from the ranks of prestigious scholars. Those who published, who received research grants, were to the left of faculty who were primarily teachers (Lipset, 1982:144-148). The logic of these findings had been enunciated earlier by people like Thorstein Veblen (1934:226-227) in 1919, Merton (1968) and Joseph Schumpeter (1962:148) in the late 1930s or early 1940s, and C. P. Snow (1954:176) and Lazarsfeld in the 1950s (Lazarsfeld and Thielens, 1958:161-163). These analysts argued in different ways that scholars gain recognition in science and scholarship for originality, for rejection of what had previously been held to be true or useful. And, they suggested that those who were innovative and critical in scholarship tend to come from the same kind of backgrounds as people who are politically rebellious or radical; in other words, that innovation in intellectual work is a form of radicalism.[5]

As I have noted, the evidence from a number of surveys agreed with the generalizations of Veblen, et al. I could not understand, therefore, how Gouldner could find differently among sociologists. I was able to gain access to a detailed unpublished analysis of his own survey done for a Ph.D. dissertation (Sprehe, 1967), and discovered that my guesses were correct. Gouldner's data showed the same pattern as the other studies. All the then extant data on sociologists, including some more recent data analyzed by Everett Ladd and myself, are presented in an article (Lipset and Ladd, 1972), "The Politics of American Sociologists." Some of the results go back to survey research among academics conducted by James Leuba in 1914 and repeated in 1933 dealing with belief in God and immortality -topics that correlate highly with political attitudes (Leuba, 1921, 1950). He found in both studies that -unlike the considerable majority of Americans, and less than natural scientists -sociologists were inclined to be disbelievers, and strikingly the "greater" among them were much more likely to reject religious beliefs than the "lesser" (1950:38, 46-47).

There is no question that those who see the academic establishment or sociology as conservative are wrong. Ladd and I also reported in detail on findings that applied to academe-from community colleges to the most distinguished research universities-as well as within the different disciplines, in our book, The Divided Academy (1976). Dealing with a sample of 60,000 faculty, we could report on each discipline. The data showed that sociology has been among the most liberal or radical fields in the entirety of academe, as it had been in Lazarsfeld's and Thielens' earlier study of social scientists.

Ladd (1969) also examined a large list of scholars who signed an anti-Vietnam war ad in the New York Times. He found more of them came from sociology than from any other field. Though the social sciences as a group are on the left, within the category, economics and political science — the disciplines that deal with established institutions — are relatively more conservative. Sociology, anthropology, and social psychology — fields more concerned with social problems — have been the most liberal to left. The research indicated that the differences among disciplines are to some considerable degree related to differential recruitment patterns, to the kinds of people who were attracted to the varying fields. Manny Rosenberg (1957) had demonstrated in the early 1950s that the choice of majors by undergraduates, as well as graduate students, reflects variation in political orientation, much the same as among faculty. The correlations increase over time, because conservatives who start off concentrating in more liberal or left fields tend to drop out of these, and the reverse occurs for liberals who enter more conservative disciplines, like engineering or business. Seemingly the image of sociology, associated with topics like stratification, poverty, racial inequality, and the like, has attracted the left oriented.

Academe as a whole is, of course, considerably to the left of other occupations and professions — a fact that is related not only to the emphasis of leading scholars and intellectuals on innovation or creativity, but also to selective recruitment. Friedrich Hayek (1949), although a major conservative figure in the American sense of the word (he thought of himself as a classical liberal, a libertarian), wrote in 1949 that as he traveled around the faculty clubs of the United States, he found that the dominant tone of the conversations was socialist, by which, of course, he meant welfare state oriented. Hayek (1949:426-427) went on to observe that the brighter figures in academe were socialists. This is a generalization, one would think, that someone with his political leanings would not have enunciated unless the reality impressed him strongly. He accounted for this observation by the contention that intellectual and scholarly activities (as well as nonprofit fields in general) attract the more left disposed among young people, while the more establishment activities, particularly business and the free professions, draw from the more conservative. Hayek's hypothesis is borne out by the Carnegie data analyzed in The Divided Academy (Ladd and Lipset, 1976). There is a variety of other findings, which I will not go into here, that also indicate academe attracts people on the left. I cannot, however, resist mentioning a 1959 survey of Berkeley freshmen by Hanan Selvin and Warren Hagstrom (1965), which found a linear relationship between aspiring to be a professor and ideological self-identification. Three-fifths of self-described leftists wanted to be academics, compared to 10% of the very conservative.

I might also add, while on the subject, that Ladd's and my findings about the ideological traits of the successful scholars were criticized by leftists who did not want to accept the generalization that formal academic achievement, receiving research grants and awards, are related to liberal-left orientations. Some of the critics argued that our indicators of achievement or elite status were inadequate, too gross; that, if we could really focus on the figures at the very top of the professions, they would turn out to be more conservative. In other words, they suggested that there is a J-shaped relationship in which there is a correlation between achievement and left views, but that at the very top, the relationship reverses. To deal with this criticism, Ladd and I obtained funds to study the most prestigious people in academe, namely the members of the honorific societies, the National Academy of Sciences, the American Academy of Arts and Sciences, and the American Philosophical Society. If there is a J-shaped relationship, these scholars should turn out to be more conservative than the upper level of academe, as classi-·fied in sample surveys. But the relationship continued to be linear. Our sample of the members of these elite organizations found them to be on average somewhat more liberal-left than the people in the top universities (Lipset, 1982:150-153).

These findings had little or no impact on the opinions of the student and left activists who emerged in the 1960s. They continued to regard the academically successful as "sellouts." And sociology, living up to its image of being among the most leftist fields in academe, provided a disproportionate number of such protesters in the United States and abroad. These activists not only turned on the university in general as a center of support for the reactionary establishment, for the war, and other various nefarious activities, but those in sociology challenged the discipline itself. Their writings denounced the leaders of the field as right-wingers, as supporters of the status quo. They sought to demonstrate that the dominant theory, as well as most empirical research, was status quo oriented. The postwar consensus behind a positivist view of sociology, including the widespread acceptance of structure functional theory and quantitative methodology, broke down with a vengeance. One sociologist, himself on the left, Norman Birnbaum (1971:230), described the "Tower of Babel," which had emerged within the discipline. No theoretical or methodological orientation, especially functional analysis and statistical emphases, commanded wide acceptance any more. Marxism and other forms of "critical" thought took over. Sociologists took to denouncing each other. Many faculty supported student activism and the radical critiques of the university. Others, including myself, did not.

Cleavages over reaction to student activism were bitterly divisive. The newer and younger sociologists were most disposed to reject the old consensus, to put forth what they described as conflict theories-which derived from, if they were not themselves-some explicit form of Marxism. Many departments were bitterly split. A certain amount of mobility can be traced to these divisions. Berkeley lost sociologists to other universities, while six who stayed at the university moved to other departments. Harvard, which once prided itself on rarely losing faculty to other institutions, had to witness the departure of six tenured sociologists. Nothing comparable occurred with any other department at these universities. The Columbia department both lost some members and became bitterly fractionated, divisions that still remain. The relative degree of intellectual unity that had characterized earlier periods was at an end and has not been restored. Even today, the departments I know best -Berkeley, Columbia, Harvard, and Stanford-are bitterly divided (Berkeley less than the others), although the manifest content of their current intramural controversies are for the most part not ideologically political.

I must confess, however, to some uncertainty as to the extent that the internecine conflict within sociology is a function of greater ideological division and strength of adherents of leftist views -although I feel certain these have affected developments from the 1960s on. After writing a first draft of this paper dealing with the last 40 years, as I experienced them, I decided to explore earlier periods. I had known that my graduate department, Columbia, had experienced severe controversies between its two best known 1930s scholars, Lynd and MacIver, which paralyzed the appointment process (Page, 1982:47).[6] At the same time, the Harvard Sociology Department witnessed bitter tensions, first between Sorokin and Parsons, and from the 1950s on between Parsons and Homans. The Chicago department was notorious for internal fights before and after World War II. Ogburn was at odds with Wirth and Park. As noted, at least two major figures, Blumer and Riesman, left in the 1950s in large part because of tense relations with colleagues. Princeton, a new postwar department, which recruited many stars, soon deeply divided. And as Charles Page (1982) notes, the differences "worked against a strong departmental solidarity and now and then caused trouble in our ranks" (Page, 1982:153, 168).

Overtly, the pre-1960s conflicts among sociologists tended to emphasize methodological and theoretical issues, not ideology. The record clearly indicates that sociology, from its formative days on, has interested students who want to reform society. As Leuba's early surveys indicate, sociology recruited from the ideologically incorrect, from the irreligious, more disposed to be socially and politically concerned. Lewis Coser, writing of the turn of the century founding fathers of the discipline, stresses their "reformers' zeal" (Coser, 1954:15, 29). He reports that "Ward, Small, Ross, Veblen and Cooley ... all propose[d] to supplant American capitalist society with a different social system. The more conservative Sumner and Giddings were 'detail' rather than 'structural' reformers" (31). As Edward Shils (1980) has emphasized, there was strong support for the view that the field is or should be an "oppositional science meaning thereby that sociology is a factually documented denunciation of the society in which it is carried on." Marxism and socialism apart, whether conservative, progressive, or radical, the "major sociologists . . . all found their contemporary societies wanting" (41-42).

> The most weighty figures of American sociology before the great upsurge which preceded the Second World War were William Graham Sumner, Robert Park, William I. Thomas, and Charles H. Cooley. With the exception of Sumner, who expected nothing reasonable from any society and demanded only individual freedom — and who, therefore, found himself at home in the free-booting capitalistic America of the turn of the century-all of these men practiced a sociological analysis which was in accordance with a severely critical assessment of the American society which was taking form during their lifetime (42-43).

While sociology's truly radical period began in the 1960s, Shils contends that it is related and derivative from the earlier alienation, that it only accentuates certain traditions that have been present within the field. "Sociology has the tendency to reduce most motives to motives of self-aggrandizement and particularly all beliefs to self-deception and the self-deception of others . . . ." Sociologists have been characterized "by ethical repugnance for what they regard as the injustice of bourgeois society" (43).[7] Stephen and Jonathan Turner (1990:24) also point out the role of the discipline's reform constituency: "For most [early] sociology departments at both the graduate and undergraduate levels, then, one of the basic 'resources' of the emerging discipline was student demand for courses oriented to amelioration and reform." The Chicago School, which dominated the discipline from 1915 until World War 11, while heterogenous theologically and methodologically, was always interested in social reform (46-49). Mary Jo Deegan (1988), in a report on the Chicago School from 1892-1918, also concludes that "despite their internal differences . . . . Social reform was intrinsic to their conception of sociology" (162). And the hypothesis may be hazarded that scholars with reformist propensities will politicize intellectual, discipline, and personal controversies.

Not surprisingly, the American Sociological Society (ASS; later renamed "Association"), has been severely divided almost from its start in 1905, Fights among its leaders and their followers were intense. Unlike the situation in the great majority of other discipline organizations, contested elections for the presidency and other offices of the association go back at least to the 1920s (Rhoades, 1981:15). Bannister (1987) discusses "the annual wrangling over the presidency of the A.S.S." as of 1929, involving the "Chicago crowd," "the old guard" and "the younger men," which produced references to "deep laid political plots" and "conspiracy" (41).

During the 1930s there were "a series of battles within the American Sociological Society," which involved various organizational issues, but basically reflected tensions over the approach of the field (189). Some pointed to "a generalized anti-elitism [which] fused private grievances, career-related anxieties, the shock of the Depression, and dissatisfaction with the structure of the profession . . ." (190). Humanists were pitted against positivists and believers in "value-free" science" against "social activists" (190). Long before the 1960s, a non-ideological "anti-establishment" animus seemed to affect electoral outcomes. Less prestigious scholars were able to defeat, often easily, leaders of the discipline in the ASS and ASA elections. Ideology, however, became central from the 1960s on. The organization began to debate political resolutions, intended to put it and the discipline on record regarding various issues, particularly the war. But it should be noted that membership referenda and surveys taken in the 1960s and early 1970s found that while the great majority, supported the activist positions, a plurality voted against the organizations going on record with respect to policy issues (Rhoades, 1981:60). In effect, they reaffirmed the original 1905 Constitution of the Society that had explicitly barred "approving or disapproving specific sociological doctrines or specific schemes of social betterment" (Rhoades, 1981:5).

Political conflicts penetrated the discipline more deeply than ever. They lowered morale in various departments. This is not to make any judgment as to who was right or wrong about the issues, but to conclude that the politicization of academe in the 1960s and early 1970s, stronger in sociology than in most disciplines, undermined the field. Given the disdain, if not open antagonism, expressed about research and outside funding, some very able younger sociologists were never able to establish themselves as scholars.

As the country, academe, and sociology moved beyond the conflicts precipitated by the Vietnam War, the situation changed. The intensity, the overtness, of conflict diminished. The scientific consensus and intellectual unity, however, did not return. This remains true to the present. And sociology remains far to the left of the country and the bulk of academe. The most recent national survey of 5000 academics conducted by the Carnegie Foundation for the Advancement of Teaching early in 1989 found that 43% of those who identify themselves as in the social sciences (anthropology, political science, sociology, and social work) said they were liberals, an additional 29% were moderate liberals, while only 14% were conservatives (12% moderately so). Other social sciences were much less liberal: economics, 18%; psychology, 28%.[8] Unfortunately, the 1989 study did not differentiate sociology as compared to political science and anthropology.

However, the University of Virginia's Survey Research Center demonstrated anew in 1991 that sociologists remain much more leftist than political scientists. In a national survey of the two disciplines, 26% of the sociologists identified their politics as "extremely liberal," compared to 16% of the political scientists. Combining the categories extremely liberal, liberal, and slightly liberal produces 74% among sociologists and 56% among political scientists. As of 1991, only a minuscule 4% of the sociologists chose one of the three conservative positions to describe their politics. It may be, however, that some of the humanities, particularly the language and literature disciplines, which became quite radicalized in the 1970s and 1980s are now to the left of sociology. The Modern Language Association seems much more aggressive politically than the ASA. The percentage among "humanists" reporting themselves as liberals in the 1989 Carnegie Foundation Survey was practically the same as for social scientists, 42%.

The politicization of sociology affects the way we look at each other. There appears to be much less consensus in sociology than elsewhere in the social sciences about which theoretical, methodological, and empirical approaches are best, about which scholars are the most important in the field. Thus, the 1977 Ladd-Lipset national survey of American academics that inquired into the top three individuals in their respective disciplines found a larger proportion of economists, political scientists, and psychologists — even English professors -picking the same person as number one than was true for sociologists. Economists revealed the greatest consensus among social scientists; even their third-ranking member was cited by three-fifths, as compared to less than a third (31%), among sociologists. The three leaders among the economists were Friedman, Samuelson, and Arrow: the first, a noted laissez-faire libertarian; the second a Keynesian; and the third a socialist. A substantial majority voted for each. Comparable discipline variations occurred with respect to the prestige ranking of departments. There was much less consensus among sociologists.[9]

The ASA remains more politicized in its elections than the organizations in allied fields. In 1981, the American Political Science Association (APSA), which had contested elections for the previous decade, stopped having them, not because of any legislative action, but because the left-wing group within the discipline -the Caucus For A New Political Science — decided that it made no sense for them to contest the elections, to take part in "sand box" politics. Ever since then, APSA elections have been unanimous. The nominating committee, appointed by two preceding presidents, presents a full slate, one candidate for each office. Opposing candidates may be nominated by petition, but almost none have been since 1981. Economics also does not have contests for office in the American Economics Association. Sociology, as we know, continues to be marked by elections, often bitterly fought ones. Our high or low point was reached a few years ago when six people ran for the presidency. In 1993, we had three candidates. The number running in 1994 is four.

We are all aware, too aware, that to some limited degree we are an endangered discipline. A few leading universities have closed down their sociology departments. These include Washington University, once the most radical departments of all, and the University of Rochester. There have been serious proposals to drop sociology at Utah, Yale, and San Diego State, and to merge others, as at Southern Methodist in the spring of 1993.[10] While each situation is distinct and can be related to special problems at particular schools, I would note the evidence that, generally, administrators are less supportive or more hostile to sociology than to other fields. In a recent national survey of reactions to nine disciplines (Lynch and McFerron, 1993), a sample of 144 deans were asked to rate "departmental quality in teaching and research .... [S]ociology comes out last in both dimensions" (3). Lynch and McFerron "conclude that departments of sociology are not random targets of administrative violence . . . . [T]heir deans (and presumably their deans' superiors) honestly believe that sociologists do inferior teaching and research" (7). And possibly related to these judgments, Lynch and McFerron report that at the same schools as the deans, sociologists are "the most subjectively disfranchised group we studied" (7), i.e., feel they do not influence university policies. "The general picture of sociology departments which emerges is one of political befuddlement which we believe has led to many of the departments being in serious trouble with their deans" (7).

I am not convinced that these judgments about teaching and research are the primary source of administrative discontent. Lois DeFleur (1991), a first-rate sociologist, who is also the President of the State University of New York at Binghampton, described the situation as she and her administrative peers see it in a talk to the 1991 ASA convention:

> I have found over the years that when I meet with administrators, as soon as they find out I am a sociologist, they all have a woeful story to tell about how they just can't understand how their Sociology Department can continue to fight among themselves, and that if that continues, they will in fact write them off. They won't channel resources to a department which is incapable of keeping its own house in order; that does not support the professional development of junior faculty or that seems more interested in petty squabbling than the atmosphere and reputation of the university. There are, in fact, many worthy competitors for funding (7).

A highly placed dean at one of the most eminent universities in the country reported comparable administrative malaise with sociology across the country. She also blamed it on intradepartment bickering over personnel matters that are brought to the administrations to resolve, and that leads them to want to get rid of the troublesome discipline. I can testify from personal experience at different research universities that sociologists tattle and snitch on each other, that they are less able to settle their internal squabbles without running to the administration than other fields. Repeatedly minorities have gone to the deans or other campus officials to complain about the other members of their department; they have tried to demonstrate to deans and provosts that most of their colleagues are professionally incompetent. Not surprisingly, as we have seen in the results of the survey of deans reported earlier, many wind up believing sociologists are inadequate in research and teaching. And administrators report that this kind of quarrelsome behavior is not to be found to a comparable degree in other fields. It is noteworthy that when Parsons and Lazarsfeld retired from Harvard and Columbia, each was soon thereafter asked by the chairs of their departments, with whom they had been at odds, to vacate their offices.

I do not know the story of all the dissolved and threatened departments, but it is clear that the one at Washington University literally killed itself by bitter internal denunciations (Etzkowitz, 1988:95-113). Utah came close to having the same outcome for similar reasons. At a session on the state of sociology at the 1992 ASA meetings, we heard a report on the Yale situation, which put the responsibility for the problems of sociology there entirely on the administration, on the supposed fact that university officialdom was in the hands of humanists, who did not like sociology. During the discussion, I mentioned the point I have made here about backbiting among sociologists as a major source of our problems. After the meeting, two people came up to me to say the same thing had occurred at Yale.

As another example of the way we harm ourselves by our internal conflicts, I can cite the elections to membership in the National Academy of Sciences. The National Academy created a Behavioral and Social Sciences Division in the late 1960s. This division includes all the social sciences. Sociology was able to elect a small number of members in the first few elections. But that has been almost the end; few get elected anymore, though one did in 1993. The procedure that the academy follows at elections is to have each discipline run a kind of primary in which members vote on nominees in their field. Candidates who receive the support of two-thirds of those in a specialty go on to another evaluation among a group of related disciplines, and finally to a ballot that is sent to all members in all fields. Very few, if any, sociologists are on the final ballot each year in part because not enough sociologists will vote for each other. The same does not occur to anywhere near the same extent in other fields. Natural scientists consider it extremely important for colleagues to be elected to the academy. They caucus before elections, seeking to obtain agreement on slates. Sociologists have attempted to do the same, but usually without success. As with appointments to departments, sociologists divide bitterly over the qualifications of their fellows. They would rather see nobody chosen than someone whom they do not approve of.

Conclusion

There is, unfortunately, one more quantitative indicator of the less than happy position of the field. Bill D'Antonio (1992) has reported on the discipline variations in GRE, Graduate Record Exam, scores. Our results have been declining steadily from the mid-1960s to the late 1980s, while other fields have not (110). Except for education students, sociologists are at the bottom, have the lowest scores (112). As a discipline, we clearly have not been attracting the best and the brightest, although the leading departments do get students with good scores. I have no hypothesis to explain this other than the assumption that our image does not make us appear intellectually challenging.[11]

More depressing than GRE scores is the finding of a survey of faculty in nine disciplines, that in agreement with the opinions of the deans in the same schools, reported earlier, "sociologists rated their own teaching less positively than teachers in the other eight disciplines," and see their own research as average (Lynch and McFerron, 1993:3). These judgments may reflect the disdain they have for sociologists other than themselves.

There is some indication of the beginning of acceptance of intellectual, even perhaps political, diversity. Every effort to evaluate the status of departments over the last fifteen years indicates that one known almost exclusively for its emphasis on quantitative methodology, not its politics, Wisconsin, has been in the lead. But as noted, there is much less agreement about such rankings than in other fields. Though I will not give the names of the two leaders in sociology in the 1975 faculty survey, because the sample of sociologists was too small, I can say that the top two as well are known as quantitative methodologists and are relatively conservative politically. Three of the last four presidents of the ASA, Coleman, Upset, and Etzioni, are not politically correct from a left point of view. These developments suggest that a decline in the politicization of the discipline may be underway, even though the overwhelming majority remain considerably to the left of the average American or professor.

What is the state of sociology? I am afraid that I still must say, "Not very healthy."[12] What can be done about it? I do not know. Obviously, preaching to ourselves to do better, to be more friendly to each other, to be willing to accept those with whom we have intellectual or political differences does not seem to work. It has been tried within our part of the National Academy of Sciences to little avail. Thus, I must report that we still appear to be a self-destructive discipline. I will be interested to see to what extent people agree with me, and if they do, what solutions they offer, if any. I would also suggest the need for some intense self-study, to find out the differences between sociologists -students and practitioners and those in other fields. I would note too that Herb Blumer demonstrated in the 1950s and early 1960s what a catholic sociology, one that emphasized competence, not adherence to specific approaches, could accomplish. But, I suppose, it could also be argued that by stressing diversity he created a time bomb that finally exploded.

Acknowledgments

I am indebted to the Woodrow Wilson International Center for Scholars and the Hoover Institution of Stanford University for support, and to M. Scott Billingsley for research assistance.

Notes

1. This is an elaboration of an American Sociological Association presidential presentation to a plenary session of the Southern Sociological Association on April 2, 1993.

2. Al Gouldner and I lived across the street from each other in the Bronx when we were in high school. But since he was in the YCL, the Young Communist League, and I in the YPSL, the Young People's Socialist League, we did not associate much, either there or at the Columbia Graduate Department.

3. On Parsons' activities as a student, see Lipset and Ladd (1972:78).

4. Sociology led the way almost everywhere. As Cohn-Bendit and Cohn-Bendit (1968:47), leaders in the French movement, noted, "student agitation since 1960, abroad as in France, has been rife among sociologists far more than among other social scientists and philosophers . . ." (see also Gouldner, 1970:10; Riesman and Harris, 1969:63; Lipset and Ladd, 1972:68).

5. It may be noted that the majority of those involved in Project Camelot — a Defense Department financed enterprise, designed to study revolutionary situations in the Third World in the early 1960s, including its Director, Rex Hopper — were on the left. Hopper was a disciple of C. Wright Mills. He argued that since the project was unclassified, its findings would be available and helpful to revolutionaries (see Horowitz, 1967).

6. During the years of rivalry between MacIver and Lynd, Columbia's sociologists became increasingly divided between support of one or the other, and in 1939 matters came to a head with the issuance of lengthy statements by each of the protagonists on the desirable future of the department" (Page, 1982:47).

7. On the general role of alienation and alienated sociology, see Friedrichs (1970:63-75).

8. These findings were generated by a secondary analysis of the data by the Roper Data Library at the University of Connecticut.

9. We never published these results since a 5000 national sample only yielded 100-200 persons per discipline, too small to give reliable estimates for given persons or units. But the overall PC. generalizations hold.

10. In making the proposal, the dean, James Jones (Cronfel, 1993:1). proclaimed, "Sociology as a discipline has been in intellectual disarray all across the country."

11. D'Antonio notes that these results may be affected by the fact that "sociology student cohorts are the most likely to include larger proportions of women and minorities than any of the other disciplines listed, both groups that have traditionally scored less well on these kinds of exams" (110).

12. For a more optimistic point of view, see Collins (1986).

References

Bannister, Robert. 1987. *Sociology and Scientism: The American Quest for Objectivity.* Chapel Hill: University of North Carolina Press.

Belk, Daniel. 1967. *Marxian Socialism in the United States.* Princeton, NJ: Princeton University Press.

Birnbaum, Norman. 1971. *Toward a Critical Sociology.* New York: Oxford University Press.

Cohn-Bendit, Daniel and G. Cohn-Bendit. 1968. *Obsolete Communism: The Left-Wing Alternative.* New York: McGraw-Hill.

Collins, Randall. 1986. "Is 1980s sociology in the doldrums?" *American Journal of Sociology* 91(5):1336-1355.

Coser, Lewis. 1954. *Toward a Sociology of Social Conflict.* Ph.D dissertation, Columbia University.

Cronfet, Natalie. 1993. "Anthropology, sociology, may be combined." *The Daily Campus* (Southern Methodist University), (April 11):1, 4.

D'Antonio, William V. 1992. "Recruiting sociologists." In T. C. Halliday and M. Janowitz (eds.), *Sociology and its Publics*: 99-136. Chicago, IL: University of Chicago Press.

Deegan, Mary Jo. 1988. *Jane Addams and the Men of the Chicago School.* New Brunswick, NJ: Transaction Books.

DeFleur, Lois B. 1991. "Strengthening the position of sociology within the university." *Address to the American Sociological Association Convention,* Cincinnati, OH, August 25.

Etzkowitz, Henry. 1998. "The contradictions of radical sociology." *Critical Sociology* 15(2):95-113.

Friedrichs, Robert W. 1970. *A Sociology of Sociology.* New York: The Free Press.

Glazer, Nathan. 1961. *Social Basis of American Communism.* New York: Harcourt, Brace and World.

Gouldner, Alvin W. 1970. *The Coming Crisis of Western Sociology.* New York: Basic Books.

Hayek, Friedrich A. 1949. "The intellectuals and socialism." *The University of Chicago Law Review.* 16(2):417-433.

Horowitz, Irving L. 1967. *The Rise and Fall of Project Camelot.* Cambridge, MA: MIT Press.

Ladd, Everett C., Jr. 1969. "Professors and political petitions," *Science* 163:1425-30.

Ladd, Everett Carll Jr. and Seymour Martin Lipset. 1976. *The Divided Academy*. New York: W.W. Norton.

Lazarsfeld, Paul and Wagner Thielens, Jr. 1958. *The Academic Mind*. Glencoe, IL: The Free Press.

Lazarsfeld-Jahods, Marie and Hans Zelsel. 1932. *Die Arbeitslosen von Marienthal*. Leipzig: Hirzel.

Leuba, James II. 1921. *The Belief in God and Immortality*. La Salle, IL: Open Court Publishing.

———————. 1950. The Reformation of the Churches. Boston, MA: The Beacon Press.

Lipset, Seymour Martin. 1950. *Agrarian Socialism: The Cooperative Commonwealth Federation in Saskatchewan*. Berkeley: University of California Press.

———————. 1982. "The academic mind at the top." *Public Opinion Quarterly* 46:143-69.

Lipset, Seymour Martin and Everett Carll Ladd, Jr. 1972. "The politics of American sociologists," *American Journal of Sociology*. 78(7):67-104.

Lipset, Seymour Martin, Martin Trow, and James S. Coleman. 1956. *Union Democracy*. Glencoe, IL.: The Free Press.

Lynch, David M. and J. Richard McFerron. 1993.   "A discipline in trouble: Why more sociology departments may be closing shortly." *Footnotes* 21(2):3, 7.

Merton, Robert K. 1968.   *Social Theory and Social Structure*. New York: The Free Press.

Michels, Robert. 1962. *Political Parties: The Sociological Study of The Oligarchical Tendencies of Modern Democracy*, E. and C. Paul (trs.) New York: The Free Press.

Page, Charles. 1982. *Fifty Years in the Sociological Enterprise*. Amherst: University of Massachusetts Press.

Parsons, Talcott. 1954. *Essays in Sociological Theory*. Glencoe, IL: The Free Press.

———————. 1956. *Structures and Process in Industrial Societies*. Glencoe, IL: The Free Press.

Rhoades, Lawrence. 1981. *A History of the American Sociological Association: 1905-1980*. Washington. DC: American Sociological Association.

Riesman, David and T. George Harris. 1969. "The young are captives of each other: A conversation with David Riesman and T. George Harris." *Psychology Today* 3(October): 28-33, 43-67.

Rosenberg, Morris. 1957. *Occupations and Values*. Glencoe, IL: The Free Press.

Schumpeter, Joseph. 1962. *Capitalism, Socialism, and Democracy*. New York: Harper & Row.

Selvin, Hanan C. and Warren Hagstrom. 1965. "Determinants of support for civil liberties." In S. M. Lipset and S. S. Wolin (eds.), *The Berkeley Student Revolt: Facts and Interpretations*: 494-518. New York: Doubleday Anchor Books.

Selznick, Philip. 1949. *TVA and the Grassroots*. Berkeley: University of California Press.

Shils, Edward. 1980. *The Calling Of Sociology and Other Essays on the Pursuit of Learning*. Chicago: University of Chicago Press.

Snow, C. P. 1954. *The New Men*. London: Macmillan.

Sprehe, J. T. 1967. *The Climate of Opinion in Sociology: A Study of the Professional Values and Belief Systems of Sociologists*. Ph.D. dissertation, Washington University, St. Louis, MO.

Stouffer, Samuel. 1954. *Communism, Conformity, and Civil Liberties*. Glencoe, IL: The Free Press.

Strodtbeck, Fred. 1994. Personal correspondence, February 14.

Turner, Stephen Park and Jonathan H. Turner. 1990. *An Institutional Analysis of American Sociology*. Newbury Park, CA: Sage Publications.

Veblen, Thorstein. 1934. "The intellectual pre-eminence of Jews in modern Europe." *Essays in Our Changing Order*. New York: Viking.

13

The Transformation of the American Sociological Association

Ida Harper Simpson and Richard L. Simpson

The American Sociological Society began as a group of scholars, formed for the purpose of exchanging knowledge and research-based ideas. Its objective was to advance the discipline of sociology, and it retained that focus through the 1950s. Since the 1950s, ASA has expanded its activities beyond its original disciplinary focus. It has taken more interest in nondisciplinary activities and has expended effort and resources on them. It has become not just a body of scholar/researchers, but increasingly a professional association. ASA's emphasis on applied sociological practice has grown, as has its attention to devising formal ways to improve undergraduate teaching. The Association has also become more responsive to political interests of its membership. It has supported the pursuit of social justice in the world at large. It has taken steps to democratize its own structure, seeking more representation and participation of previously excluded or disadvantaged groups as ends in themselves.

These actions embody cherished democratic values, but as organizational goals and actions they have blurred the disciplinary focus of ASA. They have structurally differentiated ASA's disciplinary functions from its professional and adaptive activities, and the different functions now compete for resources. The changes have diluted the control of the Association by disciplinary elites and have channeled ASA resources into activities that do not advance the discipline. This transformation of ASA and some of its consequences for the Association are the topics of this paper. Most of the data are from official proceedings of the ASA. We did not have copies of the proceedings for all years, and as a result the time periods we have used are not systematically selected. We do think, however, that our sample captures the history of ASA and that our lack of data on a systematically selected set of years does not distort our findings or conclusions.

Pressures on ASA, and its Responses

Membership in the American Sociological Society (renamed "Association" in 1959) grew from 3,522 in 1950 to 6,345 in 1959 (Riley, 1960), an 80% increase. It grew another 135% over the next thirteen years, to 14,934 in 1972. In 1972 there were more than four times as many ASA members as there had been twenty-two years earlier. One would expect such growth to influence the way an organization operates; but growth by itself would seem likely to affect chiefly the structure of organizational maintenance and coordination, and should not necessarily produce shifts of emphasis from one kind of goal or activity to others. In this period of rapid growth, ASA faced other kinds of pressures from its membership, including direct political pressures. ASA's responses to these pressures produced shifts of the latter kind, with new functions coming into prominence. Below we trace these changes in ASA activities, and interpret them as responses to pressures from outside and inside the Association. The newly emerging constituencies were non-academic sociologists, political activists, women, minorities, and sociologists as teachers.

In 1959, the American Sociological Society was compelled by the licensing of psychologists to try to gain formal public recognition of sociology as a distinct discipline, in order to protect the rights of sociologists to practice their discipline as a profession. Not only were sociological social psychologists at issue; sociologists employed in government wanted recognition of their discipline as an occupational category, as did other applied sociologists in corrections, industry, and other fields.

The 1960 Program Committee asked Talcott Parsons in his role as chair of the Committee on the Profession to prepare a paper on problems confronting sociology as a profession as a basis for discussion at a General Session on Analysis of the Sociological Profession. Parsons (1959:547) conceived of a profession as "a category of occupational role which is organized about the mastery of and fiduciary responsibility for any important segment of a society's cultural tradition...." He went on to note that professional roles are of two types: those in which the professional functions are performed and those of collectivities formed by fellow-professionals for the purpose of promoting the interests of their field. The objective that had directed the founding of the Society more than fifty years earlier in 1905, as stated in the Society's constitution, was "the encouragement of sociological research and discussion, and the promotion of intercourse between persons engaged in the scientific study of society." The Society had been founded around the discipline.

Unlike applied fields such as medicine, sociology is a scientific discipline dedicated primarily to the advancement and transmission of knowledge in its field and only secondarily to the communication of such knowledge to nonmembers and to its utilization in practical affairs. The formal organization of sociologists around the discipline of sociology defines the central goal of ASA as the promotion of the discipline of sociology through the sharing of research among its members and through the training of students who will carry on the research function. From a disciplinary perspective, the training of graduate students who will pursue the discipline is the central instructional interest of the association, not the teaching of undergraduates who are unlikely to become sociologists, or the teaching of professional students in other fields. The disciplinary interest is not in teaching, but in the training of graduate students. Graduate programs in sociology are the reproductive units of the discipline.

While sociologists are expected first and foremost to be scientists dedicated to developing the discipline of sociology and training their successors, like all sciences sociology can be applied, and sociologists have the "responsibility for facilitating the use of sociological knowledge for practical interests ..." (Parsons, 1959). The discipline has applied implications, and sociologists are responsible for bringing their disciplinary knowledge to bear on social matters. But this responsibility does not alter the fact that the discipline of sociology is institutionalized in the research university, not in the society at large. This bifurcation between the discipline as inquiry set within the university and the application of its knowledge made applied interests the most serious problem facing ASA in the late 1950s and the early 1960s.

In the thirty-five years since the General Session on the profession for which Parsons prepared a position paper, the relation of the profession to nonacademic employment has remained a breeding ground on issues confronting the Association. Some concerns are essentially the same as those of the 1950s, whereas others pertain to the position of practitioners in ASA and their access to associational resources. Since sociological practice lacks an institutionalized role, its market is controlled by employers, not by the Association. Nonacademic sociologists wanted ASA's help to try to establish and gain some control over a market for themselves as sociologists. Applied nonacademic employment has produced three kinds of issues that have come before ASA for action: (1) licensing and certification of sociologists - i.e., defining a market for sociological practice, (2) ethics - how sociological knowledge will be used, and who will define how it is used, and (3) legitimation of a practice specialty within the discipline and within ASA, so as to give practitioners visibility and an audience within the Association. ASA has responded to these pressures in different ways, including the establishing of a standing committee on practice and the sponsoring of a journal, which failed to attract enough subscriptions to keep it afloat. Despite this one failure, practitioners have secured a visible position in the Association.

Another challenge to the Association has come from the larger society and its social problems. Sociology in the United States developed around social problems. This concern with the real world linked the development of U. S. sociology to empirical research and helped to institutionalize it in research universities as an empirical discipline, in contrast to the philosophical emphasis of sociology in Europe. The deep affinity of sociology for social issues has long been evident in the values and ideology of sociologists. Sociologists identify with the underdog, and support the rights of the less privileged and the outcast. The institutionalization of the discipline as an empirical science in the first half of the twentieth century evolved norms of research to limit the penetration of social ideology into the discipline. Weber's (1946) essay on science as a vocation, with the researcher role as a dispassionate lens, was the disciplinary model of scholarship that was widely accepted as a norm for graduate education and research. Following World War II, disciplinary elites assumed implicitly that this value-neutral model governed their association, the ASA.

The social movements of the 1960s and 1970s challenged the presuppositions of the inward-looking disciplinary model. In contrast to disciplinary associations, client-oriented professional associations have institutionalized roles for individuals to express their social values. Medicine has charity work; law, pro bono work; and the ministry, visitation. Such institutionalization protects associational boundaries, limiting the infusion of social issues into the professional association. Sociology has no institutionalized community-based roles for individual sociologists to address social concerns. The association is thus directly subject to penetration by external social movements.

Two different kinds of challenges came out of political movements, both in the form of caucuses. The impetus for the first was the Vietnam War, with an initial challenge made at the 1967 Annual Meetings in San Francisco - a demonstration and a resolution calling for the end of the war successfully sponsored by the Sociology Liberation Movement. From this beginning, militants who embraced liberation ideologies organized themselves as a radical caucus and successfully navigated the passage of resolutions at Business Meetings for the ASA to take public stands on ideological issues. They rejected the Weberian model in favor of an externally-oriented activism that would align ASA with revolutionary actions. Resolutions initiated at the Business Meeting became items on Council's agenda and increasingly competed with disciplinary matters for Council's time. For instance, in 1975 at its midyear meeting in Washington, "With all eighteen members present, (the 1975) Council acted on a wide variety of items but spent most of its time debating the merits of seventeen resolutions passed at the Annual Business Meeting in Montreal" (Footnotes, 1975:1). Included were resolutions calling for protest, censure and sanctions, as well as resolutions proposing revisions of some of the By-Laws of ASA.

Another pressure on ASA was political activism by caucuses of women and African Americans, who demanded in the late 1960s that their respective groups be accorded more power and more opportunities for participation in ASA affairs. These minorities wanted formal recognition within the Association, and each pressed its interests under a banner of group representation. Unlike another pressure group that arose at about the same time - the Sociology Liberation Movement, whose main activity was symbolic pronouncements about political affairs in the larger society - the caucuses of women and minorities contested the power structure of the Association itself. The ASA Council acceded to many of their demands. For example, in 1968, Council endorsed a resolution presented the Caucus of Black Sociologists by "resolving that the ASA shall make every effort to ensure that black sociologists are brought into the fullest participation in all aspects of the governance and other activities of the Association" (Rhoades, 1980:1). In 1970, Council endorsed a Black Caucus recommendation that a staff position be established concerned with problems of Black sociologists. The position was filled in 1972, and a year later it was enlarged and renamed Executive Specialist for Women and Minorities. The Women's Caucus was also active at this time, with its resolutions favorably received. The 1970 Council instructed the 1971 president to establish an ad hoc Committee on the Status of Women. By the mid-1970s, ASA had embraced major interests of women and of minorities, creating programs and committees designed to increase their numbers and participation. Other disadvantaged groups have followed, receiving sympathetic responses from ASA to their requests that it be attentive to their interests.

The caucuses of collectivized members brought their collective identities into their ASA participation, challenging the Association to adapt to their collective interests on the grounds of social justice. The Association, composed as it is of persons whose predominant values are with underdogs and who champion social justice in the society, voted new goals and charges for itself - to become more open, to represent the societal minorities among its members. New kinds of concerns were added to its governance and daily functions.

In earlier times there were separate collectivities of sociologists in regional and specialty societies, but these groups had been formed around disciplinary issues, unlike the later pressure groups. The Association dealt with these specialized groups in much the same way as it dealt with the later ones. It brought them into the system of governance. Regional societies were given Council seats. But in time the Association, whose Council had become unwieldy because of its inclusion of members whose interests were centered in their own subdisciplinary or regional groups, reconstituted the Council to include only members elected at large by the entire ASA electorate. Everett C. Hughes (1962) had opposed the inclusion of regionally-elected Council members on the ground that ASA was a disciplinary and not a professional association. Professions, Hughes argued, are organized as federations with representatives from local and state societies. In 1967, a constitutional change eliminated from the Council the representatives from regional and affiliated societies and the editors of ASA publications, on the premise that the Association should be a society of individual sociologists. The Faris Committee, which recommended the constitutional change, retained vestiges of regional representation by recommending that the Committee on Committees and the Committee on Nominations be elected by members in six equal-size voting districts.

Another pressure on ASA arose from still a different societal situation. Baby boomers swelled the demand for higher education. New universities were established in the 1950s and 1960s as branches in state systems, in city universities, and in two-year community colleges. Sociology had a market in them, which, when added to course demands in older institutions, pushed undergraduate enrollments to the highest levels either before or since then. Undergraduate sociology was a big consumer item. Sociology in secondary schools had long been served by a standing committee of ASA, but in the mide-1970s, undergraduate college education became visible within the Association. Under the sponsorship of the Section on Undergraduate Education, a teaching service program was assigned to the Executive office in 1978-79; the 1979 Council expanded ASA's teaching functions by creating a standing Committee on Teaching, enlarging the teaching services program, authorizing the development of a Departmental Subscription Service, and establishing an annual award for distinguished contribution to teaching. A journal on teaching was also established. Teaching had joined practice as a professional concern. Proponents of the teaching emphasis saw it in essentially the same light as Parsons had. At an ASA-supported task force meeting in November 1974 in Chicago, participants, who were members of the Section on Undergraduate Education, noted that "few students develop a commitment to the discipline' from their undergraduate courses (Footnotes, 1974:1).

ASA reacted to these pressures of the 1960s and 1970s mainly by absorbing the pressure groups into its structure. A result has been to expand the goals and functions of the Association beyond its initial disciplinary objective. Functions are more differentiated now, encompassing more professional and activist interests. Functions of the Association are of four main kinds: disciplinary functions that relate ASA to the field of sociology, professional functions that deal with work issues other than research and graduate education, adaptive functions that relate the Association to the socio-political environment, and functions that maintain the organization and ensure its viability. We shall call these functions, respectively, disciplinary, professional, adaptive, and maintenance. (These categories are adapted from Simpson, 1988.) Our thesis is that disciplinary interests have declined as new interests have competed for organizational resources, and that their decline has diluted the control of the association by members in research universities with Ph.D. programs, the reproductive structure of the discipline. Committee deliberations, Council actions, and other activities of ASA will be discussed below to chart the shifts in ASA functions.

ASA Activities and Functions

ASA conducts its affairs mainly through three structures: The Council, committees, and the Executive Office. The Council governs ASA, acting as both a legislative and judicial body, in both proactive and reactive ways. Table I classifies motions acted on by five councils in yearly meetings from 1960 through 1992, and shows two main patterns. The 1970 and later councils dealt with markedly different kinds of issues than the Executive Committee had in 1960. (For 1960, the Executive Committee's minutes were analyzed rather than Council's because the 1960 Council included representatives of regional and affiliated societies, and matters that came before it appear to have been more routine than those coming before the Executive Committee.) Disciplinary motions made up more than half of all actions taken by the 1960 body; in subsequent years they hovered between a quarter and a third of all decisions. In 1979, when they were nearly a third of

Council's actions, President Blalock took a proactive stance on disciplinary matters. His presidential report to Council asked, "What can the ASA do to advance the quality of the discipline in terms of our research, teaching, and publications?" The proportionate decrease in disciplinary actions reflected increases in adaptive and maintenance decisions. As councils dealt with thorny political issues, their disciplinary decisions became increasingly routinized around approving committee recommendations on editors for journals, scholarship awards, and annual programs.

Table I
Categories of Council Actions, 1960-1992*

Year	Disciplinary (%)	Professional (%)	Adaptive (%)	Maintenance (%)	Total
1960	52.6	15.8	10.5	21.1	19
1970	25.3	12.0	25.3	37.3	83
1979	32.5	13.5	19.0	34.9	126
1987 - 88	29.1	13.6	21.4	35.9	103
1991 - 92	25.4	13.6	25.4	35.6	59

*1960 actions are for the Executive Committee of the Council; minutes of full Council meetings do not report actions taken by Council. Meeting, March 25, 1960, reported in *American Sociological Review* 25 (1960): 410-411. 1970-1992 figures are for all actions taken by Council for that year. In 1979 it met four times, but in the other years only three times. Sources: 1970: *American Sociologist* 6 (1970) : 59-71; *American Sociologist* 7 (1971) : 63-68. 1979: *Footnotes* 7 (1979), No. 1 (January) :11; No. 4 (April) : 8-9; No. 6 (August) :18-19; No. 8 (November) : 7. 1987-88: *Footnotes* 15 (1987), No. 8 (November) : 15-16; *Footnotes* 16 (1988), No. 5 (May) : 14-16; No. 9 (December) : 21-22. 1991-92: *Footnotes* 20 (1992), No. 2 (February) : 14-16; No. 5 (May) : 21-22; No. 10 (December) : 14.

The growing functional and structural differentiation of ASA elaborated its maintenance functions. The organization needed more tending. Besides the shifts in the functions affected by decisions, there were also a rise and fall in the number of decisions from 1960 through 1992, approximating a bell-shaped curve. This pattern parallels the institutionalization of the adaptive and professional functions in ASA, so that by the late 1980s there were fewer issues to deal with than in the 1970s.

A similar tale is told by ASA committee reports analyzed in Table II. Slightly over two-thirds of the 16 committees in 1960 were disciplinary; six years later, disciplinary committees had declined to 45% of all committees, mainly as a result of an increase in the total number of committees. The absolute number of disciplinary committees remained relatively constant, ranging from 9 to 12, except in 1971 when they dropped to 7 and in 1987 when they increased to 16. Proportionately, however, they declined over the thirty years. The proportionate share they lost was picked up by professional and adaptive committees, with inroads being made chiefly by professional committees in the 1960s and by adaptive committees in the 1970s. Maintenance committees grew absolutely, but proportionately they hovered from around a quarter to a third of all committees, except in 1984 when they dropped to 20%. In 1992, ASA was considerably less a disciplinary society than it had been in the 1960s.

Table II
Categories of Committees of American Sociological Association, 1960-1992*

Year	Disciplinary (%)	Professional (%)	Adaptive (%)	Maintenance (%)	Total
1960	68.8	6.3	0	25.0	16
1966	45.0	20.0	5.0	30.0	20
1971	29.6	33.3	3.7	33.3	27
1977	43.5	17.4	13.0	26.1	23
1980	40.0	23.3	13.3	23.3	30
1984	34.3	31.4	14.3	20.0	35
1987	34.8	34.8	13.4	34.8	46
1992	26.2	31.0	14.3	28.6	42

*Subcommittees are excluded from the tallies. Data are from *American Sociological Review*, *The American Sociologist*, and *Footnotes*. In 1977, committees listed in the annual program included three that were not mentioned in *Footnotes*, and one listed in *Footnotes* was not in the annual program. Since the annual program was not available for earlier years, the list in *Footnotes* was used.

The growth of professional and adaptive functions and the relative decline of disciplinary ones is also visible in the expenditures of ASA. Table III compares expenditures for 1960 and 1991 by functional categories. Disciplinary expenditures dropped proportionately by almost half in the thirty-year period, while professional and administrative expenditures rose sharply. Now, with professional and adaptive functions firmly institutionalized, almost as much of the annual budget is allotted to professional as to disciplinary items, and 169% as much of the budget is spent on administrative/bureaucratic activities as on disciplinary ones. For every dollar spent, only a little over a quarter goes to promote the discipline, compared with a little over a half thirty years earlier.

Table III
ASA Expenditures, 1960 and 1991

Type of Expenditure	Percent of Total Expenditures	
	1960	1991
Disciplinary		
Publications	45.0	21.2
Annual Meetings	4.7	6.3
Sections	2.6	0.6
Total	52.3	28.2
Professional/Associational		
Committees & related	6.6	2.5
Nonjournal publications	5.8	4.1
Program services	—	17.3
Total	12.4	23.9
Bureaucracy/Administrative		
Office	20.4	28.3
Other	14.9	19.6
Total	35.3	47.9
Total Expenditures	$154,694	$3,287,117
Total Staff	2*	24

Sources: 1960: "Financial report from the Executive Office, April 1961," *American Sociological Review* 26 (1961): 629. 1991: "1991 ASA Audit: Limited resources, good financial health." *Footnotes* 20 (1992), No. 7 (September): 10-11. * In 1960 the staff consisted of an Executive Officer, Gresham Sykes, and an Administrative Office, Janice Hopper.

Organizational Trends: A Mixed Picture

At the same time that ASA has diversified its functions and bureaucratized its operations, sociologists' commitment to the Association has weakened in some respects but strengthened in others. One measure of commitment to ASA is its number of members. People pay money to join. Membership increased steadily from the end of World War II through 1972; then it declined fairly steadily for the next twelve years, though at a slower rate than it had grown before 1973. In the 1970s, when ASA was said to have become a more open association that provided more services to its members, memberships dropped, declining by just under a quarter from 1972 to 1984. The democratization and professionalization efforts in the 1970s had failed to enlist and retain members. (See Figure I, reprinted from Collins et al., 1989:2.) The upturn in memberships since 1984 has been fairly soft, with student memberships, known to be unstable, growing at a slightly higher rate than other memberships.

Figure I
Transformation of the ASA

ASS/ASA Membership for all available years (Source: ASA)

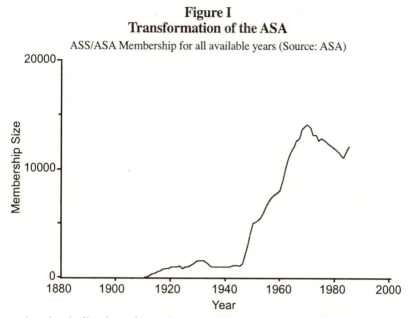

Another indication of member commitment is voting. Table IV shows a steady decline in the percentage of eligible voters returning ballots. In 1959 just under two-thirds of the electorate voted. The percentage decreased steadily through the 1960s to 55.4% in 1970, continued to decline at about the same rate through 1980, tumbled to just over a third voting in 1987, and then declined gradually over the next five years to just under a third voting in 1992. The decline in voting paralleled the decline in disciplinary activities in ASA.

Table IV
Percentage of Eligible Voters Returning Ballots, 1952-1992*

Year	Percent Voting	Eligble Voters
1959	62.3	2,689
1964	60.1	3,204
1966	56.9	3,870
1970	55,4	4,936
1975	49.9	4,153
1980	44.4	9,017
1987	35.6	8,127
1992	32.4	10,272

* Data are for general elections only. Sources: *American Sociological Review* 24 (1959): 562, 29 (1964): 583; *American Sociologist* 2 (1966): 63-68; *Footnotes* 3 (1975), No. 5:1; 8 (1980), No. 6:1; 15 (1987), No. 6:1; 20 (1992), No. 6:1. Carla B. Howery, ASA Deputy Executive Officer, supplied data for 1970.

A third participatory trend in ASA is in section memberships. Sections' smaller memberships provide more opportunity for members to participate in disciplinary activities than does the regular ASA program, whose sessions have larger numbers of papers submitted. Paralleling the differentiation of ASA functions, the number of sections and their memberships have grown. From 1960 through 1987, sections increased fivefold, from five to twenty-five, and total section memberships more than quintupled (see Table V). During the twenty-seven years from 1961 through 1987, the proportion of ASA members who belonged to one or more sections nearly doubled, rising from about a quarter to about half. Of the section members, nearly half in 1987 belonged to multiple sections, compared with a quarter in 1961. Although ASA members increasingly joined sections, half still belonged to no sections in 1987. Members of multiple sections are more likely than other ASA members to vote in ASA elections (Ridgeway and Moore, 1981; D'Antonio and Tuch, 1991) - a seeming anomaly since multiple section membership has risen while voting has fallen. The multiple memberships crosscut different disciplinary specialties, thus reducing possible fragmentation of the discipline. This may create a heightened sense of unity that increases the propensity to vote.

Table V
Section Membership, 1961 and 1987

	1961		1987	
	N	%	N	%
Number of sections	5		25	
Membership in one or more sections	1696	25.4	5890	49.2
Membership in one section	1258	18.9	3119	26.0
Membership in multiple sections	438	6.6	2771	23.2
Total section memberships	2252		11,499	
ASA members not in a section	4966	74.5	6078	50.8

Who were the members who belonged and did not belong to sections? If section affiliation is a way to participate in disciplinary activities, albeit activities limited to one's specialty, then we expect members most identified with the discipline to embrace sections proportionately more than members who are more identified with professional activities of practice and undergraduate teaching. A sample of 198 members from the 1990 directory was selected, with the first-named nonstudent member from every other page and their type of employment and membership in sections observed. Table VI, based on these data, shows that section members are about equally employed in research universities, in non-Ph.D. academic programs, and in nonacademic settings, though nonmembers are employed mainly in non-Ph.D. academic programs and applied settings. Of the Ph.D. department faculty members, 80% belong to a section, compared with around 60% of applied sociologists. Judging from this limited sample, sections promote discourse among members employed in different settings, and involve members in the discipline through their subspecialties.

Table VI
Type of Employer of ASA Section Members and Nonmember, 1990*

	Number	% Section Members	% of Employment Type
Section Members	130	65.7	
Ph.D. sociology department	45	34.6	80.4
Non-Ph.D. sociology department	38	29.2	57.6
Applied**	47	36.2	61.8
Nonmembers	68	34.3	
Ph.D. sociology department	11	16.2	19.6
Non-Ph.D. sociology department	28	41.2	42.4
Applied	29	42.6	38.2

* Data are a sample consisting of the first listed ASA nonstudent member to appear on every other page of the 1990 Biographical Directory of Members.
** Applied includes employment outside the academy as well as in research divisions of universities with Ph.D. sociology programs, but not in the Ph.D. sociology department.

The Disciplinary Elite and its Dilution

As we have mentioned, the central goals of a scholarly or scientific discipline are research and the training of future researchers. The fountainheads of U. S. disciplines are major graduate departments in universities. A small number of departments produce a large share of the most seminal research, and reproduce themselves by training a large proportion of the Ph.D.'s who will work in similar departments (on the latter, cf. Gross, 1970).

To observe elite reproduction, we compared the kinds of departments where the full-time faculty members of top-rated graduate sociology departments, and of less-highly rated graduate departments, had earned their doctorates. We defined as "elite" faculties those in the ten departments rated highest in a 1992 survey of chairs and directors of graduate studies (Webster and Massey, 1992), and as elite givers of Ph.D's to these faculty the ten departments rated highest in a 1969 study by Roose and Andersen (1970).[SVS1]1 Of 280 elite faculty members, 65.4% had doctorates from elite departments. Nearly all the rest had doctorates from second-ten departments. In contrast, only 39.3% of 1,828 less-elite faculty members had elite doctorates. (Our tabulations omit foreign doctorates.)

The reproduction of sociologists includes the commitment of graduate students to the discipline, in addition to training them. Are top-rated departments more successful in this function than lower-rated departments? We assume that graduate students who join ASA are more likely than nonjoiners to be strongly committed to the discipline, and more likely to become major research contributors. To see if elite graduate programs are more effective in disciplinary reproduction, we drew a sample of U.S. graduate student ASA members listed in the 1990 Biographical Directory of Members (American Sociological Association, 1990), tallied them by departments they were enrolled in, and calculated the ratios of sample students to total graduate enrollments in the 102 sociology departments that awarded Ph.D. degrees in 1990-91 (American Sociological Association, 1992).[2] As we expected, we found more student members of ASA in elite than in less-elite departments. Of 1,141 graduate students in the ten elite departments identified in 1992, 25.9% were in our directory sample, as contrasted with 15.2% of 5,301 students in the 93 less-elite departments.

While it makes sense to identify in the 1990s a disciplinary elite of top-ranked graduate departments, the pattern of dominance by a very small number of departments has declined over the years. Until the 1960s, the main reasons why the number of highly productive departments grew were simply that the number of graduate departments grew, and the sizes of both new and old departments-but especially of new ones-grew. This growth made possible a spreading of high-quality disciplinary work from a small to a large elite group of departments. There were more disciplinary stars to go around, and the older elite departments did not grow enough to absorb them all.

Since the 1960s, however, the numbers of graduate departments and of graduate students have been fairly stable, yet the dilution of disciplinary elite dominance has continued. In particular, the leadership of ASA has become increasingly diffuse in institutional affiliation, with a decline in the proportion of leaders who are in elite departments (cf. Wolfe, 1992). We have no data to support any assertion about causes of this trend, but it has coincided with a broadening of ASA functions and goals to emphasize professional and adaptive activities more and disciplinary activities relatively less. Since about 1970, more and more ASA officers appear to have been nominated and elected for reasons other than disciplinary eminence. "Honor in the profession is [now] more politicized..." (Wolfe, 1992:768).

Elite dilution in the reproduction of sociologists is evident in the declining percentage of U.S. sociology Ph.D.'s granted by the top ten departments. Riley (1960) shows this for degrees awarded in the decades from the 1920s through the 1950s. She defines the top ten departments as the ten that awarded the largest numbers of doctorates. We have continued the time series through the 1980s, 3 though we used a sample of ASA members and she used all members, and we defined the top ten departments by quality evaluations for each decade of Ph.D. receipt (Cartter, 1966; Roose and Andersen, 1970; Jones, Lindzey and Coggeshall, 1982). Elite dominance measured in this way declined continuously from the 1920s through the 1970s, then leveled off in the 1980s. The percentages of U.S. Ph.D.'s that were awarded by the top ten departments, and the N'S of Ph.D.'s or sampled Ph.D.'s on which they are based, are: 1920s, 79.5% (N=88); 1930s, 71.4% (N=210); 1940s, 67.7% (N=359); 1950s, 53.8% (N=1,127; 9160s, 47.8% (N=278); 1970s, 30.4% (N=685); 1980s, 29.9% (N=585).

This broadened distribution of doctoral training probably accounts for some of the elite dilution among ASA officers. But it does not explain all of it, for the training backgrounds of officers have changed much faster in recent decades than those of sociologists in general. We have departmental quality rankings for 1957 (Keniston, 1959), 1964 (Cartter, 1966), 1969 (Roose and Andersen, 1970), 1982 (Jones, Lindzey, and Coggeshall, 1982), and 1992 (Webster and Massey, 1992). The numbers and percentages of ASA officers - presidents, vice presidents, secretaries, and at-large council members - in those years whose jobs were in the top ten departments as evaluated in the years of their service declined by half or more, from 60% in 1957, 80% in 1964, and 67% in 1969 to 33% in 1982 and 36% in 1992 (see Table VII). Concentration of officers in elite departments declined sharply from the late 1960s to the early 1980s.

Table VII

Percentages of ASA Officers from
Top Ten Departments of Sociology, 1957-1992

Year	Percent	Total Officers
1957	60	15
1964	80	15
1969	67	15
1982	33	15
1992	36	14

Elite dilution resumed after the slight blip of 1992. The 1993 Committee on Nominations slate for 1994 election had fourteen candidates for seven offices (Footnotes, 1993:1). Only three of these, 21%, were in departments rated in the top ten in 1992. (When two candidates with nonacademic affiliations are removed from the denominator, the figure rises to 3/12 = 25%.) No candidate was from Wisconsin-Madison or Chicago, the top two departments according to the most recent survey. The biggest plunge in disciplinary elite representation among officers occurred during the 1970s, a decade when ASA was aggressively broadening its agenda to put more emphasis on undergraduate teaching, applied practice, broadened ethnic and gender representation and participation, assistance to disadvantaged groups, and other professional or adaptive concerns, all of which are nondisciplinary.

At the same time, there may have been little if any elite dilution in purely disciplinary activity. Nothing is more disciplinary than publishing in the American Sociological Review. Table VIII shows the types of employment of ASR article authors in 1963, 1973, 1983, and 1993. Authors in the more recent years were more concentrated in Ph.D. - granting departments and in institutes and other programs in Ph.D. - granting universities than were authors in the earlier years. We speculate that the growth of energy devoted to undergraduate teaching, applied practice and other nonresearch endeavors may have weakened interest in the kind of disciplinary research and theorizing that ASR publishes. The differentiation of the Association by function may also have structurally differentiated the membership so that the research function became more concentrated in research universities.

Table VIII
Type of Employment of Authors of Articles in *American Sociological Review,* 1963-1993*

Year	PhD Soc Dept (%)	Research Univ (%)	Non PhD Soc Dept (%)	Applied (%)	Foreign (%)	Total
1963	78.0	—	10.2	10.2	1.7	59
1973	87.3	—	7.3	5.4	0.0	55
1983	78.5	12.3	7.7	1.5	0.0	65
1993	81.6	10.2	0.0	2.4	4.1	49

* If more than one author, the one to whom correspondence is to be directed is counted for 1983 and 1993 and the first-listed author for 1963 and 1973. Research uninversity refers to employment at a research Ph.D. university, but not in a department of sociology. This distinction could not be made for 1973 and 1963, when correspondence address was not given. Employment for those years is grouped as Ph.D. sociology department. Most authors of articles published in 1973 and 1963 were known to the writers and few if any errors in classifying these years were made.

Some might argue that the growth of elite concentration of ASR authorship reflects lessened opportunity to do ASR-style research in the age of high-powered quantitative analysis if one is not located in a research university. We would disagree, and assert that research opportunity has become more widespread than ever before. Up-to-date computers and other search facilities are accessible in colleges and nonacademic settings that did not have them until the 1980's or 1990's. Internationally available machine-readable data sets make research quicker and cheaper than it was when researchers had to conduct their own surveys or archival searches. Moreover, there is less competition for space in ASR and other journals than there was twenty-five years ago, because fewer articles are being submitted to them. If elite concentration in disciplinary work has grown, the reason would appear to be that sociologists in non-elite settings are doing other things instead.

Concluding Comments

In summary, the American Sociological Association has undergone fundamental transformation during the past three decades. It is no longer the scholarly society dominated by a disciplinary elite that it was in the 1950s, when it had its first major growth spurt. It has come to resemble a professional association of organized subgroups with diverse demands that have led to diversification of its functions. In responding to these pressure groups, ASA has added new goals and activities, aimed at advancing the groups' interests, and in time the interests have become institutionalized as established programs of the Association. These programs have contributed to sociology by helping to enhance the status of its minorities and to improve undergraduate instruction. This turn toward pluralism and professional services has given visibility and power to new groups, who now stand alongside the disciplinary elite in the Association. More than half of ASA committees and its Council actions, and more than two-thirds of its budget, are now concerned with nondisciplinary functions.

A consequence of this functional differentiation has been a decline in the control of ASA by disciplinary elites. Paradoxically, the democratization of governance and the diversification of associational functions do not appear to have promoted the increase in participation among the membership that was intended. Proportionately fewer members vote, and sociologists in non-elite settings are less likely to publish in their premier journal, than when the Association was more elitist.

On the other hand, section memberships have grown so that half the members now belong to sections. Sections provide an opportunity for participation in the discipline. As Collins et al. (1989) note, the sections promote discussion among members who share research interests. They also help to uphold norms and standards of scholarship through giving awards for distinguished works and careers. The small size of the sections allows their members to get to know each other and to develop esprit de corps around disciplinary interests. Participation in ASA's annual program still seems preferred over participation in a section program; if so, participation in sections appears to serve distinct functions that the regular ASA sessions may not. The sections do not appear to be structural alternatives to ASA; instead, they attach members to it. These parallel developments suggest that many members are disaffected from ASA - at least, from its governance - but are not turned off from sociology, the discipline.

Some degree of functional differentiation of ASA was necessary if the Association was to survive in a changing environment. The pressures for change were powerful. They originated in the environing society and were brought into ASA by blocs of members who wanted new things done and old things done differently. These blocs became constituencies that a politically-run association had to attend to. Had the ASA tried to ignore them, it might have stonewalled itself to death, with separate organizations splintering off to serve the diverse constituencies. Another logically possible response when an organization must come to terms with environmentally-based groups that seek change is to try to coopt them (Selznick, 1949); but this strategy will not work when the new groups are organized, sophisticated, and aware of what is going on. Instead, ASA adapted to a more complex environment by elaborating its structure and diversifying its functions.

Adaptations of this sort can help an organization survive, but they may be overadaptations when viewed from the perspective of the original functions. Functions are interrelated. New functions may suffer if old ones wither. The original goal of ASA was the nurturing of its disciplinary base. Our observations of the transformation of ASA show an association that needs to become more attentive to its discipline. A profession without a strong discipline risks losing its moorings and forgetting why it exists. Program services may have unintended effects; for example, the means of teaching may become ends in themselves. Techniques may become standardized and applied to disparate student bodies, and they may become so removed from the subject matter that the intellectual challenge of teaching is lost. Sociological practice may ossify into rote application of yesterday's wisdom. For sociologists in varied employment settings to feel unity and move forward as a discipline, a revitalization of disciplinary leadership is needed.

Acknowledgments

We are grateful to Carla B. Howery of the ASA Executive Office for tracking down and giving us some elusive historical information, and to Kenneth C. Land and Alejandro Portes for comments on an earlier draft.

Notes

1 The 1969 data on backgrounds of current faculty were the closest available to the decade of the 1970s, when the model sociologist of the early 1990's was trained. Data on degrees of recent faculty are from American Sociological Association, 1993.

2 Our sampling procedure was to count the first two and last two U.S. student ("SA") members listed on every page of the directory for whom the information showed clearly that they were graduate students in identified departments.

3 Our sample was the first and last sociology Ph.D. identified on every page of the 1990 ASA membership directory (American Sociological Association, 1990), omitting those with pre-1960 or foreign degrees. We recalculated Riley's figures to exclude foreign doctorates. When departments were tied for tenth place, we used those whose universities' names came first in the alphabet.

References

American Sociological Association. 1990. *Biographical Directory of Members*. Washington: American Sociological Association.

————. 1992. *Guide to Graduate Departments*. Washington: American Sociological Association.

————. 1993. *Guide to Graduate Departments*. Washington: American Sociological Association.

Cartter, Allan M. 1966. *An Assessment of Quality in Graduate Education*. Washington: American Council on Education.

Collins, Randall, John McCarthy, Marshall Meyer, Pamela Oliver, and Jonathan Turner. 1989. "Future organizational trends of the ASA." *Footnotes* 17 (September):1-5, 9. (Report of ASA Council's Ad Hoc Committee on ASA Future Organizational Trends.)

D'Antonio, William V. and Steven A. Tuch. 1991. "Voting in professional associations: The case of the American Sociological Association." *The American Sociologist* 22:37-48.

Footnotes (no author indicated). 1974. "Sociologists fly-in for workshop on undergraduate education." *Footnotes* 2 (January):1, 3.

————. 1975. "Council acts on resolutions from annual business meetings." *Footnotes* 3 (February):1, 16.

————. 1993. "Candidates for ASA offices, Council, and committees." *Footnotes* 21 (December):1, 10.

Gross, George R. 1970. "The organization set: A study of sociology departments." *The American Sociologist* 5:25-29

Hughes, Everett C. 1962. "Association or federation?" *American Sociological Review* 27:590.

Jones, Lyle V., Gardner Lindzey, and P. E. Coggeshall, eds. 1982. *An Assessment of Research-Doctorate Programs in the United States*, 5 volumes. Washington: National Academy Press.

Keniston, Hayward. 1959. *Graduate Study and Research in the Arts and Sciences at the University of Pennsylvania*. Philadelphia: University of Pennsylvania Press.

Parsons, Talcott. 1959. "Some problems confronting sociology as a profession." *American Sociological Review* 24:547-559.

Rhoades, Lawrence J. 1980. "Association reaches zenith in tumultuous sixties." *Footnotes* 8 (November):1, 4, 5.

Ridgeway, Cecilia and Joan Moore. 1981. "Voting in the American Sociological Association: Investment, network, and interest." *The American Sociologist* 16:74-81

Riley, Matilda White. 1960. "Membership of the American Sociological Association, 1950-1959." *American Sociological Review* 25:914-926.

Roose, Kenneth D. and Charles J. Andersen. 1970. *A Rating of Graduate Programs*. Washington: American Council on Education.

Selznick, Philip. 1949. *TVA and the Grass Roots*. Berkeley; University of California Press.

Simpson, Ida Harper. 1988. *Fifty Years of the Southern Sociological Society: Change and Continuity in a Professional Society*. Athens: University of Georgia Press.

Weber, Max. 1946 (1919). "Science as a vocation." In H. H. Gerth and C. Wright Mills, trans. and eds., *From Max Weber: Essays in Sociology*: 129-159. New York: Oxford University Press.

Webster, David D. and Sherry Ward Massey. 1992. "The complete rankings from the U.S. News & World Report 1992 survey of doctoral programs in six liberal arts disciplines." *Change*, November/December: 20-52

Wolfe, Alan. 1992. "Weak sociology/strong sociologists: Consequences and contradictions of a field in turmoil." *Social Research* 59: 759-779

14

Institutional Perspectives On Sociology[1]

Joan Huber

Introduction

Recent years have been stressful for sociology as a discipline. Many sociologists sense that all is not well (Cole 1994, p. 129). Journalists and others have alleged that sociology lacks intellectual integration. Moreover, compared to the other social sciences, underemployment was more common among sociology/anthropology Ph.D.'s from 1973 through 1989, and median earnings declined more and revived less strongly in sociology than in other fields during this period (Roos and Jones 1993).

Perhaps most ominous was the demise of departments at the University of Rochester and Washington University in St. Louis in the 1980s and the threat of severe reductions at San Diego State and Yale universities in the early 1990s;[2] currently, there are rumors of potential splitting of some graduate departments and termination of others. Two recent articles (Wright 1990; Lynch 1993) published in the ASA newsletter, Footnotes, have intensified the impression of a troubled discipline.[3]

This essay analyzes sociology from an institutional perspective in order to distinguish between problems that affect all disciplines and those that more often affect sociology and that therefore may be more amenable to change by sociologists. My biases are those of a sociologist turned administrator. Especially in bad times, administrators tend to think like ecologists because they must deal with competition for a pie never big enough to go around. They must choose, in effect, between a semistarvation diet for everyone or the starving of weaker units in order to give stronger ones a chance to flourish. Cuts across the board may please feeble units, but they enrage strong ones and weaken the institution.

The first part of this essay presents an institutional perspective on problems common to all academic departments: the fiscal situation in higher education, the anachronisms of academic organization, and what deans, provosts, and presidents really want in departments. The second part discusses aspects of sociology that affect administrators' perceptions of it: its attraction for students with reformist or radical agendas, the ease with which its research can be trivialized, a cognitive style that leads faculty to be more pessimistic about their field than the areas of other scientists, the liabilities of a weak disciplinary core, and the currents of antirationalism that may affect administrators' perception of sociology as a science. The third part discusses what departments might do to strengthen their institutional niche. I first discuss the fiscal problems of higher education, the most important single source of trouble for ail disciplines.

The Fiscal Context of Higher Education

Disciplinary troubles are thrown into relief whenever severe fiscal problems afflict higher education-especially research universities, whose departments are academia's reproductive units (Simpson and Simpson 1994). Rapid growth traditionally enabled administrators to fund new programs without terminating existing ones (Cole 1993, p. 9). Now new growth will most likely be funded either by cuts across the board or selective retrenchment. Administrators, constrained by the need to maximize both institutional prestige and financial security, tend to avoid cutting across the board. Instead, they typically use a mix of criteria to determine a unit's level of support: quality of faculty and students, centrality (the extent to which its courses are required across the university), and student demand.

Of these criteria, centrality (best exemplified by mathematics and English composition) is least amenable to department control. Sociology's claim to centrality is tenuous (although the social sciences together have a solid claim). Thus, hard times require that sociologists improve what lies within their power to improve: quality of faculty, students, and courses.

The thesis underlying this essay is that academia's current fiscal problems result from a convergence of factors that will likely exacerbate problems of resource allocation for some time. Prudent departments must therefore examine their competitive position in the institution. What evidence supports the thesis that fiscal problems will persist?

First, higher education funding is affected by the federal budget deficit. A nation that must adapt to global economic competition is also averse to raising taxes to levels that would provide adequately for basic education and broad social welfare programs. Public universities now compete at the state level not only with primary and secondary education but also with social welfare and exponentially rising medical costs. Moreover, as public four-year colleges have moved from normal school to teachers' college to state college to state university over the last 40 years, they have come to compete with major public universities for graduate program funding (Clark 1983, p. 217).

A deficit-related factor that affects private as much as public universities concerns science funding, which rose sharply during World War II. Combining easy federal money with faculty incentives to produce students resulted in exponential growth of a system of Ph.D. production that no government could sustain.[4] Meanwhile, research universities became dependent on federal funding. The present and future cost of much frontier science is now so high that only government can finance it (Nichols 1993, p. 199). Academic science now faces an instrumentation deficit plus escalating costs of state-of-the-art equipment. The long-run challenge of sustaining university research capacity appears endless (Geiger 1993, p. 325). And ongoing federal budget deficits make academic science a low funding priority.

A second reason for higher education's funding problems concerns enrollment trends. The greatest program growth has always occurred in periods of the greatest enrollment growth (Carnegie Council 1980, p. 102). Enrollments have risen ever since the industrial revolution made knowledge for use and the production of new knowledge centrally important (Carnegie Foundation 1977). Whether this historic expansion rate will level off or decline depends in part on the response to two questions that are seldom addressed: What proportion of a nation's adults can be supported in "nonproductive" activities like education, whatever the future payoff to individual quality of life or national economic growth? And what proportion of high school graduates can learn at a level that will attract high quality teachers? Whatever the answers to these two basic questions, future enrollment trends will differ from the past ones.

High school completion rates, the major stimulus for enrollment expansion over the last century, cannot rise much higher. By 1993, 89% of all 35-45-year-olds had completed high school (Bureau of the Census 1994, P. 1).

After World War II, several factors pressed federal and state governments to expand higher education. The dramatic rise in high school completion rates from 1930 to 1940, along with legislation making college affordable for veterans, flooded colleges with students after the war. As that flood subsided, the baby boom cohort continued the pressure on enrollments, which doubled in the decade ending 1967-68. Income and expenditures tripled, plant expenditures rose fourfold, and foundation support increased fivefold (Cheit 1971, p. 5). Academia doubled every 15 years from 1880 to 1960 but tripled from 1950 to 1970; in 1980, 80% of academics held positions that had not existed 30 years earlier (Metzger 1987, p. 124). In parallel, college completion rates rose from 5% in 1940 to 21% in 1989 (Kominski 1990). The huge undergraduate increase since 1966 was concentrated in two-year colleges (Astin 1985), which now account for more than two-fifths of all higher education institutions; in 1993, they constituted two-thirds of all new institutions (Evangelauf 1994). No other nation so embraced open access to higher education (Carnegie Council 1980).

Unfortunately, institutions' dependence on enrollments to remain solvent tended to erode their autonomy and academic quality (Bowen 1980, p. 221). The need for tuition dollars may tempt administrators to lower academic standards in order to admit more students. By the end of the 1970s, most public institutions were running their educational programs almost entirely with funds from tuition and enrollment-based state appropriations. Private institutions depended on tuition for the bulk of their revenue. Most federal and state funds came via student grants, which encouraged student access but weakened literacy and quantitative skills (Carnegie Council 1980, p. 86). More institutions became part of multicampus universities or were subjected to increasingly detailed state regulation, which also decreased their autonomy and tended to erode their academic quality (Bowen 1980, p. 221).

A third reason for persistent fiscal problems is the relative rise in operating costs: instructional and research equipment (and personnel to run it), computers, laboratories, staff to comply with federal rules, and litigation pressed by disgruntled administrators, faculty, staff, and students.[5]

Some administrators worry that a freshet of recent books critical of higher education (e.g., Sykes 1988; Smith 1990) may also exacerbate its fiscal problem, although such criticism historically has had no apparent effect on high public esteem (Carnegie Council 1980, p. 23). Prewitt (1993, p. 88) claims that the current alleged loss of public confidence is based on anecdotal evidence and is incorrect. According to NORC data from 1972 on, leaders in the arenas most closely linked with research universities (science and education) were highly regarded by a larger part of the public in 1991 than in the early 1980s.[6] Except for "college president," only eight occupations ranked higher than "college professor" in prestige; 726 ranked lower. Fiscal problems, therefore, reflect government budget problems more than low public confidence in universities (Prewitt 1993, P. 96).

The Anachronisms of Academic Organization

The unique organization of academia intensifies the impact of retrenchment on departments because those departments have weak governance mechanisms that tend to become even weaker when the parent discipline is troubled. Under heavy fiscal constraint, the orderly restructuring of colleges and departments is therefore especially difficult.

Coleman (1973) describes academia as an organizational anachronism. It has no effective mechanisms for corporate decision making. It has a communal governing structure but it lost its communal character. The secularization of universities over the last century or so decreased their control over members' personal and religious lives, giving faculty the behavioral latitude of employees of the modern corporation. Yet in one respect faculty have far more latitude than corporate employees. Except for teaching, faculty are free to use their time or to sell it as they see fit. Independent professionals control their time but receive no salaries. Corporate employees receive salaries but do not control their time. The basic flaw in academic organization is the failure 'to exact control of faculty time in exchange for salary (Coleman 1973, p. 383).[7]

Faculty also control their classroom activities. They may reduce preparation time without constraint. Were the university a real community, reduced performance would be controlled by communal norms. Paradoxically, only when universities ceased being communities were the deviant opinions that test academic freedom tolerated; the informal controls that enable a community to punish bad teaching can also suppress deviant teaching (Coleman 1973, p. 310). Thus, department chairs often overlook the behavior of faculty who flout classroom norms. For example, if a faculty member is reputed to give finals in the last week of classes despite an institutional ban on giving them except as scheduled, a chair can gather the information needed to justify sanctions only by behaving more like a police officer than an academic, which most chairs are reluctant to do.

The lack of university mechanisms for corporate decision making can be a short-run advantage to a fractious department in a fragmented discipline. Terminating a department is not easy in the absence of rules that permit orderly governance of choice (Carrter 1974; Cole 1993). Prudent administrators avoid abrupt termination, preferring instead a long period of attrition before putting a department out of its misery. This gives a troubled department time to redeem itself. However, redemption is not easy even under optimal conditions and is quite difficult under fiscal constraint. This policy appears to be the one that was pursued by Washington University. After the sociology department suffered severe problems in self-governance (Etzkowitz 1989-90), the administration constrained the department's efforts to improve for some years while its national ratings dropped sharply (Hargens 1990, p. 207). Only then did the administration deliver the final blow.

What Do Deans Really Want?

What do deans really want in an academic department? Because of the way their own professional success is measured, most academic administrators have two primary goals: to enhance an institution's prestige and ensure its survival. Prestige requires hiring the faculty who contribute most effectively to scholarship and enrolling the most talented students. Ensuring survival requires fiscal prudence in weighing alternatives. Judgments are often difficult because in practice the two goals often conflict; for example, administrators may struggle with whether or not to admit less well qualified students (despite adverse effects on institutional prestige) because the tuition they pay will help balance the budget.

Provosts value deans who recognize departmental quality and who use common sense and fairness in allocating rewards selectively among units. Departmental quality can be defined by many criteria. A common indicator is faculty prestige, an assessment of research quality based on nationwide peer judgment. Administrators, especially in research universities, are much aware of these rankings. Provosts and deans typically ask external department reviewers how faculty activities compare with those in the discipline's most highly regarded departments. Another important indicator of quality is departmental reputation for teaching. It is bad news if complaints about teaching reach the dean or provost. Private universities (because of high tuition) are especially vulnerable to criticism that they fail to meet their teaching responsibilities adequately.

Deans, in turn, value department chairs who reward quality and manage well. Because chairs must deal directly with faculty and students, administrators also value the political skills that foster a productive community with high morale and reduce the chances that disgruntled faculty and students will pester the dean or provost.[8]

Problems With Elective Affinities For Sociology

In addition to the problems that afflict all academic disciplines, sociology has some that stem from the nature of the discipline itself. Certain characteristics, which may have both benefits and costs, increase the probability of attracting negative attention from administrators, other departments, and the public: a tendency to recruit reformists, the ease with which its research can be trivialized, a cognitive style that tends to make sociologists pessimistic about the field's intellectual vitality, a weak core, and some affinity for the antirationalist ideas currently emanating from some areas in humanities. Many of these features would resist change (nor would we necessarily want to change all of them) but we should be aware of their potential costs.

An Affinity for Reformists

Until the late 1700s, the humanities accounted for a huge share of the curriculum, including prolonged doses of Greek and Latin taught as grammar, not literature. This share was eroded by the appearance of factual findings incompatible with reigning theories.[9] The physical sciences emerged from philosophy during the 1800s. The social and behavioral sciences emerged from moral philosophy in the late 1800s, among a plethora of disciplines born in a period when college enrollments were tripling (Carnegie Council 1980). Spawned by economics in the 1880s (Metzger 1987, p. 130), sociology was an undefined residual category in the social sciences. It included reformist topics (e.g., charities and corrections) with no academic home. A primary resource base continued to be student demand for courses on social amelioration (Turner and Turner 1990, p. 23). Pressures to become a science were probably greater in the land grant universities, which emphasized knowledge for use, than in the older private universities where humanist interests blunted that drive Smelser 1992, p. 53; cf. this university education with the one described in Cobban [19751).

From the beginning, sociology attracted students with reformist concerns and sociologists have long remained to the left of most academics (Hamilton and Hargens 1993). The benefit of attracting reformists comes from their intellectual stimulation of the field. The best sociologists typically include those who are willing to entertain unorthodox ideas as to how modern societies function (Lazarsfeld and Thielens 1958, p. 161). To study human organization in itself whets curiosity about alternative arrangements.

The cost of attracting reformists results from its giving a discipline the appearance, justified or not, of being politically partisan. A discipline's reputation for lopsided political sympathies can annoy legislators. In turn, vexed legislators worry administrators in public institutions because lawmakers vote on the state subsidy. However, in both public and private institutions, the ultimate cost of attracting reformists results from the impression they make on boards of trustees and regents, who tend to be successful business persons. Trustees are supposed to ensure that the institution's officers, from president on down, exercise prudence in running it. Presidents, whom trustees hire and fire, get the brunt of praise or blame. Trustees ordinarily stay out of department affairs, but they tend to become uneasy if they see their institution become prey to radicalism. Regardless of their personal values, provosts and deans cannot ignore trustees.

The cohort entering the field after World War II included persons with reformist, even radical, concerns. However, they tried to separate their politics and scholarship (Lipset 1994), which reduces (but does not eliminate) the cost of reformists' affinity for sociology. Later on, the concept of the unity of theory and practice turned the goal of the separation of politics and scholarship upside down. This view, which tends to raise the cost of sociology's attraction for reformists, is encouraged by the antirationalist currents in academia to be discussed later.

The Ease of Trivializing Research

All research can be misinterpreted, especially by the mass media, because compression distorts results. In print journalism and television, for example, survey research findings from a particular time and place are often given without details as if they were timeless and universal truths (Weiss and Singer 1988).

Sociological research tends to suffer more than other types from the ease with which it can be not only distorted but also trivialized (see Molotch 1994, p. 221). One source of difficulty stems from the unavoidable practice of stating research problems in terms that laypersons assume they understand. For example, when I was a department head at the University of Illinois in Urbana-Champaign, the dean called me in to discuss the title of a sabbatical research proposal. The faculty member, a demographer, wanted to study two-sex life tables. "You have to come up with another title," the dean said grimly. "I can't send that to the trustees. They'd have a fit."

Another source of trouble is that journalistic treatment reduces some topics to triviality; journalistic norms emphasize accuracy, but news stories must sell papers. Sociological research attracts reporters who want the kind of human interest stories that make deans and department chairs wince. For example, the stories on the annual meetings of political science and sociology in the Chronicle of Higher Education in 1983 served sociology poorly. Political scientists were reported to be criticizing research on the presidency. The story on sociology was entitled "You Drink What You Are and Other Reports from the Annual Meetings of Sociologists." It began: "What you are may determine what and how you drink. That was among the many research findings-on topics ranging from boredom to the aesthetic training of chefs-presented by scholars at the Annual Meeting of the American Sociological Association" (Watkins 1983, pp. 7, 8). It is not difficult to imagine the public perception of scholars whose research topics range from boredom to the aesthetic training of chefs.

Disciplinary Type and Faculty Discontent

According to Hargens and Kelly-Wilson (1994), scholars' pessimism about research quality in their own field may affect the way administrators, other faculty, and research foundation personnel perceive that field. Administrative perceptions adversely affect the discipline, hindering a department in the competition for institutional support and external research funds. One disciplinary-level source of pessimism is scholarly anomie, the loss of solidarity following a breakdown in the exchange of information. Specialists lose the capacity to talk to each other, making it hard for scholars to obtain recognition for their work, and leading to a belief that the field is stagnant (Hagstrom 1964, p. 187). Another source of pessimism is wide disagreement on the relative importance of research topics and on the theories and methods appropriate for a given topic, which may also diminish scholarly recognition. Disciplinary size and differentiation also make it hard for sociologists to be recognized for their work (Collins 1987).

Using the 1984 Carnegie survey, Hargens and Kelly-Wilson (1994) examined variation by discipline in faculty assessments of their own field's vitality. As predicted, pessimism about one's field is much higher in the social sciences and humanities than in the physical and biological sciences. Furthermore, despite sociology's portrayal in journals and media as a discipline that lost its sense of purpose, Carnegie surveys in 1969, 1975, and, most recently, 1984 show that the proportion of sociologists who are pessimistic about their field has been very stable over time. The good news: pessimism about sociology has not increased. The bad news: this factor continues to disadvantage sociologists compared to physical and biological scientists.

A Weak Core

A department in a discipline with a weak core is more subject to scrutiny when fiscal difficulties intensify than are other departments. The core of a discipline, college, or university is the body of knowledge needed for an adequate overview of that area. What constitutes an "adequate overview" may be contentious because the concept tends to surface in hard times when departments and colleges are at risk of being reduced in size or terminated. Pragmatically, a disciplinary core is what must be retained if the discipline is to continue to exist. In sociology, many scholars see demography, social organization, and social stratification as the core because these areas yield the replicable data most needed to understand how societies work.

When departments are evaluated as a basis for resource allocation, those whose disciplinary cores are weak make problems for administrators.[10] Both the internal and external peer opinion on which deans depend may be unclear or inconsistent, giving inadequate guidance to decision makers. Some department chairs try to avoid the dilemmas of a weak core by insisting that everything their faculty does is important. This is a political mistake. It damages department credibility and may force the dean to decide which research is most significant.

Portes (1994, pp. 4, 6), analyzing the causes and consequences of competition among disciplines, has pointed out that a weak core makes a discipline subject to intrusion by other disciplines. Sociology became sufficiently fragmented in the second half of this century to become the target of economics and sociobiology. Social scientists in target areas greeted the innovations with attention but the eventual reaction was mixed.

In principle, of course, science might be better served if certain subareas in one discipline became part of other disciplines. The current disciplinary division of labor owes much to historical accident; the configuration may look quite different 200 years hence. However, in practice, the loss of a major subarea would seriously damage any discipline, defining it as a loser in academia's zero-sum games.

Antirationalism in Academia

Today, an unknown proportion of sociologists feels that there are no standards of rationality, objectivity, or truth. Another (also unknown) proportion believes that sociology has a viable academic niche only as a science. The intellectual chasm is unbridgeable. What is at stake is the scholarly idea of the disinterested observer seeking objective truth with universal validity that is based on the notion of a reality independent of human thought and action (Searle 1993, p. 69). This idea is at the heart of any discipline's claim to be a science; that is, to be producing replicable research.

Antirationalism tends to be a problem for those disciplines that harbor it because administrators typically lack sympathy with a view that undermines the tradition of Western science. Antirationalist currents, strongest in languages and literature, appear mostly in the humanities, some social sciences, and some law schools but have had little influence on philosophy, natural and physical science, economics, engineering, and mathematics (Searle 1993, p. 76).

Postmodernism, the encompassing name for these trends, assumes that the rationalist philosophy that has sustained Western European civilization is bankrupt and on the point of collapse (Gross and Levitt 1994, p. 5). Postmodernists are complete relativists who see science as an intellectual device to further the ends of those paying for research rather than a way to discover truth about the universe. They tend to identify science with technological achievements that caused controversy, like atomic power stations and military research in the Vietnam period (Ben-David 1991, pp. 477, 491).

Antirationalist currents washed into sociology along well-established channels and through new channels opened in the late 1960s.[11] In sociology, I have the impression that there is a tendency (but only a tendency) for the more susceptible individuals and groups to be those that identify more with humanities than with sciences. In addition, Gross and Levitt (1994, p. 108) argue that some members of groups long excluded from science have come to feel that the dominance of research methods linked to Western rationalism is a major factor in their exclusion. Feminist criticism of science originally claimed, correctly, that women were virtually excluded from participation. In contrast, the new criticism of science as a masculinist enterprise goes to the heart of science's methodological, conceptual, and epistemological foundations. Even physics and mathematics have been accused of succumbing to the use of patriarchal methods.[12]

These currents affected sociology by spurring the growth of a more relativistic sociology of science in Britain in the 1960s (Ben-David 1978). The sociology of science that emerged in the United States in the 1950s, the work of Merton and his students, had opposed relativism (Merton 1973). The British version saw scientific norms and "truths" as changing from field to field and time to time more as a result of "negotiations" between opposing interests than of new discoveries. This view implies that scientific truth depends on the power of the negotiator more than on a complex relationship to an external reality that the negotiators cannot control.

What Should Departments Do?

Thus far, I have tried to demonstrate two theses: that higher education's persistent fiscal problems will pressure departments in all disciplines to make their claim on university resources as strong as possible and that some of sociology's characteristics tend to make its departments especially vulnerable to budget cuts. What should departments do? Falk (1991) and DeFleur (1992) have suggested that they should seek special niches in their respective institutions, keep their houses in order, serve the university, and strengthen their undergraduate and graduate programs.

Some data strongly suggest that graduate programs need attention. Sociology graduate applicants suffered from the general decline in GRE scores in arts and sciences that had resulted from a sluggish academic labor market and growing opportunities in law and business, a decline exacerbated by a 30-year decrease in the percentage of doctorates awarded by research universities (Bowen and Sosa 1989, p. 173). [13] By the early 1980s, sociology GRE scores were the lowest in the social sciences (D'Antonio 1991).

Report: Task Group on Graduate Education

As ASA president-elect in 1988, I was aware of information circulating among a network of sociologists with experience in reviewing graduate programs, including highly ranked ones, that reported instances of unclear standards, doubtful course rigor, a smorgasbord curriculum, and inappropriate graduate student participation in governance. [14] However disturbing, these data provided an inadequate basis for action because they were anecdotal and had to remain anonymous. Yet to do nothing seemed imprudent. I therefore appointed a task group, originally chaired by Richard HUI, to address these concerns. It was composed primarily of persons with administrative experience in graduate departments and ultimately included four ASA presidents. [15] The task group strongly agreed that it could only recommend actions: disciplinary association cannot tell departments what to do. The report's purpose was to stimulate late discussion. Submitted to the ASA Council early in 1992, it was neither approved nor circulated to the membership for discussion. Below I paraphrase the report's discussion of administrative criteria for budget cuts, the reasons for sociology's vulnerability, graduate department Ph.D. requirements, and final recommendations.

> The hostile fiscal environment of the 1990s makes it likely that administrative administrtors, who try to be rational, will use these guidelines in making selective cuts:
> 1. Strength will be protected. An excellent department or one nearly so will be spared to the extent possible.
> 2. Core departments will be protected. No university will terminate its mathematics department just because it is weak. Is sociology a core discipline? Probably not. Other undergraduate programs rarely require specific sociology courses.
> 3. Universities will protect the departments that contribute most to the institutional mission. Favored departments will be those (a) that take their undergraduate mission seriously, as evidenced by their controlling of grade inflation, their offering of rigorous courses and a strong honors program, and their reforming the curriculum as appropriate, all of which require collective action; (b) that provide a structured curriculum for high-quality graduate stu-

dents with an opportunity for hands-on research; (c) that have faculty engaged in high-quality research, and (d) that have faculty who demonstrate university citizenship by appropriate service activities.

In meeting these challenges in a hostile fiscal setting, sociology is vulnerable. It tends to be characterized by individualism and fragmentation, making it especially hard to do the things that need to be done.

Sociology's reputation among legislators and trustees tends to be that of a pusher of unpopular causes. One legacy of the student movements of the 1960s and early 1970s is that administrators often see sociology departments as centers of radicalism. Sociology tends to prosper during surges of public concern with social problems and to languish in conservative periods. This cyclical pattern almost always antagonizes higher-level administrators who remain fearful of hotbeds of leftist action.

Another legacy of the 1970s is the denial of sociology's status as a science, which undercuts the methods and research strategies that had long been seen as the discipline's underpinning, needed for its legitimation. Compounding this legacy was an antisociology coalition within some of the older humanist fields, which helps to account for some of sociology's weakness in the Ivy League.

A serious legacy of 1969 is an extreme ideology of democracy that permits graduate student participation in decision making on faculty recruitment and graduate curriculum. Other departments tend to assign such responsibility solely to faculty. Departments can be paralyzed when students become a political force through formal representation in governance or through their own organizing capacity. Students tend to fight for "freedom" and against "structure," against quantitative and language training, against repeated evaluation, and for "input" and "voice" in curriculum, admissions, and personnel matters. Given the choice, a sizable majority of graduate students would probably opt for a less structured program with few courses in quantitative methods, even though most students who reluctantly go through a tough program later credit it with creating the human capital from which they have been able to draw at will in academic or nonacademic careers.

Sociology's growth rate in the 1960s has left departments heavily staffed with faculty now near retirement, making these units tempting targets for deans hunting for programs to terminate.

In times of retrenchment, sociology's interdisciplinary strength can make it vulnerable. Many administrators laud links across disciplines but seldom note dangers. In one major department, 14 of 21 appointments are joint. Such a unit is easy to close because tenured faculty can be appropriately absorbed elsewhere.

Our interdisciplinary strengths may also produce overspecialization. In the Guide to Graduate Departments, some departments list more specialties than faculty members.

In turn, lack of a well-defined core coupled with an ideology of limited terms for department chairs leads to less stable leadership. Overly rapid turnover erodes the prestige of the position and reduces relations of trust with the dean.

The task group asked William DAntonio, then the ASA Executive Officer, to gather data on the requirements in the 104 Ph.D.-granting departments listed in the Guide to Graduate Departments. Their major requirements, from most to least common, appear in Table I.

Table I
Ph.D. Requirements in Sociology Departments, 1990

Requirement	% of Departments
Dissertation	99
Oral defense	98
Dissertation proposal	92
Comprehensive examinations	90
Research methods	78
Theory course(s)	72
Speciality area examination	49
Foreign language	46
Total credit hours	44
Coursework	42
Residence	40
Core area examination	39
Statistics course(s)	37
Area of specialization	34
Teaching/research requirements	22
Time limit	14
Specific number of area courses	13
Empirical paper	13
Specific quantitative methods course	9
Specific qualitative methods course	9

The most striking fact about the list of major requirements is its lack of substance.[16] An observer who wanted to identify sociology's core could hardly infer it from this list. It is also notable that only the dissertation, its proposal and defense, comprehensive examinations, and a requirement in research methods and theory are common to more than half of the departments. Fewer than half of the departments require a specialty area examination. A little more than one-third require any statistics courses. Yet the ASA executive office had emphasized that the association is slowly but surely making the point among federal agencies that sociologists share statisticians' and psychologists' statistical skills. These data make it hard to refute the charge that graduate education in sociology fails to reflect a central core.

The task group does not foresee the ASA's setting standards or monitoring programs; instead, the ASA should provide a forum for discussion through general interest programs. The teaching journal could encourage a dialogue on graduate education. Although the task group believes that attention to its six recommendations would improve a department's position in the university, departments remain responsible for the way they manage their teaching and research.

The task group's six recommendations are given below:

1. *Departments need to address the extent of graduate student influence on faculty decision making.* Departments are poorly served by having graduate students (especially as voting members) on curriculum committees or committees that establish or oversee graduate programs.

2. *Many departments need to confront the problem of loosely structured design-your-own programs that have little quality control, no solid general hurdles, and minimal faculty oversight.* These problems can be exacerbated by the presence of large numbers of students from abroad.

3. *Most graduate programs are probably spread too thin.* Departments often try to do too many things. They might better focus on few areas, depending on faculty size and quality. Once a department has chosen its areas, it should get enough faculty to work together to build real strength. Students in a given area should have a core program whose methods and substance are suited to one another.

4. *Although research funding is a general problem, many departments do too little to encourage research training before the dissertation.* They fall into patterns of funding students as teaching assistants and they overemphasize examinations.

5. *All students should be required to master the research methods needed to work in government or applied settings.* The discipline's claim to produce skillful statisticians must be based in reality, even if many sociologists choose to emphasize qualitative methods in their dissertations or postgraduate work.

6. *Courses required for the undergraduate major and the graduate program should reflect sociology's central core*: demography, social organization, and social stratification. Too often a radical discontinuity separates faculty research from what is being taught at the undergraduate level.

The Organization of the ASA

That the ASA Council did not circulate the report on graduate education for discussion is perhaps not surprising. Since the early 1970s, the ASA Council and its governance structure have increasingly reflected the interests of constituencies whose primary focus is not on graduate education: nonacademic sociologists, political radicals, women, minorities, and sociologists as teachers. These groups mobilize around intellectual, practical, and ideological issues (Collins et al. 1990, p. 5), a practice which tends to politicize the association and reduce its ability to address disciplinary issues such as graduate education.

Simpson and Simpson (1994, pp. 260-65) recount how the ASA has dealt with several constituencies. When nonacademic sociologists wanted ASA help to establish and control a market for themselves, the ASA set up a standing committee on practice and sponsored a journal (which .attracted too few subscriptions to survive). In response to external social movements, the ASA Council established in the early 1970s an executive specialist for women and minorities along with committees and programs designed to increase their participation. In response to enrollment decrease in the 1970s, the council enlarged the Teaching Services Program, created a standing Committee on Teaching, a departmental subscription service, and an annual teaching award.[17]

In roughly the same period, the number of ASA sections grew from five to more than 25; the proportion of ASA members who belonged to one rose from about one-quarter to about one-half (Simpson and Simpson 1994, p. 270). The increase was not driven by association size, which peaked in 1972 (Collins et al. 1989). Some growth occurred in areas with applied interests; other sections are offshoots of political interest groups that have retained resources won from the ASA in periods of militant mobilization.

Once the process of adding new sections was well established, however, it became part of normal organization politics (Collins et al. 1989, p. 4). Setting up a new section is now routine for any group that mobilizes. Knowledge of the process is widespread. Thus, sections have become a major part of ASA politics although, ironically, participatory movements make organizations more complex and bureaucratic in structure (Collins et al. 1989).

As a result of these organizational changes, only a quarter of every dollar spent now goes to promote the discipline, compared to about half 30 years ago (Simpson and Simpson 1994, p. 268). Decreasing the emphasis on the discipline did not increase membership, which peaked in 1972 and declined by just under a quarter from 1972 to 1984, with a soft upturn since 1984. Nor did the shift in focus increase voting. In 1959, just under two-thirds of the members voted. The percentage of voting decreased to just over one-third in 1987 and just under one-third by 1992.[18]

Along with the broadening of ASA functions to reflect professional and adaptive activities, more and more ASA officers appear to have been nominated and elected for reasons other than eminence in the discipline. A rough indicator of this practice is that only three of the 14 candidates named by the 1993 Committee on Nominations for the 1994 elections were from a top ten department; none was from the top two, the University of Wisconsin-Madison and the University of Chicago (Simpson and Simpson 1994, p. 273).

Discussion

Higher education's fiscal problems highlight aspects of sociology that increase departmental vulnerability to selective budget cuts. Although weakness in departmental self-governance occurs across campus, some of sociology's other characteristics are less widely shared: an elective affinity for students with activist and unrealizable reform agendas, the ease with which research can be trivialized, a low consensus on substance and method that lead to pessimism about the field's vitality, a weak core, and some affinity for antirationalism. Such features tend to attract negative attention from deans. In addition, the politicizing of the ASA over the last two decades has decreased its ability to deal with disciplinary issues.

Some attributes, like the affinity for reformists, would be hard to change and most sociologists would not want to change this attribute even if they could. The practical question is how to minimize negative effects that can be caused by this predilection. There are other aspects of sociology, however, whose costs tend to outweigh any benefits. Two of them stand out.

First, antirationalist forays into the discipline incur potentially heavy costs with no compensating benefits. As sociologists, we should resist our admirable tendency to tolerate differences when it requires tolerance of perspectives that involve aggressive efforts to undermine everyone else. There may be no universal intellectual standards, but some are certainly much less contested than others and it is naive to expect administrators to give resources to those who proclaim unwillingness to respect, honor, and advance such standards. Cultivating skepticism cuts both ways. The vulnerability of the antirationalists is that they also put forth standards (however tacit and incoherent) just as they claim others do, but theirs are more blatantly self-serving than most of what they criticize (Rytina 1994).

Second, sociology's lack of a core puts departments at competitive disadvantage in the struggle for resources. It is hard for administrators to get adequate information about the quality of faculty research. If a department chair stonewalls the dean by claiming that all faculty research is equally important, the dean may conclude that it is all equally unimportant.

Lack of a core also makes it hard to design a graduate program. Sociology's extreme popularity and rapid growth in the 1960s left behind diverse, often mutually hostile camps. Many departments accommodated these differences by evolving decentralized graduate programs that allowed subdisciplinary groups to award degrees to students indifferent to or willfully ignorant of the core. Yet a discipline that awards degrees or faculty positions to those with no respect for its broader legacy will not live long. How could such persons hope to convince administrators to devote scarce resources to a discipline that they themselves do not value?

Nothing is inherently wrong with a house that has many rooms (Stinchcombe 1994). But the rooms need a common entryway. Furthermore, the presence of too many rooms without a logical throughway is an invitation to knock down some and board up others. I do not argue that sociology should be limited to a single substantive dimension of research. That would be impossible and disastrous. But to claim that nothing can be done to evaluate the merit of subareas is a defeatist obeisance to relativism. It seems likely that nothing will be done unless a department agrees that it risks losing ground in the struggle for resources. Certainly, nothing will be achieved without academic civility. Faculty must ask themselves who and what they are and then address the ways that their diversity can contribute to the central core.

The core is embedded in disciplinary history. Few will disagree that the founders were concerned with society writ large, how it was changing the problems attending change, and what might be done about those problems that was possible and just. The founders also agreed that the working of society was subject to scientific study, whatever the problem attending that approach. To maintain historic continuity requires that the discipline examine the way societal organizations function and change in order to clarify the problems experienced by individuals and groups This task requires the sharpest theoretical and methodological tools Surely most subareas in sociology can accommodate and contribute in some way to this core.

Concretely, sociologists need to consider the discipline's niche as producer of knowledge. As Davis (1994, p. 181) notes, "In the lingo of our dear friends the economists, we need some comparative advantage In plain English, we have to be able to do something that somebody wants and do it better than our competitors." Universities exist because taxpayers and other publics are willing to pay for them. What does the public get in return for supporting sociology? A critical task no other discipline handles is to supply the knowledge needed to run welfare states. Practical problems have always spurred social science development by stimulating pressure for action, attracting resources, and testing extant theories (Portes 1994, p. 22). Sociologists have a natural affinity for education, health, and welfare institutions. If we do not believe that we can increase human knowledge and understanding, we cannot expect others to believe in or pay for our efforts. Sociologists need to address the consequences of the way that modern societies change, as Weber and Marx did (Sciulli 1989). They need to work on increasing the solid fact that may be sociology's greatest contribution (Davis 1994, p. 184). Data are needed to address an abundance of nontrivial social problems. Let's get busy.

Notes

1 I am grateful to William Form, Lowell Hargens, Barbara Reskin, Steven Rytina, and the AJS reviewers for comments that greatly improved this paper and to Richard Haller for technical assistance. Correspondence should be addressed to Joan Huber, Department of Sociology, 300 Bricker Hall, 190 North Oval Mail, Ohio State University, Columbus, Ohio 43210.

2 Washington University's vice chancellor of public affairs (Volkman 1991) now proffers advice on how to terminate departments.

3 Wright (1990), analyzing claims in the 1989 Fiske Guide to Colleges that sociology departments were weaker than other social science departments, noted the nonrandom sample and unstated N. (The 1994 Guide, using the same methods, depicts sociology as a less popular major.) Lynch et al. (1993) wanted to explain why more departments of sociology might be closing shortly, but their methods (McFerron et al. 1991) made their findings on faculty and chairperson opinion hard to interpret.

4 The marketing and production functions are nearly divorced in Ph.D. production. Industrial producers must attend to the market to survive, but academic producers can ignore the market, and those who produce a marginal product are often less likely to adjust output to demand than those with the highest reputation for quality (Carrter 1974, P. 274).

5 The cost of education is determined primarily by the money that can be raised. Institutions raise as much as they can and spend it all. The question as to what education ought to cost is posed only from the outside (Bowen 1980, p. 15).

6 The data are calculated from the GSS Codebook, University of Chicago, 1992 (Prewitt. 1993, p. 99).

7 Because universities subsidized them, this flaw made professors cheap hires as consultants for federal projects after World War 11, but it limited their undergraduate teaching (Clark 1983). By the late 1980s, complaints that research conflicted with teaching led to an exaggerated and anecdotal literature on that topic (Geiger 1993, P. 327).

8 According to one sociologist-administrator, anecdotal evidence suggests that sociologists carry fights to the dean more often than do other faculty members (DeFleur 1991). My experience differs, perhaps because I usually met with deans and provosts from the Midwest, the location of three of the top five sociology departments (Webster and Massey 1992).

9 By the mid-1800s, this curriculum had made colleges much less popular. Despite rapid population increases nationwide, some enrollments actually declined (Veysey 1973, p. 2)

10 One indicator of a weak core is the absence of fairly consistent requirements across graduate programs for the Ph.D. Data on this issue will be presented below.

11 See Huber and Loomis (1970), Huber (1973), and van den Berg (1980). The antirationalism that appeared in the 1970s was far more hostile to Western ratio-

nalism than was the Deweyism of the 1930s (Veysey 1973, p. 20).

12 For references to feminist criticism of science as a masculinist enterprise, see Ferber and Nelson (1993, p. 8) and Gross and Levitt (1994, chap. 5). In sociology, feminists are divided on these issues (Sprague and Zimmerman 1989).

13 A research I university offers a full range of baccalaureate programs, gives high priority to research, annually receives at least $40 million in federal support, and awards at least 50 doctorates annually; 59 public and 29 private universities currently meet these criteria (Carnegie Foundation for the Advancement of Teaching 1994, P. xix).

14 For example, one department, the only one in its university to do so, gave graduate students voting parity on all committees. A faculty majority wanted to tighten requirements but graduate students persistently prevented it.

15 The task group included Michael Aiken, James Coleman, Lois DeFleur, Barbara Heyns, Kenneth Land, Stanley Lieberson, Franklin Wilson, William Julius Wilson, Mayor Zald, and me. The report was enriched by comments from senior sociologists experienced in program review.

16 In contrast, undergraduate and graduate programs in economics typically require a year of microtheory, a year of macrotheory, and a year (or more) of statistics courses (Hansen 1990; Siegfried et al. 1991).

17 The AM Council discussion at the time made it clear that one incentive in emphasizing teaching was the hope of luring new members from the burgeoning two-year and community colleges.

18 Network factors (membership in a section, Sociologists for Women in Society, a Ph.D.-granting department, or annual meeting participation) predict ASA voter turnout more often than demographic factors (D'Antonio and Tuch 1991).

References

Astin Alexander. 1985. *Achieving Educational Excellence*. San Francisco: Jossey Bass.

Ben-David, Joseph. 1978. "Emergence of National Traditions in the Sociology of Science." Pp. 197-218 in *The Sociology of Science*, edited by Jerry Gaston. San Francisco: Jossey-Bass.

————. 1991. *Scientific Growth*, edited by G. Freudenthal. Berkeley and Los Angeles. University of California Press.

Bowen, Howard. 1980. *The Costs of Higher Education*. San Francisco. Jossey-Bass.

Bowen, William, and Julie Ann Sosa. 1989. *Prospects for Faculty in the Arts and Sciences*. Princeton, N.J.: Princeton University Press.

Bureau of the Census. 1994. *Current Population Reports*. Special Studies Series P-23, no. 187. Washington, D.C.: Government Printing Office.

Carnegie Council on Policy Studies in Higher Education. 1980. *The Next Twenty Years for Higher Education*. San Francisco: Jossey-Bass.

Carnegie Foundation for the Advancement of Teaching. 1977. *Mission$ of the College Curriculum*. San Francisco: Jossey-Bass.

————. 1994. *A Classification of Institutions of Higher Education*. Ewing, N.J.: California/Princeton Fulfillment Services.

Carrter, Allan. 1974. "The Academic Labor Market." Pp. 281-307 in *Higher Education and the Labor Market*, edited by Margaret Gordon. New York: McGraw-Hill.

Cheit, Earl. 1971. *The New-Depression in Higher Education: A Study of Financial Conditions at 41 Colleges and Universities*. New York: McGraw-Hill.

Clark, Burton. 1983. *The Higher Education System*. Berkeley and Los Angeles: University of California Press.

Cobban, Alm. 1975. *The Medieval University*. London: Methuen.

Cole, Jonathan. 1993. "Balancing Acts: Dilemmas of Choice Facing Research Universities." *Daedalus* 122:1-35.

Cole, Stephen. 2000. "Introduction" in *What's Wrong with Sociology*, edited by Stephen Cole. New Brunswick: Transaction Publishers.

Coleman, James. 1973. "The University and Society's New Demands upon It." Pp. 359-99 in *Content and Context: Essays on College Education*, edited by Carl Kaysen. New York: McGraw-Hill.

Collins, Randall. 1987. "Is 1980s Sociology in the Doldrums?"
American Journal of Sociology 91:1336-55.

Collins, Randall, John McCarthy, Marshall Meyer, Pamela Oliver, Jonathan Turner.
1989. "Future Organizational Trends of the ASA." *Footnotes* 17
(September): I-5, 9.

D'Antonlo, William. 1991. "Recruiting Sociologists in a Time of Expanding
Opportunities." Pp. 99-136 in *Institution Building in Sociology*, edited by
Terence Halliday. Chicago: University of Chicago Press.

D'Antonlo, William, and Steven Tuch. 1991. "Voting: The Case of the American
Sociological Association Revisited." *American Sociologist* 21 (Spring).
37-48.

Davis, James. 1994. "What's Wrong with Sociology?" *Sociological Forum*
9:179-198

DeFleur, Lob. 1992. "Strengthening the Position of Sociology within the
University." *Footnotes* 20 (November): 3, 4.

Etzkowitz, Henry. 1999-90. "The Brief Rise and Early Decline of Radical
Sociology at Washington University, 1969-1972." *American Sociologist*
20:346-52.

Evangelauf, Jean. 1994. "A New Carnegie Classification." *Chronicle of Higher
Education* (April 6), A17-A26.

Falk, William. 1991. "Strengthening Sociology's Position in the University."
Footnotes 19 (November); 1, 4.

Ferber, Marianne, and Julie Nelson. 1993. *Beyond Economic Man.* Chicago:
University of Chicago Press.

Fiske, Edward. 1988. *The Fiske Guide to Colleges 1989.* New York:
Times Books.

———. 1993. *The Fiske Guide to Colleges 1994.* New York: Random House.

Geiger, Roger. 1993. *American Research Universities since World War II*
New York: Oxford University Press.

Gross, Pad, and Norman Levitt. 1994. *The Higher Superstition: The
Academic Left and Its Quarrels with Science.* Baltimore:
Johns Hopkins University Press.

Hagstrom, Warren. 1964. "Anomy in Scientific Communities." *Social
Problems* 12: 186-95.

Hamilton, Richard, and Lowell Hargens. 1993. "The Politics of the
Professors: Selfidentification, 1969 to 1984." *Social Forces* 71:603-27.

Hansen, Lee. 1990. "Educating and Training New Economics Ph.D.'s: How Good a Job Are We Doing?" *AEA Papers and Proceedings* 80:437-50.

Hargens, Lowell. 1990. "Sociologists' Assessment of the State of Sociology, 1969-1984." *American Sociologist* 21 (Fall): 200-208.

Hargens, Lowell, and Lisa Kelly-Wilson. 1994. "Determinants of Disciplinary Discontent." *Social Forces* 72:1177-95.

Huber, Joan. 1973. "Symbolic Interaction as a Pragmatic Perspective." *American Sociological Review* 38:274-84.

Huber, Joan, and Charles Loomis. 1970. "Marxist Dialectic and Pragmatism." *American Sociological Review* 35:308-18.

Kominski, Robert. 1990. "Educational Attainment in the United States: March 1989 and 1988." *Current Population Reports. Population Characteristics*, ser. P-20, no. 45 1. Washington, D.C.: Government Printing Office.

Lazarsfeld, Paul, and Thielens, Wagner. 1958. *The Academic Mind*. Glencoe, IL: Free Press.

Lipset, Seymour Martin. 1994. "The State of American Sociology." *Sociological Forum* 9:199-220.

Lynch, David, Richard McFerron, Lee Bowker, and Ian Beckford. 1993. "A Discipline in Trouble: Why More Sociology Departments May Be Closing Shortly." *Footnotes* 21 (February): 3, 7.

McFerron, Richard, David Lynch, Lee Bowker, and Ian Beckford. 1991. "Teaching and Research Support in Higher Education." Working paper Indiana University of Pennsylvania, Graduate School.

Merton, Robert. 1973. *The Sociology of Science*. Chicago: University of Chicago Press.

Metzger, Walter. 1987. "The Academic Profession in the United States." Pp. 123-208 in *The Academic Profession*, edited by Burton Clark. Berkeley and Los Angeles: University of California Press.

Molotch, Harvey. 1994. "Going Out." *Sociological Forum* 9:221-39.

Nichols, Rodney. 1993. "Federal Science Policy and Universities." *Daedalus* 122: 197-224.

Portes, Alejandro. 1994. "Contentious Science: The Forms and Functions of Trespassing." Paper presented to Dean's Symposium, University of Chicago, May 6.

Prewitt, Kenneth. 1993. "America's Research Universities under Public Scrutiny." *Daedalus* 122:89-101.

Roos, Patricia, and Katherine Jones. 1993. "Women's Inroad into Academic Sociology." *Work and Occupations* 20:395-428.

Rytina, Steven. 1994. Personal communication.

Sciulli, David. 1989. "The Deserved Marginality of Theory." *American Sociologist* 20 (Summer): 249-5 1.

Searle, John. 1993. "Rationality and Realism; What Is at Stake." *Daedalus* 122: 55-83.

Siegfried, John, Robin Bartlett, Lee Hansen, Allen Kelley, Donald McCloskey, and Thomas Tietenberg. 1991. "The Status and Prospects of the Economics Major." *Journal of Economic Education* 22:197-224.

Simpson, Ida Harper, and Richard L. Simpson. 1994. "The Transformation of the ASA." *Sociological Forum* 9:259-78.

Smelser, Neil. 1992. "External Influence on Sociology." Pp. 43-59 in *Sociology and Its Publics*, edited by Terence Halliday. Chicago: University of Chicago Press.

Smith, Page. 1990. *Killing the Spirit*. New York: Viking.

Sprague, Joey, and Mary Zimmerman. 1989. "Quality and Quantity: Reconstructing Feminist Methodology." *American Sociologist* 20 (Spring): 71-86.

Stinchcombe, Arthur. 1994. "Disintegrated Disciplines and the Future of Sociology" *Sociological Forum* 9:279-92.

Sykes, Charles. 1998. *Profscam*. New York; Regnery Gateway.

Turner, Stephen, and Jonathan Turner. 1990. *The Impossible Science*. Newbury Park, Calif.: Sage.

van don Berg, Axel. 1990. "Critical Theory: Is There Still Hope?" *American Journal of Sociology* 86:449-78.

Veysey, Laurence. 1973. "Stability and Experiment in the American Undergraduate Curriculum." Pp. 1-63 in *Content and Context: Essays on College Education*, edited by Carl Kaysen. New York: McGraw-Hill.

Volkman, Frederick. 1991. "Closing Academic Units." Washington, D.C.: Council for Advancement and Support of Education.

Watkins, Beverly. 1983. "You Drink What You Are and Other Reports from the Annual Meetings of Sociologists." *Chronicle of Higher Education* 27 (September 14): 7. 8.

Webster, David, and Sherri Ward Massey. 1992. "The Complete Rankings from the U.S. News & World Report 1992 Survey of Doctoral Programs in Six Liberal Arts Disiciplines." *Change* 27 (November/ December): 20-52.

Weiss, Carol, and Eleanor Singer with Phyllis Endreny. 1988. *Reporting of Social Science in the National Media.* New York: Russell Sage.

Wright, Richard. 1990. "Fiske on Sociology Departments." *Footnotes* 18:8

15

Sociology: After the Linguistic and Multicultural Turns

Paget Henry

In the view of C. Wright Mills, the promise of sociology was a theoretical framework in which men and women could interpretively link their personal troubles and public issues to broader changes of history and social structure (1977: 3-24). Today, because of such changes, it is the personal troubles and public issues of our discipline that need the light of the sociological imagination. Since the mid-eighties, both in and outside of sociology, there has been the recognition that our discipline has entered a period of decline. The troubles and issues produced by this decline have been the subject of several analyses. These can be put into two broad categories. The first is the politicized or value influenced nature of knowledge production in sociology. The second is that the technical conditions of production are not strict enough. The analyses offered by Horowitz(1993) and Lipset(1994) reflect the over-politicized view, while those of Wallace(1988) and Collins(1994) represent the under-technicized position.

I am willing to grant that there is room for improvement in both of these areas, but I do not think that the absence of these improvements are the primary causes of our present crisis. One reason is that our current political and technical practices are quite similar to those of our period of high growth. Second, they are certainly not worse than those of our sister social sciences. In other words, the equally politicized practices of economists have not thrown economics into a similar crisis. The differences in technical conditions of production reflect the more qualitative nature of sociological data. In contrast to the above positions, I would like to suggest that the roots of our crisis are to be found outside, rather than inside, the discipline. Like the people in Mills' text, our troubles and issues go beyond the limited confines of our disciplinary milieu. They are to be found in our inadequate response to sets of structural changes that have been taking place in a number of closely related academic markets. The first set of changes is related to the resurgence of economic theory and the challenges it has presented in the more technical/ instrumental aspects of sociological production. On the whole, rational choice sociologists have made a very credible response to this challenge. They have clearly established themselves as significant players in this market. However, because sociologists have imported more from this market than we export, the discipline has a negative intellectual trade balance with economics.

The second set of changes are the result of major increases in the theoretical status and institutional representation of linguistic and racial discourses within the larger academic community. The growing presence of these discourses has presented a major challenge to the hermeneutic and cultural aspects of sociological production. However, the response to this challenge by interpretive and other sociologists has been far from credible. Indeed, it has been quite inadequate. Let us hope that we are not soon confronted by similar challenges on our third front - the historical aspects of our practice.

In this new competitive situation, sociology has been losing its share of a number of academic markets and its quasi-monopolistic claims on others. This has been true in areas such as race, gender, Third World studies, popular culture, and the criticism of the arts. Focusing on the area of race, I will examine how the rise of Afro-American Studies, together with its heavy reliance on post-structuralist theory, have provided sociology with one of its new competitive challenges. This is all done from the perspective of a development sociologist who currently heads an Afro-American Studies department. I conclude the paper with some suggestions for how we may better meet these challenges.

The Linguistic Turn

The linguistic turn refers to a fundamental shift in the relationship between language and the disciplines of humanities and social sciences, and hence between language and the explanation of human behavior(Levi Strauss, 1963: 1-97, Rorty, 1967). We can describe this shift as the gradual releasing of language from imprisonment in its communicative role, as modern cultural systems continue the process of internal differentiation. In its communicative role, language has been severely restricted by the communicative needs of everyday speech and specialized discourses like sociology. Now that it is able to do more, language is emerging as a powerful explanatory principle of human behavior. As these new capabilities of language emerge, different aspects have been appropriated as founding analogies for new explanatory or interpretive strategies. Thus the communicative (Habermas, 1984), the semiotic (Derrida, 1984), the categorical (Foucault, 1973) and semantic (Austin, 1962) aspects of language have been employed in this way. Exploring the possibilities inherent in these strategies slowly secured this turn to languages not just as a theory of texts, but also as a theory of social behavior.

The gradual solidifying of the linguistic turn produced a number of new discourses that have changed the composition and social organization of disciplines in the academy. Among the more important of these new discourses are Semiotics, Cultural Studies, Critical Legal Studies, and Postcolonial Studies. These new fields employ one or more of the above linguistically-based approaches to theory. They offer new explanations that compete with those coming from sociological subfields such as interpretive theory, sociology of mass culture, sociology of law and development. In these fields, sociological explanations now find themselves in competition with linguistic explanations from these new discourses and the older humanities, such as literature and philosophy that have also been influenced by the linguistic turn.

In addition to the rise of these new discourses, the linguistic turn has also produced two important epistemological shifts that have significantly affected sociology's competitive position. The first of these was its contribution to the decline of the neopositivist philosophy of science that had its roots in Popper(1965) and extended to Lakatos(1970) and declined with Feyerabend(1979). In the current post-positivist environment, epistemological and methodological pluralism has become more the norm. As a result the non-scientific epistemic claims of the new linguistic theories of the humanities have found a much more receptive audience than they might have in the high days of positivism. Thus the edge that our scientific techniques gave us in the past vis-a-vis the humanities has declined in the post-positivist period.

Second and closely related was the contribution of the linguistic turn to the dethroning of rational, Cartesian models of the knowing subject in which language was confined to its communicative role. Many subfields in sociology made use of these Cartesian models. They have now been replaced by more linguistically inscribed models that are closer to the assumptions of ethnomethodologists, who have been marginal to the sociological enterprise. In these new models, thinking is shaped by logic as well as by language. Consequently social action is not only institutionally but also linguistically determined. With this conceptual shift, language emerges as a relatively autonouous domain of human self formation and behavior regulation. As with the first epistemological shift, the decline of the rational subject has lowered the epistemic advantage that sociology derived in the past from its over-dependence upon rationalism.

In short, the linguistic turn has given rise to new discourses that have changed the division of intellectual labor within the academy. It has also changed relations with old ones such as philosophy and literature that have decreased the edge sociology had because of its more rational and scientific orientation.

The Multicultural Turn

The multicultural turn is also grounded in an important discursive shift This time it is between ethnic discourses and the established disciplines of the social sciences and humanities. As in the case of the linguistic turn, we can also describe this shift as a process of discursive differentiation that has given rise to new discourses, programs and departments within the academy. Unlike the linguistic turn, this is not a case of diffentiation that is driven by the adaptive needs of basic institutions, but by changes in patterns of racial and ethnic inequality.

The ethnic hierarchy of American society has been and continues to be primary sources of the personal troubles and public issues of dominated racial and ethnic groups. Since the 1950s, the most important changes in those hierarchies were produced by the period of African American resistance known as the Civil Rights era. This resistance changed not only the institutional framework of white/black domination, but also the mode of its discursive representation. As we will see, this would also bring to an end sociology's quasi-monopoly on race within the academy.

In addition to the above changes, African American resistance produced an outbreak of what Stephen Steinberg has called "ethnic fever"(1989: 40). Since that outbreak, the demand for ethnic information has been growing steadily. An increasing number of social groups have reclaimed suppressed ethnic heritages and have been demanding space within the academy. These demands have dramatically increased the number of ethnic discourses seeking academic recognition. As a result, we now have programs or departments of Afro-American Studies, Asian American Studies, Latino Studies or Ethnic Studies in many universities. Programs of race and ethnicity are also being housed in English and American Studies departments. It is the institutionalizing of these ethnic discourses that has multiculturalized the study of race and ethnicity. These new discourses have posed a competitive challenge to the sociology of race that is comparable to the challenges from the new linguistically-oriented discourses and from economic theory. Similar shifts and related processes of differentiation have supported the institutionalization of feminist discourses within the academy.

These ethnic and gender discourses have also made unique contributions to the epistemological pluralism of the present period. Along with the linguistic turn, they have contributed to the dethroning of the Cartesian subject by exposing his concealed white and male identities. From their perspective, the knowing subject is particularized not only by language, but also by gender and ethnicity. These concrete identities do not disappear in moments of abstract universalism. As an always gendered or ethnic agent, the knowing subject brings the special hermeneutic of an insider to the tasks of ethnic or gender knowledge production. Discursive recognition for such gendered or ethnically marked hermeneutic processes has increased in this period of epistemological pluralism. The truth claims of these insider hermeneutics are, of course, contestable and offer no absolute guarantees. But this increase in philosophical legitimacy for ethnic and gender discourses also means increased competition for the sociology of race, whose quasi-monopoly rested in part on more abstract models of the epistemological subject.

The New Competitive Challenges

If the above interpretations are correct, then the new competitive challenges confronting sociology are at least partially the result of the new discourses that have found a place in the academy because of the linguistic and multicultural turns. Whether it is Afro-American Studies, semiotics, post-colonial studies or Women's Studies, these programs are attracting students and producing explanations that compete with those of sociology. It is important to note that these discourses are not offering propositions that have been produced with greater scientific or technical rigor. It is not their technical or empirical power that is making them competitive. Their's is not the instrumental challenge of economic theory. Rather it is their ability to deconstruct identities, to interpret, and to explain behavior in terms of systems of linguistically structured meanings that provide them with influence.

More than disciplines like economics or political science, these changes in the academic marketplace have been particularly hard on sociology. The primary reason for this is that sociology has no exclusive institutional or social property. That is, there is no institutional or social process that it can claim in the way that economists claim the economy, political scientists the state, or psychologists the psyche. Because sociology has no such protected area to provide a buffer against market competition, the rise of the new linguistic, gender and ethnic discourses have been pretty hard on us. As a discipline, we survive and grow by entering already occupied markets with explanations that both producers and consumers in these markets find useful. The impact of political sociology on political science is a good case in point. Whenever our share of these external markets contracts sharply, we enter into a state of crisis.

Because of its special market conditions, sociological practice often takes place at the interface of two or more analytically distinct discourses. Thus whether it is the sociology of race, literature, science or religion, sociological explanations must compete with the accounts that producers of works in these fields have of their own production. The continuing crisis in sociology is the outcome of changes in patterns of cooperation and competition in areas where sociology has been sharing a market with another discipline or set of disciplines. The resulting tensions between the sociological and non-sociological accounts will necessarily produce periodic swings in the evaluation of sociological explanations in particular markets.

For example, in the Fine Arts, the Marxist revival of the late sixties brought a renewed interest in sociological explanations of art. This revival competed successfully with the formalism of the "new critics," and peaked in the works of Arnold Hauser(1982), Theodore Adorno(1972), George Lukacs(1975) and Lucien Goldman(1978). However, the subsequent rise of structuralism and post- structuralism has produced a new formalism that has led one historian of ideas to the following observations: "the trend has been away from psychological and sociological theories ... and toward theories that recognized language in all its density and opacity as the place where meaning is constituted, and that have their more general theoretical articulation in linguistics, philosophy and literary criticism." (Loews, 1987:881) This swing back to formalism in the fine arts is a good example of the competitive challenges we have been facing.

In short, the linguistic and multicultural turns have dramatically altered the nature of the marketplace for interpretive sociology. They have changed its organization, the major players and the level of competition. As new theoretical and interpretive products enter these markets, our's are being pushed out. This is the meaning, I attach to Horowitz' "post-sociological environment" (1993: 169) rather than that of "decompositon." To continue this developmental analogy, our exports to important markets are falling, and our products are finding buyers only in our small domestic market. The latter is small precisely because of our lack of exclusive institutional or social property. Here lies the primary source of our private troubles and public issues. These are the larger forces of history and social structure that have deposited them in our lap. Here is our new challenge. We are not beyond the reach of these forces because we study them. No, the only advantage sociology gives us is the ability to understand our unease in terms of our location at "minute points of intersection of biography and history within society". (Mills, 1977: 7) However, before dealing with our responses to this larger set of interpretive challenges, I will examine more closely the case of the sociology of race.

The Sociological Discourse in Race

During the decade of the 1920s, sociology gradually replaced biology as the home of race/ethnic studies in the academy. The securing of this quasimonopoly was facilitated by the failure of biologists to find genetic support for white supremacist claims regarding African American inferiority. It was also facilitated by the exclusion of African Americans and African American discourses from the classrooms of the academy. However, emerging when it did, the new subfield interfaced with biology, anthropology, psychology, African American scholarly discourses, and the everyday discourses of both European and African Americans. The parameters of the sociology of race were also shaped by increasing conflicts between blacks and whites, and the tensions that accompanied the arrival of large numbers of European ethnics.

Between the 1920s and the early sixties, we can distinguish at least four distinct theoretical approaches to race and ethnicity by sociologists: the social Darwinist, the assimlationist, the intergroup relations, and the culture of poverty approaches. Although some of these theories were progressive in their day, as a group their constructions of the African American sociopolitical identity and their policy recommendations have left a lot to be desired. In these theories, African Americans did not find revealing reflections of their personal troubles or their public issues. Consequently, it is not difficult to understand why these theories were surpassed by the multicultural turn.

Social Darwinism was sociology's first theoretical offering on race as it moved to replace biology. Although critical of biological claims, this approach was heavily indebted to biology. It did not change the basic way in which the race problem had been formulated. It was still cast in terms of what to do with an unassimilable, inferior population that was now a

permanent part of the American landscape. To explain the differences between European and African Americans, sociologists resorted to the principle of natural selection. The inferiority of African Americans was the result of the limited mental capacities that life in Africa required that they
develop—capacities that were seen as inadequate for the American terrain.
Sociologists such as Ross, Cooley, Giddings, Sumner and Ellwood were
caught in this twilight zone between sociology and biology. At the policy
level, Jerome Dowd sanctioned the status quo by declaring the race problem insoluble (1926: 360). Thus, at a time when African Americans were
proposing full civil rights, black nationalism or an end to apartheid, sociologists were declaring them to be unrealizable solutions.

In contrast to the bipolar, black/white world of the social Darwinists,
was the broader framework of culture contact and assimilation formulated
by Park(1950). Applied to the experiences of European immigrants in
America, Park saw two possibilities. Anglo-conformity or a melting pot of
mutual influencing. Along with this theoretical shift came Park's open
involvement with African Americans, and his reformism. But in spite of
these significant moves, his policy recommendations were in the main
noninterventionist. Reform was reform within the racist socio-political
order of American society. Only hard work and education were useful
activities in the face of white domination. It was for this reason that
Gunnar Myrdal placed Park and other assimilationists in the category of
"do nothing" liberals.

The more interventionist stance of the intergroup relations approach derives from two sources: its association with the New Deal of the Roosevelt
administration, and the increasing militancy of African Americans as evi-
denced by the organizing activities of A. Phillip Randolph, and the Detroit
riot of 1943. The theoretical center of this approach was the work of Robin
Williams, who shifted the conceptual framework from Anglo-conformity
to ethnic pluralism with a system of shared values (1947). Williams attempted to formulate a dynamic theory of the tensions that signifiers of
difference such as race and ethnicity created within this system of shared
values. Propositions for reducing such intergroup tensions were generated
and tested. Education emerged as the primary instrument of intervention.
Whites needed to be educated about their attitudes, and blacks needed
education for social mobility. Thus, in spite of the revolt that was partly
responsible for the hightened interest in reducing racial tensions, there was
no serious thematizing of the persistent insurrectionary consciousness that
distinguished the African American experience from that of European ethnics.
Finally, we have the culture of poverty approach. Essentially, this is the

social Darwinist approach with a twist. Instead of defects being located in the specific adaptations of national cultures, this approach hypothesizes a universal culture that emerges whenever a human group adapts to poverty. This culture makes mobility, integration or assimilation into the mainstream extremely difficult. Although originating with the work of Oscar Lewis, this approach has been most influential in sociology through the work of Moynihan and Glazer (1970). For these authors, the melting pot was an existing reality. Thus, the problem becomes why haven't groups like African Americans and Puerto Rican Americans made it into the mainstream. The answer is the culture of poverty, with its peculiar patterns of family disorganization. Because in the view of the authors this culture reproduces itself independently of the order of domination that produced it, state intervention and political resistance are of little help here. The more helpful strategies were the "bootstrap" activities of family reorganization and the acquiring of achievement values.

From this brief review, it should be clear that the intellectual and institutional space created by the sociology of race was a cramped one for African Americans. Access was limited. The discourse was controlled by white males. Its policy recommendations were weak. Its representations of Africa and its culture remained unsatisfactory. And so also were its representations of African Americans and their political capabilities. These representations constrasted sharply with the portrayals of African Americans in works of W.E.B. DuBois(1899), C.L.R. James(1939), Johnson(1941), Oliver Cox(1948) and E. Franklin Frazier(1957). For James, African Americans represented "potentially the most revolutionary section of the population"(1939).

In short, African Americans did not find illuminating reflections of their unease about identity misrepresentation and institutional exclusion in the sociological imagination of these four decades. This failure was both interpretive and political in nature. One result of this failure, was the attempt to establish a "Black sociology" that was distinct from "White sociology." Joyce Ladner's The Death of White Sociology was the manifesto of this movement In her introduction, Ladner links the rise of Black sociology to the claim that white sociology "had seldom advocated the kinds of progressive changes that would insure that Blacks no longer experience the subjugated status in American society to which they have been subjected."(1973) Thus, dissatisfaction with the white identity of sociology and its conservative policy recommendations were major stimuli to the rise of the Black sociological movement of the sixties. The political failures of the sociological discourse on race point to dimensions of the ideological issue that do fit the paradigms of Lipset and Horowitz. It suggests that ideology, like the empirical factors, can contribute to the rise or the decline of a field. Which of these two possibilities will be realized depends on the competitive context. As we will see, it is not just the technical propositions of the new discourses that have made them competitive. It is also their ideological stances and their interpretive or cultural capabilities.

Afro-American Studies. Multiculturalism and Poststructuralism

The Civil Rights Movement significantly changed the discursive representation and institutional organization of race/ethnic studies in the academy. Segregated schools and universities were forced to desegregate, while those that discriminated informally came under pressure to increase enrollments of African Americans and other excluded groups. In addition to these quantitative issues, there was the qualitative impact on various academic disciplines. This manifested itself in the greater representation of African American contributions in courses, the growth of studies of race in English and American Studies departments, the growth of Black sociology and in the rise of programs and departments of Afro-American Studies.

For sociology, these shifts produced significant changes in the competitive and intertextual dynamics of its discourse on race. The highly restricted border relations with African American scholarly discourses were replaced by more open ones. Long ignored African American intellectuals such as DuBois, Johnson, Frazier, Reid and Cox experienced a rebirth. This more cooperative attitude in textual production also changed sociology's relations with the everyday discourses of African Americans. Whether integrationist, black nationalist, black Islamic, Pan Africanist or separatist, the racial or insider hermeneutics of these discourses joined those of European Americans to become a basic stock of predefined meanings that guided the sociological analysis of race.

In the short run, these shifts strengthened sociology's competitive positions as the home of race relations within the academy. They provided African Americans and other excluded ethnic groups with new opportunities to articulate, confirm or disconfirm the central claims of their scholarly traditions and everyday discourses. In other words, both the discursive space and the institutional framework that sociology provided for the study of race was now less cramped.

One important indication of these changed intertextual relations was Robert Blauner's *Racial Oppression in America* (1972). Reflecting also the Marxist revival of the period, this work took the analysis of American race relations outside the framework of existing theories and placed it squarely within an internal colonial framework. It rejected the claim that African Americans were just another ethnic group by thematizing a history of oppression that made their experiences comparable to those of external colonies. This change of framework reflected tendencies in a number of black scholarly and everyday discourses. Thus the initial impact of the Civil Rights Movement was a strengthening of sociology's dominant position in the field of race and ethnic studies.

However, the above strengthening of sociology's competitive position did not last very long. By the early eighties, the rise of newly formed Afro-American and other ethnic studies departments brought new suppliers of race/ethnic knowledge to this market. Increasing competition from these departments, the linguistic turn in the humanities, and a political shift to the right have all combined to erode sociology's position. Until this period, race relations was as close as sociology came to owning exclusive social property. The institutionalizing of the multicultural turn transformed this defacto monopoly into the more competitive pattern that holds for most of sociology's subfields. Thus conditions of textual production in the sociology of race have moved closer to conditions in the sociology of literature, the sociology of religion, or political sociology.

The increased competition for the sociology of race derives from the qualitatively different nature of Afro-American and other ethnic studies departments. In the case of Afro-American Studies, departments are usually interdisciplinary and focus more exclusively on the experiences of continental and diasporic Africans; intertextual relations with the wide variety of black scholarly and everyday discourses are more open, and faculty are often predominantly African American. These differences have resulted in distinct contexts for studying race. Consequently, students now have choices that did not exist before.

Another important factor that currently distinguishes the Afro-American Studies approach to race is its greater openness to the linguistic turn than the sociological approach. Because of its interdisciplinary nature, AfroAmerican Studies registers with equal weight important shifts in both the humanities and the social sciences. In the sixties and early seventies, it was the socio-political writings of African Americans that dominated the discourses in Afro-American Studies departments. They were also the texts that were important for sociologists like Blauner, Ladner, Nathan Hare and Robert Staples. Hence the strong social science influence on Afro-American Studies, and the significant parallels with the sociology of race.

However, by the early eighties, the spectacular growth in African American fiction and its criticism turned many Afro-American Studies departments in the direction of the humanities. It was the search for interpretive tools to analyze this body of fiction that opened Afro-American Studies departments to poststructuralist theory. Evidence of this linguistic turn in Afro-American criticism can be seen in works of Houston Baker(1984), Cornel West(1989), and Henry Louis Gates(1988). In the area of popular culture, it can be seen in the works of Michael Eric Dyson(1993), Tricia Rose(1994) and Wahneema Lubiano(1991). From these sites it has spread to others, creating tensions with older Pan Africanist or black nationalist approaches. The work of the Jamaican/ British sociologist Stuart Hall(1978; 1980) provides us with interesting locations where these currents have intersected. This shift toward poststructuralist theory might have been avoided had African American critics made the sociology of literature their theoretical point of departure. But in literature, the sociological approach was being eclipsed by new formalism of poststructuralist theory. Hence the linguistic turn in Afro-American Studies.

Many of the features and trends we described above also hold for Hispanic and Asian American Studies programs, and the more inclusive ethnic studies departments. These institutional and discursive changes are increasing the disciplinary choices available to the student of race/ethnic relations. In other words, the multicultural turn has dramatically changed the nature of competition in this field. It has divested sociology of its disciplinary monopoly and has transformed the field into a more interdisciplinary market, whose many players have more specialized interests. To survive under these changed conditions, sociologists must now do more than write for each other. We must make available texts that producers and consumers in this now interdisciplinary market will find useful.

Sociology's Response to the New Challenges

As I see it, the roots of sociology's continuing crisis are to be found in the inadequacy of its response to changes in its competitive situation. These changes are not confined to sociology of race. They have also affected areas such as theory, the sociology of the arts, social change and development. Our loss of shares in these markets is due primarily to a theoretical challenge that is hermeneutic in nature. The new discourses are not offering propositions that are more ideologically neutral or logically rigorous. Rather what they are offering are propositions that make good use of linguistic theories of meaning and difference.

With regard to the multicultural turn, sociology's response has been ambivalent without being genuinely innovative. Some sociologists have embraced multiculturalism, but in ways that do not adequately address basic sociological concerns. The recent volume edited by Margaret Andersen and Patricia Hill-Collins *Race, Class, and Gender* (1995) is a good case in point. The editors situate race in a general theory of difference that is broader than Robin William's, and rejects his emphasis on common values. In Derridian fashion, this theory draws analogically on linguistic notions of difference that polarize binary oppositions such as male/female, sacred/profane or white/black. Racism or sexism thus becomes a categorical difference that is projected onto a group. However, this categorical orientation opens a cleavage with the institutional aspects of racial or gender domination that Andersen and Hill-Collins do not successfully negotiate(1995: 1-9). Achieving such a sociolinguistic or socio-semiotic synthesis would constitute an important advance over what currently exists.

However, not all sociologists have been this open to the multicultural turn. Some, such as Glazer, have responded by defensively reasserting the claims of the culture of poverty or assimilation paradigms(1983). These conservative responses have gained significant support from the political shift to the right. The retreat from the position of the sixties that this shift has produced are also evident in Wilson's *The Truly Disadvantaged*.

As a response to multiculturalism and the rise of Afro-American and other ethnic studies departments, this ambivalence is inadequate. For those who embrace the multicultural theory of difference, they need to tailor it more specifically to the institutional concerns of sociology. The link between semio-linguistic and social structures must be more fully theorized, so that contributions not derivable from the semio-linguistic alone can be made. Without such distinct contributions, we won't get the full theoretical benefits from this linguistic import.

To compete with the particularizing of the modern subject that ethnic departments have institutionalized, race needs to be more centrally located within the sociological discourse on modernity. The latter has been centered on processes of rationalization and industrialization. This is too narrow as it excludes the complex processes of racializing, cultural mixing and creolization that have been such basic parts of the modern experiences of non-whites. Like India and other Asian countries, Africa needs to be included in the classical analyses of modernity. African modernization needs to be freed from its ethnographic construction as the quintessential site of pre-modernity, and included in Weberian and Marxian accounts of modernizing processes. We now need to be ethnically and racially specific in our accounts of the rise of the modern world. To resist these processes of diversification and particularization in the face of the increasing differentiation of race/ethic discourses will only decrease our capacity to survive in this increasingly complex market

Finally, to deal with the experiencial and organizational difference between sociology and ethnic studies departments, we will have to examine more carefully the institutional and discursive spaces that we offer to non-whites. This is still a major problem. Afro-American students and faculty still do not feel quite at ease in sociology departments or in the subfield of race and ethnicity. The persistence of a Black sociology suggests this. Sociology's record in historically and empirically documenting the reality of racism remains very strong, if not unsurpassed. However, it has been lacking in bold policy recommendations, innovative institutional changes, and illuminating interpretive mirrors for African Americans and other ethnic groups. Dealing with these issues will be critical to our survival in the field of race/ethnic relations.

With regard to the linguistic turn, our responses have been even less adequate. We have not appropriated the strength of this discursive event to maintain or widen the appeal of sociological theory, nor have we successfully deployed sociological theory to guage the limits of this turn. For the most part, we have ignored it, hoping that this spectre would soon go away. But it hasn't, because behind it is a process of institutional differentiation within the academy. This process has been more difficult to see because its institutional patterns have been more fragmented and dispersed than those of the multicultural turn. Linguistics, the basic locus for the study of languages, continues to study them as detached systems of communication. However, the behavior regulating and identity forming consequences of language have found institutional space in programs like cultural studies, postcolonial studies, and literary criticism. As the dust settles on these specific programs, it becomes clear that the current hermeneutic challenge is not rooted in them specifically, but in the new explanatory power of language (made available by linguistics) that brought these programs into being. In other words, the institutional separation between linguistics and the study of linguistically coordinated social action has made the increasing differentiation of language and its intellectual consequences for sociology difficult to see.

In addition to this ambiguity, sociology's response was further complicated by the fact that the linguistic turn peaked at a time when interpretive sociology had entered a period of decline. As the most linguistically oriented styles of sociology, symbolic interactionism, ethnomethodology, and Schutzian phenomenological sociology would have been the likely sites of creative engagements with the linguistic turn. Schutz attempted to outline a phenomenological semiotics (1964: 287-356). Berger and Luckman's principles of social constructionism, have been central to poststructuralist applications of linguistic theory. So also have been the conversational strategies of ethnomethodology. This was the group of sociologists who were best positioned by interest and training to engage the linguistic turn. They were the ones to respond to it, the way rational choice theorists responded to the technical/ instrumental challenge from economic theory. However, it was at this time that they began to disintegrate.

Among the earliest responses to the linguistic turn was Charles Lemert's. Lermert very clearly perceived the changing role of language in the academy. "Sociology," he noted, "has never produced a forthright theory of language practiced, of discourse" (1979: 14). However, addressing this gap was not Lemert's concern. Rather, it was the implication of Foucault's critique of homocentrism for sociological theory.

The work of Richard Brown is indicative of the affinity between interpretive sociology and the linguistic turn that I noted earlier. Brown very successfully uses the new linguistic theories to enrich his interpretive sociology (1987). However, his polemical use of the category of rhetoric reinforced rather than weakened tensions with empirical and historical sociologists. Nevertheless, it is primarily from these two sociologists that the interpretive response to the linguistic turn has come.

Responses have also come from outside of the interpretive tradition. Among the functionalists there was Parsons' attempt to engage the thought of Levi-Strauss. However, Parsons' systemic interests pushed him to conceive language in instrumental terms that made it analogous to "steering media" like money and power (1967). This orientation took it away from his theory of symbolism(1981), and contained the new linguistic possibilities that Levi-Strauss was exploring. In the Loubser et. al volume, *Explorations in General Theory in Social Science*, several Parsonian scholars took up the problem of language in functionalist theory, and how it could be used to supplement the analysis of meaning. However, the push in this direction was eclipsed by the rise of neofunctionalism.

From the neofunctionalists we have Alexander's clear recognition of "the hermeneutic challenge"(1987: 281). However, the challenge was perceived primarily in relation to Parsonian theory and not to the competitive position of sociology as a whole. In this context Alexander characterized the turn as a form of sociological idealism which reduced everything to meaning. Thus, caught up in the search for a post-Parsonian multi-dimensional synthesis, Alexander missed the new explanatory powers of language before they reached the condition of sociological idealism.

By far and away, Habermas has provided sociology's most innovative response to the linguistic turn. He has perceived with great clarity the increasing differentiation of language in modern societies, and the challenge it poses to theories of meaning that are grounded in intentional subjects. Choosing the pragmatic/ communicative aspects of language over the semiotic and semantic, Habermas attempts to reformulate the development of sociological theory in relation to this process of linguistic differentiation. His re-reading of Marx, Weber, Durkheim, Mead and Parsons have all been shaped by this linguistic turn(1989). However, the more Habermas has moved in this direction the less influential has been his work on sociology. The dissatisfaction appears to be with the degree to which linguistic/ communicative structures have eclipsed social structures in Habermas' work. His formulation of the dialectical interplay between these two has not won the approval of most sociologists. On this particular issue, Pierre Bourdieu with his nation of cultural capital seems to be closer to the mark, even though his synthesis is not as explicitly worked out. However, Habermas' reformulation remains our most innovative response to the linguistic turn. It has clearly stimulated the work of Ben Agger(1989) in this area.

Finally, from the rational choice theorists we have had little or no response. In Coleman's *Foundations of Social Theory* we have a highly instrumental and economistic model of sociology that expands the technical/ empirical dimensions of the sociological imagination at the expense of its interpretive dimensions. Coleman's legal reconstruction of norms is particularly indicative of this will to instrumentalization(1990: 241-55). With such a strong turn in the direction of economics and away from the humanities, it is understandable why rational choice theorists have had so little to say about the linguistic turn.

Given the wide influence of this turn on both the humanities and the social sciences, it should be clear that ours has indeed been an inadequate response. The resulting decline in theoretical influence has not been restricted to interpretive sociology. On the contrary, it has been a discinplinary wide decline. This points to the interconnected nature of the three dimensions that make up the sociological imagination. In *Knowledge and Human Interests* Habermas reinforced this three dimensional view from an epistemic perspective. If, inspite of the tendencies to diverge and fragment in three separate directions, we accept this integrated view, then it should be no surprise that a major crisis for interpretive sociology has become a crisis for the discipline as a whole. All need to be concerned even when only one of these three pillars of our imagination is confronted by an external challenge of this magnitude. At such times, we need to put internal differences on the back burner and face the challenge together.

Although a little late, sociology needs a strategy to address the long-term changes in academic markets that have come with the linguistic turn. These changes are indicated by the claims that are being made for language by the producers of linguistic theories of social behavior. In his recent book, *The Construction of Social Reality,* John Searle makes the argument for the linguistic nature of social institutions. If we are to meet this challenge, two processes of differentiation within sociology must be more firmly institutionalized.

First, we need to encourage the growth of the sociology of language. This particular interface has become extremely important, but this subfield has not experienced a corresponding boom. This is a measure of inflexibility that we cannot afford, given our particular mode of market insertion. More resources must be put in this subfield and graduate students encouraged to enter it. In these times, we must not only be politically and ethnically correct, we must also be linguistically correct.

Second, we must institutionalize more firmly the slowly emerging division of labor between theory construction and metatheory. Our metatheorists would be largely responsible for the general models of societies that derive from the classical tradition and their relationships to new models arising in other social sciences or the humanities. The stream of ideas that gave birth to the classical tradition has not stopped. The linguistic turn demonstrates clearly the need for a group of theoretical sociologists whose primary responsibility is indeed the impact of movements in this stream for sociological theory. If we want to regain our position as net exporters of theory, this is a market in which we must be competitve. The metatheoretical field would then have a relationship to the history of ideas that the sociology of religion or literature has to religious or literary studies. Except in this case, we would have a very special interest in a particular set of ideas. In the past, we have relied too heavily on the big theorists to do this work. The time has come for us to train more ordinary graduate students in metatheory, just as we do in all other subfields. As a group, they should be able to respond to sociology's interpretive, empirical and historical interests vis-a-vis new developments in the history of ideas.

Without this capacity, we will not be able to respond effectively to new theoretical challenges, hermeneutic or otherwise. Internal fragmentation will continue and so will the loss of market share. At some point on this path, we would have to redefine ourselves on a more restricted model, such as Coleman's. But, such contractions would be particularly costly for sociology as we have no distinct institutional property. Because the social dimension cuts across all institutions, being competitive in these institutional markets that are dominated by specific disciplines is extremely important for sociology. We are at our best when we can hold our own in these markets. And to do our best we need all three cylinders working together.

To keep all three cylinders working, there must be significant changes in our patterns of resource allocation. The contrast between our inadequate response to the hermenentic challenge and the more credible response to instrumental challenge, points to a structural imbalance in need of correction. The inadequacy of the interpretive response reflects a lack of personnel, resources and internal organization. Between Lemert and Habermas, are the fragments of a response that was never mobilized. To do it, more attention and more institutional support must be given to the interpretive wing of our discipline. To the extent that ideological factors maintain this imbalance, they will be contributors to this and other crises.

Conclusion

I've argued that the continuing crisis in sociology is the result of our inadequate responses to new competitive challenges that have been produced by the multicultural and linguistic turns. This position reflects the troubles I've had in reconciling the increasing appeal of Afro-American Studies and postcolonial studies over the sociology of race and the sociology of development in the minds of many of my students. Although primarily a historical sociologist, the impact of these changes has moved me to look more closely at the state of interpretive sociology. I am convinced that they have increased the competitive pressure most directly on the interpretive pillar of sociological production. Consequently, it is the interpretive and cultural power of sociological explanations that is especially in need of revitalization, not the empirical, the historical, or the ideological. If there are problems with these, it is how we relate them to each other. This revitalization can only take place if there are shifts in resource distribution, and a greater sense of collective responsibility among sociologists as a whole.

As Mills often reminded us, the cultural significance of sociology is realized when through its lenses people see their personal troubles and public issues in a new and more familiar light. As a result, they gain a new understanding of themselves, they experience a change of identity or a transvaluation of values. These are the cultural, interpretive gifts of the sociological imagination. It is in this area that we are being surpassed by Afro-American Studies, postcolonial studies and other new discourses. We cannot be content with the production of empirical and historical generalizations. As Weber suggests, it must be the primary responsibility of some sociologists to employ these generalizations in the understanding of particular situations. Only then is the cultural significance of sociology realized. Consequently, the more immediate challenge confronting us is the revitalizing of this cultural function in an era in which the multicultural and linguistic imaginations are also changing identities and transvaluing values.

References

Adorno, T. & Horkeimer, M. 1975. *Dialectic of Enlightment*. N.Y.: Contenum.

Anderson, Margaret and Hill-Collins, Patricia. 1995. *Race Class and Gender*. New York: Wadsworth.

Agger, Ben. 1989. *Socio(ONTO)logy*. Chicago: University of Illinois Press.

Alexander, Jeffrey. 1987. *Twenty Lectures*. New York: Columbia University Press.

Austin, JL. 1962. *How To Do Things With Words*. New York: Oxford University Press.

Baker, Houston. 1984. *Blues, Ideology and Afro-American Literature*. Chicago: University of Chicago Press.

Blauner, Robert. 1972. *Racial Oppression in America*. New York: Harper and Row.

Brown, Richard. 1987. *Society as Text*. Chicago: University of Chicago Press.

Coleman, James. 1990. *Foundations of Social Theory*. Cambridge: Harvard University Press.

Collins, Randall. 1994. "Why the Social Sciences Won't Become High Consensus, Rapid Discovery Science," *Sociological Forum* 9: 155-177. [Reprinted in this volume]

Cox, Oliver. 1948. *Caste Class and Race*. Garden City: Doubleday.

Derrida, Jacques. 1984. *Grammatology*. Baltimore: John Hopkins University Press.

Dowd, Jerome. 1926. *The Negro in American Life*. New York: Century.

Dubois, W.E.B. 1899. *The Philadelphia Negro*. Philadelphia: University of Pennsylvania.

Dyson, Michael. 1993. *Reflecting Black*. Minneapolis: University of Minnesota Press.

Feyerabend, Paul. 1979. *Against Method*. London: Verso.

Foucault, Michel. 1973. *The Order of Things*. New York. Vintage Books.

Frazier, E.F. 1957. *Black Bourgeoisie*. Glencoe: Free Press.

Gates, Henry. 1988. *The Signifying Monkey*. N.Y.: Oxford University Press.

Glazer, Nathan. 1983 *Ethnic Dilemmas* Cambridge: Harvard University Press.

Goldman, Lucien. 1978. *Toward a Sociology of the Novel*. London: Tavistock Publications.

Habermas, Jurgen. 1971. *Knowledge and Human Interests*. Boston: Beacon Press.

————. 1984. *The Theory of Communicative Action, Vol I*. Boston: Beacon Press.

————. 1989.*The Theory of Communicative Action,Vol II*. Boston:Beacon Press.

Hall, Stuart. 1978. *Policing the Crisis*. N.Y.: Holmes and Meier.

————. 1980. *Culture, Media, Language*. London: Hutchinson.

Hauser, Arnold. 1982. *The Sociology of ALI*. Chicago: University of Chicago Press.

Horwitz, Irving. 1993. *The Decomposition of Sociology*. New York: Oxford University Press.

James, CLR. 1939. "Preliminary Notes on the Negro Question" *Internal Bulletin* No. 9 p.2-18.

Johnson, Charles. 1941. *Growing Up in the Black Belt*. Washington, DC: American Council on Education.

Ladner, Joyce. 1973. *The Death of White Sociology*. New York: Vintage Books.

Lakatos Imre. 1970. *Criticism and the Growth of Knowledge*. Cambridge: Cambridge University Press.

Lemert, Charles. 1979. *Sociology and the Twilight of Man*. Carbondale: Southern Illinois University Press.

Levi-Strauss, Claude. 1963. *Structural Anthropology*. New York. Basic Books.

Lipset, Seymour. 1994. "The State of American Sociology" *Sociological Forum* 9: 199-215. [Reprinted in this volume]

Loews, John. 1987. "Intellectual History After the Linguistic Turn" *American Historical Review* 92: 879-907.

Loubser, Jan C., et al. *Explorations in General Theory in Social Science: Essays in Honor of Talcott Parsons*. New York: Free Press, 1976.

Lubiano, Wahneerma. 1991. "But Compared to what? Realism, Essentialism and Representation in Spike Lee's *School Daze* and *Do The Right Thing*" *Black American Literature Forum* 25.2: 253-282.

Lukacs, George. 1975. *The Theory of the Novel*.Cambridge, MA.: MIT Press.

Mills, C. Wright. 1977. *The Sociological Imagination*. New York: Oxford University Press.

Moyniham, Daniel and Nathan Glazer. 1970. *Beyond The Melting Pot*. Cambridge: MIT.

Park, Robert. 1950. *Race and Culture*. New York: Free Press.

Parsons, Talcott. 1967. "The Concept of Political Power", in *Sociological Theory and Modern Society*. New York: Free Press.

——. 1981. "The Theory of Symbolism in Relation to Action", in *Working Papers in the Theory of Action*. Westport: Greenwood Press.

Popper, Karl. 1965. *The Logic of Scientific Discovery*. NY: Harper and Row.

Rorty, Richard. 1988. *The Linguistic Turn*. Chicago: University of Chicago Press.

Rose, Tricia. 1994. *Black Noise*. Hanover: Wesleyan University Press.

Schutz, Alfred. 1964. *Collected Papers I*. The Hague: Martinus Nijhoff.

Steinberg, Stephen. 1989. *The Ethnic Myth*. Boston: Beacon Press.

Wallace, Walter. 1988. "Toward a Disciplinary Matrix in Sociology" in Neil Smelser (ed) *The Handbook of Sociology*, 23-56 Beverly Hills: Sage.

West, Cornell. 1989 *The American Evasion of Philosophy*. Madison: University of Wisconsin Press.

Williams, Robin. 1947. *The Reduction of Intergroup Tensions*. New York: Social Science Research Council.

Wilson, William Julius. 1990. *The Truly Disadvantaged: The Inner City, the Underclass, and Public Policy*. Chicago: University of Chicago Press.

16

Writing From Sociology's Periphery*

Carolyn Ellis & Arthur P. Bochner

Scene: Over breakfast in the kitchen of a married academic couple. Carolyn, a sociologist, and Art, a professor of communication, are conversing intermittently while drinking coffee and reading the newspaper.

Carolyn: (lays down the business section): What's wrong with sociology?

Art: (from behind the sports page) Huh? What are you talking about?

Carolyn: I was thinking about the chapter Stephen Cole invited me to do for his book, *What's Wrong with Sociology?* There's so much I want to say, but I can't decide how to write it.

Art: What's the problem?

Carolyn: Well, the other contributors are primarily mainstream sociologists, and I assume the book's audience will be mainstream as well. I'm so out of contact with them. This is a good opportunity to showcase the kind of sociology we do, but I'm not sure how to write it without alienating the people I want to persuade. I'd like to be experimental, and not follow the singular form demanded by the conventions of academic sociological discourse (see Richardson 1990: 16).

Art: We've said over and over that there is no *one* right way to conceive of social science inquiry. Why let these conventions limit you now? I'm sure Steve wants you to do what you do best, which obviously is unorthodox.

Carolyn: But I'm concerned that I need to follow some of the standard

---

*We thank Stephen Cole and Laurel Richardson for insightful comments.

practices for writing sociology or I'll lose my audience up front.

Art: Not if you stick to "what's wrong with sociology." That's why readers will read the book, to see what different scholars have to say about sociology's deficiencies.

Carolyn: Yes, but readers also will have their answers to the question. What they think is wrong with sociology relates to their own experiences over the years as sociologists — what's happened in the course of their graduate educations, their careers, their successes and failures, the work they've chosen to do. Whatever I say — well, some people will relate to it, but others may not have the foggiest notion of what I'm talking about.

Art: (Now engaged, Art lays down the sports section and focuses his attention on what Carolyn is saying.) But that's not a problem, it's a reality. There *are* multiple versions of what sociology is and what purposes it serves. Sure, different sociologists view the goals of sociology differently. That's a strength, not a weakness.

Carolyn: But how do I get that point across?

Art: Talk about your own experiences as a sociologist. Your story will not be the story of all sociologists, but it will have elements that touch other sociologists' biographies. If there's interest in a book on "what's wrong with sociology," it's because a lot of people think there's something wrong with the way it is currently conceived and practiced.

Carolyn: Well, I like the idea of incorporating my own story, but I don't want readers to dismiss it as only one person's unique history.

Art: (chiding) You just want to make sure the orthodoxy takes you seriously.

Carolyn: Of course I do. I've had to take them seriously my whole career. Besides, one of my main arguments is that if scholars in the center don't take people on the margins seriously, there may be nothing left of sociology in a few years.

Art: Well, you've been reading other accounts lately of what's wrong with sociology, what do they say?

Carolyn: They're typically presented as macro-political (see Davis this volume; Smith 1995), professional (Halliday and Janowitz 1992), or organizational and institutional accounts (Huber, this volume; Simpson and Simpson, this volume; Turner and Turner 1990) with little mention of the biographies of the writers.

Art: But aren't there some fairly recent books about sociology that work from an autobiographical perspective? I'm thinking of Berger's *Authors of Their Own Lives*, Riley's *Sociological Lives*, and Goetting and Fenstermaker's, *Individual Voices, Collective Visions: Fifty Years of Women in Sociology*. These writers don't camouflage the "I."

Carolyn: (laughing) You know more sociology than many sociologists. My piece would fit with those works, although my goals are somewhat different. I want to focus explicitly on my approach/avoidance orientation toward sociology and use my own movement away from orthodox sociology to theorize sociology's dilemmas. I especially want to comment on the relationship between the center and periphery of sociology.

(Carolyn pauses for a moment to reflect.)

You know, I could start with a brief excerpt from *Final Negotiations* and ask readers: Is this sociology? How do you decide what fits within sociology's boundaries?

Art: I like that. Starting with a story might provoke readers to think differently about sociological practices and to question why some kinds of writing are viewed traditionally as outside sociology's boundaries. But you know it'll be difficult to engage readers in the experiences you write about in *Final Negotiations* in a short snippet.

Carolyn: I'll give it a try.

* * *

Settling into Maxwell's Plum, the tension dissolves under the influence of champagne and gourmet food. Cost does not concern us. Like new lovers, we hold hands and look into each other's eyes. Like old companions, we talk about death and the shortness of time we have left together. We cry softly as we admit the lowered numbers on pulmonary tests have reaffirmed our worst fears.

Then Gene says angrily, "Why does Dr. Silverman pretend there's hope, when there isn't any? Why doesn't he just say so?"

"He does, Gene. He said there was no cure in your lifetime." A pall spreads over our conversation.

"But then he says the shuffling of the medicine will help. It won't," replies Gene, still angry.

"That's true. But think of his position. He wants to be honest, yet not depress you or make you feel there's no hope for improvement. So he confronts us with the stark reality of your deterioration, and then gives us a ray of hope to hang on to. It isn't dishonest. He wants to have hope too."

"I guess," Gene replies, softening with resignation. Then, because

*nothing reminds us of our love in quite the same way as facing the loss of it,
Gene connects with my eyes, and mouths silently, "I love you." As the
feeling of love flashes back and forth between us, my fear subsides.*

*"At least we have each other," he continues, now changing sides. "And
who knows. Maybe I'll live longer than anybody thinks. There's always the
possibility of a lung transplant."*

*Sure, I think ironically, but say sincerely, "Anything is possible. I'm just
glad to have this time now. I guess our situation is not really worse than
others. Everybody will die."*

*"This champagne is wonderful," Gene says. "Taste it in the back of your
throat. It's so full and dry."*

*So began a tradition of having lunch at Maxwell's Plum after each doctor's
visit. Without fully realizing it at the time, the two of us were being
socialized into the roles of dying and grieving. I rehearsed how to show
Gene love, yet shut out pain and fear; Gene practiced how to face his
illness, yet escape assuming the role of a dying person.*

*The doctor's candid opinion, supported by the declining test results,
confronted us with the reality of Gene's impending death. We began to
relate to the disease much as the doctor had — facing the inevitable and
then looking for some reason to be hopeful. Ambivalence as a coping
mechanism offered comfort yet left room for reality. These afternoon lunches
provided opportunities to integrate hope and reality, a balance that would
tip toward reality as the illness took over* (Ellis 1995b: 55-56).

* * *

How do you, the reader, respond to this brief episode? Does it fit within
your conception of sociological writing? Am I, the writer of this story, aptly
considered a sociologist? What do your answers say about your premises
regarding practices of sociological research and writing? This passage comes
from *Final Negotiations: A Story of Love, Loss, and Chronic Illness*, which
I published in 1995. In this book, I present two stories: the central story is a
nonfictional narrative of my relationship with Gene, my ill and dying
partner; the second story frames the narrative and chronicles my move from
writing orthodox sociology to writing autobiographical narrative as
sociology.

Gene and I were two sociologists engrossed not only in living through
the mystery and tragedy of chronic illness but also in trying to create a
meaningful life out of our situation. We used our sociological perspective to
co-construct a meaningful relationship that, in many respects, acted back
reflexively on how we thought of ourselves as sociologists and partners.

After he died, the writing of *Final Negotiations* became part of my continuing search to make sociology meaningful and relevant to my lived experiences and to overcome some of the alienation I had encountered as a sociologist.

* * *

Art: (That afternoon, Carolyn hands Art a copy of the above. After reading it, Art responds.) So, what you're trying to do is provoke readers to consider how being sociologists impacts upon the rest of their lives, and how their own life experiences influence how they practice sociology. You're drawing connections between living in a social world and writing from a sociological perspective about one's world--whether or not that's something truly embraced under the rubric of sociology.

Carolyn: Yes, but I also want this passage to lead into a discussion about what's going on at the periphery of sociology. There's no doubt in my mind that what I'm doing is on the margins. My guess is that any sociologist trying to use literary modes of writing to communicate sociological ideas occupies a peripheral location within the field. But all sociologists need to think seriously about the relationship between what's on the margins and what's in the center of sociology, a relationship that has changed rather drastically.

Art: Is that going to be the next part of your paper?

Carolyn: I think so. I'll draft the next section, then let's talk about it. (Carolyn heads up to her office and doesn't emerge until late that night. She is at work early the next morning, and Art doesn't see her until the next evening when she hands him the following.)

* * *

Sociology: Center and Periphery

Whether sociology's center will hold, the theme of The Southern Sociological Society annual meeting in 1992, is an issue that has been replayed in various forms time and again. The "field" often seems obsessed with defining and claiming the illusive center of the discipline of sociology, worrying about the weakness (Huber this volume) and inconsistency (Davis this volume) of the theoretical core, its lack of substantiality and resilience (Crane and Small 1992), the sturdiness of its "handle" (Davis this volume), and the intrusion of other disciplines onto "our turf" (Smith 1995: 68; 1991; Huber this volume). In the second half of this century, sociology's center has become fractionated, fragmenting into a multitude of small specialized groups and Sections in the American Sociological Association (Collins 1986; Huber this volume; Wolfe 1992), which makes sociology appear less as a single discipline and "more as an archipelago of poorly connected islands of specialization" (Halliday 1992: 25). Since members write primarily for each other, sociology has been unable to develop broad public appeal (Rule this volume; Wolff 1992) or get much recognition from the media or government (Molotch this volume; Turner and Turner 1990).

Few in the "elite" center have paid much attention to what is happening on the periphery, except as a source of sociology's misery. Orthodox sociologists blame postmodernists — their metonymy for the periphery — for "perpetuate[ing] sociology's inferior status and weakness" (Smith 1995: 68), causing a less than unified picture of sociology to be represented to the outside world, depleting resources, and producing organizational and departmental malaise (Huber this volume; but see Denzin 1997a; and Gamson 1992). Political fractionalization in the ASA is sometimes blamed for the loss of sociology's organizational core (Simpson and Simpson this volume; Wolff 1992). Otherwise the periphery is largely ignored.

The periphery about which I speak does contain numerous sociologists who have been influenced positively by postmodernism, which opened spaces for us to practice a different kind of sociology. And, many of us criss-cross the political factions that have gained influence in the ASA, which now are in danger of being co-opted by the center. Yet, just as often we maintain multiple group affiliations and research perspectives, and we are loyal to focused outlier groups (such as Society for the Study of Symbolic Interaction, Society for the Study of Social Problems, or Humanistic Sociology), associations in other disciplines (such as Speech Communication Association or American Anthropological Association), or regional societies (such as The Midwest Sociological Society), instead of, or as well as, political factions of ASA (see Turner and Turner 1990: 155-159; Wolff 1992: 769).

Indeed, a large part of sociology's periphery is incommensurate with the center. We don't read the same books, speak the same language, or care about the same issues. Many of us feel the heart is as important as the head, that concrete details are as interesting as theoretical abstractions, and that the activity of consuming knowledge is less important than using it.

Moreover, orthodox sociology is losing its hold on a major segment of the periphery. It no longer provides a benchmark for the way many of us on the margins, who think of ourselves as sociologists, understand the goals of our work. As the core of sociology strains to hold tight, many of us are reconsidering our loyalties and finding few reasons to read mainstream sociology, send our articles to its journals, or champion its causes. We no longer assume mainstream sociology will provide outlets or audiences for what we do.

To understand the whole of sociology, mainstream sociologists must "go outside" their own small communities. As sociologists, we have a long tradition of recognizing that you cannot understand society's mainstream without understanding its margins (see Molotch this volume). Shils (1975) maintains that this outermost structure binds a society together. Those in the center should not continue to assume, as they have in the past, that the periphery will always rally under the umbrella of sociology and the ASA, clamoring to be "let in." From the margins, many of us have formed working alliances with colleagues in other disciplines and in the public domain, seeking broader audiences for our work (Tierney and Lincoln 1997; Richardson 1997). If the periphery continues going in this direction, it really doesn't matter whether the center holds or not; there can be no core without a supportive periphery.

* * *

Art: (looks up from reading) Do you have evidence that the periphery is going elsewhere?

Carolyn: Aren't my experiences, observations, and conversations with other sociologists enough?

Art: Of course, but have you found confirmation for these impressions in other writings by sociologists?

Carolyn: (chiding) Isn't there already enough citation authority here for you? (Art grins. Carolyn looks down at the notes she has prepared for just this occasion and continues.) Well, Turner and Turner (1990: 159) conservatively estimate we now have over 300 journals for sociologists, compared to 9 in 1933, and Simpson and Simpson (this volume) claim there is more concentration of the presumed power elite (meaning those from Ph.D. granting departments) publishing in *ASR* in recent years and less competition for publishing in the top journals because fewer people from "nonelite" settings are submitting to them. Although *ASR* editor Paula England reports in *Footnotes* (April 1995: 13) that new submissions are up for the last two years of 1993 (368) and 1994 (361) from the steady decline in 1990 (386), 1991 (371), and 1992 (327), the increase fails to come close to the jump in submissions reported by Turner and Turner (1990: 152) of 200 to 800 a year between 1950 and 1970.

Art: Ok, ok! I believe you. But let's go back to the issue of how postmodernism has impacted both the center and the periphery of sociology, indeed all of social science, over the past fifteen years or so. The "crisis of representation" (Clifford and Marcus 1986; Geertz 1988; Marcus and Fischer 1986; Turner and Bruner 1986) has allowed a more sober understanding of words like "truth," knowledge," and "reality." Many of us on the margins have become more comfortable with contingencies of language and human experience; and we no longer feel we have to treat social science as completely distinct from literature. But the "crisis" also led others to cling even more tightly to the notion that there is Truth to be found and criteria that do not depend on our utterances or modes of inscription. The orthodoxy still sees subjectivity as a threat to rationality and holds to the belief that differences of opinion can be arbitrated by objective criteria beyond dispute. So the crisis has deepened our divisions and made it more difficult to talk to each other. But mainstream sociologists delude themselves if they think postmodernism and poststructuralism are going to disappear. Some of the intellectual currents of postmodernism may have been excessive, and some excesses are being counteracted, but we can never return to an undaunted belief in neutral observation and language-free truth.

Carolyn: The configuration of the smaller, but contentious center and the increasing segmentation of the periphery of sociology from it seems yet another example of what postmodern fragmentation is all about. Take the American Sociological Association, for example. Simpson and Simpson (this volume) note that in recent years ASA has become more diversified in its interests and has turned increasingly to professional and activist issues such as maintaining itself as a bureaucracy, sociological practice, politics, and teaching. As a result, there has been a dissolution of concern with disciplinary issues and a decrease of the control of the discipline by so-called "disciplinary elites" (which Simpson and Simpson define as top-ranked graduate departments). While some of this adaptation is a response to the inherent demands of a growing bureaucracy and a pluralistic clientele, I think it is associated also with disagreement about what the goals of the discipline should be.

Art: My point is that we don't have to agree. We must come to terms with how we can live with our differences and appreciate the legitimacy of different goals for sociology. The more the center endeavors to make all sociology the same, to come up with a single solution--the more problems will be created. There is no one solution, no one sociology.

When I say we can't go back to the way things were, I mean we have to accept and nourish sociology's multiplicity.

Carolyn: Wolff (1992) and others (see Molotch this volume) have suggested there are many sociologies, each with its own rituals, membership criteria, hierarchies, and expectations. And, as Stinchcombe (this volume: 290) says, this may be the optimum state of affairs. Calhoun (1992: 184) goes so far as to suggest that disciplinary divisions may be counterproductive to our general understanding of social life and that there might not need to be disciplinary boundaries around a field called sociology.

Art: I don't want to touch that one. But if the question "what's wrong with sociology?" assumes there is an answer that will make everyone subscribe to the same goals and visions--well, that's an illusion.

Carolyn: I don't think that's what Steve has in mind. If he did, he wouldn't have invited papers from people like me.

Art: Still, most of the authors in this book are older, white males who speak basically from the center of sociology.

Carolyn: That's true, but at least they're mainstream dissidents. Most don't buy into the orthodoxy uncritically.

Art: "Mainstream dissidents." An interesting term.

Carolyn: So how can we live with our differences without intolerance and power struggles? Lipset (this volume; 216; see also Huber 1995) says that faculty in sociology departments have a reputation for intradepartmental bickering and complaining to administrators about each other, which then leads administrators to feel less supportive of sociology than other fields.

Art: You'd think sociologists would know how to play the game of university politics better than that, wouldn't you? But I'm more interested in talking about differences in respect to the domination of imagination by rigor in sociological practice.

Carolyn: If sociology is going to embrace its periphery, it will need to foster greater creativity.

Art: Could you write a section about how sociology construes data, subjects, and norms of research, to make that point?

Carolyn: That's something you've written about before (Bochner 1994; Bochner, Ellis, and Tillmann-Healy, 1998). Why don't you draft a short section on the norms of orthodox social science for this piece?

Art: (mumbling with pencil and paper in hand) Ok. How'd I get into this?

* * *

Orthodox Sociology

Most of the research texts sociologists produce do not display the felt experiences of particular lives. Sociologists do not call the people they study characters or actors; they call them "subjects." Subjects have no names, no apparent life apart from participation in research procedures. Researchers ask subjects to tell about their lives. What is told of lived experience is called data, then used to test hypotheses. Sociologists plot peoples' stories on graphs, then analyze the graphs on which lives have been plotted, discarding details in favor of abstractions, postulating causes where once there were meanings. Researchers twist and turn peoples' lives into variables, explanations, and theories. The end product is a text called a research report, a highly conventionalized rhetorical form that brushes aside particulars to get to generalities and in which, typically, there are no characters to provoke our empathic connection, no expansive plot line to hold us in suspense, no emotions to evoke our involvement, no temporal sweep to convince us we are witnessing the flux and flow of evolving relationships, little psychological depth that compels our attention, no bodies that remind us we are finite human beings, and no mention of spirituality to suggest that people may act on the basis of more than rational choice.

The first loyalty of orthodox sociologists is not to the lived reality of the lives studied but rather to colleagues, the community of social scientists in which membership is sought. The badge of membership is conveyed only after young scholars have been socialized to accept without question or skepticism the conventions and practices of artless, rigorous social science, which include such time-honored principles as: (1) keep your own feelings out of your research and erase any indications from your text that you may have been emotionally involved by virtue of your own life experiences or involvement with your "subjects" (your work is only to account for the "objective" experiences of others, not your "subjective" experience of yourself); (2) use concrete details only in the service of abstraction (it's the theory and concepts that count; you cannot learn anything without analysis); (3) rule out all rival hypotheses or explanations and never let it be known that you may have struggled and suffered to gain this knowledge or that you may still be uncertain about what knowledge to claim (there should be no loose ends; analysis is incomplete if any mystery remains unresolved); (4) do not worry about whether the people whose experiences you are representing would understand or concur with what you write about them (you can assume "they" would find your writing confusing and obscure because they are not "academically" trained; rest assured that this rule relieves you of any responsibility to communicate what you have said about them *to them* or to include their construction and feelings about you as part of your text); (5) assume that your readers want to "receive" your knowledge passively, not enter into the experiences or put themselves in the place of your subjects (the text must be "academic" and generalizable, not accessible and particular) and; (6) never question the rules to which you have been asked to conform (these rules are natural and constitute a transcendent power of unquestionable authority).

* * *

Carolyn: (finishes reading and turns to Art) I like what you've written, but I hope readers understand the implications of seeing the process of traditional sociology as socially and rhetorically constructed. As Steve Cole (personal communication) says, "Even writing a standard *ASR* paper frequently involves making up a story. It's just that the style of the paper hides the social construction." Latour (1981: 69) argues that the research process "is nothing *more* and nothing *less* than the rest of our daily world and daily stories of fictions and disorder."

Art: Certainly I agree with Steve, and I don't think we need to hide or camouflage the reality of what we do. Who are we trying to fool? It's time to be *self-critical* about our institutional practices, to see sociological method as means to an end and to question whether the end justifies these means. If sociology has different purposes, we must appreciate the need to understand the different ways these purposes can be achieved.

Carolyn: Then it doesn't have to be either/or. There's a need for prediction and control, and there's also a need to learn how to understand and talk to people different from us. The former, science does well; the latter has been the province of great literature and the best sociology like *Tally's Corner, Street Corner Society*, and *Everything in its Path*.

Art: I agree, and I like that you've begun to clarify different legitimate goals for sociology.

Carolyn: But we still have this problem of how those on the periphery and in the center can live in a world that both refer to as sociology. I don't want to fall into the same trap that we criticize the sociological orthodoxy for — that they over-simplify the positions of others and make their case by talking about what's wrong with what everybody else does.

Art: Reminds me of what Jane Tompkins (1992) says about academic discourse at conventions and in journals. People demolish each other's work in the name of science. The symbolic violence is like the "shoot-out at the Ok Corral." Whoever's left standing at the end is the winner. She asks whether there isn't some better way.

Carolyn: The "better way" may be to learn to live with our differences, but let's not forget that these differences have real consequences. Many orthodox sociologists do seem to live in a world very different from mine.

Art: They must — the desire to control life is substantially different than the desire to cope with it. The first sees the contingencies of life as unpleasant and tries to overcome them; the second understands the mysteries of life and tries to deal with them.

Carolyn: Makes me think that even if those in the center learned to tolerate each other, I'm not so sure they would be willing to hold hands with the periphery.

Art: Reminds me of that incident at ASA, you know, at the storytelling session.

Carolyn: Oh yes, the only mainstream session I've attended at the ASA in the last decade. The Special Session on "Social Theory, Social Research, and Storytelling." The room was overflowing; four mainstream, white, older, male sociologists participated. They were from Chicago, Harvard, and Princeton, and several were quantitative methodologists. I asked why qualitative sociologists were not included on the panel — given our history of using storytelling in research — and got brushed off without a meaningful response. Another woman in the audience failed to get a response when she asked why no women or people of color were on the stage. When I tried to talk to the organizer after the session, he said, "If qualitative people had been involved, the session wouldn't have been as effective. Everybody expects qualitative researchers to be sympathetic to storytelling. We know what they will say. But when quantitative sociologists say it, everybody listens." "By that logic," I responded, "we should make sure that no women are on panels to talk about feminism, since we know what they will say and it won't be as effective." He replied, "I'm not going to have this discussion," and walked off in a huff, waving his hand furiously in dismissal. I stood there dumbfounded, practically hyperventilating. So much for connecting the center and periphery — a perfect opportunity gone awry.

Art: That's a good example of how little intersubjectivity exists between those in the center and periphery. Incredible, really. But are you saying that you want them to want you?

Carolyn: I'm not sure. Frankly, I enjoy being on the periphery where I don't always have to justify the work I do to people who don't understand it. But it's not as though we don't have our disagreements and draw our boundaries out here.

Art: You sure have vacillated on this in the six years I've known you, from demanding your work be considered sociology to moving away from seeing "sociologist" as a vital part of your academic identity.

Carolyn: I know. The vacillation reflects my frustration that sociology can't be what I want it to be, yet sociology has been so important to me.

Art: I guess almost every sociologist feels that way at least some of the time. But there's a new problem on the horizon these days called "public accountability." The public is increasingly hostile towards social science. They won't tolerate the game where we write critically to and for only a small group of scholars. They're asking tough questions about our research. Do we write for our colleagues in order to get tenure or merit increases...

Carolyn: (interrupting) Or release from teaching?

Art: Yes, don't forget that. They want us to show how our work is useful to a wider audience. The Florida legislators want to withhold public funds to support research that doesn't clearly contribute to the public good. They want to know who our users are. How do people read sociology? How do we want them to read our work? We haven't really given those questions enough thought. I'm not on the legislators' side; most of them are completely uneducated about what we do and don't really care to learn. But we still have to respond.

Carolyn: This is where artful sociology comes in. It has a practical bent. It is written in accessible prose for a wider audience.

Art: Perhaps now is the time for you to introduce artful sociology.

* * *

Artful Sociology

Artful sociology (see Brady 1991; 1993: 264, who writes about "artful science") works against taken-for-granted notions of doing orthodox research. It revels in opening up, not closing down, the mysteries of life. It attempts to evoke experiences and feelings in readers, who are offered an opportunity to engage the author's text actively, rather than receive it passively. Artful sociology stays close to peoples' experiences and strives to be "life-like," allowing us to "relax a bit into a multidisciplinary imagination"

(Molotch this volume) where emotions, bodies, cognition, personality, spirituality, and the market are given their due. Told in detail, artful sociology shows how concrete experience is made possible and limited by social structure, and how the autobiographical and ethnographic, the personal and cultural, and the historical and biographical are intertwined (Mills 1959: 6).

Artful sociology seeks a fusion between social science and literature, a space "where you are partly blown by the winds of reality and partly an artist creating a composite out of the inner and outer events" (Bateson 1977: 245). It eschews the relationship with economics or natural science that many sociologists desire (Cole this volume). The problems that others, Cole for example, see in sociology — that nonscience values such as political ideology and personal experience influence choice of problem and findings — become part of the strength of artful sociology, which openly includes autobiographical details and explicitly specifies the position from which we speak.

Artful writers experiment with forms of presentation, employing creative non-fiction, short stories, poetry, personal stories, autoethnographic accounts, performance, multi-voiced, co-constructed, and interactive discourses (see Benson 1993; Denzin 1997b; Denzin and Lincoln 1994; Ellis and Bochner 1996; Ellis and Flaherty 1992; Tierney and Lincoln 1997; Richardson 1994a; 1997; Ronai 1995). They make use of scripts and dialogues; italics, fonts, formatting, and character styles (Molotch this volume); spacing and strategic placement of text on the page. They borrow heavily from literary devices used in effective novels, creative nonfiction, and poetry, such as metaphor, character development, scene setting, dramatic tension, and dialogue. Works often take the form of temporal portrayals of action, in which characters, who are developed in ways that allow readers to experience their lives, move dramatically along or around an engaging plot line. While there may be some resolution in the story itself as the characters play out the dramatic plot, the author need not produce a single meaning to be taken from the story. At the same time, authors often examine reflexively the meaning the stories they tell have for their own lives.

A primary goal of artful sociology is for it to help us — author and readers —cope better with our lives and improve the social world. Artful sociologists offer companionship to people struggling through day-to-day events and epiphanies and an avenue for a writer to work through her own crises and meanings. One of the uses of artful sociology is to allow another person's experience to inspire critical reflection on our own, what Rorty (1996) calls "the inspirational value of reading." You recontextualize what you already knew in light of your encounter with someone else's life or culture. Writers want their work to be inspiring, hopeful, and potentially self-transforming; at the same time, they often confront human experience head on, without necessarily giving way or offering a place for themselves or readers to stand outside it. Rather than asking, "how is it true?" artful sociology begins with the question, "how is it useful?" Our goal is to produce work that concentrates on helping us "know how to live" (Jackson 1995), which may include knowing how to know. Ultimately, we judge our work by considering how other people take it in and use it for themselves (Coles 1989: 47).

* * *

Autobiographical Sociology

Art: A good overview, but I think you need to show readers what artful sociology might look like.

Carolyn: Well there are many forms of sociology that fit the framework I've laid out above, and there are probably other forms that we would like to call artful sociology that wouldn't quite fit with what we've said. Most of what I've done as artful sociology has been autobiographical.

Art: That's what's missing in this paper. An appreciation of how a sociologist's biography ties in to her responses to the question "what's wrong with sociology?" You've claimed the relationship between the center and periphery of sociology is changing, discussed the orthodox rules of sociological method, and introduced artful sociology. But you haven't told readers how you got here. What alienated you from orthodox sociology but also kept you inspired to work and think and live as a sociologist, albeit a different kind?

Carolyn: I told a lot of that in *Final Negotiations*.

Art: I think you should tell it here as well. Many young sociologists are alienated by their graduate education, which socialized them away from the passions that brought them there in the first place. Perhaps they can take comfort in a story that says, "I survived an orthodox education."

Carolyn: (laughs) It still won't convince their committee members in mainstream programs to let them write artful sociology. Wish I had a dollar for every time a graduate student has complained to me about that.

Art: You can't solve all the problems in one article.

Carolyn: OK, I hear you. I'll tell my story as briefly as I can.

* * *

Socialization into Sociology

I grew up in Luray, Virginia, a protestant working class community of three thousand people located in the middle of the Blue Ridge Mountains, and cut off from the rest of the world by surrounding mountains. Living in a small town laid the groundwork for my interests in sociology. There, concrete experience, stories, and dialogue were privileged over abstract and general knowledge. Telling tales about mundane day-to-day life, epiphanies, and crises provided an important way to pass the time. Rarely were issues of the political economy, culture, stratification, or society mentioned. Rarely did we read newspapers other than the local weekly, which concentrated on births, obituaries, hospitalizations, and traffic tickets. The television programs we watched consisted of sitcoms, soaps, and weekly court and murder mystery serials.

I first "encountered" sociology while taking a career placement test in ninth grade. As I chose "social work" as my subject of interest, I noticed "sociology" under it. At home that evening, I looked up sociology in the dictionary, where it was defined as "the study of social relationships." *That's what I'm interested in,* I thought. The lack of stimulation in Luray had allowed much time for observing myself, my relationships and family, and analyzing the local people and small town culture. Granted, my analysis was limited, given that I had never been outside Luray and had little to compare.

My parents, like most people I knew, had spent their lives in Luray, without the benefit of much education; both had gone through elementary grades in a one-room school house. Yet they were remarkably supportive emotionally and financially of my desire to go to college "to study sociology," I told them, although they knew even less than I about what that meant.

My formal introduction to sociology came in 1969 when I entered the College of William and Mary in Virginia as a sociology major. Without exceptional effort, I had been at the top of my small class in high school. Now, working as hard as I could, I struggled to compete against valedictorians from large metropolitan high schools. I vividly remember calling my mother after my first biology test to tell her I had gotten 27 out of 100 points and was flunking out of school. Amid my tears of humiliation, she said soothingly, "Well, don't worry, you'll just come home if that happens." I felt relieved and loved, yet there was a part of me that understood already that "coming home" was not an option. Now that I had tasted life outside of Luray, I knew I could never go home to live.

At William and Mary, I was introduced to Erving Goffman's *Presentation of Self in Everyday Life*. Like many students before and after me, I fantasized that I could be like him. It was hard to believe I got college credit for reading Goffman's books; I would gladly have read them for fun. I took the maximum number of sociology classes allowed. Even when I sometimes grew restless and bored by what I heard in class and read in sociology books, I assumed it had to do, not with sociology, but with the particular professor or text. Researching and writing an ethnographic honor's thesis about an isolated fishing island provided my most rewarding experience. Thankfully, I did not have the problems with sociology that I did with biology, and I graduated magna cum laude.

After college, I spent a year as a social worker working with foster children in the black ghetto in a nearby town. What else did one do with a sociology degree? Disillusioned with social work and missing campus life, I applied to graduate school in sociology at SUNY at Stony Brook. I wanted to study with Eugene Weinstein, whose work on interpersonal influence I had read in social psychology classes.

In Stony Brook's sociology department, I was faced with cultural as well as intellectual shock. I was intimidated by the elite, northeastern, intellectual bantering and Jewish repartee I encountered, which celebrated abstract thinking and knowledge of macro-political issues. I also was not accustomed to calling on higher authorities as I talked. ("Marx said...." "According to Weber...or Durkheim...or Simmel...." "In *The New York Review of Books*...."). The only higher authority we had called on as I was growing up had been God (in church), and occasionally my father (when I was in trouble). Instead, I found it more rewarding to call on my feelings and everyday experiences and compare them to the experiences of those around me, whom I always watched carefully.

The contrast between the abstract discourse I encountered in graduate classes and the worldly experience of social work was hard to assimilate. I learned early on that my sentiment that sociology should "help people" was best left unexpressed publicly. My socialization "took," and soon I shared the hierarchical notion that it was important to separate sociologists (the knowers) from social workers (the doers). Still I continued to wonder whether sociology shouldn't strive to open peoples' eyes to the world they lived in and assist all people in living better lives. For the most part, I could not connect my life to what was being taught in classes. How could those outside this tribe connect their lives to what we were doing? The reality was that only a few scholars I encountered tried to connect sociology to lived experience. I dared not speak on this subject for fear my professors would regard me as a "touchy-feely" type, or someone who lacked appreciation for grand sociological theory. Nevertheless, I had become hooked on the stimulating academic environment of the university and the intellectual climate Stony Brook represented. By the middle of my first year in graduate school, I knew I wanted to think and talk like other academics, requirements for full membership in this tribe.

I continued my work on isolated fishing communities for my dissertation (Ellis 1986), comparing two isolated fishing villages in terms of their connections to mainstream society. Although the unit of analysis was community, I was inspired by a microanalytic approach that sought to understand face-to-face interaction and the emotionality of community members. Although I wrote theoretically about social organization, social change, history, family, and work, what excited me most was writing vignettes that offered insight into interactional processes. While I read all the standard sociology assigned in graduate school, I longed to immerse myself in a good story with a dramatic plot. These were foreshadowing events; it would take a life crisis — several of them — before I became aware of the radical implications of these early whispers. I didn't yet realize that sociology could be more engaging than it was and that I might have writing and research interests not being tapped by my graduate education

My comparative ethnographic study of fishing communities at least gave me the real world connection I was looking for in sociology. During this project, I lived and participated with the people whose lives I was studying. Mostly I followed the rules for doing grounded theory fieldwork. Yet, while in the communities, I often experienced conflict between remaining uninvolved and distant, as I had been trained, and participating fully, which was my impulse; between recording only my "objective" observations of fisher folks' actions and speech, and noting my experience of their emotional lives. When I began to write my dissertation, I felt constrained by the detached and abstract social science prose and the authoritative and uninvolved voice in which I was asked to write. It was difficult to capture the complexity of the lives of the fisher folk using social science categories, and I often felt unsure of the conceptual distinctions I was forced to make.

Mostly I was invisible in the writing of the story. Any effects I might have had on what the fisher folk said and did, or what I might have learned through their reactions to me, took a back seat. I never admitted how much my own emotional experiences in the communities influenced what I saw and wrote.

Not until later would I recognize how important it was to give more voice to community members, show myself in interaction, and confront how these conventional strategies may have hurt those I studied (Ellis 1995a). Not until later would I realize that the situation of the fisher folk — who lived largely apart from mainstream society and had began having more and more contact with the outside world — paralleled my own transition from a small southern town to the metropolitan northeast. As a sociologist governed by orthodox writing practices, I did not understand how to connect my work and life to my research and writing.

During my six and one-half years at Stony Brook (1974-1981), my relational life interacted closely with my work. At the end of my first year in graduate school, I began a romantic relationship with Eugene Weinstein, the professor with whom I had gone to Stony Brook to study. It lasted until he died from emphysema nine years later.

Our relationship had a strong impact on my graduate career —both adding to and helping resolve the conflicts I experienced there. Gene became my significant other not only romantically but also as a benchmark for what counted in sociology. Gene was fond of saying he liked "my eye," which was the ability to pick apart the most common interpersonal episode and talk on different levels about "what is really going on here." "You're so perceptive about what people are feeling, thinking, and what motivates them," Gene once said. "Too bad there isn't a way to turn that into sociology" (which for him meant abstraction). Shaking my head in agreement, I quickly squelched the question struggling to get out, "And why isn't this sociology?" Gene was a successful sociologist and the smartest person I knew; I trusted that he knew what constituted sociology.

Gene and I loved talking about group process and interpersonal relationships, and people's emotions, motives, and strategies. As time went on, we increasingly talked about his illness and its intersection with our relationship. He fed my hunger to understand macropolitical and macrohistorical processes, as well as formal social psychological theory, and he told engaging stories that connected all of it back to my life. In our conversations around the kitchen table, I learned more sociology than I ever learned in classes. But when we left the kitchen table, the only knowledge that seemed respected was the abstract conclusions we had drawn, not the stories we had told.

Within a short time, I had been socialized fully into my closely connected career and relationship world where abstraction and theory were valued. In public, I no longer presented myself as a small town southern girl who loved to tell stories, talk about feelings, and compare concrete events. In private though, there was nothing I liked more.

Since sociology uncritically became my religion, I tried desperately to mold myself into the best sociologist I could be, rising as far in the status system as I could. Although I never gave up my qualitative approach for a quantitative one, I attempted to write qualitative sociology scientifically for a mainstream audience, as I had been taught. As I practiced and taught sociology as science, I ignored my growing suspicions that it was not a very successful one, and that this approach limited topics I could address — the very questions of meaning and emotionality that interested me most.

At an ASA convention in 1979 I experienced a career crisis. Searching for a job, I was intent on appearing intelligent and demonstrating that I was worthy of membership in the sociological tribe. I paid more attention than usual to the academic discussions occurring around me. But the harder I tried to fit in, the more alienated I became. I experienced conversations as posturing about irrelevant ideas that failed to enlighten me about my life or the world in which I lived. Instead, I heard "you rub my status and I'll rub yours" couched in irrelevant jargon. Hadn't anybody read Goffman? Was I the only person who could see through this facade?

"[Little girl], what's your dissertation about?" Gene's friend, a middle-aged man with puffy eyes and balding head asked casually. [In 20 words or less. You have two minutes to impress me before I glaze over and move to the next hungry student.] That's what I heard; all he actually said was, "What's your dissertation about?" But his posture, head tilted and nodding slowly, his glancing sideways as I talked, his quick dismissal, all implied much more. *Three by five card. I must have my dissertation topic on a three by five card,* I remember thinking. To impress them, I knew I had to recite the most abstract notion first. Then be ready to supply the details — the categories and sub-categories. Few sociologists celebrated good description. Few showed active interest in the concrete details about how people felt and created meaning in their lives. They wanted a "definition of the problem," and then, succinctly, the "outcome." But doing research inductively meant I wouldn't have answers to those questions until the project was almost done, if then.

I hesitated, stuttered as I tried to tell the theoretical story I had practiced with Gene for just such an occasion. ["Uh, huh, as I suspected, you're just Gene's young blonde girlfriend. Next."] was the message I read in his face, just before he turned to the young woman beside me, hoping, I suspected, that if she failed to measure up intellectually, she at least would not have a romantic attachment.

Waking up in tears the next morning, I told Gene I wasn't leaving the hotel room. "I don't like these people," I blurted out, not caring how he interpreted what I said, "who judge me by the quickness of my tongue, how many sociologists — read baseball players — I can name, including university where employed, history of Ph.D. and former places of employment, number and titles of books and articles published — read team, when traded where, earned run average or batting average, and games won against which teams.

"And don't forget most recent work published, with preferably a synopsis following of the faulty reasoning in or what's left out of each person's work — read as a complete analysis of the last world series," I added facetiously. Gene listened carefully, but said nothing.

"You should hear yourselves," I continued, "competing for recognition, who has the latest information, who can top whom. It's all a game, and not a game I like playing."

Gene took my hand and said softly, "What a horrible time for this to happen to you. You're just feeling insecure. All graduate students go through this. You'll get over it," which, I heard as, "You'll never make the big leagues. I love this game. I excel at it. I need to go play now." After trying unsuccessfully to console me, Gene left the room.

Several hours later, I went to the lobby and took notes on what I saw. *"Maybe this way,"* I thought, *"I can get a handle on this, convert my negative feelings into a project, and turn my "eye" on sociological practice.* I watched sociologists scan across crowds and look furtively at who might be passing (them) by as they postured with each other — one talking, the other waiting to talk or escape to the company of someone more important. I watched some graduate students scurry about, trying to be noticed, read badges and identify the important people, get an audience of superiors for even a minute; while others hid in the corners, looking as though they were reading something that absolutely had to be read at that moment. I had played both roles; I was playing the latter one now. What I observed didn't help my emotional state. *Maybe I'm not tough enough or smart enough for this,* I contemplated. Given my background, this explanation certainly seemed possible.

After this ASA meeting, I was too frightened to think about how I felt about sociology. I had come too close to deciding the sociological world didn't provide enough meaning. What did I do then? I didn't want to leave the stimulating world of the mind, a world where I thought I would have control over my time and activities, to return to the difficult and constrained practice of social work. Instead, I concentrated on jumping the hurdles I had to clear to keep my options open — a dissertation, then a book, then eventually tenure. I couldn't continue to raise such existential questions and succeed. In the process of clearing hurdles, I became a sociologist.

In spite of my doubts, these were some of the best and most stimulating years of my life, although the excitement too rarely took place in classes or writing assignments. But I remember fondly sociologists who inspired me; the lively conversations Gene and I had nightly; and a graduate student study group that met weekly, in which we studied Parsons and Durkheim, but only after watching "Mary Hartman, Mary Hartman" at 11:30 p.m. In that group, I came to learn and appreciate classical theory. I also remember the thrill of living on the edge as young "experience junkies" of the mind, body, emotions, and soul.

As sociology baby-boomers have reached and some surpassed the peaks of their careers, the turmoil in sociology, the questions being raised about what's wrong with sociology, all are products of the complexities of life experienced in the 1970s. Most of us live now in the sociological hinter-land, geographically if not intellectually as well.

Transition to Artful Sociology

A major transition began shortly after I got my first job at the University of South Florida in 1981. In January 1982, my younger brother was killed in a commercial airplane crash on his way to visit me (Ellis 1993). At the same time, Gene, who had moved to Florida with me, entered the final stages of chronic emphysema. Mocking my fears and hopes, flashbacks of live TV footage of passengers from my brother's plane floundering in the Potomac River were interrupted in real life by Gene choking and yelling for me to untangle his oxygen hose. Suddenly the scientifically respectable survey of jealousy Gene and I were working on seemed dreadfully insig-nificant.

Instead I wanted a way to understand and cope with intense emotion, especially the excruciating pain I felt about the sudden loss of my brother and Gene's deterioration. I wanted to tell my stories to others because it would be personally therapeutic, offer companionship to others going through disastrous experiences (Mairs 1994), and provide sociological insights about an important part of life. All that had to wait until early 1985 when *Fisher Folk* was in press, and I was promoted to Associate Professor. Now it felt less risky to write something other than traditional social science. Now I could better afford to challenge the boundaries of what counted as legiti-mate sociology, an endeavor that became a passion after Gene died a few weeks later.

Not long after Gene's death, my dog of fourteen years (who had attended all my graduate classes) died, and a few months later my father passed away suddenly from a heart attack. Reading sociology provided none of the comfort, coping strategies, and meaning I was seeking. What I couldn't find in sociology, I located in literature and personal stories of illness.

In 1986, the advent of a section in the American Sociological Association called "Sociology of Emotions" legitimated the study of emotions as a proper arena of research. I was soon disappointed, however, to see many colleagues follow a "rational actor" approach to emotions research, busily handing out surveys, counting and predicting emotional reactions, observing facial muscles contracting on videotapes, categorizing people, and rushing to abstract generalizations from lived experience. Emotion was in danger of becoming simply another variable to add to rational models of social life. What about emotion as lived experience and interaction? I vowed to resist the rationalist tendency to portray people exclusively as spiritless, empty husks with programmed, managed, predictable, and patterned emotions (Ellis 1991a,b).

In this context, I became absorbed with writing about my loss experiences. What I had been unable to find in writing traditional sociology, I finally found in writing personal and emotional narratives.

Writing *Final Negotiations*

It took nine years to construct and reconstruct the story of my relationship with Gene, to work out satisfactorily a version of what this relationship had been and had meant to me, and to tell a story that cohered both with what I remembered and what my life had become (Crites 1971). During this time, I moved from conceiving of my project as science to viewing it as interpretive human studies and narrative inquiry (Bochner 1994), transforming the process of writing the text from realist ethnography to a story, and my primary goal from representation to evocation.

Writing about this relationship was so difficult that I kept notes on the writing process in the same way I had written field-notes on the actual relationship and illness process. These notes eventually became the basis for telling how I transformed ethnographic fieldwork into a story that I hoped would speak therapeutically to a mass audience and sociologically to an academic one.

As I wrote *Final Negotiations* as an intimate conversation about the intricacies of feeling, relating, and working, I was confronted once again with the deficiencies of traditional social science research for dealing with day-to-day realities of chronic illness and relational processes. From the beginning, I violated many taken-for-granted notions in social science research: making myself the object of my research and writing in the first-person infringed upon the separation of subject and researcher

(Jackson 1989); writing about a single case breached the traditional concerns of research from generalization across cases and focused instead on generalization within a case (Geertz 1973); the mode of storytelling fractured the boundaries that normally separated social science from literature; the episodic portrayal of the ebb and flow of relationship experience dramatized the motion of connected lives across the curve of time and thus resisted the standard practice of portraying social life as a snapshot; and the disclosure of normally hidden details of private life highlighted emotional experience and thus challenged the rational actor model of social performance that dominates social science.

Along the way, more canons of social science research were called into question. I began to advocate research and scholarly writing as healing; being emotionally involved with what we study; writing social science as creative non-fiction with scene setting, dialogue, and unfolding dramatic action; showing details instead of telling abstractly; evoking readers' experiences and feelings in addition to analytic closure as a proper goal of research; and adding bodily and spiritual dimensions of living to rational and emotional expressions. When I was finished, I judged the product of my labors by the "lifelikeness" (Bruner 1986: 16; Brady 1991: 15) of my stories, not the Truth of my arguments.

* * *

What's Wrong With Sociology?

Carolyn: (Carolyn hands the segment above to Art, who is in his office reworking the section on orthodox sociology.) I hope this autobiographical account shows the juxtaposition of my work and relational life and my struggles to connect my identity with a meaningful conception of sociology as I moved away from conventions of sociological discourse in the writing of *Final Negotiations*. It seemed so important to understand sociologically what had happened to Gene and me and to convey how a sociological perspective had helped me cope with chronic illness and loss.

Art: In effect, you returned to the values of Luray, the importance of storytelling and talking about mundane and conflictful life events.

Carolyn: (laughs) Yes, but I hope with a more sophisticated view.

Art: Does your story end then with *Final Negotiations*?

Carolyn: In some ways, it could start there. My relationship with you has continued this trajectory.

Art: How serendipitous it was that I attended the talk you gave in the Department of Management on introspection (Ellis 1991a). Early 1990, wasn't it?

Carolyn: You better remember when it was! (Both laugh.) How could we have been on the same campus for six years and not run into each other? Our interests were so similar.

Art: Easy. We were in different departments and colleges. The humanities were separated from social sciences.

Carolyn: I'm sure glad we found each other.

Art: (laughs) We do play off each other, don't we?

Carolyn: Sometimes I don't know where my ideas stop and yours start. Maybe we should co-author all our pieces. I feel like together we've managed to make the activity of doing sociology and communication personally meaningful, connecting our work and personal lives.

Art: Victor Turner's (1982: 97) memorable line captures it well. We've tried to make our work something more "than a cognitive game played in our heads and inscribed in--let's face it--somewhat tedious journals."

Carolyn: What do you think readers will think about this chapter?

Art: I don't know. Some will probably say, "Hum, that's interesting, but I don't see why she considers herself a sociologist."

Carolyn: Should that bother me? I used to care so much. Now perhaps the field ought to be concerned that people like Laurel (Richardson 1996; 1997) and me care little about whether or not the central gatekeepers recognize our work as sociology.

Art: It seems absurd that they wouldn't. After all, most of your books and articles are published and cited as sociology. As Laurel (Richardson 1994b) says, if it appears in a sociology publication, it's sociology. (Art and Carolyn laugh.)

Carolyn: True enough, but the last four articles I published appear in psychology, education, and communication journals.

Art: Still, most of your articles were written for a sociological audience. And what about all those sociology journals in our library upstairs? They must mean something.

Carolyn: Sure, they do. But I can finally admit that I rarely get anything out of the esoteric, dry mainstream journals. The subject is often so narrowly defined that I can't locate myself or my interests in these works. Did I tell you I canceled *Social Forces* after subscribing for almost twenty years?

Art: Why didn't you cancel *AJS* and *ASR* as well?

Carolyn: I don't want to lose touch completely with the center. I keep hoping the editors will realize there's a whole interesting world going on out here in the hinterland that they might like to tap into. I was heartened to see the current editor of *ASR* say that she would welcome ethnographic papers (*Footnotes* April 1995: 13). But I think it's going to take more than just a "welcome."

Art: It's going to take people like you submitting to them.

Carolyn: Why would we, given what these journals have become? I haven't sent anything there since I was a graduate student.

Art: Our fifteen-foot floor to ceiling bookcase certainly tells a story of our careers, doesn't it?

Carolyn: Yes, years and years of *ASR* and *Social Forces* occupy the top shelf; *AJS* is only one shelf lower.

Art: Way up there with my statistics books and *Human Communication Research.*

Carolyn: I can't believe you made your early career as a statistician and methodologist. And now we read ethnographies, personal narratives, novels, cultural studies, interpretive and qualitative journals.

Art: You mean the ones at eye level in our library?

Carolyn: (laughing) Yes, those.

Art: Living with you, I know you're deeply immersed in a network of sociologists who publish and edit sociology journals. And you've never lacked for good students who want to study sociology with you, even while your alienation from the center of sociology has moved you toward joint appointments in other departments at South Florida.

Carolyn: Those moves have more to do with the local situation — the interpretive social science focus of the Communication Program and the excellent Ph.D. students there, for example, and the problems with getting an interpretive program going in the Sociology Department — than with my alienation from sociology. I'm still ambivalent though.

Reminds me of when I requested the move of my faculty line to the Communication Department. One of your communication journals came in the mail that day. I leafed through it and started to cry because I didn't know any of the authors. Nor did I care much about many of the topics. *This isn't who I am,* I thought. Then I noticed the new ASA convention program also had arrived. Glancing through it, my tears turned into laughter. I didn't know many of the people listed there either, nor was I interested in most of the topics. So where do I fit?

Art: Where does any of us fit? In the social sciences, a department discipline is mainly a bureaucratic convenience or a resource for professional identity. In most departments, colleagues often have little in common with each other.

Carolyn: Except for the concerns of their national organizations.

Art: So being classified as a sociologist comes down to one's commitment to the ASA?

Carolyn: When you look at that as a criterion for being a sociologist, I fit. I've participated in nearly every ASA meeting since I was a graduate student and been active in the governance of the Section on Emotions for almost a decade. Simpson and Simpson (this volume) suggest a relationship between identification with the discipline and section membership. That makes sense, but sometimes I feel most alienated from sociology when I'm in the center of activity at ASA, like I sometimes felt as a graduate student. *Is this what I work so hard for?* I ask myself.

Art: Are you a sociologist then? Should sociology embrace a person like you? Or should it encourage you to leave the field because you aren't committed to the conventions of orthodox sociology?

Carolyn: I think this is a good place to leave it. Let the readers decide. (Carolyn turns to her imagined readers.) *What do you think is wrong with sociology?*

Bibliography

Bateson, Gregory. 1977. "Afterward." In *About Bateson*. ed. J. Brockman. New York: Dutton.

Benson, Paul. 1993. *Anthropology and Literature*. Urbana: University of Illinois Press.

Berger, Bennett, ed. 1990. *Authors of Their Own Lives: Intellectual Autobiographies by Twenty American Sociologists*. Berkeley: University of California Press.

Bochner, Arthur. 1994. "Perspective on Inquiry II: Theories and Stories." In *Handbook of Interpersonal Communication*, 2d ed., ed. Mark Knapp and Gerald Miller. Newbury Park, CA.: Sage.

Bochner, Arthur, Carolyn Ellis, and Lisa Tillmann-Healy. 1977. "Mucking Around Looking for Truth." In *Dialectical Approaches to Studying Personal Relationships*, ed. Leslie Baxter and Barbara Montgomery. Mahwah, NJ: Lawrence Erlbaum.

Brady, Ivan, ed. 1991. *Anthropological Poetics*. Savage, Md.: Rowman and Littlefield Pub., Inc.

———. 1993. "Tribal Fire and Scribal Ice." In *Anthropology and Literature*, ed. Paul Benson. Urbana: University of Illinois.

Bruner, Jerome. 1986. *Actual Minds, Possible Worlds*. Cambridge: Harvard University Press.

Calhoun, Craig. 1992. "Sociology, Other Disciplines, and the Project of a General Understanding of Social Life." In *Sociology and Its Publics: The Forms and Fates of Disciplinary Organization*, eds. Terence C. Halliday and Morris Janowitz. Chicago: University of Chicago Press.

Clifford, James, and George Marcus, eds. 1986. *Writing Culture: The Poetics and Politics of Ethnography*. Berkeley: University of California Press.

Cole, Stephen. 2000. "What's Wrong with Sociology?" In *What's Wrong With Sociology?* ed. Stephen Cole. Transaction Press.

Coles, Robert. 1989. *The Call of Stories: Teaching and the Moral Imagination*. Boston: Houghton Mifflin Co.

Collins, Randall. 1986. "Is 1980s Sociology in the Doldrums?" *American Journal of Sociology* 91: 1336-1355.

Crane, Diane and Henry Small. 1992. "American Sociology since the Seventies: The Emerging Identity Crisis in the Discipline." In *Sociology and Its Publics: The Forms and Fates of Disciplinary Organization*, eds. Terence Halliday and Morris Janowitz. Chicago: University of Chicago Press.

Crites, Stephen. 1971. "The Narrative Quality of Experience." *Journal of the American Academy of Religion* 39: 291-311.

Davis, James. 2000. "What's Wrong With Sociology?" In *What's Wrong With Sociology?* ed. Stephen Cole. XXX Press.

Denzin, Norman. 1997a. "Institutional Perspectives on Sociology: A Response to Huber." *American Journal of Sociology.*

————. 1997b. "Performance Texts." In *Representation and the Text: Re-framing the Narrative Voice*, eds. William Tierney and Yvonna Lincoln. Albany: SUNY Press.

Denzin, Norman and Yvonna Lincoln, eds. 1994. *Handbook of Qualitative Research.* Thousand Oaks: CA: Sage.

Ellis, Carolyn. 1986. *Fisher Folk: Two Communities on Chesapeake Bay.* Lexington, Kentucky: The University Press of Kentucky.

————. 1991a. "Sociological Introspection and Emotional Experience," *Symbolic Interaction*, 14(1): 23-50.

————. 1991b. "Emotional Sociology." *Studies in Symbolic Interaction.* 12:123-145.

————. 1993. "'There Are Survivors': Telling a Story of Sudden Death," *The Sociological Quarterly*, 34(4):711-730.

————. 1995a. "Emotional and Ethical Quagmires in Returning to the Field." *Journal of Contemporary Ethnography*, 24(1):711-730.

————. 1995b. *Final Negotiations: A Story of Love, Loss, and Chronic Illness.* Philadelphia: Temple University Press.

Ellis, Carolyn, and Arthur Bochner, eds. 1996. *Composing Ethnography: Alternative Forms of Qualitative Writing.* Walnut Creek: AltaMira Press.

Ellis, Carolyn, and Michael G. Flaherty, eds. 1992. *Investigating Subjectivity: Research on Lived Experience.* Newbury Park: Sage.

Erikson, Kai. 1976. *Everything in Its Path: Destruction of Community in the Buffalo Creek Flood.* New York: Simon and Schuster.

Footnotes. April 1995. 23(4). American Sociological Association Office.

Gamson, William. 1992. "Reactions to the TAGGE Report." August, ASA Office.

Geertz, Clifford. 1973. *The Interpretation of Cultures: Selected Essays.* New York: Basic Books.

————. 1988. *Works and Lives: The Anthropologist as Author.* Stanford, CA: Stanford University Press.

Goetting, Ann, and Sarah Fenstermaker, eds. 1995. *Individual Voices, Collective Visions: Fifty Years of Women in Sociology.* Philadelphia: Temple University Press.

Halliday, Terence. 1992. "Introduction: Sociology's Fragile Professionalism." In *Sociology and Its Publics*, eds. Terence Halliday and Morris Janowitz. Chicago: The University of Chicago Press.

Halliday, Terence, and Morris Janowitz. 1992. *Sociology and Its Publics.* Chicago: The University of Chicago Press.

Huber, Joan. 1995."Institutional Perspectives on Sociology." *American Journal of Sociology.* 101(1):194-216. [Reprinted in this volume]

Jackson, Michael. 1989. *Paths Toward a Clearing: Radical Empiricism and Ethnographic Inquiry.* Bloomington: Indiana University Press.

———. 1995. *At Home in the World.* Durham, NC: Duke University Press.

Latour, Bruno. 1980. "Is It Possible to Reconstruct the Research Process? Sociology of a Brain Peptide." In *The Social Process of Scientific Investigation*, eds. Karin Knorr, Roger Krohn, and Richard Whitley. Dordrecht, Holland: D. Reidel Pub. Co.

Liebow, Eliot. 1967. *Tally's Corner.* Boston: Little, Brown.

Mairs, Nancy. 1994. *Voice Lessons: On Becoming a (Woman) Writer.* Boston: Beacon Press.

Marcus, George, and Michael M. J. Fischer. 1986. *Anthropology as Cultural Critique: An Experimental Moment in the Human Sciences.* Chicago: University of Chicago Press.

Mills, C. Wright. 1959. The Sociological Imagination. London: Oxford University Press.

Molotch, Harvey. 2000. "Going Out." In *What's Wrong With Sociology?* ed. Stephen Cole. New Brunswick: Transaction Publishers.

Olson, Richard. 1982. *Science Deified and Science Defied: The Historical Significance of Science in Western Culture.* Berkeley: University of California Press.

Richardson, Laurel. 1990. *Writing Strategies: Reaching Diverse Audiences.* Newbury Park: Sage.

———. 1994a. "Writing as a Method of Inquiry." In *Handbook of Qualitative Research*, eds. Norman Denzin and Yvonna Lincoln. Thousand Oaks, CA: Sage.

———. 1994b. "Nine Poems: Marriage and the Family. *Journal of Contemporary Ethnography* 23:3-13.

————. 1996. "Educational Birds." *Journal of Contemporary Ethnography* 25(1):6-15.

————.1997. *Fields of Play: Constructing an Academic Life*. New Brunswick, NJ: Rutgers University Press.

Riley, Matilda White. 1988. *Sociological Lives*. Newbury Park: Sage.

Ronai, Carol Rambo. 1995. "Multiple Reflections of Child Sex Abuse: An Argument for a Layered Account." *Journal of Contemporary Ethnography* 23:395-426.

Rorty, Richard. 1996. "The Necessity of Inspired Reading." *The Chronicle of Higher Education*, February 8, A48.

Rule, James. 1994. "Dilemmas of Theoretical Progress." *Sociological Forum*. 9(2):241-257. [Reprinted this volume].

Shelton, Allen. 1996. "The Man at the End of the Machine." *Symbolic Interaction* 18(4):505-518.

Shils, Edward. 1975. *Center and Periphery: Essays in Macrosociology*. Chicago: University of Chicago Press.

Simpson, Ida Harper, and Richard Simpson. 1996. "The Transformation of the American Sociological Association." Sociological Forum 9(2):259-278. [reprinted in this volume]

Smith, Joel. 1991. "A Methodology for Twenty-First Century Sociology." *Social Forces* 70:1-17.

————. 1995. "Emancipating Sociology: Postmodernism and Mainstream Sociological Practice." *Social Forces* 74: 53-79.

Stinchcomb, Arthur. 1994. "Disintegrated Disciplines and the Future of Sociology." *Sociological Forum* 9(2):279-291. [reprinted in this volume]

Tierney, William and Yvonna Lincoln, eds. 1997. *Representation and the Text: Reframing the Narrative Voice*. Albany: SUNY Press.

Tompkins, Jane. 1992. *West of Everything*. New York: Oxford Press.

Turner, Stephen P. and Turner, Jonathan. 1990. *The Impossible Science: An Institutional Analysis of American Sociology*. Newbury Park: Sage.

Turner, Victor. 1982. "Dramatic Ritual/Ritual Drama: Performative and Reflexive Anthropology." In *A Crack in the Mirror: Reflexive Perspectives in Anthropology*, edited by Jay Ruby. Philadelphia: University of Pennsylvania Press.

Turner, Victor and Edward Bruner. 1986. *The Anthropology of Experience*. Urbana: University of Illinois Press.

Whyte, William Foote. 1955 [1943]. *Street Corner Society*. Chicago: University of Chicago Press.

Wolfe, Alan. 1992. "Weak Sociology/Strong Sociologists: Consequences and Contradictions of a Field in Turmoil." *Social Research* 59:759-79.

Contributors

Howard S. Becker, Professor of Sociology, University of California, Santa Barbara

Peter L. Berger, Fellow, Institute for the Study of Economic Culture, Boston, MA.

Arthur B. Bochner, Professor of Communications, University of South Florida, Tampa, FL.

Maria Cole, Professor of Sociology, State University of New York at Stony Brook

Stephen Cole, Professor of Sociology, State University of New York at Stony Brook

Randall Collins, Professor of Sociology, University of Pennsylvania, Philadelphia, PA.

James A. Davis, Professor of Sociology Emeritus, Harvard University and Research Director National Opinion Research Center, Chicago, IL.

Carolyn Ellis, Professor of Sociology and Professor of Communication, University of South Florida, Tampa, FL.

Richard B. Felson, Professor of Sociology, Pennsylvania State University, University Park, PA.

Paget Henry, Professor of Sociology and Professor of African American Studies, Brown University, Providence, RI.

Joan Huber, Professor of Sociology Emeritus, Ohio State University, Columbus, OH.

Seymour Martin Lipset, Professor of Sociology Emeritus, Stanford University, Stanford, CA. and Professor of Sociology, George Mason University, Fairfax, VA.

Harvey Molotch, Professor of Sociology, University of California at Santa Barbara

William C. Rau, Professor of Sociology, Illinois State University, Normal, IL.

James B. Rule, Professor of Sociology, State University of New York at Stony Brook

Ida Harper Simpson, Professor of Sociology, Duke University, Durham, NC.

Richard L. Simpson, Professor of Sociology, University of North Carolina at Chapel Hill

Arthur L. Stinchcombe, Professor of Sociology Emeritus, Northwestern Universtiy, Evanston, IL.

Mayer N. Zald, Professor of Sociology, University of Michigan, Ann Arbor, MI.